MEN AND SHIPS AROUND CAPE HORN 1616-1939

THE EDINBURGH ACADEMY

PRIZE FOR

2nd in Class

Name A.J.M. Watson

Class IV B

Date 1970~71

_____ Rector.

OPPOSITE: "Where there's a will is a way." Device engraved on the stern of the famous English clipper *Cutty Sark*.

ENDPAPER MAP: Map of the Cape Horn region reproduced in the voyage of Gouin de Beauchesne, 1699.
COVER: Aquatint by F. S. Ferner, Bordeaux, 1833.

MEN AND SHIPS
AROUND CAPE HORN
1616-1939

by JEAN RANDIER

Translated from the French by M. W. B. Sanderson

ARTHUR BARKER LIMITED
5 Winsley Street London W1

SBN 213 76476 8

First published in France by Librairie Hachette under the title Hommes et Navires au Cap Horn 1616–1939 © Librairie Hachette 1966.

Phototypeset by BAS Printers Limited, Wallop, Hampshire and
Printed in Great Britain by Unwin Brothers Limited, Woking and London.

Contents

Figurehead of the four-masted barque *Herzogin Cecilie*. Formerly sail training ship of Nord Deutsche Lloyd. She at one time belonged to the Gustav Erikson fleet in 1920 and carried grain.

Preface

"The Cape", as it is known colloquially, is a term that almost defies definition. In reality Cape Horn is simply a specific geographical point on the immense chart of the World. But it is not only a dreaded headland at the extreme tip of South America, rearing its malevolent head to the skies. For those who have rounded this sinister point, it is, because of its reputation and strength, something else.

Firstly, Cape Horn stands as the symbol of an era which has altogether gone for ever, a glorious age of great discovery of unknown lands and, moreover, a symbol of men overcoming the most terrible perils and dangers which beset them. It is the story of men breaking down the barriers of ignorance and with the aid of better navigation and geographic knowledge being able to thrust into new seas. The Cape is also a reminder, an unforgettable memory, of an age when men were brought closely together to combat the most primitive forces of nature; it is a tribute to their courage, endurance and resistance to physical suffering and a spirit of self-sacrifice which was never found wanting aboard the ocean-going sailing ships. Finally, the Cape marks the nostalgia of youth, whereby young sailing captains and their crews were able to exert their enthusiasm to penetrate the utmost secrets of the winds and seas throughout the world in order to carry the great white ships to every corner.

That is what Cape Horn means to us, the survivors. The subject is so vast and complex, that it may seem presumptuous to attempt to put into the pages of one book such a great assembly of facts and impressions, of methods and opinions, of dreams and reality, of history and legend. That such an attempt has been made is entirely due to one who loves the sea, who has navigated it many times and understands many of its secrets. It was necessary to penetrate deep into the mentality of the Cape Horners themselves, to bring to the surface all the richness of their experiences and their memories of those seas. Such a book must steer between the Scylla of the over-use of technical terms and the Charybdis of flowery and insipid language which many writers use in their poetic descriptions of life at sea, often devoid of truth. Such a book, moreover, must avoid too much quotation and abridgement which may lead to exaggeration and a drawing of hasty conclusions; and, at the same time, remain within the strict limits imposed by modern writing. In all these respects, it was necessary for the author to possess that rare ability to bring back to life an age which he did not know, with accuracy and truth. Above all, it was necessary that we, the Cape Horners, in reading the text and examining the wealth of fine illustrations throughout, should find ourselves portrayed in this book. And it is this very impression that we do find; and this is perhaps the greatest compliment that we can pay to Jean Randier. We salute this work, which is his own and which, without doubt, will remain one of the finest which has ever been written upon this great subject, the story of the men and the ships of Cape Horn.

LÉON GAUTIER

[International Grand Master and President of the French section of the Society of Cape Horners.]

PART I

To the East Indies on a Westerly Course

All roads lead to Rome. So, too, do all lead to the Moluccas—the sea routes, the desert paths, the mountain passes, the caravan trails, the tracks of sailing ships and oared galleys.

For centuries, the caravans that brought spices, precious stones, and costly silks overland from the Orient to Christendom had operated under the control of the Arabs. To attempt to emulate them would have been folly. Another way had to be found—by sea.

But such intentions would have remained only a dream, without the means of realizing them, had not courageous seafarers been willing to risk the perils and uncertainties of the world's great oceans. The men of the Renaissance, emerging from the maritime obscurity of the medieval world, responded to this great challenge. They feared nothing; faith and confidence in their abilities fortified them. They built vessels capable of withstanding the fiercest storms and slowly, step by step, ventured farther and farther across unknown seas until at last they reached the Spice Islands. Thus one great part of the world was clearly marked out, defined, and charted. To their spiritual satisfaction was added the spur of material prosperity. As a result, control of the wealth from the East gradually passed from the Arabs to the Portuguese.

Since the world was round and could be circumnavigated eastwards, why not also westwards? The Spaniards leapt at this possibility, but encountered the great barrier of the continent of America. Was this China, they wondered? To their dismay, having crossed the Isthmus of Darien, they found the Pacific before them, immense and seemingly impassable.

At this critical moment, it was Magellan who sought and found a chink in the armor of the American land chain. Westward from the South Cape, he sailed on day after day across the broad Pacific to the Isles of Wealth. His ship arrived there without him, but the first circumnavigation of the globe had been achieved. In consequence vast areas of the world were assigned as dominions of the two great European powers of that time: Spain and

Detail from the planisphere of Sebastian Cabot, 1544. *(Bibl. Nat. Cartes et plans)*

Dutch merchant ship of the 15th century, an engraving signed W. A. 1470.

Portugal. But, as so often happens in the granting of special privileges, the beneficiaries slept while those who felt endangered prepared to retaliate.

The English and the Dutch entered the exploration lists and sought to control sea routes elsewhere. Their navigators searched for a northeast passage to Cathay; others sought in vain for a northwest passage through the frozen Arctic Seas. At the same time, European statesmen and financiers began to take advantage of the new discoveries and wealth of the East.

Every route to the Orient seemed guarded by the Spaniards and Portuguese, and all its wealth remained the exclusive preserve of their merchants and navigators; there appeared no way of gaining access to the riches of the East without openly contesting the Spanish and Portuguese monopoly. But one route did remain—certainly the most difficult and dangerous—whereby the East Indies could be reached in a westerly direction from Cape Horn.

THE WONDERFUL SPICE-MERCHANTS

Once long ago far to the East, beyond Baghdad and Calicut, beyond Malacca and Pekin, lay the Fabulous Isles, unknown to the great cartographers and upon whose shores no Christian vessel had ever beached. Winged serpents, fierce gryphons and legendary monsters guarded their coasts and in the middle of an impenetrable forest reposed an enchanted orchard. There was the garden of spices.

Camphor and cardamon; incense, myrrh and cinnamon; cloves, mace, ginger and nutmeg grew in fertile profusion in this garden, cultivated by celestial gardeners. Such were the Spice Islands.

This little fable could have been a description by a medieval traveller. The magic words which spoke of distant lands, of great voyages to the ends of the world, of unknown perils, and of fabulous monsters, went straight to the hearts of the men of that age and made them forget, far more than any economic argument could, the exorbitant prices that were charged for the spices from such a distant paradise. It was no wonder, therefore, that the consumers remained content and the merchants were honest in their dealings. It only required a little imagination, and a portion of mystery and oriental enchantment to invest aloes and rhubarb, balsam and mace, with magic powers over body and mind.

The apothecaries in their round or sugar-loaf hats made their fortunes through the spice-merchants. In addition to the blood-lettings and the purgatives, a few grains of pimento helped the sick to regain consciousness. Those who recovered fell on their knees in thanksgiving. Their gratitude echoed back, over the Red Sea and the Yellow Sea, to the Spice Islands whence the remedies had come.

Grain and spice merchants of the 16th century. (*Ordonnances de la juridiction de la prévosté des Marchands de Paris*, 1528)

The harvesting of cinnamon in the East Indies from Thevet's Universal Cosmography, 1575. (*Bible. Nat. Estampes*)

The port of Lisbon in the 15th century. From de Bry's Grands Voyages, 1595. *(Bibl. Nat.)*

English merchant of the late 16th century. Anonymous engraving after a drawing by Titian.

How could one ever think of hesitating to pay a little more for these Indian fruits, whose effects were, in turn, so stimulating, relaxing and erotic?

In the castle kitchens of that age, even the meanest scullery maid knew the value of spices. Scarcely anything, food or drink, was served up without first being generously sifted, sprinkled, stuffed and larded with aromatic herbs.

Encouraged by doctors and gourmets, the merchants did not lag behind in meeting the demand. At Venice, Marseilles, Barcelona, Bruges, London, Lübeck, Bergen, and Novgorod, the spices were brought in and marketed. From the markets held during the Venetian fairs, German merchants—the famous "Tedeschi"—carried the goods across the Brenner and Saint Gotthard passes and ensured their distribution to the great commercial cities of Northern Europe.

Bruges—the Venice of the North—was the terminus for the Mediterranean galleys and the Hansa ships. The Hanseatic league formed a powerful link between the maritime trade of the North Sea and the Baltic and had for three centuries, thanks to a strict protectionist policy, been able to dominate the commerce of Northern Europe. It was not, however, the Hansa sailors or ships which had originated the spice trade, but the Portuguese. It was Lisbon, port of call on the voyage from Venice to Bruges and furnisher of wines to ships en route, that assumed leadership in the crusade against the monopoly of Islam. The expeditions launched from Lisbon, and partly supported by German money, culminated in 1510 in the complete displacement of the Arabs' maritime trade with the East.

Side by side with the gold standard, there existed a pepper standard. A substantial market in peppercorns flourished. The Company of Pepper

Merchants of London, founded by patent in 1179, negotiated loans and gave advice to kings. From there it was only a short step to fit out a fleet, appoint its commanders, and by one way and another wrest control of the maritime trade from Islam. Was not this a fascinating traffic—vessels laden with perfumes from the East, jewels from India, silk from China, spices from beyond the seas? But first, how much was known of this long-distance traffic, whose wealth the Arab world had so long kept in its possession?

Very little was known, as a matter of record. D'Ibn Vahab and Soleyman (9th century A.D.) discuss it in their *Voyages en Chine*; there are also relevant passages in Sheikh Edrisi's: *Récréations de celui qui désire parcourir les pays* (Sicily, 1154), and Rabbi Benjamin of Tudela's: *Voyage en Méditerranée*. The first important description from the geographical point of view, however, was that given by Marco Polo (1298). During twenty-five years of wanderings, he gained considerable practical experience of the Spice route to China—both the sea voyage via India and overland through Tartary. Then follow two other accounts; one by a monk of Seville (ca. 1300) which, for the first time, mentions the famous "Prester John"; the other, by an Italian monk named Odoric of Pordenone which is full of details about the cultivation and harvesting of pepper. Finally there are the diverting accounts contained in the writings of Sir John Mandeville. His travels are now known to be fictitious, and thus unreliable guides for a voyage of exploration.

By means of these remarkable narratives however, it is possible to gain some idea of the immense journey involved in bringing the spices from the Moluccas. About A.D. 1000, when the original inhabitants had been driven out by the Chinese, Malacca became the great entrepôt of the spice trade. In its busy harbor Malay praus, already taxed by the Sultan of Malabar upon their arrival from Amboina, transhipped their previous cargoes to Arab dhows bound for the ports of India and Arabia.

According to the prevailing monsoon, whole fleets plied back and forth between Aden, Muscat, Ormuz and the Far East. At the same time the great overland caravans traversed the empire of Tamerlane, laden with cloves, pepper, silk, and perfume. From port to port, and town to town, the merchandise rose in price as it was taxed in succession by emirs, caliphs, and sheikhs. At last, having crossed Anatolia or the Red Sea, it reached Constantinople or Alexandria, whence Genoese or Venetian ships carried it on the last stage of the journey to Western Europe. Christendom indeed felt a certain bitterness at having to submit to the frontier tolls and charges exacted by pagans; but neither religious faith nor the dictates of trade could make any headway against the problem.

Only the Venetian republic was able to profit from all these transactions. On the one hand it kept control of the monopoly upon the distribution of goods from Islam; on the other, it derived great benefit from the lucrative contracts negotiated with the crusaders to bring them to the Holy Land. Regarding the Crusades, their miserable fate is well known: the disintegration of vast armies dispatched eight times between 1096 and 1291 to fight in the wastes of the desert and, finally, the capture by the Turks in 1453 of Constantinople, the last bastion of Christianity.

One of the wonders of the world and also the first beacon used by ancient navigators—the lighthouse of Alexandria (200 B.C.); wood-burning, a principle which was continued in use until the 18th century. From John Harris' "Voyages"; London, 1764. (*Service hydrographique, Paris*)

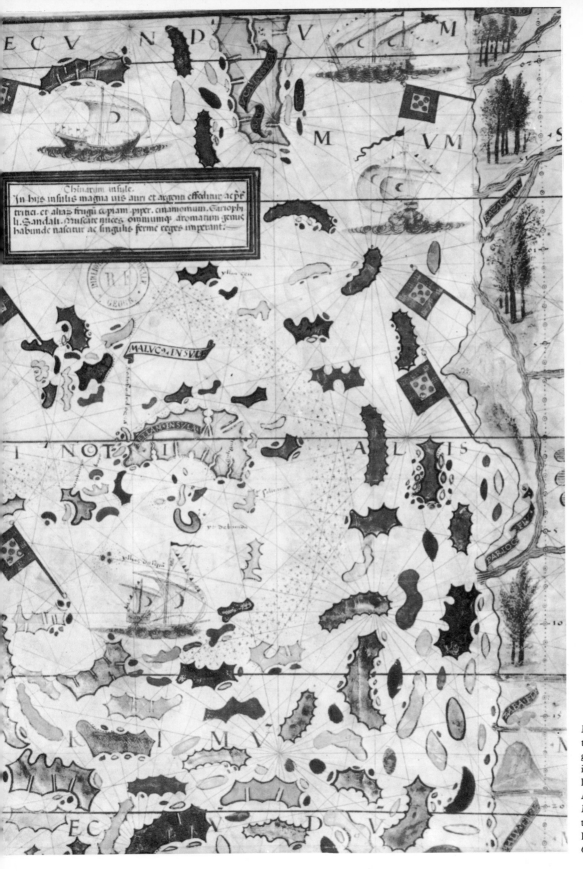

More picturesque than useful to navigators, portulan charts gave only an approximate idea of the earth's surface and lacked any nautical precision. A portulan chart of the Moluccas on vellum. From the Portuguese atlas of Lopo Homen, 1519. *(Bibl. Nat. Cartes et plans)*

Henry the Navigator (1394–1460) at Sagres, surrounded by sea captains and cartographers. From a painting by E. Lopez, end of 19th century.

THE HERMIT OF SAGRES

Lusitania, situated in the western extremity of the Iberian peninsula, remained for five hundred and sixty-nine years the Atlantic boundary of the Roman Empire. Occupied in turn by the barbarians and by the Arabs, this land had been wrested from Islam by Alfonso II of Castile. Later, Alfonso III of Portugal had enlarged the kingdom to the south by gaining control of the Algarve. This territory he gave to his son Prince Henry, who set up court at Sagres (the Sacre of the Ancient World), near Cape St. Vincent. It was from Sagres that the era of "Great Discoveries" began.

The young prince was no general, and although he had only once before sailed the seas—during the capture of Ceuta in 1415—his name has justly come down through history as Henry the Navigator. The prince's intelligence, imagination and patronage were such as to attract to Sagres all who were interested in geography and navigation—cartographers, professors, navigators. Fifty years before, King Ferdinand had already sought to encourage the art of navigation by exempting shipbuilders from paying taxes. Such a maritime destiny came naturally to a country so much in contact with the great Atlantic Ocean.

Upon a Majorcan world map dated 1375, opposite Cape Noun, one can see where the cartographer has written: "Here is the end of the world". At that very point, Henry the Navigator believed the route to the Indies began. Nothing was spared, either by way of material or research, in launching one expedition after another farther and farther southwards.

At the end of seventeen years of effort, the navigator Gil Eanes succeeded in rounding the formidable Cape Bojador (1433), beyond which: "the heat was so intense that ships foundered and seamen suffered in a boiling sea".

Not without loss, the Gulf of Guinea—or Guiya, the country of the negroes —was discovered between 1434 and 1462. Cape Lopez was reached in 1475; and the navigators marked their progress along the African coast by erecting a series of emblazoned cairns which could be recognized again.

In 1487, Bartholomew Diaz rounded the "Cape of Storms" mentioned in Camoens' "Lusiad". His ship dropped anchor in what is now Mossel Bay and the estuary of the Great Fish River. He sailed back to Lisbon in 1488, with the certain knowledge that he had reached the southern point of Africa.

Thus, the Genoese pilots were superseded by the Portuguese. The Pope recognized their achievement in acknowledging Portugal's suzerainty over all lands discovered up to one hundred leagues west of the Azores.

THE INDIAN OCEAN

Between 1415 and 1487, the Portuguese had in five stages, and at the expense of launching fifty expeditions, determined the African coastline down as far as its junction with the Indian Ocean. Covilham and Payra, sent through the Mediterranean in search of the lands of Prester John, continued overland eastward as far as Ormuz and Calicut. Thence Covilham sent back to King John II important directions, which were relayed to the masters of vessels about to set out from Sagres, round the Cape of Good Hope: "When they reach the Indian Ocean, your mariners must ask for the course to Sofala, the Island of the Moon. There they will find pilots who will guide them to the Indies".

This was excellent news and could not have happened at a more appropriate time, since Columbus had just returned from his famous first voyage and the papal bull of Alexander II (1493) and the Treaty of Tordesillas had defined the geographical lines of division of the unknown world between the Spaniards and the Portuguese. For all future possessions, the vertical line of demarcation was redrawn at three hundred and seventy leagues to the west of the Azores.

Young Don Manuel, who succeeded John II on the throne of Portugal, chose Vasco da Gama, his brother Paulo and Nicolas Coelho, to lead an expedition beyond the Cape of Good Hope. Four square-rigged vessels, displacing 200 tons, were fitted out with a wide variety of supplies, including the best nautical instruments available. In all, the crew numbered one hundred and eighty (including several "degradados"—prisoners under sentence of death), and victuals and stores sufficient for three years. The detailed planning of the expedition even extended to the inclusion of letters of introduction to Prester John.

Having set sail from Belem on 18 July 1497, the navigators shaped course for the Fortunate Isles (Cape Verde Is.). Below the equator their ships were blown off course by storms and becalmed for many days. Severe gales were also encountered off the Cape of Good Hope; they watered at Vaqueros but there lost one store ship. On 25 December they sighted land which they appropriately christened Natal. Here some of the crew mutinied. At this critical moment Vasco da Gama stood firm. Giving orders that all the money nd navigational instruments be thrown overboard, he said to the sailors: rom now on, God alone shall guide us. If the mission given to me cannot accomplished, I shall not return to Portugal".

Oriental spices carried on the backs of camels being put on board ship. From Thevet's: Universal Cosmography, Paris, 1575. (*Bibl. Nat.*)

Vasco da Gama (1469–1524). Anonymous engraving. *(Bibl. Nat.)*

A short time later scurvy struck down his men. At the next landing-place a marble column was erected, inscribed on one side with the legend: "By order of the Sovereign of Portugal, the Kingdom of Christians"; and, on the other with the royal arms of Portugal.

At Mozambique trouble occurred with the local chieftain. But matters improved at Malindi, where an able "degradado" named Juan Machado, conducted negotiations with the local inhabitants. Fortunately he encountered one of the Arab pilots mentioned in Covilham's letter and found him to be in possession of an excellent chart, a quadrant and declination tables.

The pilot warned him: "In the Indies you must be restrained in both manner and speech, so as to give offense to no one".

The monsoon carried the voyagers across the ocean to Calicut where they arrived on 23 May 1498. An extraordinary spectacle greeted them there: spices and precious stones in profusion and a great variety of aromatic herbs sold in the market place by the quintal. In the harbor five hundred vessels rode at anchor. Mistrustful of the inhabitants' curiosity, intrigues and professions of goodwill, da Gama did not wait long before setting out on the long return voyage.

Lisbon was finally reached on 10 July 1499, the expedition having sailed a total of twenty-four thousand miles in six hundred and thirty days and lost two-thirds of its men (including Vasco's brother, Paulo) from disease. Two ships had been lost, but the survivors received a rousing welcome on their triumphal return. At the time, Columbus was on his second voyage to America, and had failed to bring back evidence of having reached what he believed to be the Indies, "... only parrots and feathered Indians".

Six months later the thirteen ships of Pedro Alvarez Cabral's fleet set sail across the Atlantic, arriving first at Brazil and proceeding from there to the Cape of Hood Hope. The result of this expedition was to supplant the Arab merchants at the court of the King of Calicut. Even before Cabral had begun his return voyage, da Gama set sail once more for the Indies in 1502.

In 1506 a new expedition was launched: a fleet of sixteen ships under the joint command of Alfonso d'Albuquerque and Tristan da Cunha. D'Albuquerque called at Ormuz and Socotra en route and during the nine ensuing years, destroyed the Arabian forts and bases in the Red Sea, until Islam accepted Portuguese terms of peace. As a result, the traditional balance of the spice trade was disturbed. Turkey, Egypt and Venice declared war upon Portugal in the Mediterranean; d'Albuquerque, Viceroy of the Portuguese Indies since 1509, dispatched one squadron after another to the east. His captains reached the Sunda Islands, captured Malacca (1509) and were congratulated by the Pope for extending the boundaries of Christendom.

Amboyna, Ceram, Bali and Java were occupied. Da Gama followed d'Albuquerque's lead by sending an expedition to Cochin (1524) and detachments to Borneo and the Celebes (1526). A Portuguese colony was established in China, and Japan was reached in 1542. In point of fact, however, only Macao began to flourish as a trading center after 1558.

It is easy to see what immense profits Portugal was able to make as mistress of the Orient trade for several decades. But the Portuguese failed to appreciate the importance of consolidating their commercial advantage by developing a strong administration and an adequate military defense. Did not Albuquerque dream of stealing the remains of Mahomet to barter them for Jerusalem, and plan the ruin of Egypt by deflecting the course of the Nile? But when the Dutch came to the East, they were altogether more realistic; in the ebullience of their newly-won independence, their mode of action was based on one premise: the Portuguese Empire will collapse.

Alfonso d'Albuquerque (1453–1515), founder of the Portuguese Empire in India. Anonymous engraving. *(Bibl. Nat. Estampes)*

The town of Calicut at the height of the Portuguese Empire. Anonymous engraving. *(Bibl. Nat. Estampes)*

Christopher Columbus (1451?–1506). Engraving by Thiriet, from an anonymous painting in the Naval Museum at Madrid.

The *Santa Maria* from a drawing attributed to Columbus. (*Extract from the Epistola Christoforo Colombi, 1494*)

COLUMBUS AND THE SPANISH NAVIGATORS

The theories put forward by the Florentine astronomer Toscanelli first gave Columbus the idea of reaching the Indies from the West. All other evidence seemed to be confirmatory: vegetation found on the coast of the Azores, bits of carved wood carried westwards by the oceanic current. Inspired by his plans, Columbus first sought the support of King John II of Portugal. The latter, however, clung to his plan for circumnavigating Africa and refused to help.

We next find Columbus at the court of Ferdinand and Isabella of Spain. It proved to be a propitious time, for the serious state of the Spanish treasury at the end of a long struggle against the Moors required desperate measures to ensure its replenishment. The outcome was that on 3 August 1492, Columbus, armed with the Toscanelli chart, weighed from Palos with *Niña*, *Pinta* and *Santa Maria* at the start of his celebrated voyage. The little flotilla dropped anchor in the estuary of the Tagus on 4 March 1493, the ships' holds "laden with Indians and parrots".

Having paid a courtesy visit to King John II, Columbus set sail once more, for Barcelona, where he was received at the court of Queen Isabella on 15 March 1493. The general conclusion there was that the voyage had achieved only a limited success since the Spaniards' preference was for more gold and fewer birds and Indians. Columbus did not receive further financial support from Isabella but convinced her of the need for a second voyage. He sailed westward once again, made landfall in the Caribbean and ultimately returned to Spain, certain that he had come within a hundred leagues of Hangchow, the capital of Cathay.

His third voyage brought him to Venezuela. There everything went wrong. Instead of returning laden with gold, he arrived at San Lucar on 6 October 1500, bound in chains in the ship's hold. This was the same year in which Pedro Alvarez Cabral, in search of favorable winds, had arrived off the coast of Brazil. In any event Columbus, oblivious to the failure of the previous expedition, set out at the age of seventy once again in a final voyage. This time he believed he had reached to within: "... one or two weeks' sailing distance of the mouth of the River Ganges". Right to the end, therefore, his belief that he had discovered the Indies remained unshaken.

His dream was finally fulfilled by the Portuguese navigator Perez d' Andrade, who sailed through the Straits of Sunda and ultimately reached Canton. Then in 1508 the Spanish voyager Pinzon discovered the estuary of the Amazon. From there he sailed deep into the Gulf of Mexico and founded Nombre de Dios on the Isthmus of Darien. He, too, believed he was in Asia. His own opinion and that of his colleagues was that only a slight penetration of the hinterland was necessary to bring them to the goal they had sought so long, but they were unaware that Portuguese ships, following the eastern route, had already brought back to Lisbon spices, precious stones, finery, and porcelain from the Indies.

One can well imagine, therefore, the astonishment and disappointment felt by Vasco Nuñez de Balboa in 1513 after having crossed the Isthmus of Darien. Instead of reaching Asia, he suddenly saw before him the vast Pacific Ocean. It was a cruel deception, and taking possession of the great sea in the name of His Catholic Majesty was hardly a suitable recompense.

One of the three Pizarro brothers (Francisco: 1474–1541) from a drawing by José Maca and an engraving by Rafael Esteve. (*Bibl. Nat. Estampes*)

Indians bringing treasure to Vasco de Balboa, the discoverer of the Pacific (1513). From de Bry's: *Voyages. (Bibl. Nat.)*

The meeting between Montezuma and Cortez in 1519, after an Aztec drawing.

The discovery was as serious a reverse for the Spanish geographers and navigators as it was for the ancient cartographic theories first propounded by Ptolemy. Accordingly, the great chart of Juan de la Cosa had to be redrawn. But time was pressing, gold had to be found and the cost of the expeditions met. In the New World the discoveries were followed by military expeditions and the systematic conquests of Peru and Chile.

Ferdinand Magellan (1480–1521). From an anonymous engraving of the 16th century. *(Academia San Fernando, Madrid)*

MAGELLAN

Was Magellan aware of Schöener's world map, published around 1515–1520, in which, strangely enough, there is shown inserted between the southern tip of the known American continent and the northern shores of the "Southern Continent", a narrow channel linking the two oceans? This information suggests that at some time explorers had passed down the Cordillera chain of mountains and discovered Tierra del Fuego and the strait. Otherwise, might not the symmetry of the continents on the shore have struck Magellan forcibly, showing him that the rounding of America could be achieved in the same way that Africa had been circumnavigated?

Whatever the real explanation, it is certain that the theory became the mainspring of Magellan's life. Wounded in Morocco fighting against the Moors, invalided out of the army with a miserable pension at the age of thirty-five, this Portuguese who had followed d'Albuquerque to the Indies and Abren to the Moluccas thought only of this realization of his dream. Rejected by his native land, he turned to Spain, offering his services to the "Casa de Contratacion" at Seville.

Magellan certainly did not lack confidence. He had access to the Portuguese Hydrographic Office—that curious organization which punished with death anyone who divulged information about its charts or nautical instructions to strangers. He rubbed shoulders with mariners and navigators and pored over the track-charts used by the expeditions to Brazil. He was sure of the existence of another sea passage to the west, besides that of the estuary of the River Plate, mistakenly believed to be the true exit. His arguments finally convinced everyone—the young Emperor Charles the Fifth, his tutors and advisers, including Columbus' sworn enemy, the Bishop of Fonseco. The gold of

Peru, the treasure of the Incas were desirable in themselves; but since this was the only way the Spaniards could reach the Indies from the west and prevent their neighbors, the Portuguese, from gaining the whole prize, the passage must at all costs be attempted.

This small, silent man exuded confidence and on 22 March 1518, a contract was signed. At Seville Magellan fitted out five ships, and five months later the little fleet, ready at last, floated down to San Lucar before venturing into the open sea. A young Italian named Antonio Pigafetta became the principal chronicler of the voyage and its commander's biographer (the account by Magellan's friend, Pierre Martyr, was later burnt in Rome). Magellan weighed anchor on 20 September 1519, ignoring all the confusion caused by a plot amongst his Spanish captains. The young emperor, who was one of his keenest supporters, gave the sailing orders:

Your principal aim will be to explore all those parts of the ocean which are on the other side of the line of demarcation. You are also enjoined to discover there all that has not yet been discovered, taking every care neither to cross the limits agreed upon with the King of Portugal, nor to give him any other cause for offense, but to keep strictly within the bounds of our own line of demarcation.

The Emperor added:

Knowing that the spices are to be found in the Moluccas and that your main task is to seek for them, my command is that you should shape your course directly for those islands.

Nothing could have been more in agreement with Magellan's own intentions.

On 13 December 1519, St. Januarius' Day, after eleven weeks at sea, the fleet entered the Bay of Rio, which had not then been fortified by the Portuguese. The seamen disembarked from their ships and were captivated to find there: "Young women whose only clothing was their head of hair". But Magellan was impatient to proceed, to round Cape Santa Maria and then enter the strait which he expected to find about latitude 40°S. The fleet sailed southwards as far as: "a wide expanse of sea" which they crossed, looking for the channel but after a fortnight's beating back and forth found that there was none. This "wide expanse" was in fact the estuary of the Plate.

For two months, in a climate becoming increasingly unfavorable, the ships held their southerly course until resolve began to waver and the crew to murmur: "How can these lonely mountains, lowering clouds, this gray and broken sea be the way to the islands of Paradise?".

Magellan shrugged his shoulders and remained silent to every question. Ought he have told his men that he had made a mistake? No. Never for a moment did he consider confessing his fears. Winter came. Instead of returning to the north, thus giving his crew the chance of deserting, Magellan chose to winter his ships at the harbor of St. Julien, which was situated in a small, gloomy and completely isolated bay, but safe and sheltered from the westerly winds. There mutiny broke out. Magellan repressed it ruthlessly; two ships' captains were executed and later a third officer and a mutinous priest were similarly treated.

During four months of an appalling winter he worked his men to exhaustion. Spring came at last and with it a strange figure that appeared one day

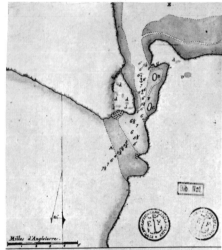

Manuscript plan of Port St. Julien. French version, after Anson's voyage, 1741. *(Bibl. Nat. Cartes et plans)*

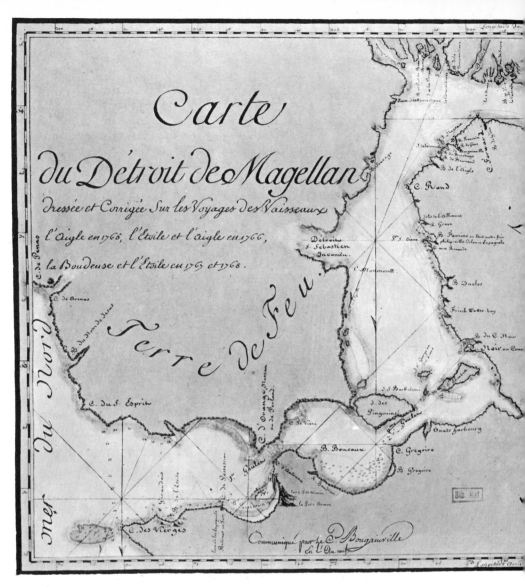

Chart surveyed by the cartographers of the Bougainville expedition, aboard *L'Aigle, La Boudeuse* and *L'Etoile*, 1765–1768 (North is below, Atlantic to the left and Pacific to the right). *(Bibl. Nat. Cartes et plans)*

standing on the top of one of the hills. It was a savage, clad in an animal's skin, through the paws of which his legs and arms protruded. His name was Patagon. A thousand wiles were used to entice aboard this giant, with his harsh voice and hair tonsured like a monk; a few other savages followed him. Two were captured but the rest escaped. Magellan then dispatched one of his ships to reconnoitre further to the south; it was wrecked but the crew were saved.

At the end of August a great feeling of despair swept the fleet. Weeks of inaction went by before it got under way again on 18 October 1520. On the 21st the Cape of A Hundred Thousand Virgins was reached. On the advice of his pilots, Magellan passed beyond it and then sent two of his vessels into the "fjord" as scouts. Nothing happened for five days and then the sound of cannon fire. The *San Antonio* and *Concepcion* rejoined the fleet; they had found salt water at the head of the channel.

On All Saints' Day the flotilla of four ships threaded their way through a

24

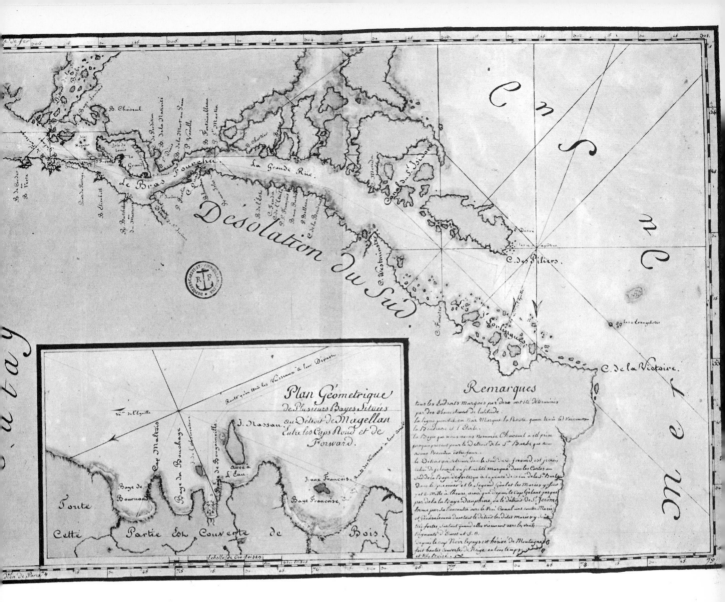

labyrinth of dark and treacherous waters. Everything combined to make navigation dangerous—shallows, sunken rocks, sandbanks, currents. For the first time Magellan conferred with his companions; remembering what happened at St. Julien, they agreed to go on. But this did not prevent the Spanish captains from defying him: "This Magellan", they told themselves, "is Portuguese. He wants to leave us to die in these icy regions while he returns to Portugal with the rest of the fleet."

After a storm had arisen, one of the ships which had been sent out on reconnaissance returned to Europe. The others pressed on. To the north lay Patagonia, to the south Tierra del Fuego. In the second part of the strait, beyond the most southerly cape—today known as Cape Froward or Forward —the weather changed; there were trees, fresh water and vegetation. They fished for dorado, tunny, bonito and flying fish. On 27 November 1520, Cape Desire hove in sight and then, at last, to the astonished gaze of the mariners, the open sea. Thus, after twenty-eight days of suspense, the one hundred

25

and ten mile channel had been negotiated. By amazing good fortune, fine weather lay upon the ocean. But the pilots now wanted to return to Spain because scarcity reigned on board ship.

We have only foul water aboard (wrote Pigafetta) fragments of biscuit, full of worm and stinking with the urine of ants. We soaked in the sea the old skins covering our gear. When they were softened after four or five days, we cut them into portions and ate them; some of the crew's gums became so swollen that they could no longer chew. Sixteen of the crew are dead, including our giant Patagonian. Now we have sailed several thousand leagues across this great abyss of ocean for three months and twenty days without ever having sighted land.

At last on 6 March 1521, the Ladrone Islands were reached, after which the fleet set course for the Philippines, where on 26 April 1521 Magellan was killed by natives. There, also, one of his ships which would no longer sail properly was burned. Between 8 November and 11 February calls were made at Timor and at Ternate and Tidor, on both sides of the island of Gilolo. At this point a cargo of spices was taken aboard. One ship was so damaged that it had to be sent back to Darien.

Magellan's ship, the *Victoria*, with her crew almost dead from famine, thirst and scurvy, made the return voyage under the command of El Cano. She dropped anchor at San Lucar near Cadiz on 7 September 1522; the last

In the Strait of Magellan; Mount Sarmiento, seen from Cape Froward. After the chart made by King and Fitzroy in 1831. (*Le Tour du Monde*)

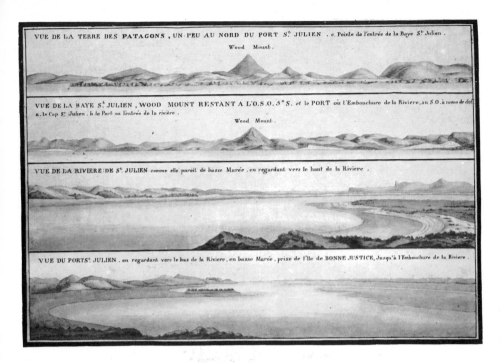

VUE DE LA TERRE DES **PATAGONS**, UN PEU AU NORD DU PORT St JULIEN . c. Pointe de l'entrée de la Baye St Julien .

Wood Mount .

VUE DE LA BAYE St JULIEN , WOOD MOUNT RESTANT A L'O.S.O. 5° S. et le PORT où l'Embouchure de la Riviere, au S.O. à 1000 de dist.
a. le Cap St Julien . b. le Port ou l'entrée de la rivière .

Wood Mount .

VUE DE LA RIVIERE DE St JULIEN comme elle paroit de basse Marée . en regardant vers le haut de la Riviere .

VUE DU PORT St JULIEN . en regardant vers le bas de la Riviere , en basse Marée , prise de l'Ile de BONNE JUSTICE, jusqu'à l'Embouchure de la Riviere .

View of the Patagonian coast, from Anson's chart, 1741. *(Bibl. Nat. Cartes et plans)*

part of the voyage was made non-stop except for a brief call at the Cape Verde Islands. King Manoel of Portugal had ordered that Magellan's ships should be seized and their crews executed as pirates. How many of them survived the voyage? Only eighteen of the sixty who had set out from the Moluccas and of the one hundred and eighty from the Philippines. The *Victoria* had sailed 14,460 leagues in thirty-seven months and curiously, one day seemed to have disappeared from the calendar in the process.

It is the first time, [wrote Charles de Brosses in his *Navigations aux Terres Australes*] that an opportunity was given of observing this fact so often repeated subsequently, namely, that in circumnavigating the world by following the sun's path, one day is gained in three years, just as one is lost if the voyage is made in the opposite direction.

The same de Brosses added :

When Sebastian Cano and his men appeared at the emperor's court, they were received with the acclamation which their achievement deserved. Cano gave Charles V two letters, one from Corada, King of Ternate, the other from Almanzor, King of Tidor —two islands in the Moluccas—in which they acknowledged themselves vassals of the Spanish crown. Several Indians of the Moluccas were presented to the Emperor, amongst whom there was one so commercially minded that the first question he asked, as soon as it could be rendered into Castilian, was if any one could tell him how many reals made a ducat, how many maravedis made a real, and how much pepper was needed to equal one maravedi? The Emperor was so impressed that he forbade this man to leave the country, but the others were sent back to their own land.

Accordingly, at a cost of the deaths of two hundred mariners and of untold suffering, the world was encompassed and the Spice Islands shown to be

William of Orange Bay. A wood engraving made from an anonymous photograph. *(Le Tour du Monde)*

A ship whose structure has hardly changed through the centuries. A Macassar prau, from a sketch made by Admiral Pâris. *(Le Tour du Monde)*

attainable from the west as well as from the east. Magellan's dream had come true, and the Spice Islands had been won for Spain.

Charles V, having claimed and acquired these islands at the Treaty of Badajoz—in which the line of demarcation was once more redrawn—then sold them back to his brother-in-law, John III of Portugal, for 350,000 ducats or 150,000 florins.

Before long the Strait of Magellan was forsaken, and its existence forgotten, although for a brief moment Drake brought it again into the limelight. Communication with the Pacific was principally maintained overland via the Isthmus of Darien, although many began to doubt the safety of the route, with robbers and buccaneers attacking the mule trains as soon as they arrived on the west coast.

The expedition of Carjaval and Ladrillera (1523), in which three out of the four ships engaged were lost, was one of the last attempts made by Spain upon the straits. Two hundred and fifty men were left to die there, abandoned by the only ship that managed to escape. In 1535 the Portuguese navigator Simon de Alcazova determined to attempt the passage. But bad weather threatened and he reached its entrance without having taken on fresh water. A shortage of water followed and his men had to drink wine for fifty days. This was enough to bring the expedition to a complete standstill. The Spaniard, Alfonso de Carmayo, tried without success to navigate the channel in 1539. Twelve years before, the Frenchman Villegagnon had made a similar attempt which ended in fiasco. The general feeling was that, in the circumstances, it made more sense to strengthen the fortress at Nombre de Dios and so give greater protection to the Darien route. This was, in essence, an admission that the Strait of Magellan was impracticable, and that it was better that they "should be deliberately neglected".

It was subsequently learned that the return passage across the Pacific eastwards from the Moluccas to Mexico was full of difficulty. One of Magellan's ships, *La Trinidad*, had made the passage to New Spain under the command of Saavedra. Later the same vessel voyaged again to the Moluccas under the command of the monk Urdaneta. He discovered that the most favorable winds for the passage were to be found along the 42° north parallel of latitude. Thus originated the passage between the East Indies and New Spain, henceforth known as Urdaneta's route.

The Spaniards now began to colonize the Pacific: the Philippines (Ruiz Lopez de Villalobos, 1542), Manila and Luzon (Lopez de Legaspi, 1565). It seemed for an instant as if Portugal and Spain might divide the world between them, like two halves of an apple, the coast of Africa and the Indian Ocean going to the Portuguese, America and the Pacific to the Spaniards. But this arrangement did not last very long. The English lost no time in preparing a fleet and the Dutch, until then masters of coastal trade in Europe, began to turn to long-distance commerce. But before witnessing the entry of these two powers upon the stage and the eclipse of two ancient empires, it is first necessary to assess what was known of navigation in Magellan's day and to say something about the men and their ships since the future destiny of the colonies was closely interwoven with the spread of sea voyages.

In the Patagonian channel. Photograph taken aboard the *Amiral Scharner*, 1965.

Magellan's ship *Victoria*. Anonymous engraving.

MEN, SHIPS AND NAVIGATION
IN THE AGE OF DISCOVERY

Magellan's ship *Victoria* sailed 43,380 sea-miles in her voyage of circumnavigation, if one includes the frequent tacking necessary with a sailing ship; in other words, more than 78,000 kilometers had been furrowed by her keel.

For the first time a voyage had been made in all seasons and weather in the search for trade. The ship had held her course despite all the hazards of navigation; in spite of disease, famine, and injury, she had returned safely to port, laden with a full cargo of spices brought from the other side of the world. The techniques of naval architecture, navigation, and seamanship had reached such a pitch that the great oceans could be challenged. It is of interest to consider the various aspects of maritime life at this threshold period, particularly as almost two hundred years were to pass before there was any marked change in maritime ways and customs.

A SHIP TO ENCOMPASS THE WORLD

Ever since the time of da Gama, the Portuguese had adapted the medieval caravel to their uses, with ships capable of sailing close to the wind and of maintaining a good rate of sail. Well-built, of low displacement and suitable for working close inshore, these vessels had crossed the Indian Ocean. However, as seamen became traders, new types of hull and rigging came to be developed by the Dutch and the Venetians.

These were the carracks, a fine reproduction of which may be seen in an engraving by Van Eyck entitled *Spanish Carracks and Galleons*, preserved in the National Library at Brussels. It was this type of ship, deep-waisted and

The carrack, a late 16th century European merchant ship. Drawing by Morel-Fatio.

square-rigged, that Columbus used to cross the Atlantic. The carrack featured three masts and a boom; a square foresail, a mainsail with topsail above and a mizzen; the whole vessel being squat, held solidly together by dowel-pins and bolts, and built to meet heavy seas and carry big cargoes. Towards the end of the fifteenth century the round stern became a square transom. The upper works—forecastle and poop—were joined to the main hull by continuous planking. Attached to the ship's sides and strengthening the internal joists, were massive ribs, juxtaposed in relation to the bilge-keel, the projection of which certainly did not improve the hydrodynamic qualities of the hull. Other features included a continuous deck running from stem to stern, pierced only by a hatch into the hold; an orlop deck with a number of ports through which protruded the muzzles of cannon only then beginning to be relied upon as fighting weapons.

Describing the battle of Lepanto, Montaigne declared: "Firearms have such little effect, except upon the eardrums, that their use has been abandoned".

The dimensions of this vessel were: length overall, 23 meters; beam, 7 to 8 meters; depth, 4·10 meters. Everywhere there was paintwork in vivid colors, while the sails were emblazoned and embroidered with designs. Figureheads, however, had not yet appeared. Ensigns and pennants flew from the trucks; the mainmast supported a crow's-nest—a sort of wooden basket, where the topmen operated, and whence doubtless Columbus' lookout first caught sight of the shores of America. Such was the *Santa Maria*, displacing a little more than a hundred tons and upon which Magellan's five ships were modelled.

Since it was a question of navigating in all seas and weathers and of undertaking long voyages of circumnavigation, it was no longer possible to shelter from bad weather, as in the past; more, therefore, depended upon the inherent quality of the vital parts of a ship. At that time, the lack of textbooks on naval architecture meant that ships owed their excellence to the art of the shipwright and carpenter, and to their imagination and experience. The backbone of the ship was the keel, with side and cross-members forming a perfectly balanced framework of wood, whose gaps were skilfully filled with timber and then caulked with pitch and tar. Below water the hull was smeared with tallow. The shroud-stays jutted out prominently, held in place by wrought-iron chains and surmounted with colossal muttonheads. Shrouds of Lithuanian hemp supported the masts, which were themselves lashed together here and there with rope in order to provide added strength.

The base of the shrouds was copper plated. Heavy as were the beams and planks, the hull still rode too high and light. It was necessary, therefore, to achieve trim by ballasting with stones and sand. This tended to counterbalance the effect of the wind upon the sails—perhaps too much, since the rolling of the ship was very severe. In distributing the ballast, attention had to be paid to the head of the ship's pumps which dipped down to the bilges, where trickles of sea water and condensation gathered. The pumps were operated from the deck and fitted with large pistons to insure maximum discharge.

There was also ample stowage for spare parts—sails, rope, hawsers, blocks and, until the time of Bougainville, ships carried an impressive quota of anchors and chains. The chains were coiled, in a "lion's den" or dark hole

Dutch merchant vessels of the 16th century. Anonymous engraving.

A large grain-hopper, a primitive machine used for discharging cargo from ships at Amsterdam. Anonymous engraving. (*Bibl. des Arts décoratifs*)

31

Galley sailing ships, steered by rhumb lines for compass points and not by degrees. The compass rose is divided into 32 points, each representing 11°5′. Thus north, north by a quarter, northeast, north northeast, northeast by a quarter north, northeast, etc. From Père Fournier's: "Hydrographie". (*Service hydrographique, Paris*)

at the bottom of the hold. There, too, turbulent members of the crew were confined. For the purpose of heaving up the chains when the anchor was weighed, the capstan had been invented whereby the rope was wound round a drum as the chain was hauled up, dripping with water and seaweed. There were also capstans on the deck where the halyards were secured and whence the yards could be hoisted as required.

In front of the orlop were the crew's quarters. These consisted of wooden frames held together with rope or of hammocks swinging from the deckhead. Shackles in the bulkheads were used to make fast each man's seachest. In the middle hung the copper secured by chains and positioned above its own hearth. It provided the cooking for the crew. Behind the orlop lay "paradise" —the cabins for prospective passengers. Underneath lay the powder magazine, well below water level so that it could be flooded in an emergency. The base of the helm was also there; and situated at the end of the free-swinging tiller was a clever device—"the manual"—by which the helmsman could keep steering while still watching the sails. It was not until near the end of the seventeenth century that spoked steeringwheels made their appearance.

On the upper deck of the poop lay the captain's cabin and those of the first mate, carpenter, and surgeon; below were the cabins belonging to the pilot-master and boatswain, the "nostromos" of the galleys. On the deck itself were one or two ship's boats secured by lashings. Forward at the bows were the two anchors, with their wooden stocks. Twenty to thirty meters long by four to five deep—such was the space from stern to poop, in which men had to live for months on end. Nevertheless, an advance had been made since the Crusaders' ships, in which the space allocated to each man measured 1·82 by 0·65 meters.

"IT HAS MISTAKENLY BEEN SUGGESTED THAT MARINERS ARE BARBAROUS AND INCAPABLE OF LEADING MORE SENSIBLE AND REFINED LIVES."
(*Père Fournier*)

Shipowners, merchants and bankers appointed a captain-general to command the expedition, upon whom they relied for its commercial success. Da Gama, Columbus and Magellan were more administrators and leaders than navigational experts. To them fell the critical decisions, often taken without consulting the ship's officers, as Père Fournier would have wished.

Each ship in a fleet also had her own captain, a replica of the captain-general; he was the man of action, the organizer and not necessarily a seaman. He was supported on board by a ship's master and pilot, both experts selected by the general only after a minute examination of their qualifications. Both the pilot and the "leadsman" or "lodeman" (the man who heaves the lead to find the depth of water) knew full well the consequences of the ship being lost through their negligence; they would quickly lose their heads.

The master was in charge of the ship's lading, trim, course and maintenance. In this he was assisted by the boatswain and, in larger ships, by the quarter-master. The latter also had responsibility for the cargo, when there was no clerk appointed by the merchants aboard. This clerk, also known as the merchant, purser, or factor (and later the supercargo), occupied an important

Maritime transport in the Indies. A miniature from the "Livre des Merveilles" of Marco Polo, 1351. *(Bibl. Nat. Manuscrits)*

The spice harvest. *(Bibl. Nat. Manuscrits)*

The river, port and admiralty buildings at Amsterdam about 1600. From a drawing by Rembrandt (1606–1669). *(Bibl. des Arts décoratifs)*

position in certain ships, according to the nature of the voyage. It was in addition, a role of increasing significance in the eyes of insurers.

The steward or major-domo presided over the ship's "pantry", later known as the storeroom. He distributed water; saltfish and meat to the cook; biscuits and other victuals to the crew. Every Saturday he supervised the issue of rations of bread, cheese and beer. The purser assisted in these duties and kept account of the outgoings.

The ship's cook was an important person. In North European and Portuguese ships, he was responsible for preparing in his galley everything the storekeepers had given him to cook, however much the ship rolled and however bad the weather. Twice a day, soup was prepared in his copper pots, under the vigilant eye of the storekeepers. In the evening the cook cleaned his pots and put out the fire in his galley—a heavy responsibility. On most of the Spanish ships, however, "each man was responsible for his own cooking and it was not unusual to see on board eighty to one hundred cooking pots simmering at the same time".

And so, here are all those who hauled, shipped, hoisted, polished, pushed, clambered up and down, and did everything else that was required aboard ship; those who sprang into action at the first shout of the boatswain and who ministered to the ship's every need—by night and by day, in freezing cold, rainstorms, and torrid heat; sick and well, and always without enough sleep or rest. These were the sailors, the topmen, the sailmakers—who mended the rents in the sails—the coopers, the caulkers, always at work from the bilges to the peak of the topmast. As Père Fournier wrote: "The qualities needed in a sailor are that he should be hardworking, trustworthy, attentive to himself and his duties, and reserved".

Over this community reigned God the Father, who "having created the world to reveal his glory, attributes and supreme goodness to mankind ... reveals them nowhere more clearly than at sea". One remembers the terrible dictum of the seafarers: "Anybody who takes the name of God in vain will be

The port of Amsterdam about 1647. *(Bibl. Nat. Estampes)*

tied to the mast and flogged by the boatswain and moreover will give two sous to the poor".

Those caught stealing on board had on the first occasion to repay fourfold; on the second underwent the punishment of being imprisoned in the hold and receiving one hundred lashes; on the third, they were flogged and hung at the yardarm. "A seaman who struck his captain, or even raised his arm against him was punished by having one of his hands transfixed to the mast by a dagger. He then faced the terrible agony of trying to get free by opening the palm of his hand and then gripping the handle of the knife between two fingers. Any seaman who libeled his master or contracted to sail under two captains simultaneously was hung from the yardarm."

The ship's captain, who was obliged to feed and pay his crew, was responsible for the loading of enough victuals in the hold to last the entire voyage. Every man was entitled to a fixed ration of bread or flour; one pint of wine, cider or beer daily; vinegar (at that time both a sauce and a medicine); pickled beef and pork; Bayonne lard; some mutton and chicken: salted and barrelled fish; and salt, butter, oil and fat.

"Dried vegetables are good victuals because they are nourishing and can be stored for long periods, particularly rice and barley; other goods which can be stored dry, are garlic, onion, grapes, prunes, figs, walnuts and hazels." But "the best victual of all is biscuit, because it needs neither to be ground, grated, salted nor diluted and it keeps for over two years". Nor was the candle to be forgotten—wax in hot climes, tallow in cold—nut oil for the lamps, and above all olive oil, "which has no superior and which answers to so many purposes".

One can imagine the infinite care taken by the storekeeper to preserve his victuals. But inevitably he saw his grain germinate, butter turn rancid, wine sour, biscuit crumble, and meat decay. The fare, eaten by spoon by the men either individually upon their sea chests or grouped round a dish, did not contain a trace of vitamins. After a few weeks the dreaded scurvy appeared.

Père Fournier has given a terrible description of its effects. The victims seemed "afflicted with dropsy, with swellings as hard as wood upon their thighs, legs, throat and ears; their complexion inflamed and leaden-hued; their gums blackened, teeth loosened, breath foul. Even so, appetite was not lost and death often occurred in the middle of drinking and eating. It was terrible to see the great slivers of putrid flesh which rotted the gums".

Relief immediately followed a return to land; nourished with fruit and vegetables the men soon recovered. It was not until three hundred years later—a case of scurvy occurred in 1914—that a complete diagnosis was made of this terrible disease. In those days it was mistakenly believed that "this disease commonly occurs on long voyages as a result of neglect in washing, in cleaning and changing one's clothes; of the sea air; of the tainting of fresh water and victuals; of cold and of sleeping at night exposed to the dew". To avoid it, no more effective remedies could be suggested than being sober, not oversleeping during the daytime and indulging in plenty of exercise. Once stricken, there was no remedy at sea. In spite of intense research, only the supply of natural foods and fruit, especially oranges and lemons, could effect a cure. But unfortunately as no means then existed of keeping food fresh on board, scurvy continued to rage. Under these conditions, a fine physique was essential if one wanted "to go down to the sea in ships". Fed on pease-pudding, biscuit and pickles; always soaked to the skin or suffocating in the fumes of the cabin, the sailors depended on their individual constitutions for their survival. Added to these horrors were the primitive methods of surgery practiced on board and the fact that no one had the slightest inkling of medicine. Until the close of the eighteenth century, if not later, medical chests on sailing ships were so utterly inadequate as to cause only amusement and dismay.

DE L'ESTIME, ET VSAGE DE LA CARTE MARINE, Ch. XI. 717

Papier Iournal.

CHAPITRE XII.

AV NOM DE DIEV SOIT

Le Nauire nommé S. Ioseph, dont apres Dieu, est Maistre vn tel N. Esperant auec l'aide de Dieu, & de la saincte Vierge Patrone de Diepe faire le voyage de Marseille est party l'an 1636. en

Iours & Mois	Runs	Vents	Qualité de Vent	Horlo-ges	Lieues Françoi-ses	Latitu-de Esti-mee	Diffe-rence de Longi-tude	Latitu-de Ob-seruée	Decli-naison d'ay-mant	Auantures
Apuril 1	ON O O SO	NE ENE	Bon fres B	26 22	39 16 ½	50 30 50 9	3 10' 4 30	50 10	4 30'	Nous vismes l'isle d'Huit
2	O SS	E NE	P	48	18	49 50	5 50			
3	O SO	NE	M	48	38	49 10	8			Nauire Turc chasse sur nous,& faict que nous nous retirons à Brest où nous demeurons 8 Iours.
4	O SS E SE	N N	B B	8 20	12 28	48 45 48 12	8 50 6 18			

Entry in the logbook proposed by Père Fournier.
(*Service hydrographique, Paris*)

An astrolabe of about 1600. The lower half of the instrument has been removed; and could in fact only shoot the stars above the horizon. (*Danish Maritime Museum, Elsinore*)

NAVIGATIONAL INSTRUMENTS

Really to understand the splendour of the maritime world [wrote Julien de la Gravière] one must go back three or four centuries in time, study oceanic navigation from its origins. One must return to the day where behind each stationary cloud one believed one saw an island towards which lost in apparently boundless space, one followed the flight of birds who at evening all flew the same way, in the hope of being able, like them, to sleep on land.

This passage from a work devoted to seamen of the fifteenth century, makes one aware of the paucity of navigational methods and geographical knowledge available to mariners at the time of the great discoveries. One historian has stated that Magellan took with him "marvellous charts and instruments". But what exactly were these famous portulans? In fact, they had to be marvellous indeed, based upon the presentiments of a wizard. In that age, in which one was forbidden to reveal the secret of a particular chart on pain of death, there was no exchange of information whatsoever; the most glaring errors in chart making were thus repeated time and again.

In his *Histoire de la Navigation*, Marguet has this to say on portulans: "In the old charts the shape of the continents is certainly recognisable, but that is about all; if one examines them in detail, many errors are apparent and their accuracy is far below what the navigators required".

Indeed! They had no adequate methods of surveying the oceans, islands and continents. Above all, they lacked good instruments or navigational tables with which to plot a route and relate it to the globe. Since the fourteenth century, the astrolabe and tables of the sun's declination—often recorded on the same instrument—enabled noon latitude to be fixed. By holding the alidade vertically in one's hand, the height of the sun was calculated through its sights; a quick calculation obtained the latitude, at best, only an approximation since nothing was then known about declination, refraction, and parallax.

HYDROGRAPHIE
CONTENANT
LA THEORIE ET LA
PRACTIQVE DE TOVTES LES
PARTIES DE LA NAVIGATION.

Composé par le Pere GEORGES FOVRNIER de la Compagnie de IESVS.

A PARIS,
Chez MICHEL SOLY, ruë sainct Iacques au Phœnix.

M. DC. XLIII.
AVEC PRIVILEGE DV ROY.

The title page of Père Fournier's celebrated work, "Hydrographie". (*Service hydrographique, Paris*)

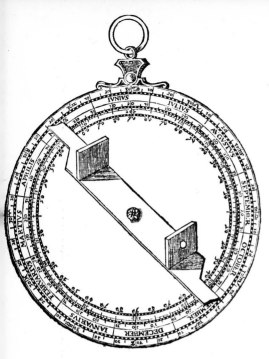

The most ancient instrument of astronomic navigation—the astrolabe, of Arabic origin. Held in the observer's thumb by its ring, the apparatus was placed in the vertical plane bounded by the star under observation, the observer's eye and the pole. Thereby the sun, the moon and the stars in the axis of the two holes in the mobile allotrope were visible; and the angle shown upon the graded circumference of the ring between the vertical and the axis of vision is the zenithal distance from which a latitude could be calculated. From Père Fournier's "Hydrographie", 1643. (*Service hydrographique, Paris*)

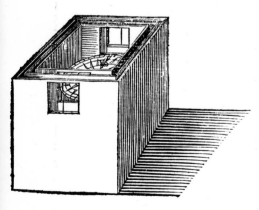

Taking a compass bearing at the beginning of the 17th century. One looked through the two holes pierced in the box and read the graduation on the compass rose pivoted inside. From Fournier's: "Hydrographie". (*Service hydrographique, Paris*)

The instrument was unreliable and great manual dexterity was necessary to obtain a reading on the swaying deck of a ship at sea.

Several remarkable solutions to the problem had been put forward: fixing a large instrument to the mast, or even installing a chair between the masts on gimbals, thus shielding the observer from the oscillation of the ship. Greater precision came with the development of the reflection instruments, particularly the octant. From the time of Magellan, latitude was obtainable with precision, but not longitude; all that was known of the latter was reckoned by the time taken to follow a certain course and at what speed. Time was measured by the hour or quarter-hour, with fragile sand-glasses which the helmsman turned over as soon as all the sand had reached the lower glass. Sometimes, tired with his trick at the wheel he turned it over beforehand. The accuracy of the hour-glasses was quite approximate, although some were calibrated in seconds.

In front of him the helmsman had the compass, housed in its binnacle. He kept as best he could the correct bearing on the course given him by the pilot, making due allowance for wind and weather. The pilot always kept asking: "Are you on course, helmsman?" But what value could such a course be, when no one realized that the compass deviated as a result of metal objects on board, and that its needle pointed as much as 20° off course? But already there existed the possibility of preparing tables of compass variations throughout the world. When he was at the Cape of Needles, Columbus had found a variation of 0°, just as in the extreme north the compass needle pointed to the Pole Star. It was thought then that latitude could be calculated by the sun's arc, and longitude by the compass. So it was they navigated by guesswork.

There remained the third element to be estimated: the speed of the ship. In this respect perhaps the greatest errors were made. It needed great skill for the eye to be able to follow a ship's speed through the water. An early method was to throw a piece of wood—a log—into the sea in front of the ship, and have a man, sand-glass in hand, stationed in the stern, who reckoned the time taken by the log to traverse the length of the ship. It was a clumsy device, soon replaced by the ship's log, a knotted rope which was unwound every half-minute from a reel, upon which the impact of ship's propulsion gave some idea of its speed.

Here again there was ample margin for error: an hour-glass in which the sand dropped in less than half a minute; distorted paying-out of the line or log; the effect of sea water in contracting the distance between the knots, theoretically fixed at fifty feet, one hundred being one twentieth of a mile. The length of this mile, according to a surveying-chain which in 1633 measured the distance as 1,866·60 meters, did not correspond exactly to its real length: 1,852 meters.

Having counted the knots that had been paid out, the pilot could make his reckonings. He examined the little pegs showing the track and speed of the vessel and then plotted his course on the chart. Had he taken account of the direction of wind and current? Was he fully aware of the prevailing tides? Deep-sea pilots of this period are often portrayed as possessors of great secrets. How had this arisen? There were more born sailors among them than men of science; the navigational resources then available did not allow them to make elaborate calculations. Thus upon their innate nautical skill depended the interpretation of the weather, the sea and the restless movement of the

elements. Without real scientific knowledge they had to return to first principles to find the ship's course and its speed and thus be able to sail from one point to another. Their best tools were the sea charts, ornamented with compass-roses, winds and a criss-cross of sailing tracks; of the latter, the crooked track between one known point and the next was far better than the straight line drawn at random.

Loxodromy, or the art of sailing by the rhumb lines—that is obliquely in relation to the meridians—is well shown in the projection of Mercator (1569), the father of marine cartography. Unfortunately, although Mercator had plotted his projection very correctly, it could not be shown mathematically; integral calculus would have been needed for that. Thus Mercator's projection shows distortion of the latitudes and the pole; the meridians are equidistant but the parallels deviate more and more as the degree of latitude increases. Therefore allowance for this distortion had to be made in measuring distances from the equator.

The ship's pilot needed great perception in order to put right the colossal navigational errors, which were the sum total of daily miscalculations accumulated during a long voyage. Above all, it was imperative he should know the ship's position because the landmarks on the chart were so often incorrectly shown. Time and again an islet or isolated rock might come into view, only to receive the wrong coordinates so that it could not be found on a future occasion. It was an age, too, of portents and omens; they reinforced the facts obtained from the sounding lead and the plummet line. The sight of birds portended landfall, as did tree-trunks and branches found at sea, and clouds over the peaks.

Weather might be forecast by studying the sea and the sky. Maybe the experienced navigators of that age could well have given accurate predictions for the regions they knew well. But how could they rely on being able to do so elsewhere, at the other end of the world? There, the only resort was to fall back upon the old sayings of the Navy. Without them, only prayer and entreaty remained.

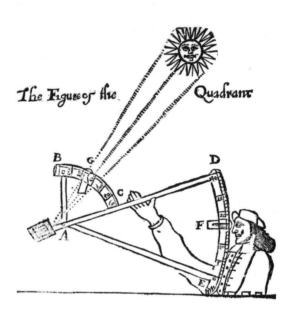

The observation of the sun by an instrument known as Davis's Quadrant, end of the 15th century. From an anonymous English sketch.

THE NEW GIANTS OF THE SEA: HOLLAND AND ENGLAND

But a new stage was now set. While Hernando Cortès disembarked at Campeche on 4 March 1519, burned his ships, and with 400 men, 15 horses and 7 cannons set out to devastate and conquer Mexico; while Francisco Pizarro with 110 foot-soldiers and 62 cavalry defeated 5000 Indians, strangled their chieftain Atahualpa and overran the empire of the Incas; while gold, silver and precious stones were brought from America by the Caribbean "flotas" to fill the coffers of the Spanish treasure; while Spain and Portugal continued to delude themselves with the illusion of each possessing one half of the world—two nations, England and Holland, awoke to their maritime destiny.

The Portuguese Empire expired slowly. It did not wait to be dismembered, but in 1580 Portugal herself disappeared, annexed by Spain for sixty years. Aware of the power of his empire, Philip II of Spain was confident of the future. But neither weapons nor arms could withstand the revolutions in thought and ideas of that era and it was precisely the Reformation which tolled the knell for Catholic Spain.

The victory of the Sea Beggars against the Spaniards at the Battle of Zuyderzee (11 October 1573). From van Stolk's atlas, Rotterdam.

The seventeen provinces of the Low Countries lived in peace, occupying the lands that are the Belgium and Holland of today. Herring fishing, clothworking, the processing and re-export of spices, coastal trade and the almost exclusive supply of many goods to the ports of Europe, had brought wealth to Holland. In 1519 the voice of Luther was heard; the Dutch became converted to Protestantism, from which sprang a fierce desire for independence; but in their lands, as elsewhere in the Spanish dominions, the Inquisition sought to impose strict orthodoxy. Thus arose the Revolt of the Netherlands—Charles V's posters against heretics, the persecution, the solemn protest by 300 Dutch and Flemish nobles at Brussels in 1566. "They are only beggars," remarked the Comte de Barleymont to Margaret of Parma in order to reassure her. But these beggars, hunted pitilessly on land and at sea, at length succeeded in throwing off the Spanish yoke and gaining independence.

By the Union of Utrecht (1579), the independence of the seven northern provinces was fully recognized, and they became the republic of the United Provinces under William of Orange. The war had fostered the growth of a Dutch navy and her destiny began to unfold, profiting from the decline in Spanish power.

Philip II, King of Spain (1527–1598), from an engraving by Vischer after a painting by Titian, 1549.

When Philip II came to the throne he had inherited a national debt of sixty-six million francs; on his death in 1598 the figure had soared to three thousand millions. The Spanish fleet was in ruins; the empire, including the Portuguese colonies, on the verge of disintegration. It now became the quarry. Dutch privateers struck terrible blows at Spanish merchantmen. On the long route of the treasure fleets, the galleons dreaded attacks of "sea-beggars" and English pirates; for now Spain had also to contend with England.

DRAKE

Drake belonged to the great line of Henry VIII's and Elizabeth's captains, to whom the Hispano-Portuguese line of demarcation was just a Papal fantasy. The English attacked everyone and everywhere; they specialized in the traffic of slaves from West Africa to the Caribbean and delighted in the support of the missionary de las Casas, who recommended the trade.

Drake served his apprenticeship as privateer and pirate under Hawkins. With him, he had a very narrow escape in 1568 following an unlucky attack against the Spaniards at San Juan d'Ulloa. From this point English hatred of Spain crystallized. Three years later, although peace still existed with Spain, Drake returned to the Caribbean in command of a fleet. Having landed at Nombre de Dios, the city was burned and pillaged, and the mule train which carried the bullion thence across the isthmus was also attacked. Unscathed, Drake returned to Plymouth with his booty. It was then that this ambitious man, the son of a yeoman, began to dream of becoming knighted. But for this he needed money, and gold was to be found in Peru. Therefore while Frobisher was wearing himself out in the search for a northwest passage, Drake decided to undertake a voyage to the west coast of South America, via the Strait of Magellan.

He equipped a pinnace and four vessels, the most powerful of which was the *Pelican* of 100 tons. On 15 December 1577, the flotilla sailed from Plymouth en route to the Cape Verdes; a Portuguese ship was boarded and a pilot found aboard her who knew Brazil. He was transferred and course was set for the River Plate. At the onset of winter, Drake found himself at Port St. Julien, as Magellan previously had done. The cold, the isolation, and the delay was as bad as ever. The squadron broke out in mutiny; but Drake had read his Pigafetta, and exacted swift reprisal. The ringleader, Thomas Doughty, who was one of his captains, was beheaded. If the authors of *The Famous Voyage of Sir Francis Drake into the South Seas* (London, 1600) are to be believed, Drake then advised his men: "each to prepare themselves for Holy Communion the following Sunday as good Christians and brethren, which had a very pacifying effect upon the company and shortly afterwards the crews returned to their ships".

Afterward, Drake got his ships under way and within two weeks passed through the strait. "We found amongst the islands of the channel great numbers of birds whose flesh was as delicious as the English goose".

At this time, too, an eclipse of the sun was observed. Having reached the Pacific, Drake sent the pinnace back to England with the news. Unfortunately the little ship was wrecked, and after being taken by Indians, Carter, the captain, did not reach England until six years later.

A violent storm struck the fleet at the mouth of the strait. One vessel

The English Admiral Sir John Hawkins (1532–1595). From an anonymous painting of the 16th century. *(Nat. Maritime Museum, Greenwich)*

Sir Francis Drake (1540–1596). Engraving by Houbraken, Amsterdam.

foundered; another, under the command of John Winter, turned back through the channel and set course for England. Having followed two or three different routes, Drake found himself alone on the 55° S. parallel of latitude. There a group of small islands with indented coastlines was discovered. However desperate the situation appeared, Drake did not give up hope. The Pacific coast had always been considered absolutely safe from attack; the effect of surprise would thus make up for lack of numbers. Drake pressed on northwards. On the way, the journal describes the discovery of islands: " ... upon which the numbers of birds almost defied belief. They are 8° within the tropics". These must certainly have been the guano islands, which were to make the fortunes of the sailing ships of the nineteenth century.

Drake passed the island of Mocha and skirted many of the Spanish coastal settlements. Of these, Valparaiso, Tarapaca, Arica and Callao were attacked and ransomed in succession. With unexpected good fortune, the Acapulco treasure galleon was captured, with 400,000 piastres aboard. Laden with booty, in such quantity as almost to sink his ship, Drake sailed north once more, searching for a channel eastwards, believed to exist near the 48° N. parallel. He discovered California and the Bay of Angels, but no channel. Course was then shaped for Mindanao, which was reached on 20 October 1579 after a 68-day passage with little food.

Pressing on, he weighed from there on 3 November and at last reached Plymouth on 26 September, 1580, more certain than ever of the merit of his achievement. Envied and condemned as the "arch-robber of the unknown world", retribution for his larceny was demanded by Philip II. But Queen Elizabeth came on board the *Pelican*, (renamed *Golden Hind*), and knighted Drake on the quarterdeck. She replied to Spanish protests:

The South Sea, as every other ocean, is open to all. The gift by the Bishop of Rome of a possession which does not belong to him is a fantasy. The Spaniards have no more right than other nations to usurp ancient kingdoms, nor to imagine that building a few huts or naming some capes and rivers entitles them to absolute possession.

After Elizabeth's support of Drake, the Pacific was invaded. English squadrons attacked Spanish treasure galleons and merchantmen in peace-time. The carriage of bullion became dangerous. But how else could it be carried?

Twice each year, in January and October, two convoys organized by the "Casa de Contratacion" crossed the Atlantic. Their escorts parted company at St. Domingo and Cuba, while the galleons proceeded alone to Portobello on the east coast of the Darien Isthmus. In the Pacific, a single galleon made the annual voyage from Manila to Acapulco, laden with spices and silk, which were then brought across the Darien Isthmus by mule train. Thereupon the Atlantic galleons returned to Europe, carrying the wealth of the East and West Indies. Henceforth fear grew that this trade, upon which Spain almost entirely depended for survival, would come to an end. The Spanish treasury could not take this risk.

Thus, when Sarmiento, sent in pursuit of Drake by the viceroy of Peru, returned to Spain via the Strait of Magellan, his proposal to Philip II that a fortress be built in the channel to bar access to the Pacific, was immediately approved. He was provided with a large fleet of twenty-three vessels, four thousand men and twenty women to populate the colony, and ample equipment and stores. The fleet was scattered in a storm, five reaching the Cape of Virgins and only two getting as far as the mouth of the strait.

Having left Seville in 1581, the Spaniards were still just beginning their task in 1584. They started building a fortress on the left bank of the entrance to the strait. Then one of the two ships returned to Europe, leaving Sarmiento alone with the other. In his account of the expedition the English navigator, King, has told of the terrible sufferings the men endured from hunger, cold, and attacks by the Patagonians.

With great determination Sarmiento held on, building a small port in the middle of the channel named San Felipe. Twice he tried to return to Rio with his ship, in order to obtain provisions for his men. He was held up by gales and finally altered course for Spain. While en route across the Atlantic he fell in with Raleigh's fleet, was made prisoner and taken back to England. Abandoned in Patagonia, the two hundred colonists he had left behind could only await a miracle for survival. Three ships hove in sight. However, it turned out to be Cavendish on his voyage of circumnavigation. The wretched Spaniards hoped in vain for a gesture of humanity by the English navigator. They finally perished from their sufferings at San Felipe, a place which history has renamed Port Famine.

Sarmiento was the last to try to fortify the strait leading to the Spanish

Port Famine, from the Atlas of Dumont d'Urville (1828). *(Le Tour du Monde)*

colonies. It was not long before they were penetrated by the Dutch and the English. For Spain there remained the isthmus of Central America and the stronghold of Nombre de Dios, and here the defenses were augmented. But Philip II turned to the invasion of England and the defeat of the Armada in 1588 marked the eclipse of his Spanish fleet.

The Americas and the Southern Continent, according to 16th century cartographers. The cartouche at the bottom of the Pacific Ocean carefully masks the ignorance of those regions at that time. From Ortelius' atlas, 1570. *(Bibl. Nat. Cartes et plans)*

THE SOUTH SEA AND AUSTRALIA

So the gray skies and the cold, the terrible wind and ice, the treacherous currents and the desolation of Patagonia overthrew most of the expeditions which had set out with flying colors to conquer the Pacific. The noisome creeks of the channel became the graveyard of countless Spanish and Portuguese seamen. The desert shore of its banks recovered the bodies of hundreds who had tried to force the passage to a new empire.

Thus had audacious projects formed on the Tagus and Guadalquivir met their untimely end. Negotiating the Strait was certainly risky and everything was against it as a regular trade route. Both Magellan and Drake had lost men and ships in so doing; others had failed to pass through, and some had been completely overwhelmed.

Of four vessels taken to the Strait in 1523 by Carjaval, Bishop of Placentia, three were lost. In 1535 Simon de Alcazova arrived at the entrance, but then died, and his squadron was compelled to return to Spain. Alfonso de Carmayo was forced to turn back in 1539 and twelve years before the Frenchman de Villegagnon failed to find the entrance.

Two ships set sail from Peru in 1552, under the command of Francisco de Ulloa in an attempt to navigate the channel from west to east, but it came to nought. In 1557 Garcia Hurtado ordered Juan Ladrillero to take two ships and retrace Ulloa's course. Ladrillero reached the Strait's western entrance, alone, lost nearly all his crew and eventually arrived back in Chile with only two men.

The English navigator Thomas Cavendish set out in 1586 to retrieve his fortunes which had been blighted by scandal at court. At the head of a flotilla of three ships he arrived at Sarmiento's harbour—San Felipe. Soon English corpses were to be added to the dead Spaniards which they found frozen to death in the huts and church. The fifty-two days taken to traverse the channel accounted for half his men: "The appalling climate and cold in this place are costing eight or nine men every day", wrote Cavendish's friend, Francis Pretty.

In 1598 the Dutchmen Simon de Cordes and Sebald de Weert were storm-bound one winter in the strait:

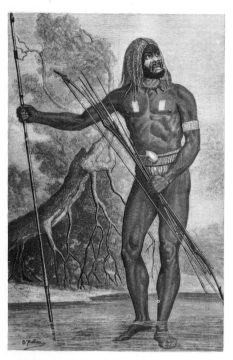

A native of New Guinea. Armed with spear, bow and arrows, he is the ancestor of the inhabitants of that great island which still today contains cannibal settlements. (*Le Tour du Monde*)

Gales were very frequent: hardly had one died down before the next came. They were so violent that many ships dragged their anchors and the men were constantly at work rescuing them. As if this were not enough, they had to endure rain, snow and hail ashore while they collected wood and water and searched for mussels or any other sustenance that could be found. Such labor was exhausting and hunger forever gnawed at them.

Men died like flies and the health of the survivors was permanently impaired. Only thirty-six of the one hundred and five men who had set out from Holland returned to the Meuse. Olivier de Noort who sailed from Rotterdam with 248 men in 1598 lost more than a hundred during the outward passage. Ten more perished in the strait, and his vice-admiral, on suspicion of treason, was cast away on a small island with a few provisions.

John Chidley set out from England in 1589 with three vessels; only one, the *Delight* under Captain Merick, arriving at Port Desire. He entered the channel but the dreadful climate carried off thirty of his men. While he struggled against wind and current to pass beyond Cape Forward, panic seized the crew. He was compelled to turn about and though the sole survivor of Sarmiento's colonists, reduced almost to the status of a wild beast, was taken aboard he died shortly afterwards. Finally he reached France again with only six men able to man the ship, but was wrecked off the coast of Normandy.

Admiral Georg Spilbergen, commissioned by the newly formed Dutch East India Company, was also faced in 1615 by the outbreak of revolt amongst his crew. At the entrance to the Strait one of his ships deserted and another sank. The rest of the fleet reached Cape Desire only with great difficulty.

With such a catalogue of frustrated effort and misery, plus so many deaths, one scarcely wonders that expeditions setting out to discover a new continent ended by reverting to piracy. As soon as the Pacific was entered, the ships invariably sailed northwards. Helped by the Humboldt Current, they came in sight of Mocha Island about 38°S. and then, according to their nationality, either called at a Chilean or Peruvian port, or filled their holds with booty. Then, carried by the trade winds, they crossed the Pacific on a westerly course to the Ladrones. It must be admitted that at this period little progress had been made in mapping the Pacific since the days of Magellan. The Polynesians with their great canoes knew how to cross that ocean far better than European pilots with all their navigational aids.

Drake had done a little exploration of the Pacific coast of North America. Apart from this, only some scattered islands in the tropics were known. It seemed that the search for the great continent of Australia, so fully shown on contemporary charts, had been abandoned as soon as the Strait of Magellan was forced and the attraction of obtaining quick commercial profit from the Moluccas became irresistible.

In fact only those areas of the Pacific near the equator were at all known, partly because pilots, steering by latitude, always kept their observations of the sun at noon at the same height on their astrolabes.

Setting sail from Mexico in 1542, Juan Gaetan reached the Solomons and in 1567 Mendaña returned home from there. In the belief that gold deposits existed, the King of Spain directed the viceroy of Mexico to take possession of the islands. Alvaro de Mendaña and Fernando de Quiros set sail for Polynesia in 1595. They were instructed to collect "all unwanted women in Peru" and establish a colony on the far off Pacific islands. Eventually they landed at Santa Cruz and the Solomon Islands.

"The islanders are barbarous" wrote Quiros in his journal, "they gaze at our clothes, plucking at them so that they can look at our bodies". When one remembers the length of the voyage and conditions on board, the haste shown by the navigators to reach their destination and find rest and sustenance, is understandable. One reads again in Quiros' journal: "On 14 January we descried a mountain peak. Our joy was unbounded and we could think of nothing but making landfall that day. Most of the crew could no longer stand and only a few skeletons were able to reach the bridge by supporting each other".

On arrival at Manila, the seamen had hardly enough strength left to drop anchor. The crew of a native canoe which came alongside were struck dumb at the sight of so many sufferers crying: "We are dying of hunger and thirst, give us something to eat, we are dying ... " Fifty people of both sexes perished on this ship during their crossing of the Pacific. Nearby another ship was found, with her sails set and the entire crew dead at the halyards. It is easy to see that under these circumstances a century had to elapse, and conditions on board ship to improve, before truly scientific expeditions could be undertaken.

One ship which formed part of the Dutch expedition of Simon de Cordes, was thrown off course by a storm in 64°S. at the exit from the Strait of Magellan. On proceeding further, her captain told of coming in sight of a land, "which resembled Norway". That seemed to confirm the existence of the continent of Australia. As for Cordes himself, he reached Japan with "only six of the crew able to move their limbs", where he and his men were

A native of Timor, whose civilization was in striking contrast to the savage customs of New Guinea. Inhabitants of Timor were peaceful, musical, artistic and fond of elaborate costumes. (*Le Tour du Monde*)

A native craft of the Solomon Islands. The picture shows the natives attempting to board the ship, one of whose boats is giving chase. *(Bibl. Nat. Cartes et plans)*

thrown into prison. To crown their misfortunes, the Portuguese Jesuit missionary who was their interpreter, felt that: "they could expect no other judgment than to be crucified".

However fate decreed otherwise. The emperor, beguiled by the industry of the newcomers, held them captive for five years and their descendants became the original Dutch settlers in the Far East. This colonization proved extremely beneficial to Holland, enabling her in time to oust the Spaniards and the Portuguese from Sunda and the Moluccas.

Quiros himself discovered the New Hebrides in 1606 and landed upon the south coast of the island of Espiritu Santo where he had an interesting parley with the local chieftain. Without an interpreter, they conversed by gestures. The king conveyed the varying sizes of islands by drawing circles of different diameters in the sand. In the case of a large country, he extended his arms and pointed to the horizon in the direction which it lay. Distance was expressed in nights rather than days and here the king cradled his head in his arms as if asleep. When he bit his arm, it meant that the islands in question were inhabited by cannibals.

SCHOUTEN AND LE MAIRE ROUND CAPE HORN

By rounding the Cape of Good Hope, Vasco da Gama had proved, much to the surprise of sixteenth century cartographers, that the "southern continent" was not joined to the southern tip of Africa, as they believed. They were certain, therefore, that this enormous land mass must be connected with South America. North of the Strait of Magellan, Patagonia formed the extremity of the American continent; to the south in Tierra del Fuego one set foot upon "Terra Australis". This supposition fitted well into the theories of that age, because they could not accept a revolving globe whose continental masses were so unbalanced.

In the north there was land everywhere: Europe, Asia, North America, Greenland, the Arctic Pole; in the south there was emptiness: the sea, a few islands, and continental extremities. As a result, both Ortelius and Mercator in their maps of the world carefully added the boundaries of a southern continent, to which they attached the coast of New Guinea. Hugging its south coast, Quiros and Torres never thought they had entered an immense gulf, nor that it formed part of an island.

So it was that navigators continued to make their voyages, still trusting in the theories of the age. The wiser venturers reached the Orient via the Indian Ocean, the bolder through the Magellan Strait to make landfall in the Ladrones.

A voyage made to the Indies by Houtman in 1595 attracted the attention of Dutch merchants. The loss of men was heavy—almost two-thirds of the ship's complement, but the profits were high. Shortly afterwards, eight ships under Admiral Jacob van Neck set sail for the Moluccas.

Commercial treaties were signed with the sultans. It seemed as if the final blow could be struck against Portuguese trade with the Spice Islands. The Dutch set up factories and overseas companies. The Amsterdam bourse soon became congested. In 1602 the government intervened to enact a charter whereby all the small trading concerns were merged into the all-powerful Dutch East India Company, which obtained an exclusive monopoly in the

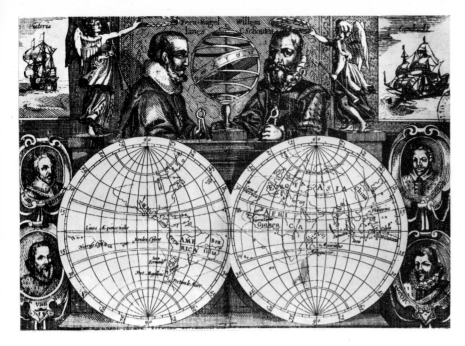

Frontispiece to Schouten's account of the voyage. It depicts two great discoverers, Magellan and Schouten face to face and surrounded by angels. The four other Pacific pioneers are also shown— Drake, van Noort, Cavendish and Spilbergen. (*Bibl. Nat. Cartes et plans*)

oriental trade. As a result, all independent Dutch traders were prohibited from sailing via the Cape of Good Hope or the Strait of Magellan. Of course, it was another matter if any bold spirit were to discover a northeast or northwest passage; but the shareholders of the company were content in the belief that none existed.

Two bold adventurers, however, the mariner Schouten and the merchant Le Maire, determined legally to overcome the prohibition. Might it not be possible to round South America through a channel other than the Strait of Magellan? A better idea of their intentions may be gathered by quoting from the preface to the account of their voyages published at Amsterdam in 1619:

As the result of a concession granted by the States-General of the United Provinces to the East India Company, all merchants and citizens of the said provinces have been forbidden to sail or trade to the Indies or any lands known and unknown, via the Cape of Good Hope or the Strait of Magellan. That being so, Isaac Le Maire, the well known merchant of Amsterdam, now living at Egmont, well experienced in foreign and local trade, and Guillaume Schouten, native of Hoorn, experienced navigator, having made three voyages to the East Indies as mariner, pilot and trader, and anxious to search for unknown lands ... have finally resolved to voyage to the southern regions of the earth and to look for a route to the South Seas, other than that via the Strait of Magellan, there having been made, in their view, little observation in the past of the environs of the Strait of Magellan.

Guillaume Schouten and Isaac Le Maire collected "as much money as they thought necessary for the enterprise and refrained from telling the other participants the true purpose of the voyage, keeping it entirely hidden".

They fitted out the ship *Concord*, 360 tons—with 65 men, 19 cannon, 12 swivels, muskets and other weapons in proportion—and the pinnace *Hoorn*, 110 tons—with 22 men, 8 cannon and 4 swivels. Officers and crew

JOVRNAL
Ou
DESCRIPTION
DV MERVEILLEVX VOYAGE DE
GVILLAVME SCHOVTEN, Hollandois natif de
Hoorn, fait es années 1615, 1616, & 1617.

*Comme (en circum-navigeant le Globe ter-
restre) il a d-scouvert vers le Zud du destroit de Magellan vn
nouveau passage, jusques à la grande Mer de Zud.*

Ensemble,

Des avantures admirables qui luy sont advenues en
descouvrant de plusieurs Isles, & peuples estranges.

A AMSTREDAM,

Chez Harman Ianson, Marchand Libraire, demeurant
en la V Varmoes-straet, a le Sereine. 1619.

The title page of the French edition of Schouten's voyage. Amsterdam, 1619. *(Bibl. Nat. Cartes et plans)*

were signed on, only "on condition that they went wherever the ship's master and merchants directed". They christened themselves "The Southern Company" and openly bruited the enterprise in order to obtain funds. Having weighed anchor from Hoorn on 16 May, 1615, they cleared the Texel on 17 June.

The trip is fully recounted in the *Journal or description of the wonderful voyage of Guillaume Schouten, Dutchman and native of Hoorn, made in the years 1615, 1616, 1617.*

The navigators sailed past Madeira and the Canaries, dropping anchor at the Cape Verde Islands where they purchased goats and tried without success to procure lemons. Skirting the coast of Sierra Leone, some of the crew developed scurvy. At a new anchorage, a stone's throw from a native village, they bartered Nuremberg knives for lemons, fish and other foods. Then they set sail once more, with a light breeze. On the 5 October a dull thud at the bows and a pool of blood in the sea alarmed the crew of *Concord*. The mystery was never explained, rather in the same way as an incident which occurred at Port Desire when the men were careening the ship and found, buried three feet in the stern below the waterline, the tusk of a narwhal. But the ship did not leak, so the voyage continued.

On 25 October, following the same wind we held upon our course. Until this moment we had proceeded without anyone knowing our destination, except our ship's master Guillaume Schouten and the trader Jacques Le Maire. Thereupon we were all told the purpose of the enterprise—to look for a passage to the South Seas other than the Strait of Magellan, which if we succeeded in discovering would lead to the finding of new lands and islands, where according to some, great riches were to be obtained. If they were not discovered we would then cross the South Seas to the Indies. All the crew were overjoyed at these tidings, both to know where they were going and with hope of individual profit from the voyage. On 1 November 1615 we passed below the sun and at midday discovered the sun to the north of us.

As they sailed south the water changed color and strange birds, fish and seaweed appeared. At about 47° S. the voyagers saw whales. On the 7 November land was sighted off Port Desire. The ships dropped anchor, the crew disembarked to search for gulls' eggs, prawns and fish. The men fished for smelt and returned on board with 150 penguins upon which they feasted. Then the westerly winds dragged the ships' anchors and they had to weigh and warp up river to a sheltered inlet. Disembarking once more, they discovered on the summits of hillocks some stone dolmens, under which were human remains they took to be of Patagonian chieftains buried there. Taking advantage of some fine weather and the spring tides they beached the pinnace in order to careen her. In the usual way they scraped the sides and then fired her; but the flames got out of control and spread to the shrouds and the upperworks, and in an instant the *Hoorn* was ablaze. There was no water near enough to put out the fire and by the next tide the superstructure was a charred wreck.

Nothing could be done except remove the ironworks and artillery and transfer them to the *Concord*.

The stay was prolonged; the search for fresh water continued with the crew scouring the country for pools. At last the decision to get under way was made. Sails were set and the expedition steered south along the coast, the sounding-lead ready for the first sign of shallows, contrary winds and current forcing them to anchor frequently. They sailed past the entrance to the Strait of Magellan and then, on 24 January 1616, they came in sight of what appeared to be the mouth of another channel:

Sounding forty fathoms and with the wind westerly, we sighted land far off to port, extending southeast and capped by several snow-covered mountains. We hugged this coast as far as we could and then saw more mountainous land to the east. These two ranges were about eight leagues distant, between which we thought there might be a channel through which the ship could proceed southwards. At noon we found ourselves in latitude 54°46′ and rode that night in a slight wind and with the current running strongly to the south. Here the number of penguins seemed infinite and there were so many whales that we kept shifting the ship's position in order to avoid an encounter with these sea monsters.

The land seen to the east they christened Staten Land, in honor of the States-General; that to the west was named after Maurice of Nassau.

Proceeding down the channel from side to side, Schouten and Le Maire noticed good anchorages, sea lions, penguins and seals. The snow on the mountain peaks led them to think of streams where they could find fresh water. The wind was fair and the current carried them south; one can imagine the anxiety felt by the pilots as they held their course. The lead sounded no bottom in the channel and at every moment they expected to meet ahead of them a range of mountains barring further progress and putting an end to their hopes. But at last . . .

. . . we met big waves and a swell rolling in from the southwest. The blue color made us think that on our starboard side away to the southwest lay the ocean, the great

"The sea wolves and sea lions have soft flesh, oily and evil-tasting; they bask in the sunshine in this way on the rocky islets and their howling and calling may be heard half a mile away." From Beauchesne's Journal. (*Service hydrographique, Paris*)

At Port Desire, the Dutch hunting sea lions to obtain their meat and fat. In this plan, north is facing downwards. (*Bibl. Nat. Cartes et plans*)

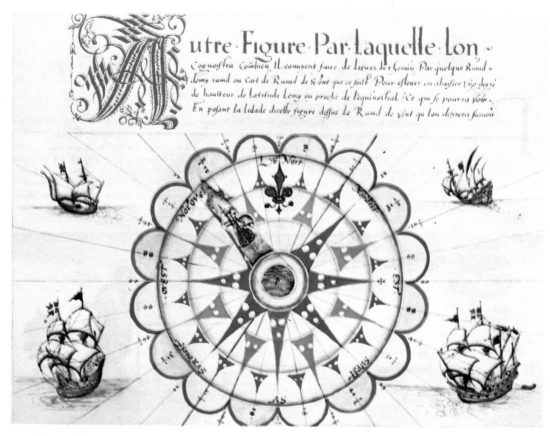

A diagram illustrating the points of the compass. From Devaulx: "Premières Heures", 1583. *(Bibl. Nat. Manuscrits)*

Part of the known world in 1583. *(Bibl. Nat. Manuscrits)*

The "Southern Continent" duly represented. *(Bibl. Nat. Manuscrits)*

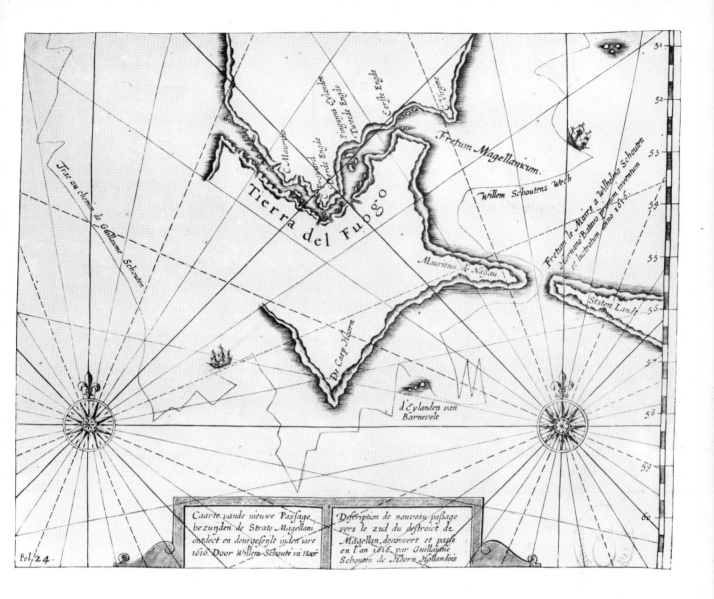

Caarte vande nieuwe Passage bezuyden de Strate Magellani ontdeckt en deurgeseijlt inden iare 1616. Door Willem Schouté vā Hoorn

Description de nouveau passage vers le zud du destroict de Magellan, deconuert et passe en l'an 1616 par Guillaume Schouten de Hoorn Hollandois

Fol. 24.

South Sea to which we had found a passage. That we had indeed discovered a channel hitherto unknown and hidden gave us great joy.

And then the albatrosses, whose wings seemed to the mariners as long as their own arms, made their appearance. It was the first time they had ever been seen and at once the malevolent relationship between the seamen and the kings of the southern ocean was established. As the birds rested on the *Concord*'s decks, flapping their huge wings, they were slaughtered by the sailors. The albatrosses fought back to the death and some of the topmen fell from the rigging, their skulls shattered by the birds' beaks.

It became terribly cold; ice coated the masts, the stays, the rigging and there were violent hail storms. Huge seas nearly stripped the *Concord* of her sails. The wind constantly veered between southwest and northwest, requiring frequent alteration of course. At dawn on 29 January the crew caught

The route taken by the ship of Schouten and Le Maire in rounding Cape Horn. This route became much admired by their unfortunate successors, because it required so few alterations of course. In the chart Staten Island was named Staten Land, because its westerly point—the only one known—appeared to belong to the Southern Continent. Once again, the area to the east of the cartouche covers the lack of knowledge of this region by the contemporary mapmakers. *(Bibl. Nat. Cartes et plans)*

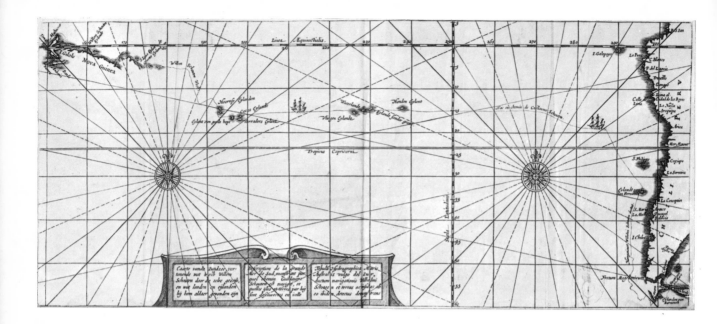

Having navigated along the Chilean coast in search of following winds, the Dutch set off across the Pacific helped by the southeast trades. In this vast waste of ocean they could hardly tell where the approaches to New Guinea lay. This was the state of hydrographic knowledge about the year 1617.

sight of two islands to starboard, "barren except for gray stones and a few rocks nearby" which they named Barnevelt. To the west the land fell away in a chaos of black cliffs tumbling down from the snowy peaks. The sea became still bluer, its swell increasing and they were in no doubt as to their having reached the Pacific.

"We found here such rain, hailstorms and changeable winds that course had frequently to be altered at every opportunity. In spite of it being midsummer, the cold was appalling and frequent southwesterly gales forced us to sail under reduced canvas."

So it was on 31 January 1616, rounding this black rocky headland, swept by wind, spray and heavy seas—the most southerly point of the American continent and frontier of the Pacific—that Schouten's men no longer doubted their achievement. In their elation, as they clung to the wind-tossed rigging and shivered in their rags of clothing and old seaboots, battered and shaken but happy, they threw their caps in the air and shouted: "We name it Cape Horn after our beloved village of Horn".

They were the first men and the first ship ever to have rounded the terrible cape from east to west. The achievement had demanded the ability of the ships to weather high seas and of the men to conquer their fear of the unknown. These men had found the real gateway to the South Seas. Under a rag of canvas and spurning the timid approach through the narrow Magellan channel, they had shown the way in both directions—for the great ships to enter one by one into the Pacific Ocean.

PART II

The Guardian of Australia

No sooner was the Cape Horn route discovered than it was abandoned. What did the Moluccas matter if gold could be found in Peru? A single galleon crossed the Pacific annually from Manila to Acapulco.

The conquered Indians now worked in the mines, whose gold and silver filled the coffers of the Spanish treasury. The Portuguese Empire was in eclipse; with the Cape of Good Hope route no longer guarded, the wolves broke into the sheepfold: the English and the Dutch reached the East Indies and China.

The windswept, gale-torn pinnacle of rock at the southern extremity of America, dividing the Atlantic and Pacific, had certainly persuaded Neptune to relent and allow Schouten and Le Maire's little ship to pass through; but future navigators would not escape her clutches. The war against the Spanish colonies brought Admiral Anson to the west coast of South America. At this new trespass, Cape Horn once again revealed her true colors: implacable, cruel, pitiless, changeable, furious and sullen. One had to accept her as she was, because the Strait of Magellan, too, had become deadly.

At the feet of this guardian of the Australian continent, merchant ships bound for the South Seas, whalers and vessels in search of unknown lands, paid their tribute in men and ships, and sometimes with everything. The appetite of this Minotaur was insatiable. It could only be defied when the mariners commanded more seaworthy ships, aptly named Cape Horners.

Slowly the hydrography and meteorology of the region became known. Slowly the narrow entrances and exits were charted, to allow the great square-riggers to sail to Chile, Peru, California, Australia, New Zealand, the Pacific Islands, China and Japan.

The discovery, colonization, and exploitation of these countries was expressed in the increasing number of sailing ships that slipped through the gap between Cape Horn and the northern limit of Antarctic ice. When maritime exploration approached completion, when it was clear that the

An 18th century frigate, from an American sketch of the period.

Cocos Eylandt
Isle de Cocos

Verraders Eylandt
Isle des traîstres

Schouten and Le Maire's ship at anchorage in the Cocos Islands (Boscawen Bay). Beyond is Keppel Island in the Solomon archipelago. (*Bibl. Nat. Cartes et plans*)

famous "Southern Continent" did not exist, when the seeds of modern world trade and industry began to take root about 1850, so many ships and men had rounded Cape Horn, that it was no longer undertaken in the spirit of discovery but rather in determination to get past an evil place as quickly as possible.

ON THE ROUTE OF THE "CONCORD"

Drake had reached the Moluccas in the *Golden Hind*. Upon his return, London merchants became deeply interested in the commercial possibilities revealed by the voyage and realized that profit could be gained by establishing regular intercourse with the East Indies. On Cavendish's return from the Indies in 1586, it was decided to promote a commercial venture, under James Lancaster in the *Edward Bonaventure*.

Out of two hundred men sent to the Indies, only twenty-five got back to England, but the cost of the expedition was largely redeemed. It was clear both to the English and the Dutch that commercial organization was needed rather than sporadic ventures, in particular the setting-up of a chartered company. But this they could not obtain from Queen Elizabeth.

However, the costs of promoting expeditions rose so steeply that it became imperative to act regardless of the political consequences. In 1600 the

Hoornse Eijlandt
Isle de Hoorn

charter of the East India Company was granted, under whose aegis James Lancaster voyaged to the Indies with three vessels. Although it cost the lives of five hundred men, this voyage made a profit of more than £200,000 and laid the foundation of English factories in the East Indies. Thus, two great powers practically supplanted the Portuguese and the Spaniards in the spice trade. The vessels of Holland and England rode at anchor side by side at Ternate, although both were at war with each other in Europe. "There is no malice in politics," wrote Tramond, "only self-interest".

So it was, that on 30 October 1616, while the Dutch vessels *Hoorn*, *Eagle* and *Loyalty* and three English ships belonging to the East India Company were taking on spices at Batavia, that Schouten and Le Maire's *Concord* entered the roadstead. For nine months she had pitched and tossed in the Pacific but had only lost four men.

Having sailed up the Chilean coast and then across as far as Juan Fernandez Island, the *Concord* had crossed the Tropic of Capricorn in search of the trade winds and then followed the 15° parallel of latitude to the Keppel and Boscawen Islands. Thereafter the north coast of New Guinea (Schouten's *Terra Australis*) had been explored in detail, before course was set for the Moluccas and Batavia. At Batavia resided the all-powerful director of the Dutch East India Company, Jan Pietersz Koenen, himself a native of Hoorn,

Schouten and Le Maire disembarking on Horn Island, in search of victuals for their crew afflicted by scurvy. The natives attempt to climb on board but are pursued. (*Bibl. Nat. Cartes et plans*)

The arrival of Schouten and Le Maire at Horn Island (Solomons). *(Bibl. Nat. Cartes et plans)*

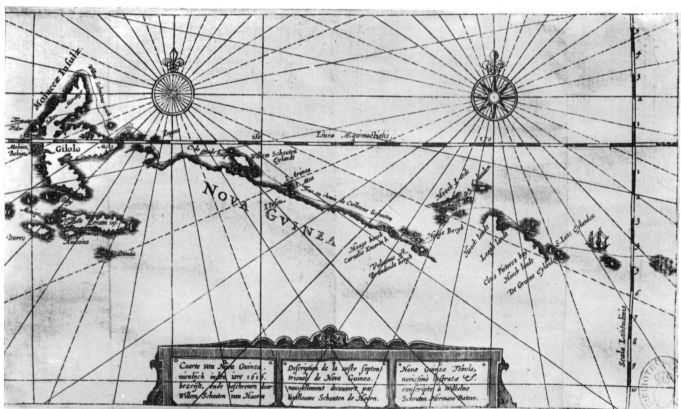

Reconnaissance of the north coast of New Guinea by the Dutch. They were aware that a southern continent lay to the south of them, but their main intention at this time was to reach the Moluccas and they did not dare to penetrate into the interior of the country, which they knew was inhabited by hostile tribes. *(Bibl. Nat. Cartes et plans)*

like Schouten, which did not prevent him from laying down the law. When Schouten and the merchants had been brought to him:

... he told them, in the presence of his assembled council, that according to the regulations of the East India Company they were obliged to place their ship and all their belongings in his hands. Schouten describes in his journal how much he was opposed to this demand, which he felt to be both wrong and unjust. But being in a minority he and his men were obliged to accept the director's demands, who added that if they believed wrong had been committed, they would obtain legal redress on their return to Holland. So they lost their ship and all their belongings. Some of the men were taken into the service of the East India Company, the rest were split up among two ships due to return to Holland, the *Amsterdam* and the *Zealand*, commanded by Admiral Georg Spilbergen.

Admiral Spilbergen was convinced that the so-called conquerors of Cape Horn were impostors. These people he thought:

... have discovered in the course of their long voyage, neither new territory nor peoples with whom one can trade. Their sole claim is to have found a passage other than that already known, which seems hardly likely since they have taken fifteen months and three days to reach Ternate. This becomes more doubtful when one considers that they had favorable winds and sailed in a single vessel, not therefore being subject to the delays always experienced by a number of ships in company.

Captain le Maye of the *Amsterdam*, who shared the views of his commander, went on to add:

The supposed discoverers, who have boasted of having found another channel, were very surprised at Admiral Spilbergen's fleet's arrival at Ternate long before them, although it comprised large ships, was frequently delayed, had taken part in a number of engagements, and visited and traded with several ports. The "discoverers" had set out only eight months after the fleet, which had spent only nineteen months in numerous operations before reaching the Moluccas.

In spite, however, of the opinions of Admiral Spilbergen and his officers, the *Concord* had indeed well and truly negotiated Cape Horn in latitude 55°59′ S.—not in latitude 57°48′ S., as Schouten had incorrectly estimated, through a faulty navigational observation made in rough weather—and reached the Pacific.

Other navigators did not hesitate to follow the new route and in proving the existence of another passage enabled Schouten and the relatives of Le Maire (Isaac's son, Jacob, died on the return voyage), to reap their just reward and retrieve their property confiscated by the Company.

In a passage in his *Navigations aux terres australes,* describing the voyage of Garcia de Nodal to "Magellanica", de Brosses tells us: "Scarcely had the King of Spain learned of Le Maire's achievement, than he expressed greater confidence in the discovery than Le Maire had received from his compatriots," and he immediately dispatched some Dutch seamen in two ships, with orders to go to the new passage between one sea and the other and "ascertain if it were possible to guard it by building two fortresses on the two (*sic*) banks".

Apparently Sarmiento's experience had not been warning enough; the idea of strongholds seemed to obsess the Spanish monarch, but in this case it was rather far-fetched, since the distance between Cape Horn and Levingston Islands was almost four hundred and fifty miles. A wide channel,

Davis's quadrant (reconstructed). *(Musée des Arts et Metiers, Paris)*

Overleaf: A planisphere of the world as known in 1700. Australia, the northwest coast of America, many islands and straits and both the North and South Poles are lacking. Also absent are reliable geographical coordinates, above all longitude, which could not be determined until the development of the chronometer. Nevertheless, one cannot but admire the extent of this cartographic work which could only be undertaken from information supplied by guesswork or by early instruments, the log, the compass and the sand-glass. From a map by Delisle, 1700. *(Bibl. Nat. Cartes et plans)*

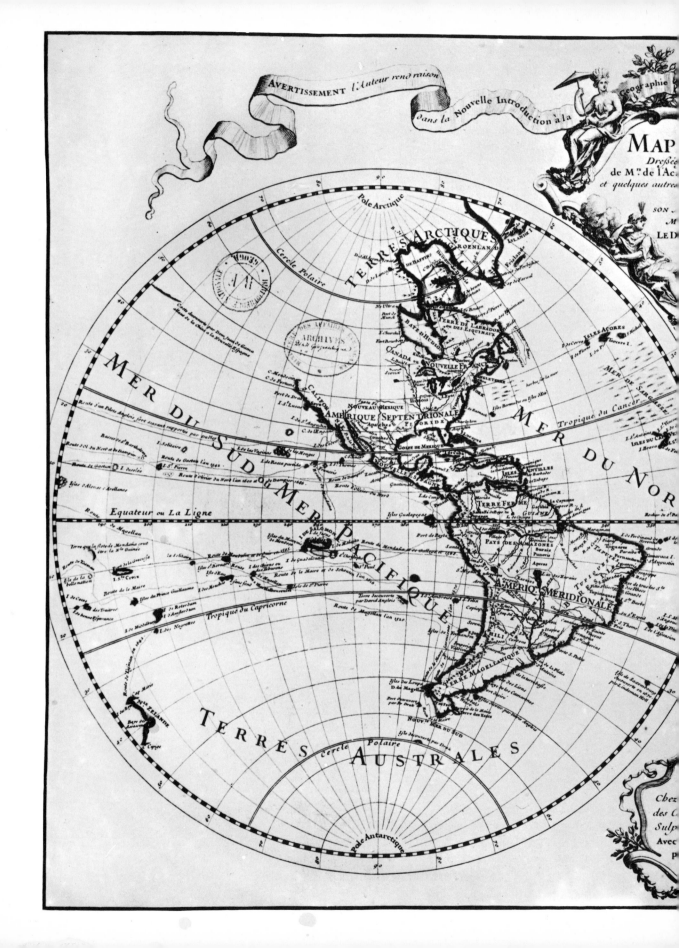

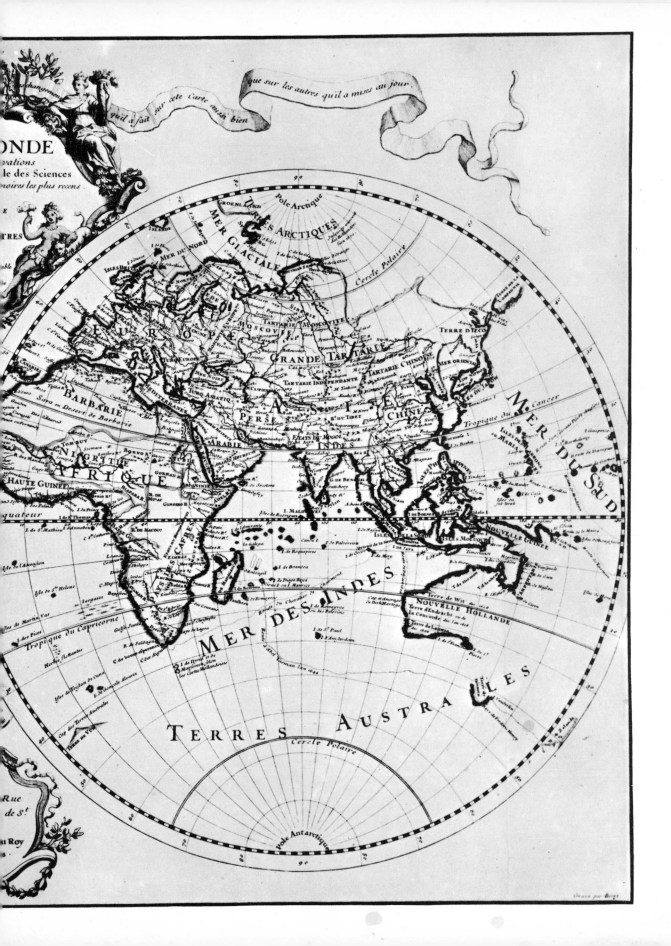

The warehouses and building sheds of the Dutch East Indies Company, about 1630. From an engraving by Mulder. *(Bibl. Nat. Estampes)*

indeed! However, every means of barring Dutch entry to the Pacific had to be attempted. In fact the Dutch admiralty were not impeded by efforts to close the Magellan Strait; they were far more concerned with the route opened by Schouten.

In 1623, eleven warships mounting 300 cannon between them, left the Netherlands under the command of Admiral Jacques l'Heremite and Hugues Schapenham "to conquer Peru". Having rounded Cape Horn, discovered an island (l'Heremite), a bay (Nassau), and another channel to the south of Tierra del Fuego, the squadron bombarded Callao, Arica and Guayaquil. The assault had little result, for the local inhabitants, whom the Dutch expected to rise against their oppressors, remained passive. L' Heremite himself died in Peru and the fleet sailed back home via the Cape of Good Hope.

For the next forty years nothing more was heard of the Strait of Magellan or Cape Horn. The expeditions had consumed too many men and too much equipment; the shipowners and merchants did not forget what it had cost Guillaume Schouten.

In the middle of the seventeenth century, politics rather than the urge for discovery stirred nations. France was at war with Spain and Colbert had just risen to power. The wealth of Holland troubled England and the Dutch East India Company reached the apogee of prosperity. The Hollanders' remarkable skill as traders was felt from the Cape to Batavia, and shareholders in their enterprises reaped profits up to 200%. The Dutch West India Company was formed in 1621 and England watched with jealous eyes the rise of the rival nation's merchant marine to world leadership. Against it, she pitted her own strength as soon as her shipbuilding program was completed.

The Navigation Act of 1651 was the English equivalent of the reforms of Colbert. Its provisions dictated English naval and commercial policy for more than two centuries. Some of the clauses were aimed directly at the Dutch merchant marine: "Foreign vessels may import into England only their own goods and manufactures. Foreign trade is reserved exclusively for English ships. Vessels engaged in English maritime trade must be built in England, under English ownership and their crew must be three-quarters English and under the command of an English captain". This was the basis of England's maritime policy. When the British Admiralty in 1652 sought to exercise these rights in the Channel, war with Holland became inevitable.

That year a fierce action took place between the English Admiral Blake and the Dutch Admiral Tromp off Dover. After a short truce in 1654, war was renewed with Blake, Monk and Deane on the English side against Tromp, de Ruyter and Evertsen on the Dutch side. The cost, £12,000,000, hit Charles II severely, whilst France recovered Dunkirk for £327,000. In such a situation there was little voyaging to "Magellanica".

The next significant occurrence took place in 1669 when two ships under the command of John Narbrough and John Wood sailed to Cape Horn. In dispatching them to the South Seas, the Duke of York included precise instructions and, for the first time in the history of navigation to that area, the objective was neither warlike nor mercenary but entirely geographical:

Your aim [one reads in the orders] is to make discoveries in the South Seas and on the coasts of the land to the south and if possible develop trade there. You will not make a landing on the American coast or even sight land, unless in an emergency, before you are south of the River Plate. You will not insult any Spaniards you may meet nor give them any ground for complaint. You will survey as exactly as possible capes, islands, bays, harbors, estuaries, shallows, sounds, tides, and currents seen in the North and South Seas.

You will take note of the trade winds and weather met with on the voyage, of anchorages in the Strait of Magellan, of all places where landings can be made; of the nature of the terrain; of fruits, trees, seeds, birds, beasts, stones, minerals and fish, fresh water and salt. You will do your best to bring back mineral and geological specimens to England and place them in the hands of his Royal Highness' secretary. You will observe the customs and manners of the local inhabitants, acquainting them with the power and wealth of the sovereign you serve. You will tell them that you have come expressly to establish trade and friendship with them; above all, it is essential that your men do not maltreat them, so that they do not have cause to fear Englishmen. On the contrary, their friendship must be sought through good behavior and you will punish any who act otherwise. Repeat all these orders to your crew, so that no one can plead ignorance of them.

Such were these curious instructions framed in an age of ruthlessness. Perhaps, the Duke of York believed that kindness might woo the people of Oceania from the Dutch who were noted for their brutality. When Narbrough reached Port Désiré he made an astonishing discovery: a post, hewn from a ship's mast and driven into the ground, upon which was nailed a lead plaque with inscriptions in Dutch, including the names of Schouten and Le Maire. There was a hole in the post in which was a small tin, eaten away with rust. Inside the tin was a scroll of parchment, quite indecipherable; on the shore loomed the burnt-out hulk of Schouten's pinnace. All was more than fifty years old. At Port Julien the pilgrimage continued, and

A flute, a type of European merchant ship. From an engraving made under Benard's direction, to illustrate naval architecture. (Bibl. Nat. Estampes)

here they came upon the grave of Thomas Doughty, the man beheaded by Drake. Eventually Narbrough and Wood got back to England with their charts, plans and sketches. Hydrographers before their time, they were the first scientific visitors to the South Seas. Their peaceful and interesting voyage was followed by others of quite a different nature—the buccaneers.

FROM THE CARIBBEAN TO THE PACIFIC

The pirate captain Bartholomew Sharp, accompanied by Dampier—who had turned from sacking towns, pillaging churches and killing Spaniards to exploration—crossed the Darien Isthmus, seized a ship, and made a "tour" of the Spanish colonies. The two men and their crew watered at Juan Fernandez, where they cast away a Mosquito Indian—a forerunner of Robinson Crusoe. They then rounded Cape Horn and passed Schouten's "Staten Land", which had subsequently been renamed "Staten Island" by Brouwer.

In this area Brouwer had been deceived in imagining there was more land to the east, the strait he followed being named by him Brouwer's Channel. This "channel" is accurately shown on contemporary charts, as is the land round about. Ought one, therefore, be surprised at Brouwer's error? No. At sea, nothing looks more like a line of distant cliffs than a mass of cumulus clouds in the setting sun. For example, off the coast of Galicia, a veil of mist over the high cliffs deceives one into thinking they are still far off, until you are suddenly amidst the rocks and the undertow. It is interesting to see on the charts of this period, that doubtful coastlines are shown with dotted lines and those which were well known, with unbroken lines.

Thus it happened that through errors in observation, the same islands were plotted in different places two, three and even four times within a 50-mile radius. Another mistake was to chart rocks, known as "lookouts", supposedly thrusting above the surface of water four to five thousand meters deep, visible to all, with the sea breaking over them and birds covering them. Was it not really a wreck or a whale that had been seen? Great care was taken on approaching these "lookout" rocks at night; sail was shortened until daylight and ears were cocked for the sound of breakers. In fog, immense detours were made to avoid them.

On returning to Virginia, William Dampier joined up with a pilot named Cowley in an expedition financed by French colonists, which planned to open up trade with Polynesia. The voyage began in 1683.

Cowley tells how, on arriving at Cape Horn, they were attacked by a sea monster. "We were amusing ourselves with choosing 'Valentines' according to the custom of our country, and discussing the fickleness of women, when a great storm got up and continued until the end of the month. It drove us southwards to 60°30′ S., farther south than any ship had yet been. From this we concluded it was a mistake to speak of women while at sea; that it brought bad luck, in this case, the storm." This tradition remained until the end of the sailing ship era.

The voyage of Cowley and Dampier continued. When they landed at Juan Fernandez Island they were greeted by the Mosquito Indian cast away there by Sharp. Amongst the works of de Brosses, this incident is recalled, as well

A buccaneer. From a drawing by Alexandre Olivier Oexmelin, 1686.

as the tale of another Mosquito Indian named Robin, who was the father of the one rescued from Juan Fernandez: whence the names Robin and Robinson. Dampier's ship pressed on northwards, touching at the Galapagos. Scurvy broke out amongst the crew and the rest of the food was completely spoiled. The spectre of famine haunted Dampier's men, as it did almost all mariners in the Pacific in that period.

"We have not had wine for sixty days," wrote Dampier "and every man is rationed a handful of corn a day. There are so many rats on board that we cannot stop them sharing it with us."

The likelihood of crossing the ocean and reaching the Ladrones within sixty days had to be carefully considered, if they were not to starve on the way. Contemporary charts differed, some placing the islands two thousand leagues from the Galapagos, others two thousand five hundred. But the captain convinced Cowley and the crew that the charts were wrong, and that with a good ship and fair winds the crossing would be made in forty days at the most. As a result, there was no need for rations beyond those required for sixty days to be carried. But he was wrong; the ship did not sail fast enough and the winds dropped. Luckily they reached Guam before the food ran out.

It proved to be just in time! "For I knew," Dampier relates, "that the crew planned to kill Captain Swan first and eat the food thus saved, and then follow it by doing the same to all those who had wished to make the voyage. 'Ah! Dampier' exclaimed doughty Captain Swan when they had reached dry land, 'you would not have been much of a meal for them!' He was right, as I had become thin and emaciated, while he remained round and plump".

A surprise awaited the navigators at Guam, in the shape of the Acapulco galleon, which had just dropped anchor on the south side of the island. What a temptation! But they had to desist, experiencing trouble in persuading the Spanish governor that their voyage was on behalf of a French company.

At Mindanao the mutinous crew cast Captain Swan adrift, where he was killed by the natives. Dampier, that strange blend of eighteenth century adventurer, pirate, businessman and writer, continued his travels in the East Indies. He nearly lost his life during a tempest while on a six-day cruise in an undecked vessel with no food or water; he then enlisted as a gunner at an English fort in Sumatra. Having deserted, he returned to London with a young Indian slave whom he sold at a profit. The publication of his journal brought fame and he became a specialist in Oriental matters. In 1699 he set out once more, this time aboard the discovery ship *Roebuck*.

William Dampier, English gentleman of fortune and culture. From an engraving by C. Sherwin. (*Nat. Maritime Museum, Greenwich*)

FRENCH VOYAGES TO THE SOUTH SEAS, AND OTHERS

In 1697 Monsieur de Gènes of St. Malo was operating in the South Seas in command of six French privateers. On 17 November of the following year Gouin de Beauchesne set sail from La Rochelle. His purpose was to develop trade in Oceania with both the Spanish colonies and the native islands. Although Père Fournier in his admirable work *Hydrographie* had recommended precision in keeping the log, Monsieur de Villefort, Lieutenant on the *Phélippeaux* in this voyage, became almost too precise in the entries he made.

St. Malo at the end of the 16th century, the port from which so many expeditions started for the South Seas. This natural harbor was well sheltered but had not yet, of course, its own wet dock. Anonymous engraving.

Having worked out at noon each day the particular reckonings made every quarter of an hour during the day, it is a simple matter to record the details in the logbook. At the top of the page you will inscribe the usual form of words which testify to the piety of our forebears and which even French heretics do not omit. In the first column you will put in the date; in the second, the course followed during the day; in the third, the wind; in the fourth, its strength; in the fifth, the time; in the sixth, the ship's position; in the seventh, the estimated latitude; in the eighth, the longitude estimated either from pricking your chart or consulting the navigational tables. In the ninth, you will record the latitude by observation and compare it with the estimated position on your chart; in the tenth, the magnetic variation; in the eleventh, any items of interest observed during the day.

In fact, however, this unusual log of the Gouin de Beauchesne expedition is full of interest, being the first account of a well organized voyage, which had profited from the experiences of its predecessors and which went to the Pacific eager to concentrate on discovery. Missing Cape Horn on the outward passage, Beauchesne went via the strait and returned around the Cape. Everything of interest—fauna, flora, the customs of the natives—was faithfully recorded in the journal by Monsieur de Villefort.

Of the savages of Tierra del Fuego who lit numerous fires while the ships lay an anchor in Port Famine, Villefort wrote:

To fight against these people would be quite pointless, as they reveal both friendship and a degree of poverty which Europeans could scarecely imagine. Here they live quite naked except for animal skins reaching only to their knees and have no dwelling except a primitive shelter covered with skins which protect them from wind and rain.

Beauchesne found the climate there no colder than in France at the same time of the year. On the other hand, the squalls that came down from the mountain tops were a menace to the ship's cables and anchors. At the mouth of the strait Beauchesne lost sight of the expedition's second ship, commanded by M. de Terville, which had set course to the north. Beauchesne followed in his wake, making for Valdivia which had been chosen as the rendezvous. On arrival and about to enter port, he suddenly saw smoke and heard the guns of the fortress firing; soon afterward, M. de Terville's ship appeared, helped by an off-shore wind. Her captain told Beauchesne that he had had to cut his cables as Valdivia was a trap and the local Spaniards treacherous.

There was no prospect of trade or victuals on that coast, which was fortified and appeared to expect an attack by corsairs. Beauchesne therefore called at the last Chilean port before the frontier of Peru, hoping for better treatment. Although there were many promises and palavers, few provisions were obtained and no trading was done. Trying further north, he sent his gig ashore, with an officer and his chaplain aboard, "the Spaniards showing great respect to priests". But they found everyone had fled except the sick and aged, who seemed to think they were English pirates. Beauchesne, however, managed to gain the confidence of some merchants, willing to cheat the government and trade illicitly. For, believe it or not, Spain in 1700 still tried to exclude all other nations from the Pacific on the basis of the old papal bull and line of demarcation. Whatever their intentions, all English, Dutch and French visitors who appeared there were ranked as pirates and corsairs.

By treaty and alliance, the Spaniards kept commercial control of their Chilean and Peruvian colonies. But English woollens and other goods were brought to South America in Spanish ships, a trade that not even the English pirates could interrupt. Such was the end of the Valdivia "incident".

After a visit to the Galapagos, which showed that nothing could be done there, Beauchesne returned to Peru. Once more he was refused wood and water by the local authorities, but managed to dispose of his cargo, including spoiled goods. Beauchesne then decided to return home and made for the entrance to the Strait. The weather was bad and the rudder of M. de Terville's ship broke. Thinking it unwise to attempt the Strait under these conditions, he pressed southwards and rounded "in excellent weather at

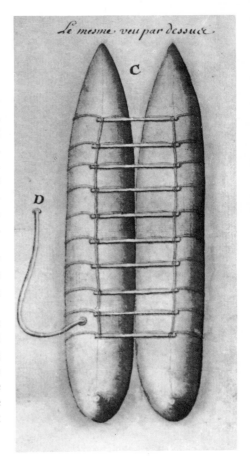

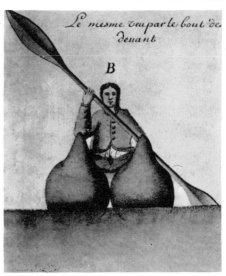

Three views of the same type of craft seen by Gouin de Beauchesne in 1799 on the Peruvian coast. This type of "Bombard", made by stitching together animal skins, was filled with air before being launched. In order to compensate for the loss of air, the passengers had to take turns to blow into a rubber tube amidships so that the voyage could continue. (Manuscript. Service hydrographique, Paris)

57° 15′ S., without sighting land. It was enough to know that passage in such a high latitude could be made without risk". Further on he discovered and charted an island which is still named Beauchesne. A surprise awaited them at Rio: "Several of my crew found prompt answers to letters which they had written at random, while I found none from the governor or the Portuguese ambassador, to whom I had written".

The great achievement made by the expedition promised well for future trade with the Spanish colonies. An island had been discovered, few men had been lost and Beauchesne himself had invented the famous "drinking tank", soon to be found on all sailing ships.

Although we were short of water and it had been rationed for some time, we found a better method of economizing it. This was to put a water butt on deck, from which everyone might drink with a mug only. In this way we soon found that much less water was consumed.

The major achievement of the voyage, however, was that it marked the first tentative attempt to establish commercial relations with Chile and Peru. The founders of the "South Sea Company"—the merchants Danycan of St. Malo and Jourdan of Paris—had warned against violence at all cost, in order to gain the confidence of the inhabitants—if not the authorities at least the merchants. This, as we have seen, was done. Both in navigating the Pacific and opening up new markets, Beauchesne had introduced new methods.

Unfortunately at this juncture, Philip V became King of Spain (1700). In order not to hurt his feelings, the "South Sea Company" was ordered to cease its activities in the Spanish colonies. In point of fact, this sacrifice of trade caused little harm, because neither of the two French companies (of the East and West Indies) had been quite as active since their foundation in 1664, as their English and Dutch counterparts. Neither had had any success in China or the Pacific. On the other hand, French companies trading in Guinea, Senegal and St. Domingo were active and flourishing. But their achievements affected Africa and St. Domingo, not the Pacific. The only resource, therefore, left to merchants operating in the South Seas was to trade illicitly. In a remarkable pamphlet entitled *French Voyages to the Pacific before Bougainville, 1695–1749* (Bougainville, born in 1729, did not enter the navy until 1763), Dahlgren gives a good description of the origins of this contraband trade. Perhaps the history of the great sailing ships around the Horn began there, at least insofar as the French merchant marine is concerned.

In France everyone awaited the removal of the ban upon sailing to Chile, as Beauchesne had done. Ultimately the subject became a political issue and an ambiguous understanding was reached with Spain. In March 1709, Monsieur Chabert, in command of a squadron of ships that had come together at Peru, brought them back to the harbor of Port-Louis (Morbihan) with thirty million pieces of gold and silver in their holds. A happy event for the Minister of Finance, who claimed it was the shipowners' duty to deposit the bullion in the Treasury in exchange for debased coinage and paper money. That duty was avoided many times. Having set sail from St. Malo, La Rochelle and Bordeaux, the contraband fleet had rounded Cape Horn incognito, sold part of their cargo in Chilean ports and then crossed the

Along the coast of Peru in 1700 the inhabitants were observed paddling a raft made of two bundles of reeds joined together. Beauchesne's Journal. (*Manuscript. Service hydrographique, Paris*)

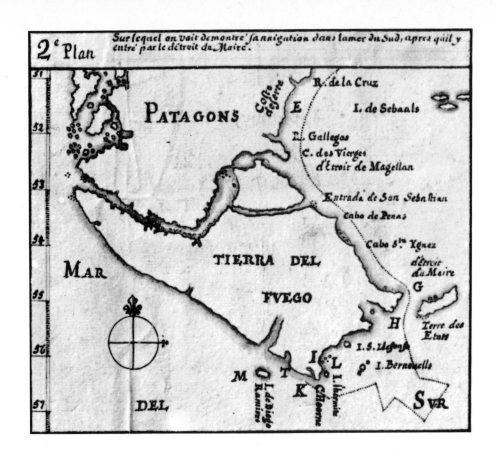

2ᵉ Plan Sur lequel on voit demonrre' sa naigation dans la mer du Sud, apres qu'il y entre' par le détroit du Maire.

PATAGONS

Costa deserta

R. de la Cruz

I. de Sebaals

R. Gallegos

C. des Vierges
d'Étroit de Magellan

Entrada de San Sebastian

Cabo de Penas

Cabo S.ᵗᵃ Ygnez

d'Étroit
du Maire

TIERRA DEL

FVEGO

Terre des
Etats

MAR

I. S. Ildefonso

I. Bernevelle

DEL

I. de Diego Ramirez

C. Hoorne

I. Inferni

SVR

1ᵉʳ Plan de la carte reduitte de Pitre Goots, que j'ay reduit a petit point, pour demonrrer qu'elle fut la naigation dudit d'Arquistade depuis son depart de Sainct Malo, jusqu'au l'Étroit du Maire.

AMERIQVE
Terre Neuve
OCEAN
EVROPE

SEPTENTRIONA.
Bermude
ATLAN. de

Tropique

AFRIQVE

MAR.

Ligne 1ᵉ Equi. 2ᵉ

noc

ttale

DEL SVR

AMERIQVE
MERIDIONA

TIQVE

DV NORD

Tropique

Capricorne

Ó Pacifica

R. de la Plate

OV MER

Étroit de Magellan
d'Étroit du Maire

C. Hoorne

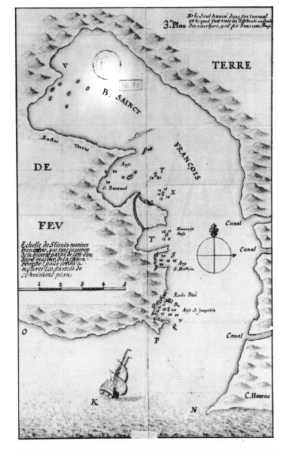

3.Plan et le seul hance dans son journal et lequel fait voir les differents endroits des ancrages, qu'il fit dans cette Baye.

TERRE

B. SAINCT

DE

FRANCOIS

Bahes Terres

Anse
S. Bernard

FEV

Canal

Maravilh
Anse

Canal

Echelle de 5 lieues marines françaises...

Rock Plat

Canal

C. Hoorne

A hydrographic chart of Cape Horn at the beginning of the 18th century. As can be seen, soundings and details of the sea bed are beginning to appear on the chart. Charts from the voyage of the *St Malo* to the Pacific, 1714–1717, drawn by Monsieur d'Arquistade and printed by Ledemaine Godalles, the royal hydrographer.

(Bibl. Nat. Cartes et plans)

Pacific to China. They had disposed of the rest in exchange for full cargoes of silk, porcelain and tea, which they sold on their return to Chile and Peru. Their ships almost awash with the quantity of bullion in the holds, they slipped back to France, using every imaginable stratagem to evade detection.

Not all were so lucky. The voyage of the *Falmouth*, commanded by Joseph Danycan and owned by Noel Danycan of St. Malo, was an unfortunate example. Having sailed from Brest on 10 November 1705, the *Falmouth*—500 tons, 50 cannon, 298 men—proceeded straight to Magellan, without stopping either at the Canaries, Cape Verde or Rio. Becalmed for many days she reached the entrance to the Strait very late, with the crew famished and scurvy-ridden. There she met another of Noel Danycan's ships, the *Danycan*, commanded by Captain Surcouf's and on her way to Chile via the Horn. The *Falmouth's* captain obtained Captain Surcouf's promise of provisions and some wine, but the next morning the *Danycan* had disappeared over the horizon.

The sick were disembarked from the *Falmouth*, but as nothing could restore their health, the voyage was resumed a week later. One hundred and sixty men were in a state of collapse and only a little fat was left to make a sort of soup. In appalling weather and with the crew utterly exhausted, it was decided to make for the Plate. One hundred and ten perished on the way. Only a skeleton crew remained and manning the sails in the estuary was beyond their strength.

They had to drop anchor off the north bank and send a boat with nine able-bodied men to seek assistance in Buenos Aires. Bad weather came and the rescue launch did not return. Those of the crew who could still stand, rather than wait any longer, set off themselves in a boat for Buenos Aires, leaving the sick between decks with a little food. Three days of high wind, rain, storm and lightning followed in the estuary. The chaplain died; the little party, weary and reeling, reached a small haven where they rested and devoured the carcass of a jaguar, which had been thrown into the sea.

At last they reached the Chuelo river and the port of Buenos Aires. There the Spanish soldiers forbade the unfortunate men to disembark, only Captain Danycan being allowed to see the governor. The exhausted men endured one more night without food or help, and on the next, all their belongings were taken from them. Five or six days passed before they had regained enough strength to return to their sick companions on the ship. Recrossing the estuary, they came across the first boat which had set out for Buenos Aires; it was empty and its occupants were dead. A further horror awaited them on board; all the sick had succumbed. Only twenty-one of the one hundred and ninety-eight men who set out from Brest had survived. Could not the cargo at least be saved?

Once more the captain went to see the governor in Buenos Aires. It was a waste of time. The governor refused not only to send anyone on board but also to allow some French vessels in the estuary to assist Captain Danycan. Five months passed, until in the end the ship was ransacked and plundered by Indians. What little was salvaged by the boats, was confiscated and sent to the treasury. Shortly afterwards, the *Falmouth* was set on fire and scuttled by order of the local authorities, under the pretext that her guns might be used by the Portuguese. It was not until 1707 that the survivors managed to return to France in a merchant ship.

Did the terrible fate of the *Falmouth* discourage or divert navigators? Not at all. In 1708, the Englishman, Woodes Rogers, sailed for Cape Horn with two ships, *Duke* and *Duchess*, and Dampier as pilot. Rogers did well to reach 61° S. (being December, ice floes had not reached the low latitudes) having passed the Falkland Islands, already discovered by Davis and re-discovered by Richard Hawkins in 1594. From that point he sailed into the Pacific without sighting Cape Horn, a straightforward course admired by the deep-water sailors who were to follow.

Rogers earned another niche in history for the rescue of the unfortunate Alexander Selkirk, castaway on Juan Fernandez for four years and four months after a quarrel with the captain of the *Cinque Ports*.

De Brosse comments: "His lonely and isolated situation was not as dreadful as most people think, especially since it arose from inevitable circumstances. Necessity is the mother of industry; simple food and temperance keep a healthy body and mind". Selkirk—Robinson Crusoe must have known something about that!

Directed against the Spaniards and French, Rogers' cruise began and ended with the sack of Guayaquil. The booty and spoils were brought back to the Downs, via the Cape of Good Hope, in 1711.

That same year, a Frenchman, Frézier (1682–1773) introduced a more scientific approach to voyages. For fifty years Cape Horners were indebted to his improvements in hydrography. In the course of two expeditions (1711–1714) to the area of Cape Horn and the Strait of Magellan, he fought the seas, explored the bays and channels and prepared plans with great enthusiasm. He began the account of his voyages, however, on a note of apology:

"The gulls of the Strait of Magellan are wiry and nervous; they stink horribly and their flesh is very bad eating." Beauchesne's Journal. (*Manuscript. Service hydrographique, Paris*)

The ship *Jean Bart* and the frigate *L'Aigrette* in the middle of a "pampero" storm which lasted for nine days at the entrance to the Rio de La Plata. From the drawing by Jacob. *(Bibl. Nat. Estampes)*

Many parts of my book can be ignored by those for whom navigation serves no purpose; but it is more important for the Republic, and the country's trade, to know about the seasons, winds, reefs, good anchorages and landings than merely strange and interesting things. More care must be given to the preservation of ships and their equipment and more recognition to those who work for their country, rather than satisfying the curiosity of idle men who prey upon hard pressed mariners, beset with many dangers.

As well as preparing excellent charts, Frézier published manuals of navigational instruction for seamen:

You can recognize the entrance to the Le Maire Channel from three headlands of the same shape, known as the Three Brothers, jutting out from the eastern end of Tierra del Fuego, between which may be seen a high sugar-loaf mountain, remote and snow-peaked ... Usually every vessel attempting to round Cape Horn should steer half a degree more to the west and south than is apparently necessary, to allow for the pull-back of wind and current ... those sailing round in winter should particularly beware of icebergs, since the nights are longer and daylight visibility worse than in England, making it difficult to avoid them easily.

It seemed as if French traders, both legal and illicit, had succeeded in reaching the heart of the Spanish colonies, in contrast to the misfortunes experienced by English and Dutch merchants on the west coast of South America. But at the Treaty of Utrecht in 1714, both England and France

72

agreed to a ban upon illicit trade in the South Seas, and two years later the death penalty was imposed in France upon smugglers.

Actually, it was a useless gesture. Marchand de Chalmont's ship, *Saint François*, sent out to Chile to enforce the ban, actually carried smuggled arms and goods aboard. Having tried in vain to check the corruption of her colonial officials, Spain paid French ships and crews handsomely to patrol the South Seas for them. In 1717, Martinet was very successful in this direction, but after France and England had declared war against Spain in 1719, the illicit trade flourished again, at the expense of the royal treasury and the privileged companies.

In 1721 Jacob Roggeween proposed to the Dutch West India Company that an expedition be sent to explore the "Southern Continent". He sailed from the Texel on 21 August, rechristened the Falkland Islands, "South Belgium", and having rounded the Horn discovered an unknown Pacific Island on Easter Day, 6 April 1722. It was thereupon named Easter Island. The islanders welcomed the mariners, already suffering from their voyage.

"They wanted our friendship," said Roggeween, "introducing their wives, offering them to us even to the extent of allowing us to take some of them back to the ships."

The provisions taken on at Easter Island—"five hundred hens and sweet potatoes which tasted almost like bread"—were soon exhausted and both ships and crew were in a bad state on arrival at Batavia, where Roggeween sought to refit. But here, as had happened to Schouten and Le Maire a century before, they came up against the power of the Dutch East India Company. Its commercial monopoly gave it the right to dispose of all the expedition's possessions, including the seamen's own clothes on the spot. Roggeween and his men had no alternative but to return to Amsterdam, recount their woes and commence legal proceedings, which in the end brought them compensation.

Despite regulations, decrees, threats and interference, the shipowners made a handsome profit out of this voyage; including four hundred million francs for those of St. Malo—enough for several years of idleness. Moreover, the experience gained by the expedition was as valuable as the material wealth acquired. It was proved that ships of size could use the route regularly and more was known of the meteorology and hydrography of the Cape Horn area. Charts prepared at St. Malo enabled navigation to be made via accurately plotted landmarks. Sounds and anchorages were shown. Science had begun to replace the allegorical figures on the charts, the mariner's cards, caravels and spouting porpoises. Quite apart from the attention to detail, these surveys revealed a degree of skill equal to the definitive charts prepared by Fitzroy, one hundred and thirty years later.

In the interval, however, between the two, there was a wealth of difference in experience of the area. According to Frézier, there was no danger in rounding Cape Horn provided a few simple precautions were taken. But Anson, for instance, had experienced such a severe ordeal during the passage, that navigators for a long time afterwards preferred to use the twisting and also dangerous Magellan channel.

A marine mercury barometer on a Cardan mounting, end 18th century. (*Mariners Museum, Saint-Malo*)

Lord George Anson, a portrait engraved by
McArdell after Reynolds. *(Nat. Maritime
Museum, Greenwich)*

THE ANSON ODYSSEY (1741–1744)

In 1741, England had been at war with Spain for two years; Spanish "guarda-
costas" sought to deny England merchantmen access to the Caribbean. The
Admiralty, uncertain of where to begin reprisals, turned to the idea of sending privateers into the Pacific. The instructions given to Commodore Anson
were very definite: "... To harry and destroy, by land and by sea, as many
of the Spanish possessions as you are able ... to take, sink, burn or disable
every ship of theirs which you meet". The route to be taken was left to him,
but he was instructed to intercept, if possible, the Acapulco galleon.

Six warships, displacing a total of 4,000 tons and carrying 2,000 seamen
and soldiers were fitted out, with two storeships in support. Anson sailed
first to Madeira, escorting a large convoy en route for St. Helena. There he
left the convoy to make its own way, and struck out across the Atlantic for
St. Catherine Island off Brazil. Two weeks out from Madeira, the charter
arrangements made with the two storeships broke down. One was prepared
to renew the freight contract; but the entire cargo of the second, the *Industry*,
had to be transferred at sea by the boats of the squadron hove-to. This
difficult operation was accomplished in three days, thanks to the skill of the
oarsmen. It was not the last time that their dexterity was to be called upon.

After the fresh winds of the trades, they were becalmed in the Doldrums.
Scurvey and ill-health struck down the crew, battened down between decks,

and the heat accounted for the remainder. Anson was thankful to make landfall at St. Catherine Island, six weeks after departing from Madeira. During the passage three hundred and twenty of his men became sick and ninety died.

The stop at St. Catherine did not, however, improve matters because one hundred and thirty more fell sick and another thirty died. For a month the squadron lay there, overhauling its rigging and equipment before facing the perils of the southern latitudes. A fierce hurricane dispersed the ships as they warped out of St. Catherine, but they were later reunited in the harbor of St. Julien, before attempting Cape Horn 450 miles away. Here a council-of-war was held in which it was decided that the next rendezvous for the fleet would be, first, the island of Nuestra Senora del Soccorro, and then Juan Fernandez. Richard Walter, the expedition's chaplain, has left a melancholy description of the Le Maire channel :

Nothing would be more horrible than the aspect of Tierra del Fuego; it affronts the eyes in a succession of rocks and screes, without any semblance of life or vegetation. The cliffs rear up in sharp pinnacles to a prodigious height, permanently snow-covered and flanked by precipices; some appear to hang in the air. The broken rocks at their base are split by numerous ravines, which seem to have been formed by earthquakes, since the fissures are almost perpendicular and run the whole length from top to bottom.

The subsequent description of rounding Cape Horn is hardly less sinister.

A bird's-eye view of the island and Cape Horn. (*Aviación militar del Chile*)

Indeed, one is surprised at the reticence of earlier voyagers in their description of the Cape. Perhaps the joy at returning home, having circumnavigated the globe and overcome so many dangers, made them forget their sufferings at the hands of the worst seas in the world. But from the time of Anson until the end of the great age of sail, the accounts are virtually in full agreement in describing the ordeals endured by men and ships in these desolate regions.

Anson certainly had little knowledge of the logs kept by those who had rounded Cape Horn before him, nor of Frézier's meteorological observations. He merely had the advice to attempt the passage only in the middle of the southern summer, that is between January and March. The end of March and the end of September was the worst for equinoctial gales. In March precisely, Anson arrived at the mouth of the Le Maire Strait. The weather suddenly changed, and a furious gale beneath leaden skies, surprised the fleet. Sail was quickly reduced, but the seas rose in violence and soon the men were at the pumps.

The dangers we have met in the last three months exceeded any which have perhaps ever been experienced by a naval expedition in the past. After the first gale, we were subjected to a period of violent weather which astonished even experienced sailors and made them revise their definition of the word "storm". There were waves of a height and closeness together which surpassed all our experience in other seas, and we were continually in fear of one breaking over the ship and sinking her. The waves, too, made the ship roll so badly that the risk of being smashed against the tiller or the ship's sides remained, in spite of every effort to hang on. Some of the crew were killed in this way, and others badly injured.

The storms were rendered more dangerous by their irregularity and by the deceptive intervals of calm which came between. After having sailed for many days under a rag canvas, or even bare poles, we did not dare to put on more or hoist full sail, because the gale would return without warning and in even greater force to tear our sails to ribbons. Nor was this all; the accompanying hail and snow covered the rigging with ice and froze the sails. Both became brittle and difficult to operate except in the most elementary way; the crew's hands and feet became numbed and frost-bitten and several developed gangrene.

Anson's fleet entering the Le Maire Channel. Staten Island is to the left, Tierra del Fuego to the right, recognizable by the three hills known as the Three Brothers. Engraving from a sketch by Lieutenant Brett.

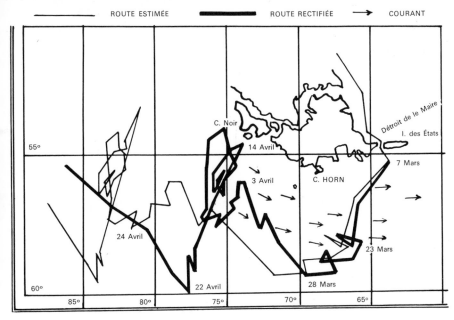

The course taken by the *Centurion* during her passage of Cape Horn, March–April 1741 (and constructed from the logbooks of the voyage). The thin line shows the course which Captain Nutt believed had been taken; the thick line shows that which was actually taken under the influence of wind and current. (*Diagram by the author*)

Three weeks had elapsed since the first storm and the squadron was still far from its goal. On 28 March 1741, it was 200 miles from the Horn in latitude 59° 30′ S.; as for longitude, who could tell after so many alterations of course? In the weather prevailing it was impossible to gauge wind and current correctly. On 31 March, *Gloucester's* main yard snapped and four days later, both *Wager* and *Anna* were partially dismasted. *Severn* and *Pearl* disappeared. On 10 April a hailstorm swept the squadron. In vain Anson searched for the other ships; only much later did he learn that two had steered north and ultimately put in at Rio, one—*Severn*—only at the end of one hundred and twelve days after parting company.

Out of the 384 men who had sailed from England in *Centurion*, only one hundred and forty-four now remained, and fourteen of these were totally incapacitated. On 14 April, one of the ships still remaining with Anson signalled that land had been sighted. Anson could scarcely believe it, thinking that they were more than five degrees further west. But there it was, looming out of the mist, Black Point on the west coast of Tierra del Fuego. Their estimate of position had erred, although allowance had been made for the drift of the current.

Disappointed, they hauled about and made a long detour to the south to avoid land, but by 22 April had made little progress westwards. After yet another gale two days later, *Centurion* lost contact with the other ships, which was not regained for seven weeks. She sailed north towards the first rendezvous, Soccorro Island. Scurvy raged among both seamen and troops. During April forty-three were committed to the deep, their bodies sewn into their hammocks and ballasted with a cannonball. In May these were followed by eighty more.

When the *Centurion* eventually reached Soccorro, the crew were nearly crazy with distress and fear; many lay shivering in their hammocks or

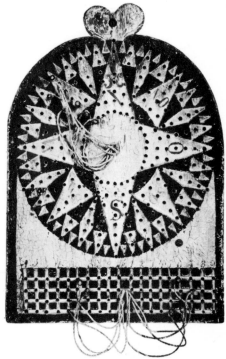

"The Fox and the Chickens." Often called simply "The Fox", one of the earliest navigational instruments. The method was to push a peg into one of the circular holes around the compass card (a circle of holes represented each half-hour of the watch measured over 8 circles), corresponding to the route followed by the ship during each half-hour. The small circle represents the first half-hour of the watch and the largest circle the last. The four lines of holes below represent the four hours of the watch. At the end of each hour a peg is pushed into one of the holes (numbered 1–20), of the corresponding line. These figures denote the speed of the ship in knots. By these means it was possible to represent on the chart the estimated course followed. (*Photo Nat. Maritime Museum, Greenwich*)

wallowing in their own excrement. For two terrible weeks the ship lay off the island, unable to anchor because of the surf. Anson then set course for Juan Fernandez, seven hundred miles away. Each day on average, six victims of scurvy were committed to the sea, while the survivors worked the pumps night and day.

Having reached the latitude of the island, but uncertain of his longitude and thinking he was farther west, Anson doubled back to the east in search of it. Two days later the coast of Chile hove in sight and he had to haul back once more. It was not until 9 June that they descried Juan Fernandez at a distance of twenty-five miles. Only two quartermasters and six seamen remained able to work the ship. They approached land as night fell, without being able to find anchorage.

The next morning, with no one in a fit state to let go the anchor, a providential gust of wind blew the ship, her anchor dragging, into Cumberland Bay. The *Tryall*, which came into the bay the following day, was in no better state. Only one lieutenant and four men remained able to man her. The sick were landed at once, but this did not prevent several from dying there.

On 26 June 1741, the *Gloucester* reached the rendezvous in an even worse plight. Anson sent food and men to her, but contrary winds which lasted for twenty-seven days prevented her gaining the anchorage. Sometimes, the wind pushed her back when she was within a mile of the *Centurion*; the effect of this torture upon the men aboard may be imagined.

Two hundred and fifty-four had perished since the departure from St. Julien. On 16 August the storeship *Anna* arrived at Juan Fernandez with a full crew, having stayed two months at Tierra del Fuego and replenished her stores. Having been condemned as unseaworthy, she was burned after everything worth saving had been taken out. The story of the last ship—the *Wager*—was not known until many years later, following an account by one of her lieutenants, John Byron.

The *Centurion* at anchor off Tinian (Marianas). Engraving from a drawing by Lieutenant Brett.

Robinson Crusoe signalling to a ship. Extract from Mame's "Voyages autour du Monde", 1846.

The bad weather had thrown the *Wager* and *Anna* together; but, whereas the *Anna* found refuge in a fjord, the *Wager* was wrecked on the beach of the Gulf of Penas, seventy miles further north. During five terrible months the drama continued. The crew mutinied, abandoned Captain Cheap, Lieutenant Byron and eighteen men, and set off amongst the maze of Fuegan channels in an attempt to reach Brazil. Of the eighty mutineers who started out in the biggest ship's boat, only thirty reached their destination. There is a story that one of them died in England at the age of one hundred and nine. Captain Cheap and three of the officers reached Chiloe, after being rescued by Indians, but their companions died on the way. The saga of the wreck of the *Wager* was not the last to take place in the sinister regions around Cape Horn.

The climate and natural wealth of Mas a Tierra (Juan Fernandez)—Robinson Crusoe's Goat Island—enabled Anson to recuperate his men and prepare his attack against the Spaniards. The subsequent events brought no particular credit to him, the punitive expedition entrusted to him by the Admiralty being carried out to the letter. The chaplain of the *Centurion*, Richard Walter, gives a picturesque description in his journal of the famous Acapulco galleon, a survivor of the heroic age of the Peruvian conquest.

In defiance of the Spanish edict of 1725, which restricted the Manila route to European vessels, the Jesuits and other religious orders chartered

The *Centurion* at Macao giving a broadside salute; the picture also shows the captured Manila galleon. Illustration from Harris: "Voyages," London, 1764. *(Service hydrographique, Paris)*

the galleon each year for their own use. Driven by the Westerlies along the 30° N. parallel—Urdaneta's route—the great ship took six months or longer to reach Acapulco. Seaweed off the Californian coast betokened the approach of shallow water, so she steered southwards towards San Lucas in Mexico. As it was quite impossible to carry sufficient water for six months, an ingenious arrangement of matting and bamboo pipes, erected between the masts and the shrouds, enabled rainwater to be collected in large jars suspended from the rigging.

The appearance of the Acapulco galleon was thus quite unmistakable, and as soon as Anson observed her silhouette on the horizon, he took the *Centurion* with her sixty guns and 227 men, immediately into action. All was soon over; a prize crew was put on board and found 1,500,000 piastres in the galleon's hold. The expedition continued on its way to China and Macao, where the galleon was sold to the Portuguese for 6,000 piastres.

Returning to England via the Cape of Good Hope, Anson dropped anchor at Spithead on 16 June 1744. He was congratulated by King George II, promoted admiral and made a peer of the realm. Of the two thousand men who had set out with him, only 145 returned on the *Centurion*. And £480,000.

The following year, a St. Malo marchant ship, bound for Callao (damaged by an earthquake and tidal wave) rounded Cape Horn in both directions with ease. But it was Anson and his experiences which were remembered. The account of his voyage inspired an uncontrollable dread in the minds of South Sea navigators for decades. For a time the Strait of Magellan regained pride of place.

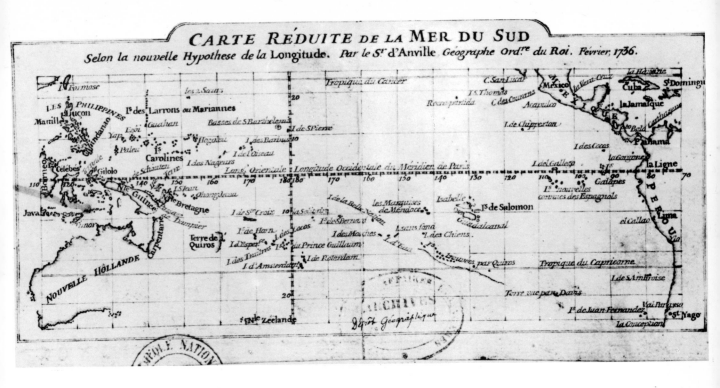

KNOWLEDGE OF THE PACIFIC

It is helpful to have a chart of the Pacific in front of one, in order to follow the succession of expeditions which fall into three distinct periods: before Byron (1764); between Byron and d'Entrecasteaux (1764–1791); and from 1800 to 1840. They were formidable undertakings when the vastness of that great ocean is realized.

In 1606, the Dutchman Widen Janszoon entered the Gulf of Carpentaria, named after Carpenter who had been there before. Another Dutchman, Abel Tasman, sent out by the Dutch East India Company in 1642, traversed the Indian Ocean far to the south and discovered Van Diemen's Land—Tasmania. Having sailed north as far as the Freycinet peninsula, he then steered northwest until he sighted what he thought was Schouten's "Staten Land". It was in fact New Ireland, in longitude 152°E. The voyage continued to Tonga and Fiji, in such a way that, without ever having sighted it, Tasman had circumnavigated Australia. In 1686, Dampier anchored in the Bay of Seals, and the Dutchman van Delft, retracing part of Tasman's track, discovered the Melville Islands in 1707.

The world chart published by Delisle in 1700 is remarkably accurate, showing what was known of the Pacific at that time. In the north and northwest the Dutch explored the coasts of Japan and Sakhalin, and around 1712, the Russians reached the Kuriles and Kamchatka. In 1728, Bering crossed the Strait which bears his name, while Russian fur traders set foot on the shores of America, at Nootka Sound. Beginning with Byron, a new phase of exploration developed. Previously much had been left to chance. Henceforth, a more systematic quartering of the unknown regions was carried out,

Small chart of the Pacific prepared by D'Anville, 1736. (*Bibl. Nat. Cartes et plans*)

TABLEAU

DE L'ACHAT, ARMEMENT

CARGUAISON, MISE=HORS, COMMISSION, ET

des armement de deux Vaisseaux de

Ligne et quatre Frégates,

COMPOSANT

UNE ESCADRE POUR UNE

EXPÉDITION SÉCRÉTE,

A LA DÉCOUVERTE DES TERRES AUSTRALES,

SITUÉES À L'OCCIDENT

DU CAP=HORN, DU CHILI, ET DU

PEROU, DANS LES MERS DU SUD ;

depuis les cinquante sept dégrès

Manuscript. *(Service hydrographique, Paris)*

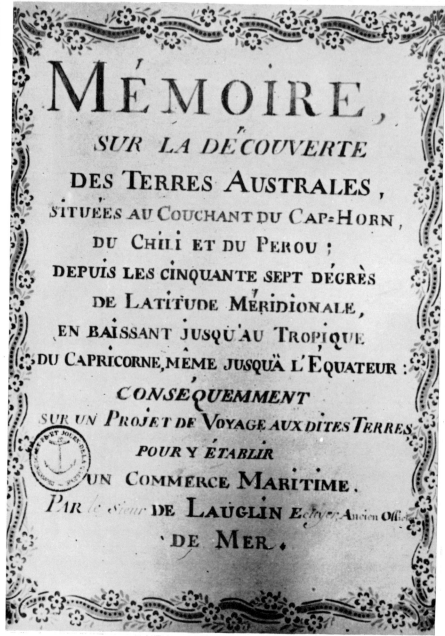

MÉMOIRE,

SUR LA DÉCOUVERTE

DES TERRES AUSTRALES,

SITUÉES AU COUCHANT DU CAP=HORN,

DU CHILI ET DU PEROU ;

DEPUIS LES CINQUANTE SEPT DÉGRÈS

DE LATITUDE MÉRIDIONALE,

EN BAISSANT JUSQU'AU TROPIQUE

DU CAPRICORNE, MÊME JUSQU'À L'EQUATEUR :

CONSÉQUEMMENT

SUR UN PROJET DE VOYAGE AUX DITES TERRES,

POUR Y ÉTABLIR

UN COMMERCE MARITIME,

PAR le Sieur DE LAUGLIN Ecuyer, Ancien Officier

DE MER.

Louis-Antoine de Bougainville (1729–1811). Drawing by Belliard. *(Bibl. Nat.)*

John Byron (1723-1786), commander of the *Dolphin*. Painting by Reynolds. *(Nat. Maritime Museum, Greenwich)*

discovery keeping pace with new instruments and methods. It was the beginning of the great scientific voyages, fostered by an era of relative peace in Europe.

In the course of his voyage, 1764–1766, Byron looked for Pepys Island in vain, visited the Falklands, re-established the position of Bouvet Island and explored the Pacific. Wallis and Carteret, in their voyage of 1766–1768, were able to plot several unknown places, thanks to better instruments and observational methods. Wallis reached Tahiti along the parallel of latitude, while Carteret took a more northerly course.

Then came Bougainville, ordered by the King to discover the "Southern Continent". In three years, 1766–1769, he voyaged to the Falkland Islands, where good relations with the Spanish governor were re-established, went to Rio, and visited the Navigator Islands, Samoa and then New Hebrides. But Australia remained undiscovered.

The Royal Society in 1768 dispatched Cook to the Pacific, ostensibly to observe the transit of Venus but also to locate the "Southern Continent", of potential interest to English trade. Having negotiated the Le Maire channel, he rounded Cape Horn. After arrival at Tahiti in April 1769, the scientists disembarked with their instruments to observe the planet's transit, while Cook set off towards New Zealand. Was this the Australian continent? In order that there should be no doubt, Cook undertook elaborate surveys of both the north and south islands in a series of charts, plans and sketches,

Resolution and *Discovery* amidst icebergs, during Cook's third voyage (1776–1780). *(Nat. Maritime Museum, Greenwich)*

The fleet of Otahiti assembling at O'Paree. From the atlas to Cook's voyages. *(Service hydrographique, Paris)*

Sandwich Islands' canoe—a sort of sailing catamaran—propelled by masked rowers. From the atlas to Cook's voyages. *(Service hydrographique, Paris)*

English missionary station at Kidi-Kidi (New Zealand). From Duperrey's "Voyage on the *Coquille*". *(Service hydrographique, Paris)*

View of part of the village of Malavae, Tahiti. *(Service hydrographique, Paris)*

James Cook (1728–1779), by Nathaniel Dance.
(Bibl. Nat. Estampes)

Port Christmas in the Kergulen Islands in the 18th century. Illustration from Cook's Voyages.
(Service hydrographique, Paris)

intending to bring them back to England via the Cape of Good Hope, as he considered the Horn route too difficult at that time of the year.

On 31 March 1770 he left New Zealand, and ten days later arrived on the coast of Australia in 38° S., opposite Cape Farewell and not far from the future Sydney. Proceeding along the coast up to Cape York, the discovery of a large continent could no longer be doubted. Having traversed the unexplored eastern coast, he took possession of it on behalf of King George III and named it New South Wales. Still following the coast northwards, he escaped shipwreck on the Great Barrier Reef, passed through the Torres Strait (whose existence had been questioned) and, via Batavia and the Cape of Good Hope, set sail for England, which he reached on 13 July 1771.

The problem of the great southern continent was not completely solved; the main result lay in the accurate charting of New Zealand. But a far greater achievement came from another direction, in the field of hygiene; throughout the entire voyage not one man died of disease.

In 1771, Kerguelen discovered the islands which bear his name. Marion-Dufresne and Crozet embarked on a voyage in the same year, which ended with Marion-Dufresne's assassination in Tasmania.

James Cook set out on his second voyage in July 1771, again in search of the southern continent but also with instructions to explore around Bouvet's Cape Circumcision in 54° S., 11° 20′ E. His *Resolution* and *Adventure*, after rounding the Cape of Good Hope, passed south and crossed the polar circle three times without being impeded by ice. Returning to the equator, the expedition then visited Easter Island, Tahiti, New Hebrides, New Caledonia and New Zealand; far to the south, South Georgia and the South Sandwich Islands were discovered. On this occasion, the search was meticulous and little remained in the southern latitudes still to be found.

Cook's third voyage began in 1776. His mission this time was to discover a passage through to the Pacific from the west coast of North America. From Kerguelen Island, he proceeded into the Pacific, revisited Hawaii, and setting course for the west coast of North America, came to Cape Flattery and the Juan de Fuca channel, now called Puget Sound.

The wintry weather in the area resulted in his decision to sail back to Hawaii. There, this great sailor and navigator, beloved by his men and acclaimed everywhere as one of the most celebrated explorers and as a just, good and brave man, was killed by natives in an unseemly and lamentable incident. To the calamity of his death was added the horror of the native's hewing his body in pieces, and Clerke the deputy commander was only able

The death of Captain Cook, 14 February 1779. Idealized drawing. From Mame's: "Voyages autour du Monde", 1845.

Jean Francois Galaup de La Pérouse (1741–1788). A rough drawing by Gorlitz. From the expedition of the *Boussole* and *Astrolabe*, 1785–1788. (*Bibl. Nat. Estampes*)

Portrait of a New Zealand native chieftain. Drawing by Parkinson. From the atlas to Cook's voyages. (*Service hydrographique, Paris*)

to recover the remains, which were reverently wrapped in sailcloth and committed to the deep.

At the end of the American War of Independence, La Pérouse set out for Bouvet Island, South Georgia and Hawaii. His instructions were to pass beyond the archipelagoes between Hawaii and New Zealand and explore the Gulf of Carpentaria, China and Kamchatka. His two ships, *L'Astrolabe* and *La Boussole* rounded Cape Horn in August 1785 and followed the Pacific coast of America, exploring it between Cook's landfall and Monterey. On arrival at the Queen Charlotte Islands, La Pérouse sent all his hydrographic papers back to France, overland via Siberia, to preserve them in case of eventual shipwreck. It was a premonition that came true, as is well known, when both his ships were lost at Vanikoro.

Australia, already circumnavigated, witnessed in February 1788 the establishment at Port Jackson, of the first small British colony, soon to be followed by the convicts, whom Governor Phillip brought with him to cultivate the new land.

Already by 1785, Nootka Sound had become an important fur trading center and there was an English trapping post there. The merchant ships engaged in the trade made valuable surveys of the area, especially of the Fuca Straits, the passage between Vancouver Island and the mainland. In 1791, Vancouver explored the southwest coast of Australia, and four years later the northwest coast of America—model undertakings of their kind.

What remained to be discovered? Details, of course, but also a more precise location of places, thanks to the advent of new chronometers and observational instruments.

Captain Hunter made hydrographical surveys of the New South Wales coast, while Bass discovered the strait which bears his name. Captain Edwards explored the Tuamotu archipelago, Duff and Mortlock the Carolines. At the same time d'Entrecasteaux and de Kermadec set out from France, via the Cape of Good Hope, in an attempt to establish the fate of La Pérouse. They visited Tasmania, New Caledonia, Amboina, Tonga, Santa Cruz, the Solomon Islands and circumnavigated Australia. Both captains died in the course of the voyage and their achievement brings to a close the great geographical upsurge of the eighteenth century which had begun forty years before.

Between 1800 and 1830, Baudin and Flinders continued the coastal survey, despite an interruption during the Napoleonic Wars. In one remarkable voyage, Baudin and a party of naturalists visited Timor and the northwest and southeast coasts of Australia. During the latter they met Flinders in Encounter Bay and went on to Port Jackson, where the English colonists rather doubted whether the expedition's intentions were solely geographical. Flinders went on to complete the hydrography of Australia.

In 1831 Fitzroy took the 10-gun brig *Beagle* to Patagonia and Tierra del Fuego, continuing a survey begun by King in 1826. Accompanying him on the voyage was the great scientist Darwin. Fitzroy's surveys of the Patagonian channels formed the basis for the cartography of that region, and their perfection has ensured their continued use in the charts of today.

The arrival of the *L'Astrolabe* at Carteret Harbor. Note the clever apparatus of the canvas funnel for bringing water from the shore to barrels in the ship's boat. From D'Urville's atlas. *(Service hydrographique, Paris)*

Laplace's *L'Artémise* in the process of being careened. This laborious operation was necessary to rid the hull of marine vegetation and animals by scrubbing it with boiling water. It was laborious in the sense that all the guns had to be removed and the upper masts taken down beforehand but nevertheless was an indispensable operation. Tahiti, 1839. Lithograph by Adolf Rouargue. *(Bibl. Nat. Estampes)*

NAVIGATION

At the time when the great voyages of discovery began (Byron 1764), navigation by dead reckoning was in its prime. In spite of the gross errors it could bring about—as for example in Anson's navigation of Cape Horn—pilots and shipsmasters thought only of how to perfect it; new methods of calculation or the use of astro-navigation were completely mistrusted.

The log, the compass, a good man at the wheel and an officer on watch to note the wind direction, were deemed quite sufficient to keep a ship on course for several weeks, even months, without sighting land. The results were often disappointing. Captain Marchand in 1790 was 3° 46′ out of true reckoning in a passage from the Cape Verdes to the Le Maire channel, although the latter's position had been cross-checked many times by the navigators rounding Cape Horn.

In the Pacific the location of the islands discovered was based upon reckoning only; the resultant effect upon hydrography from the 17th to the middle of the 18th century may well be imagined. To proliferate the types of log and compass was useless; so long as the means of determining longitude remained unsolved, further progress would not be made. The problem of position remained unsolved and advances in cartography were nil. What use was a detailed knowledge of coastlines, depths and soundings if their exact position remained unknown? As a result of this dilemma, the English Parliament of 1714 offered £20,000 to the first discoverer of a reliable way of determining longitude, half to be paid after a demonstration offshore, and half following six weeks of trials aboard a ship. In France, the Parliamentary delegate Rouille set up a fund to promote advances in navigation. The Board of Longitude was created in England in 1714, but the following quotation cited by Delambre and, more recently, by Marguet from the works of Gemma Frisius (1558), show how long the principle of calculating longitude had been known:

It is first necessary to make use of small clocks known as watches; their lightness allows them to be carried, and with a twenty-four hour movement they offer a simple means of determining longitude. Before commencing the journey, the watch should be set at the time of departure and care taken that it does not stop on the way. On reaching a certain place, the time should be calculated by use of the astrolabe, compared with that shown upon the watch, whereupon the difference will be the longitude.

The problem put this way appeared simple enough. But without an effective marine time keeper at that time, attention was first drawn to another method, unconnected with recording time by a watch on board ship. This was the method known as lunar distance, based upon the use of an instrument which calculated visually the differences of angle between the nought and local meridians. But observation was extremely difficult and the readings were inaccurate.

Hadley's octant was the ancestor of these reflection instruments, from which the sextant derived. The former was a very large apparatus, made of ebony and with mirrors of polished copper, which could measure angles to the accuracy of nearly one minute. In 1775, Borda gave definite form to the sextant.

If we return to lunar distances, we can see that the angle measured between the moon in its course and a large fixed star corresponds to a degree of meridian: the time, furnished by a nautical almanac. The observation of the

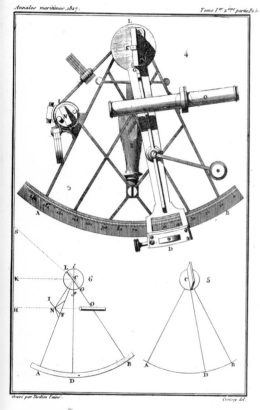

Hadley's octant of 1731 underwent a large number of improvements and amendments; but by 1827 it was perfect. The illustration shows a copper model and is the last word in its development, with vernier reversible screw, magnifying glass and astronomical mirror. But until at least 1860 primitive wooden octants continued to be used on board ship. (*Annales Maritimes de 1827*)

coincidence is made through the eye-piece of the octant, and the time recorded. Then followed a laborious calculation which in the days of Cook and Bougainville could result in a longitude being obtained within a quarter or half degree. What was still needed were accurate astronomical tables and appreciation of the limitations of the instruments. Similar methods were used by scientists aboard ship, in observation of eclipses of the sun, moon and larger planets, which when compared with simultaneous readings made elsewhere on land produced accurate determinations of longitude. The advantages of this method ensured its survival long after the development of the chronometer, partly because of the cost and scarcity of the latter, partly because of habit. Le Gaigneur in his admirable *Pilote instruit* (1781), instructs his pupils:

You must be forewarned, and not therefore surprised, by the prejudices of navigators used to routine methods; their lack of knowledge will make them mistrust even the best new developments, condemning as troublesome and complex methods which they understand little about.

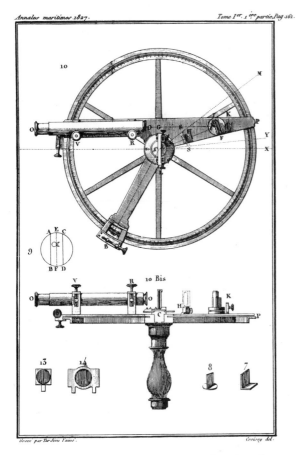

Annales maritimes 1827.   *Tome I.er 1.ere partie. Pag. 161.*

Gravé par Tardieu l'ainé.   *Croisey del.*

		PRAIRIAL, XI.e Année. (112)			
		DISTANCE DU CENTRE DE LA LUNE AU SOLEIL ET AUX ÉTOILES.			
Jours du mois	ÉTOILES orientales.	À MIDI.	À 3 HEURES.	À 6 HEURES.	À 9 HEURES.
		D. M. S.	D. M. S.	D. M. S	D. M S
2	Régulus	66. 50. 27	65. 5. 45	63. 21. 27	61. 37. 29
3		53. 3. 29	51. 21. 50	49. 40. 34	47. 59. 41
4		39. 41. 8	38. 2. 35	36. 24. 24	34. 46. 36
5		26. 43. 7	25. 7. 28	23. 32. 10	21. 57. 13
5	Epi de la m.	....	....	....	....
6		68. 10. 24	66. 37. 22	65. 4. 37	63. 32. 8
7		55. 53. 28	54. 22. 26	52. 51. 37	51. 21. 0
8		43. 50. 36	42. 21. 1	40. 51. 34	39. 22. 13
9		31. 57. 14	30. 28. 29	28. 59. 50	27. 31. 14
10		20. 9. 7			
10	Antarès.	65. 56. 30	64. 27. 43	62. 58. 55	61. 30. 4
11		54. 5. 11	52. 35. 59	51. 6. 42	49. 37. 20
12		42. 8. 49	40. 38. 44	39. 8. 30	37. 38. 8
13		30. 3. 48			
13	α de l'Aigle.	85. 29. 43	84. 11. 55	82. 54. 4	81. 36. 7
14		75. 5. 42	73. 47. 35	72. 29. 32	71. 11. 33
15		64. 43. 15			
15	Fomal- haut.	87. 36. 37	86. 8. 28	84. 40. 7	83. 11. 35
16		75. 46. 38	74. 17. 16	72. 47. 47	71. 18. 15
17		63. 49. 51	62. 20. 8	60. 50. 31	59. 21. 1
18		51. 55. 50	50. 27. 31	48. 59. 37	47. 32. 13
19		40. 24. 0			
19	α du Bélier.	101. 2. 29	99. 21. 22	97. 40. 6	95. 58. 38
20		87. 28. 48	85. 46. 20	84. 3. 43	82. 20. 56
21		73. 44. 52	72. 1. 14	70. 17. 29	68. 33. 36
22		59. 52. 24	58. 7. 49	56. 23. 9	54. 38. 24
23		45. 53. 22			
20	Soleil.	....	....	....	....
21		117. 5. 15	115. 28. 44	113. 52. 5	112. 15. 16
22		104. 9. 8	102. 31. 31	100. 53. 45	99. 15. 52
23		91. 4. 41	89. 26. 6	87. 47. 26	86. 8. 39
24		77. 53. 23	76. 14. 5	74. 34. 43	72. 55. 16
25		64. 37. 14	62. 58. 30	61. 17. 44	59. 37. 58
26		51. 19. 1	49. 39. 16	47. 59. 35	46. 17. 56
27		38. 2. 54			

Borda's reflection instrument (1775), perfected at the beginning of the 19th century. This instrument was more convenient than the earlier sextant for calculating lunar distances which necessitated measuring large angles. The instrument continued in use until *ca.* 1860, although it was not often found aboard merchant ships. (*Annales Maritimes de 1827*)

For many years after chronometers had been operating and after they had been installed on board ships, many navigators continued to calculate longitude by lunar distances which only required an approximate knowledge of the time. The above is an illustration of the calculations necessary, and these tables remained in nautical almanacs until about 1900. (*Service hydrographique, Paris*)

Commenting on Marchand's voyage of 1794, Claret Fleurieux criticized his countrymen and colleagues even more severely:

It is time that French navigators were cured of the dreadful apathy into which they have sunk through adherence to old methods. This slavery has prevented them putting to good use the advances in geometry, astronomy, and mechanics—exceeding those of all other sciences—which have been made in the last fifty years. Is it credible that there are only a hundred seamen in France, perhaps less than half this number, who are able to make proper astronomical observations at sea and thereafter calculate the meridian of longitude? What is the use of the Board of Longitude in France, like its counterpart in England, preparing elaborate tables and propounding complex theories for the benefit of navigators, and publishing them year by year, if they cannot be put into practice on long-distance voyages?

How can the clocks and watches—masterpieces of mechanical art—which have been developed for the navy by Ferdinand and Louis Berthoud, and which can determine longitude at sea every day, even several times a day, be put to the best use? How can the genius of Borda, who gave the French navy an ideal instrument for measuring the distance and height of stars at sea, be turned to advantage? If the present lethargy in France can be shaken by the example of a rival nation, I would tell our sailors that there is not a single English captain on a long-distance voyage, who does not today make full use of up-to-date methods in order to determine his ship's longitude.

English naval officer about to use a sextant. From a statuette in colored wood (1800). *(Nat. Maritime Museum, Greenwich)*

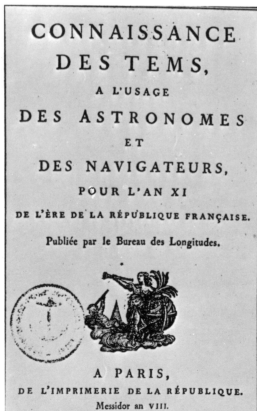

CONNAISSANCE DES TEMS,

A L'USAGE

DES ASTRONOMES

ET

DES NAVIGATEURS,

POUR L'AN XI

DE L'ÈRE DE LA RÉPUBLIQUE FRANÇAISE.

Publiée par le Bureau des Longitudes.

A PARIS,

DE L'IMPRIMERIE DE LA RÉPUBLIQUE.

Messidor an VIII.

Essential for taking ships' bearings, these astronomical tables were calculated several years ahead and were frequently used by long-distance navigators. *(Service hydrographique, Paris)*

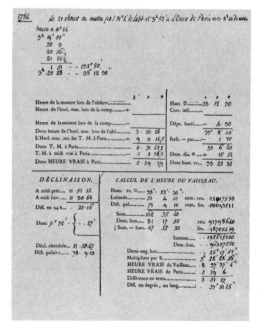

An example of the printed form for making nautical calculations (1784). (Here it was a question of calculating longitude from the difference of the time on board ship, obtained by observing the altitude of the sun and the time shown on the marine chronometer.)

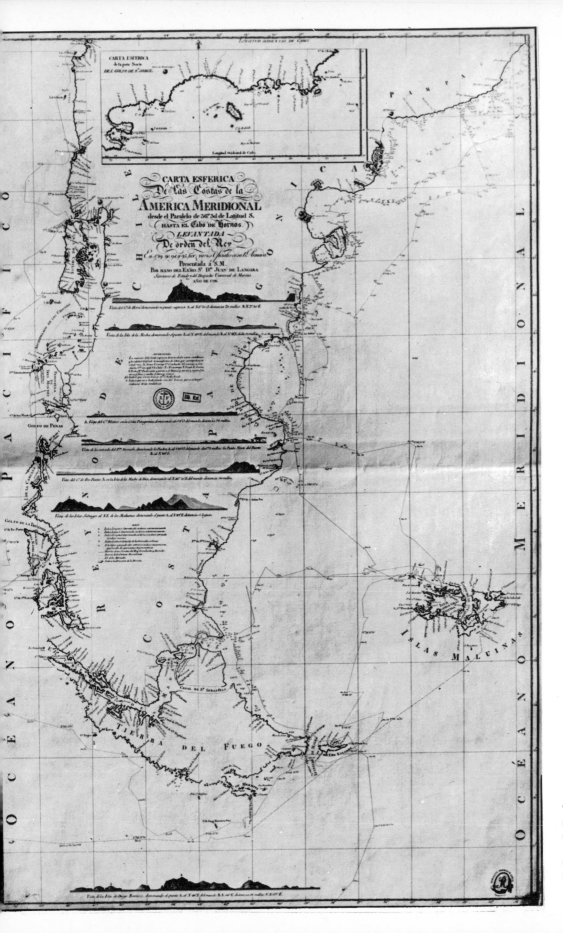

This chart of South America, surveyed by Spanish ships between 1789 and 1795 and published in 1798, enables one to see the tremendous progress made in determining longitude. *(Bibl. Nat. Cartes et plans)*

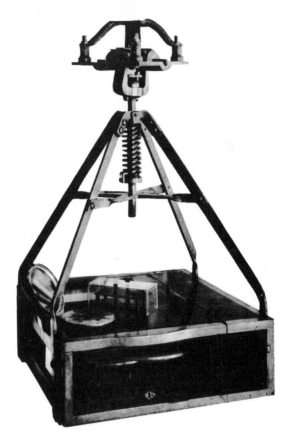

Berthoud's third Marine Chronometer (1775). It appeared about the same time as Borda's and was used at sea in 1776. (*Conservatoire des Arts et Métiers*)

Berthoud's Marine Chronometer No. 1 (1760). An instrument of great precision, although imperfect in operation. (*Conservatoire des Arts et Métiers*)

Huyghens in Holland, Sully and Harrison in England, le Roy and Brequet in France, Berthoud in Switzerland, were landmarks in the long and arduous journey which ended in the creation of the modern marine chronometer. Between Huyghens' first experiments in 1664 and le Roy and Berthoud's timepieces of 1770, lay a century of effort, hope and disappointment before success came. Even more than the frigate and the cannon, the chronometer was the real conqueror of the Pacific and the servant of modern hydrography.

Full recognition must be given to the supreme skill needed to perfect an instrument which had to remain reliable for every second of the day and determine longitude at sea to within a half-minute of a degree. The number of clocks involved, for instance Berthoud's No. 2 or le Roy's No. 4, must also be correctly appreciated, since these were essential stages in the development of the perfect instrument.

Cook took four Kendall chronometers with him on his second voyage; thereafter most English discovery-ships were so equipped, enabling them to make the most precise reckonings. The methods of determination of position, including triangulation from landmarks, had made great strides, but the

94

subsequent mathematical calculations had hardly kept pace and, strangely enough, only caught up towards the end of the nineteenth century.

Both Flinders and Poisson demonstrated the effects of magnetism aboard ship, a phenomenon of growing importance as more and more metal went into their construction. Hydrographic work carried out by several nations gradually encompassed every ocean and coastline, until by the end of the nineteenth century, the task was virtually complete. The navigators for their part were now equipped with excellent charts and reliable nautical tables.

THE SHIPS

In order to build her four thousand merchant ships, neither England, nor indeed Holland, who had six thousand at her disposal in the seventeenth century, had had to wait for the technical developments of the age of Colbert. Even if these possibly exaggerated numbers, including vessels of all types and tonnage, were reduced by a half or three quarters, they would remain far in excess of the two hundred ocean-going merchant ships which the Minister of Marine found existing in France when he took office.

A merchant marine cannot be built in a day; nevertheless, even more remarkable than the results achieved in this direction by Colbert in 1683, were the changes in technique and administration. The old methods were completely transformed, and one of the greatest achievements of Colbert's reforms was to stimulate nautical endeavour and skill. Obscure men emerged from the shadows and achieved fame because of their particular abilities.

In order to assess the size of the French merchant navy, Colbert ordered the production and collection of plans and drawings to show the different types of ship. The plate depicts a 220-ton pinnace of Nantes, used to transport cod from Newfoundland to France. *(ex-Colbert Collection, Service hydrographique, Paris)*

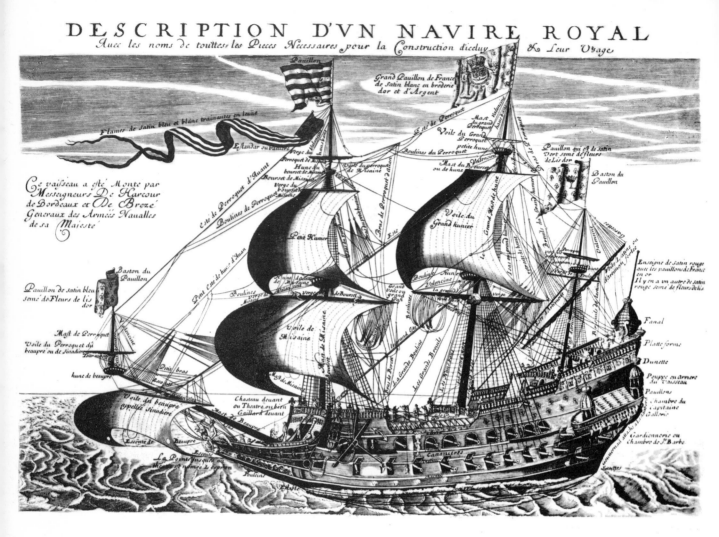

DESCRIPTION D'VN NAVIRE ROYAL
Auec les noms de touttes les Pieces Necessaires pour la Construction d'iceluy & Leur Usage

Frontispiece to Père Fournier's: "Hydrographie". This "royal" ship possessed many of the characteristics common to those of the 18th century: spritsail, bowsprit gallant, mizzen bowlines, bowlines, brails to the yardarms, enormous topsails and a high poop. (*Service hydrographique, Paris*)

Warships and merchantmen gradually took on a definite architectural form, a blend of two opposite schools: the English type of ship, preferred by Seignelay, and the Dutch. The frigate was the creation of French shipyards and a type copied throughout the world in the ratio of beam to length; 3:4 or 3:4½.

After research and trials in new methods, came standard works on the art of naval construction: Duhamel du Monceau and Ollivier. It was they who laid down the principles for choosing the raw materials and then building the ships.

It is a moving experience to study a list of the innumerable parts that together formed a complete ship, parts perfectly chosen for the function they had to perform and which are still used today in the building of many fishing vessels and pleasure craft: "Keel, stem, sternpost, stemson, apron, knees, inner and outer sternpost, lower stern-pieces, fashion-piece, flat floor timbers, raised floor timbers, crotches, lower futtocks, main timbers, top timbers, hawse pieces, wing-transom, deck beam, escutcheon beam, sternpiece beam, keelson, false stern, keelson deadwoods, filling-pieces, transverse

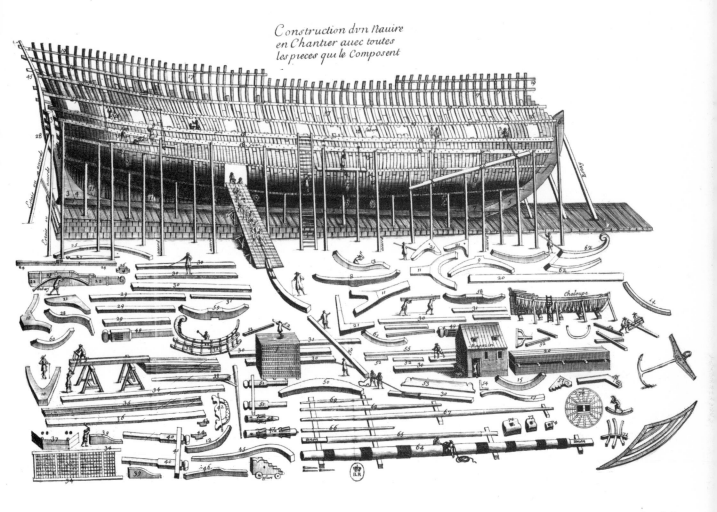

Construction d'vn Nauire en Chantier auec toutes les pieces qui le Composent

and horizontal, breast-hooks, escutcheon knees, riders, orlop beams and orlop beam knees, mainmast keelson, mizzen keelson, main and subsidiary clamping-beams, beam-ledges, carlings, iron knees, timber guttering, spirketing, lower deck strakes and planking, ceiling of the lower and middle decks, stern-frame knees, etc".

The sailing qualities of the ocean-going ships were directly related to their main sail area, of which the main and mizzen topsails and the topgallants were both large and reefed. Studding sails hoisted at the ends of the lower sails greatly increased the overall sail area. These were certainly ships of the high seas, besides which the coastal trader and the fishing vessel appeared in an entirely different design. One need not look at *L'Atlas de Colbert* to see that his dream of the evolution of typically French merchant ships had been realized.

Great changes also took place with the rigging. Comparing a diagram from Père Fournier's *Hydrographie* with the plans of d'Entrecasteaux and Baudin's ships, one can see that the running rigging is no longer fixed to the stays, the bowsprit gallant has gone, and only the yard of the spritsail remains. But

Everything by hand! The axe, adze, two-handed saw and drill-tenon remained the prime tools of naval architecture until the mid-19th century. The pieces were cut from the timber and shaped in the form required. Plate from Caron's: "Traité des Bois". *(Bibl. Nat. Estampes)*

was this sail rigged at sea? Since 1720, the superiority of the jib had become so evident that a large jib-boom was added forward with staystail stay, jib and flying jib.

The days of the deep-bellied sail were numbered; the flat well-shivered sail as an alternative showed its ability to give ships more speed, a factor which they depended on more and more. About 1770, skysails appeared above the topgallants. The vang of the mizzen, carrying the lateen-yards, was transformed in the development of the lateen-sail; the lower part being carried across into a boom, so as to form, in the case of the brigantine, the typical form of spanker-boom and crutches.

Forward, the bowsprit was solidly joined to the cutwater by gammoning— pieces of ornamented timber linking the cutwater and main hull, in the same way as the rails supported the heads and the beak. Another feature of the frigate hull were round and chubby bows, which made up for a loss in maneuverability by minimizing pitch in heavy weather (the sharp bow did not reappear until the days of the clipper).

The deck was continuous; in the stern and alongside, the quarter galleries shone with their adornments and gilded decoration. The stern was quite transformed, from being high and narrow to squat and square, and ultimately horseshoe shaped. The stern of the *Bounty,* over which the mutineers threw food to Bligh and his men sitting in the boat, was a typical example. Since 1650, the manual helm had been superseded by the tiller rope. As for the steeringwheel, it was mounted on deck; exposed to the air and the spray, the helmsman steered the ship, one eye on the compass, the other on the sails.

Soon anchor and cable-chain replaced the rope. This was a wonderful improvement that gave the ship both virtually indestructible and permanent

Diagram showing how the frames, keelsons and beams were assembled in an 18th century ship. From Duhamel du Monceau's: "Traité de construction des vaisseaux". (*Service hydrographique, Paris*)

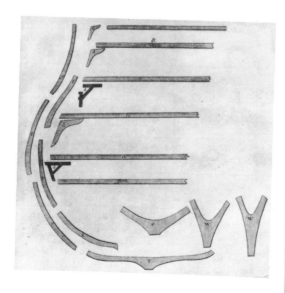
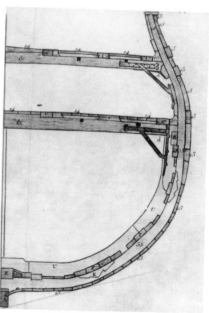

VAISSEAU QU'ON LANCE À L'EAU.

VAISSEAU SUR LE CHANTIER.

18th century shipyard: the fashions change but the methods and principles remain. Anonymous engraving. *(Bibl. des Arts décoratifs, Paris)*

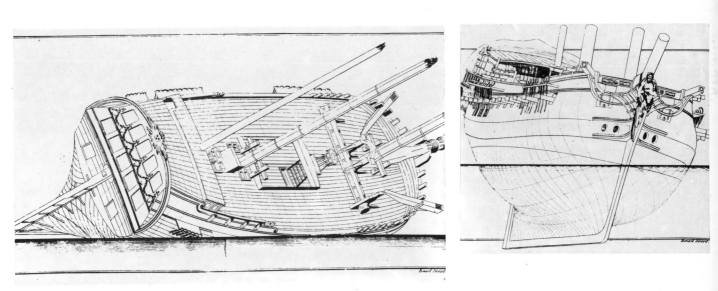

Section of a frigate: "L'Encyclopédie", 1787. *(Bibl. des Arts décoratifs, Paris)*

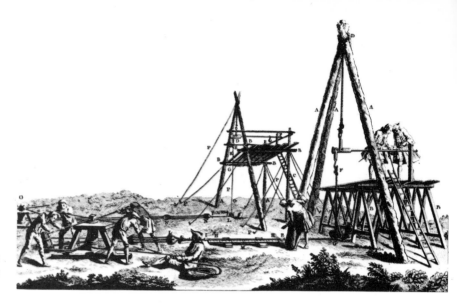

Testing marine cable. From collection of plates in: "L'Encyclopédie", 1787. *(Bibl. des Arts décoratifs, Paris)*

"New apparatus erected at Dunkirk, for loading and discharging cargoes from ships." Anonymous, 18th century. *(Bibl. des Arts décoratifs, Paris)*

Brig in graving dock. Perrot, *ca.* 1835. *(Bibl. Nat. Estampes)*

Caulkers at work on a small ship in dock. Drawing by Morel-Fatio, 1844. Print from *La Marine*.

mooring on the bottom, and fine anchorage in bad weather, provided by the weight of the chain. But in hoisting the anchor—since the chain could not be turned on the windlass like the rope—it was necessary to heave on the capstan bit by bit with a rope, whose ends were attached to the chain cable at the water line—a difficult and dangerous operation in bad weather. A sprocket-wheel mounted on the capstan was then invented so that the chain could be heaved in like cable. This was performed with suitable "heave-hos".

The ship's timbers, ribs and sides, were carefully examined against dry-rot which could reduce even the largest pieces to sponge, and the ships were frequently fumigated. Externally, protection of the hull below the water line had not yet been invented. The usual practice was to careen in order to scrape the bottom covered with barnacles, until the advent of a remarkable development that came towards the end of the era of discovery. This was to sheath the hull with copper, which at once solved the careening problem—shellfish and seaweed finding copper salts very unpalatable.

About 1805 in England, and 1811 in France, the first metal tanks were installed aboard ship, enabling water to be kept permanently fresh.

Progress in general, however, remained slow. Few contrivances could survive the severe test of working efficiently on a ship. Without mechanical aid, everything depended on the physical strength of the crew, working block and tackle, rope and spars: loading and unloading cargo, catting and fishing the anchor, working the cable and the boats. The eighteenth century was the golden age of the oarsmen, whose astonishing virtuosity extended to even the very smallest craft. The ability to lift great weights in the air depended as much upon the crew who rigged the gear, as upon those who heaved at the line to the sound of the boatswain's whistle and the songs they sang.

Besides the frigates of war and trade, there were innumerable brigs—the merchantmen of the West Indies and Pacific, the whalers of voyages round the world. Would we ever make similar voyages today in such small craft? Cook's *Endeavour* was 25 meters long and 8.50 meters in the beam.

The evolution of tonnage only came gradually; the advantage of freighting in ships of larger capacity was not yet appreciated. Companies confined

The caulker. Anonymous engraving, *ca.* 1840. (*Bibl. des Arts décoratifs*)

themselves mostly to one ship's captain, and cargo was picked up, a few tons at a time, at several ports in turn. Only with the development of the East India Companies and the realization of prosperity through bigger cargoes, did ships' displacements reach—as with the "Indiamen"—one thousand tons and more.

LIFE ON BOARD

With the exception of alterations in the build and size of ships, few changes took place in life on board, between the start of the long-distance voyages and the end of wooden sailing ships. It is only necessary to have in front of one, cross-sections of ships pictured in *L'Atlas de Colbert* (1663), *L'Encyclopédie* (1787), and of frigates of 1830, to realize the lack of progress made in seamen's conditions. On board officers and masters were installed in the stern in conditions of symbolic isolation. The crew lived between decks and practically nobody had quarters he could call his own, except under the poop, where the officer of the watch stood, close to the captain's cabin. Within the breastwork of the poop two doors led to the main deck. On the poop deck were the helmsman, the wheel, the compass and ship's bell for striking the hours. The short deck forward remained separate, and between were the hatch covers above the holds.

At the stern, on the level of the orlop deck, were the officers' cabins arranged in a square around it. They were often so small that the bunk was wedged between the beams, in space hardly big enough for a coffin. Sometimes there was even a gun port, with the cabin further congested by a cannon, and its accompanying tamping, breeching and sponge. Below the orlop deck were the quarters of the master, the purser, the supercargo, the clerk and the surgeon's assistants; being below the water line, they were entirely without natural daylight. The smell of victuals in the storeroom, the suffocating atmosphere of the hold, the stench of oil lamps and rats, the water lapping in the bilges, and the slap of waves at the stern, combined to disturb the slumbers of men living in these depths.

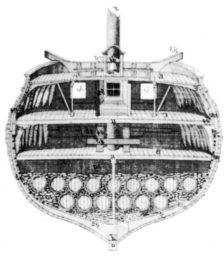
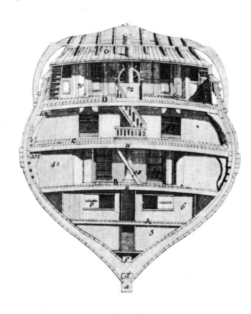

Draughts of 1787, depicting a Swedish 40-gun frigate (28 in battery). Such draughts, plans and sections show that interior details had altered little in the fifty years since the age of Colbert. The difference of a century in ship evolution may be seen by comparing the illustration on the previous page. "L'Encyclopédie", 1787. (*Bibl. des Arts décoratifs, Paris*)

The lower deck, sleeping in hammocks slung from beams between decks. Drawing by Morel-Fatio, appearing in *La Marine*, 1844.

The crew—seamen and gunners—lived in the orlop. How could they survive in the appalling conditions to be found in ships up to the beginning of the nineteenth century? It was possible to open the ports in good weather, but between decks fresh air could only be obtained by creating draught in front and behind. Dampness rotted the timbers, soaked the men's clothes and gave them rheumatism for the rest of their lives. Everything was washed with sea water, the deck scrubbed, sanded and holystoned, the waste being hosed off into the scuppers. The timbers were never dry.

At the first sign of bad weather, the ports and hatches were closed; inside, scores of men languished in the foul air, contaminated with their own acrid sweat, pipe smoke and smells of cooking from the galley. To this nausea was added the stench of foul water, rats and tarred rope. The crew ate their food with knife and fingers from the communal bowl, as they sat between the guns

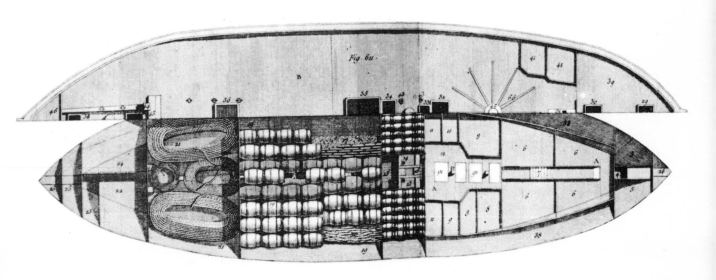

Seal Bay, New Holland. The camp of *l'Uranie* on the Peron peninsula. From Freycinet's atlas. *(Service hydrographique, Paris)*

Coupang on the island of Timor: the interior of a Timor dwelling. From Freycinet's atlas. *(Service hydrographique, Paris)*

Two frigates, weathering out a severe storm under bare poles. Lithograph by Perrot. *(Bibl. Nat. Estampes)*

or on deck. At rest they lay in their hammocks, slung between the beams, trying to sleep in wet clothes as they swung to the rolling of the ship. When it was very cold, as at Cape Horn, no form of heating existed—neither brazier nor stove—except for the fire in the galley at mealtimes.

The sanitary facilities were in the bow. One had to descend to the heads, a platform with gratings suspended between the rails; there one had to crouch down, hanging on to a rope's end or stanchion, soaked to the skin and swept with spray, and perhaps racked with fever or dysentery. The stern quarter-galleries performed the same function equally crudely for the officers. As for water for washing, even up to 1820–1830, the ration was one bucket among eight men. Drinking water was issued in very small quantities; kept in wooden casks in the hold, it was frequently foul. Inside the sea chests, at the bottom of the hold, along the beams and in the timbers, hordes of yellow-and-black beetles, cockroaches and rats scuttled, swarmed and crawled.

The ferocity and hunger of the rats remained undiminished in spite of the ravages they committed upon the stores. They not only devoured the biscuits, but chewed the staves of the casks, and gnawed the sails and rope. They multiplied despite periodic rat-hunts and fumigations, during which every hatchway had to be sealed for two days. Dead ones were thrown overboard, but, like the Phoenix, they were reborn, making life intolerable on board.

Between decks in hot weather was uninhabitable. Sleep was best taken on deck during the night watches, cooled by the sea breezes. There one could dream under the stars, lulled by the wind in the rigging, and forget for a moment the constant and close proximity of one's fellow men. There one found that essential aloneness otherwise lacking in a ship, where one slept,

View of a merchant ship in longitudinal section.

(*Service hydrographique, Paris*)

1. Flat floor timbers amidships and floor-riders; 2. Rising bow floor timbers; 3. Rising stern floor timbers; 4. Kelson or counter-keel; 5. Keel; 6, Sternpost; 7. Rudder; 8. Stem; 9. Ballast; 10. Cross-beams; 11. Knees; 12. Apron; 13. Filling chocks; 14. Head timbers; 15. Head rails; 16. Butt store. 17. Pump-well; 18. Pumps; 19. Magazine; 20. Main shot locker; 21. Cable tier; 22. Bow shot locker; 23. Knight head; 24. Scuttles; 25. Orlop beams; 26. Bread store; 27. Passageways to the stores; 28. Gun room; 29. Food ration counter; 30, Sail room; 31. Fore cockpit; 32. Magazine bulkhead; 33. Gunner's storeroom; 34. Lower deck; 35. Stern locker; 36. Tiller; 37. Main gun battery mounted on carriages; 38. Deck ladder;

39. Double capstan; 40. Mainmast, cut in section to show internal fishes and side-pieces; 41. Deck hammocks; 42. First and second bitts; 43. Single capstan; 44. Foremast, cut in section as mainmast; 45. Bowsprit; 46. Manger board; 47. Anchor cable; 48. Gun deck; 49. Mess room; 50. Pantry; 51. Companionway; 52. Mainyard halyard; 53. Mizzenmast; 54. Pig pen; 55. Hencoops; 56. Galley; 57. Oven; 58. Upper deck; 59. Main cabin; 60. Officers room; 61. Wardroom; 62. Banisters for manual operation of the tiller; 63. Bitt for belaying the mainbraces; 64. Upper deck battery mounted on carriages; 65. Vang or bowline at the base of the mizzenyard; 66. Bitt for foresail clew garnet; 67. Bitt for anchor stopper; 68. Anchor cathead; 69. Mainsail clew-garnet; 70. Downhauls; 71. Brails; 72. Foresail clew-garnet; 73. Downhauls; 74. Brails.

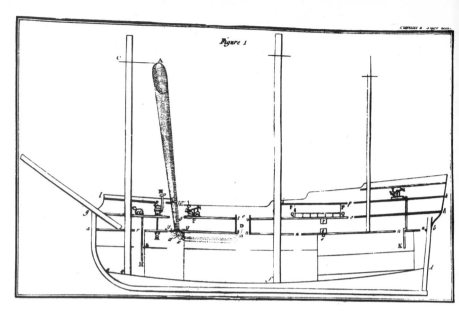

Cloth ventilator designed to aerate the 'tween decks. Could this apparatus have survived the gales of the southern seas? Duhamel du Monceau. (*Bibl. Hist. de la Marine*)

ate, washed and worked so closely together. If refuge could not be found aloft, at the tiller, or in the hold, one could always remain mute. Everybody respected the awkward silences and grumbling taciturnity to which each was prey. More terrible was the effect of the collective silence of a hostile crew upon captain or master, which if expressed in words would have resulted in immediate punishment.

In voyages of three to four years duration, with no landfall for four to six months, the characters of all these people were molded. Besides giving orders, each officer had to impose his own personality on the crew. Many failed in this responsibility, as in the case of the crisis during the Baudin voyage and the mutiny on the *Bounty*. But there were exceptional men like Captain Cook, whose death demoralized the crew.

Understanding was often more necessary than discipline. On his voyage to the Antarctic in 1738, Bouvet realized that the low morale of his crew might make it impossible to continue. They were afraid of the icebergs, "shaped as islands, fortresses and buildings", which surrounded them. "To banish these thoughts, I read out the section of my orders which promised rewards to officers and crew, proportionate to their rank, as soon as the discoveries had been made". Morale returned and Bouvet had won the men over.

Apart from the severity of sea and weather, serious problems of nutrition and disease also existed. In 1757, Lind's classic of naval hygiene: *An Essay on the most effectual means of preserving the Health of Seamen*, was published. Without being a complete panacea, it awoke public opinion and led to involved arguments amongst naval surgeons. Lind condemned the irresponsibility of the pressgang system, which brought on board released prisoners, invalids and "men whose health had been ruined on merchant ships".

The orlop decks of the ships of Anson's squadron were said to be filled with veterans—old pensioners drafted from Chelsea Hospital. Lind recalled that: "it is far better to avoid contracting a disease than have the pleasure of being cured of it". He was a strict vegetarian, recommending a gruel made with shallots, onions and garlic, in place of meat broth. Instead of beer alone, a blend of beer and brandy, with sugar, honey or a little vinegar added, should be drunk. Steps should be taken to combat the noxious fumes, exuding from the unseasoned timber of new ships, which produced fever and diarrhea. The best remedy for scurvy was strained orange juice, kept in wax-sealed bottles with some olive oil in the neck. Lind also showed how leeks and cabbage might be preserved in a cask, by sprinkling them with salt, just as cod are crated.

If it was impossible to install a wind-tunnel contraption of cloth known as "the ventilator of Mr. Hales of the Royal Society", the best means of disinfection was to scrub the decks with hot vinegar and, once the ports and hatches had been closed, to fumigate the crew's quarters with sulphur, gunpowder or tar. Lind considered the practice of blood-letting, indulged in aboard Spanish and Portuguese merchantmen, to be quite useless; far better to make generous use of tropical herbs and remedies such as ginger, quinquina and spices.

In 1774 Monsieur Poissonnier Desperrières, physician and inspector of naval hospitals, published a thesis in support of vegetarianism, which was

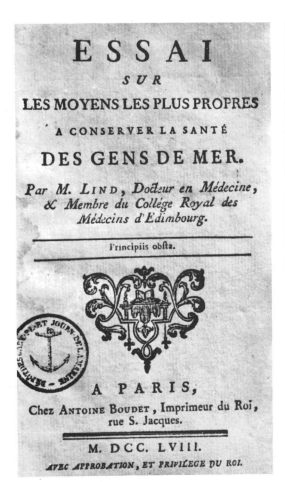

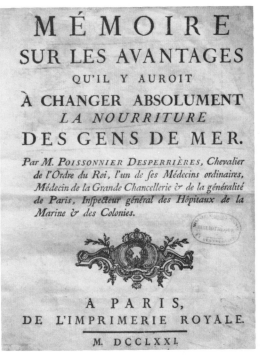

Advantage or absolute necessity? *(Bibl. Hist. de la Marine)*

An attempt which one wishes had succeeded. *(Bibl. Hist. de la Marine)*

strongly opposed a century later by Dr. Fonssagrives. Poissonnier recommended that a convalescent: " ... breakfast upon a ration of bread, an ounce of jam, and a quart of claret". The same diet was recommended for a scurvy sufferer except that the claret should be mulled. "For dinner—soup cooked with rice, chicken seasoned with onion and sorrel, a quart of wine and bread. For supper—either three ounces of barley or four of rice, with prunes cooked in brown sugar, or spiced with cinnamon, ginger or nutmeg; plus the same quantities of bread and wine as before".

For fit men, the following dinner menu was suggested: "Half the usual ration of fat and four ounces of rice to each man on Sundays and Thursdays; five ounces of rice, seasoned with half an ounce of sugar and a little ginger, on Mondays and Fridays; and six ounces of lentils, seasoned with pickled onions, salt and half an ounce of olive oil, or six ounces of either peas or white beans, for the three other days of the week."

When soup was not available, cheese or two ounces of honey could be substituted. "In this way", concludes Dr. Poissonnier, "I have done away with three meals of cod and two of salt beef". One wonders at the effect of these medical prescriptions upon the great copper cauldron, presided over by the cook in the galley, and how far they were carried out.

Captain Cook in each of his three voyages took great care of his men's health, doling out fresh fish, vegetables and fruit whenever possible: "Every day celery, leeks and a broth of peas and barley were prepared for the crews of both ships; their standard refreshment was beer".

And what about women? This problem, often recurring on lengthy sea voyages, was sometimes misunderstood. The famous definition of seamen as "simple men, supported by alcohol, who could only man ships"

Two American sailors, veterans of the War of Independence. Popular American drawing.

The return of the sailor. He has overcome the waves, but has she repulsed the advances of other admirers? But, for the moment, they are overjoyed at being re-united; his sea chest is stuffed with coins from distant lands, and the mother-in-law shares in the happiness. *(Bibl. des Arts décoratifs, Paris)*

did not, in fact, fit people who took life as it came. The sexual obsession with which they are frequently associated, applies more to the landlubber leading a so-called "normal" life. The sailor was chaste by necessity; the lack of female company aboard ship was a prerequisite of his life, which he accepted ungrudgingly in the same way as he did fatigue, discomfort and rough weather. It would not be difficult to give examples of a locket, a few letters or a fragment of a wedding veil becoming articles of extreme sentimental value. But this reserve applied only at sea; on shore Jack Tar shook off the shackles and basked in the pleasure of having "a wife in every port", or sometimes a host of women!

On this particular point, the mariners of bygone days were luckier in port than their modern equivalents. They often set up camp ashore, where, for instance, in the Pacific islands they could receive countless local sirens who conveniently happened to come bathing nearby. The women willingly dispensed their favors in exchange for beads or a few battered coins, which in those regions were worth their weight in gold.

I allowed [wrote Captain Cook] fraternization with women because I could not prevent it, but it was never encouraged, for fear of the consequences. I know that several believe these relationships to be our best insurance against the natives, and it may be right that our seamen's inclinations and needs be found amongst them. On the other hand, it is quite otherwise with passengers and navigators such as ourselves, and in these situations, affairs with women lose more men than they gain. Can one expect any other result, when the relationship is based more on lust than affection or attachment? In my considerable experience I have never come across a case to the contrary.

Seventy years later, Dupetit-Thouars in 1842 witnessed similar scenes in the Marquesas and came to the same conclusions.

Sailor's horn, decorated with a ship motif. These horns were often filled with tallow, used to preserve the sailors' needles and lubricate them while stitching the sails. *(Musée des Arts et Traditions populaires)*

CAPTAINS AND CONTRACTS

Amongst the shipping companies of the past, the powers of the merchant captain were extensive. They had full responsibility for the cargoes carried and it was not unusual for a captain to quit his ship and set himself up on shore in order to negotiate for freights, while his first mate remained on board bringing the cargo from port to port. Until the nineteenth century, a sailing ship captain's contract of engagement carried with it more than a monthly pledge; often it included either a private commission or a share in the profits. In certain instances a part of the hold space was allocated to him for the carriage of private cargo. "The master mariner was a highly esteemed person; small presents secured his cooperation, whereby private goods loaded before sailing could be transformed under bills of lading and exchanged in distant ports for merchandise which could be sold in France at a much higher price. After disembarking, the captain made his official calls in silk hat, frock coat and white cravat, twirling his umbrella. He was a frequent guest of the leading colonial families; if he liked riding—but few did—he was provided with a horse".

The following documents, quoted by C. Thiesen in the journal *Der Albatros* admirably convey the prerogatives of a merchant ship's captain. Here first, is Captain Boysen's terms of contract for a voyage to Callao in 1854:

The following contract has been made between M. J. C. D. Dreyer, owner of the three-masted barque *Fortunata* and Captain Cornelius Lorenz Boysen. Captain Boysen has been engaged by M. Dreyer to command the *Fortunata* upon the following financial basis: during repair or careening, the captain will receive half-payment, at the rate of half a thaler a month; during loading, either half or total payment according to the state of the crew; during the voyage, that is from the day of the crew's signing on,

The Loire estuary in 1836. A coastal trader, a ship and a lugger waiting the turn of the tide before proceeding up river to Nantes. Lithograph by F. Perrot. (*Bibl. Nat. Estampes*)

LE PILOTE

total payment at the rate of 25 thalers, plus 3% commission on the cargo. M. Dreyer must inform him respecting private packages or passengers.

The two contractants pledge agreement in the event of a change of command becoming necessary, and, to avoid legal complications, are in agreement that: Captain Boysen is in full command of the ship and its movements and is responsible for its safety. Equally, M. Dreyer has the right to dismiss Captain Boysen, without cause given; a decision which he must obey under any circumstances. However Captain Boysen is assured, in the event of being dismissed abroad, of free passage back to Holstein and a two-months pledge of security or 50 thalers daily from the date of dismissal. The same pledge may be paid to the captain when granted shore leave before the start of the voyage; on the other hand, the captain is only entitled to other paid leave either at a stipulated port or at the end of the voyage. The two contractants have signed and sealed this contract, and have instructed that an exact copy be made.

(Signed)   J. C. D. DREYER   Altona, 1 March 1854.
            C. L. BOYSEN

Home from a long voyage. First contact with land —the pilot. Drawing by Félix Saint-Aulaire, 1840. *(Bibl. Nat. Estampes)*

The *Merope*, an American brig *ca.* 1820. Aquatint
by François Roux. The topsails are still undivided.
(*Bibl. Hist. de la Marine*)

Port of Altona *ca.* 1830. Painting by E. Normann.
(*Danish Maritime Museum, Elsinore*)

Similar instructions, given by M. Dreyer to the captain of the *Fortunata* in 1855, ran:

Under the charter terms agreed with Messrs. M.D.F. Weber & Co., of Hamburg, you will voyage to Callao and act in full conformity with the terms of the agreement. The ship is freighted for both passages and you will receive £1,000 sterling, less current expenses, after the cargo has been discharged, remitting this sum to your account with Messrs. Weber within sixty days.

I shall need a note from you stating that the cargo has been unloaded, preferably with an accompanying document intimating that the charter valued at £10,000 sterling has been executed; but the first note will, if necessary, be sufficient as long as it is forwarded in duplicate. I, for my part, shall remit to you in duplicate a promissory note to cover your financial expenses and costs for taking on stores in port. Your expenses should not exceed 200, or at most 300, thalers in any one port, and you must arrange that they be redeemed at Callao. There, you must keep account of the thaler's exchange rate, as your expenses must be shown in pounds sterling according to the arrangements made with Messrs. Weber.

Our ship is fully insured for 38,000 marks, and its outward cargo, valued at £1,000 sterling, for 13,800 marks. The initial insurance covers every port at which you call, up to the time the return cargo is loaded aboard; the subsequent insurance is valid up to its unloading. For your own benefit I shall add an insurance policy for about 15,000 marks, covering the £1,200 sterling value of the cargo on the return voyage.

Attached is a copy of the personal instructions which I send to every captain of my ships. In the event of your decease, which God forbid, these instructions will be transmitted to your lieutenant, Richard Jappen Flohr.

(Signed)   J.C.D. DREYER   Altona, 5th May, 1855.

View of the American legation at Shanghai, *ca.* 1840. Drawing by Lancelot from an aquatint by Fisher. (*Le Tour du Monde*)

Then follows a paragraph of more detailed instructions:

Your ship and its cargo are fully insured, but the greatest care is enjoined upon you during the course of the voyage. Should, however, a disaster occur, you must submit a full written report of the damage in order that a legal claim may be made with the Hamburg insurers. Above all, do not leave the place where the damage occurred before acquainting me with the full circumstances; in such cases, there can never be too much detail. Also, I request you to provide a full account of all that happens on board, especially at the start of a new voyage. Send your reports by the quickest means—steamship, warship or mail-packet—preferably via North America, Spain, France, England, etc. You may send your reports through one of our correspondents, of whom I have given you a list.

Before leaving port, use them to acquaint me with any claims you may have or debts you may have incurred. At the start of each voyage, including those sailing from Hamburg, make sure that every member of your crew possesses a clean bill of health. In the unhappy event of one or more of them dying, throw their clothes overboard and record the event in the ship's log, so that, at Cuxhaven or any other port, you will not be unduly delayed by quarantine regulations.

Pay particular attention to the welfare of your men and reject any who appear to be carriers of disease. I recommend the use of stevedores where possible, because it will give your men less work and less need of medicines. Economy in all things is necessary, remembering that we do not wish to trade at a loss.

The Thames at Limehouse, 1793. Lithograph by Freeman after a painting by Rob. Dedd. Part of a series of views of English ports, similar to those of Vernet. (*Port of London Authority*)

Right: The Port of London, *ca.* 1860. Only the paddlewheel tug, belching black smoke, destroys the illusion of a scene a century before. Drawing by E. H. Andrews. (*Port of London Authority*)

Oregon timber being unloaded at Canada timber dock, Liverpool. Painting by Duddley, taken from *The Graphic*.

In the event of a serious accident en route, causing a change in the itinerary and, besides, difficulty in disposing of the cargo as originally intended, you will ensure that your subsequent actions do not in any way contravene the conditions agreed in the original charter.

If you bring back cash or specie on the return voyage, remember to have it heavily insured or at least inform me in sufficient time to make the necessary arrangements. A lot depends on the circumstances and the time available, but, remember, there is no way of anticipating an accident or damage.

When you arrive in the Elbe, forward a copy of the ship's "manifest" and your other letters to me before you dock at Cuxhaven, so that your affairs reach me first. The companies underlined in your list are business colleagues of mine and I direct them to your attention; those marked with a red cross, I know to be reliable and trustworthy, those unmarked, I know only slightly. If you arrive in a port where there are no correspondents as marked in my list, I suggest you try to obtain information from the others and act according to your discretion.

(Signed)   J. C. D. DREYER   Altona, April 1855.

L'Espérance of Bordeaux, Captain Alquié, aground on the Bengal shallows, 12 May 1818. These small three-masted "Indiamen" of 300 tons, were very similar to those seen in the Pacific after 1815. Sailor's drawing. *(Hayet Collection)*

At the beginning of the letter of instruction an incident is described that explains the shipowner's cautious attitude. In this, one of his captains had been compelled to obtain a loan which not only swallowed up the entire profit of the voyage but more besides.

In 1870, the *Stella* returning with a cargo of guano had met bad weather off Cape Horn and put into Bahia for repairs. There the captain, short of money, had negotiated a loan with the agent of Messrs. Thomsell & Co., of Dublin. The sum borrowed was 20,000 francs on the security of the owner of the *Stella,* and on condition that 27,000 francs was repaid within three months. Compound interest indeed! Moreover, since the moneylender was also the supplier of goods, it became a worse proposition. Rope, sails and victuals, all of inferior quality were purchased from him, to pay for which, nearly 8,000 out of the 20,000 francs borrowed was used. If the depreciation of the ship, the crew's wages and the interest on the loan be added, it can be seen how most of the profits of the venture were lost in the unfortunate episode.

Ships fighting a severe storm. It is unlikely that the crew will save them, once the cargo has begun to shift in the holds. Drawing by Perrot, 1838. *(Bibl. Nat. Estampes)*

Spirit distillery on Guam. From Freycinet's atlas. (*Service hydrographique, Paris*)

CHARTING THE PACIFIC: MAJOR ECONOMIC AND HISTORICAL PROBLEMS

The Voyage of Captain Marchand (1790–1791)

On his way back from Bengal in 1790, Captain Étienne Marchand had put in at St. Helena and there met a veteran Pacific mariner, the English Captain Mortlock. Their conversation, mostly about fur trading with China, prompted Marchand on his return to Marseilles to approach the firm of Baux, with a proposal to undertake a commercial voyage to the Pacific.

Accordingly the ship *Solide* was fitted out. Fifty men were signed on: two second officers, three leiutenants, two surgeons, three volunteers, a boatswain three marine officers, two carpenters, two caulkers, two coopers, an armorer, three storekeepers, a cook, a baker, two fur traders and twenty-two seamen and ship's boys. Not without difficulty, Marchand got official permission to load with a cargo of goods for barter: clothing, footwear, cutlery and firearms.

On 14 December 1790, the *Solide* set sail from Marseilles, on the first stage of a voyage of circumnavigation that inaugurated a century of trading by sailing ships in the Pacific. The journal kept by Claret Fleurieu and published in 1798, not only describes the voyage and its commercial success, but is in itself a pleasure to read.

Passing Planier Island on 14 December, Marchand set course for Brazil, rounded Teneriffe and reached La Praya. On 1 April 1791, Staten Island was on the starboard beam and three weeks later they were in the Pacific in latitude 50° S., having rounded in twenty days, "at a bad time of the year the dreaded Cape Horn, which even in these days inspires awe". The voyagers, moreover, had been able to find wood and fresh water on the banks of the Magellan channel. As Fleurieu wrote in his journal:

Port Jackson, New Holland. An aborigine family on the move. (*Service hydrographique, Paris*)

Since Captain Cook's discovery of the great bay of Christmas Sound on the south coast of Tierra del Fuego, with its fine anchorage and wood, water and vegetation in abundance, there was no longer any fear of the long and tortuous labyrinth of the Magellan Strait.

Setting course for the Marquesas, Marchand reached them precisely 73 days after leaving Staten Island, thanks to accurate astronomical observations. They were an island paradise where his men could rest from their exertions. Here they bartered trinkets with the inhabitants, whose ancestors the Spaniards in 1695 had hunted and fired upon as if they were wild beats.
    The Marseilles seamen had no intention of repeating these cruelties:

Quite a number of women were seen in the islanders' canoes which paddled out to us from Santa Christina and Dominica, many of them young and attractive. Their glances and gestures left little doubt of their intentions, which was confirmed when the men with them acted as interpreters. The women were allowed on board, greeted by a crew, upon whom six months of effort had not extinguished their natural feelings. After some hard bargaining, the women did not hesitate to go below deck.
    The curtain must be drawn upon what followed. Sufficient to say that at dusk the young Marquesan women reappeared on deck, laden with every imaginable trinket, which they had obtained in exchange for the only commercial asset at their disposal.

With universal regret the *Solide*, well provisioned, sailed from the Marquesas on 21 June 1791 on a northwesterly course, bent on trade. Having reached Norfolk Bay on 12 August, a month was spent trading with Indian trappers along the coast of America, who proved to be very experienced bargainers. The *Solide* sailed north as far as the Queen Charlotte Islands and Nootka Sound; by the end of the season, a great commercial success had been gained and the ship's hold was crammed with furs and skins.

But it was time to pass to the second stage of the venture, from buying to selling. The *Solide* crossed the Pacific, stopping at Hawaii on the way, and then entered Macao harbor on 27 November 1791, eager to begin trading. But here they had a setback in the shape of a recently enacted ban upon fur trading. The Portuguese descendants of d'Albuquerque had become the puppets of the Chinese mandarins.

European factories at Canton, *ca.* 1800. Annony- mous Chinese painting on rice paper. *(Danish Maritime Museum, Elsinore)*

The coast of Albemarle Island, the Galapagos archipelago. Drawing by Berard after the account of Darwin's voyage. *(Le Tour du Monde)*

Two recent arrivals, a British ship and a Spaniard, had been compelled to discharge their cargoes in bond into a customs shed, and preference in the fur trade was being given to the Russians. There was a glut of furs on the market at Whampoa and even if the ban on sales was lifted, falling prices would seriously affect sales. Moreover, the Chinese mandarin in charge of customs, under state orders to produce the same revenue every year, imposed taxes in inverse ratio to the number of foreign vessels that entered Canton River. Thus a ship of *Solide's* calibre might well be taxed 6,000 piastres.

Escaping from the restrictions, Marchand set course for Réunion. He noted in his journal:

... the Chinese taste for furs is so decided and widespread that unless the ban is soon lifted, the pressure of demand coupled with the cupidity of the mandarins will discover a means of evading the regulations, as has happened in the case of opium. Illicit traffic will make the prices see-saw, according to the quantity of furs available.

Marchand ultimately arrived back at Toulon on 14 August 1791. But his cargo of furs, taken to Lyons to be sold, was confiscated and then ruined by worm as a result of the 1793 revolution. But the voyage had not been an absolute failure; the *Solide* had circumnavigated the world without difficulty in twenty months, the crew had remained in good health, and Marchand had brought back from America and China vital information on trading conditions. Had he not seen British and American ships at Macao? The voyage opened the eyes of financiers and traders to the possibilities in the Pacific, to a degree not yet reached with regard to the "Southern Continent". Quick voyages round Cape Horn were indicated.

Chilean settlement at Punta Arenas. Engraving by Berard from a photograph. (*Le Tour du Monde*)

THE INTERMINGLING OF TRADE

Even before Lewis and Clark had crossed the United States from east to west in 1804 (Columbia River and Nootka Sound), many towns and villages on the west coast were known, having been settled in the course of the establishment of trading posts by the fur companies. They had discovered more of the Far East than any officially sponsored expedition prior to Frémont in 1845. And the latter were soon superseded by the gold rush. Ships along the east coast, from Maine to Georgia, made annual voyages to Tierra del Fuego to obtain furs.

The primitive existence of the inhabitants there was rudely disturbed, as the traders bought skins from the Indian hunters and stored them until the ships came. North of the Columbia river lay Russian America—Alaska. The ports of Sitka and Kodiak and villages in the Aleutians and along the Bering coast began to thrive through the traffic in furs and it was in order to protect and develop this trade, that the succession of Russian voyages by Krusenstern, Kotzebue and Lutke were undertaken.

In a voyage which extended over four years, 1803–1806, Krusenstern sailed from Kronstadt to the Pacific via the Horn, with two ships, *Nadeshda* and *Neva*. The expedition was sponsored by the American Fur Trading Company

Temples and huts of the village of Caieli, Bouro Island (Moluccas). From Duperrey's atlas to the voyage of *la Coquille*, 1822–1825. (*Service hydrographique, Paris*)

Settlement at Frenchman's Harbor, Alaska, during the fishing season. The area was also a center for the fur trade. From La Pérouse's atlas. *(Service hydrographique, Paris)*

Interior of Indian fishermen's hut, Nootka Sound. These people lived entirely by fishing and hunting. The trading of furs to China flourished here from the 18th century. Drawing by Webber. From the atlas to Cook's voyages. *(Service hydrographique, Paris)*

Village of Agagna, Guam. From Freycinet's atlas. *(Service hydrographique, Paris)*

of St. Petersburg. But Krusenstern was ill-received in Japan, and trading conditions both there and at Canton proving unfavorable, he proceeded to Sitka. But there, too, it was more difficult than in the past, much to the disappointment of the Czar. Nevertheless, Krusenstern brought valuable information on hydrography and trade, and some important maps back to Kronstadt.

Ten years later, as soon as the Congress of Vienna had restored peace in Europe, Kotzebue undertook two similar voyages, first with the *Rurick* and then the *Predpriarte* and *Seniavin*. After having tried to find a northeast passage back to Russia, he returned via the Pacific Islands, California, and Chile.

The *Seniavin* went to sea again in 1826, under the command of Frederik Lutke. After stops at Rio and Valparaiso, recently liberated from the Spaniards, she sailed straight to Sitka. Lutke found that the welfare of the

The quayside at Guayaquil. Engraving by Lancelot, from a photograph. (*Le Tour du Monde*)

Russian settlers at Sitka had improved since Krusenstern's previous visit. The latter had painted a grim picture of conditions, in which his countrymen had flocked there with little thought of the future and had been exploited by the agents of the American company.

Lutke wintered in the Carolines, explored the west coast of the Bering Strait and then returned to Kronstadt in 1829, having completed the third Russian circumnavigation of the world within twenty-five years. This type of voyage, however, if it were to be followed up by colonization, faced the Russians with the prospect of traversing immense distances—almost the entire Eurasian continent, 10,000 kilometers from St. Petersburg to Okhotsk. In consequence, later Russian maritime voyages were mostly undertaken by whaling ships and the empire's zone of influence in the Pacific became restricted to the Asiatic coast north of Kamchatka, with the port of Okhotsk serving as the main base for her ships.

All the European powers had by now established commercial relations with China, but, after the French revolution, only English and American ships were seen in the Imperial ports. English ships, displacing a thousand to twelve hundred tons, carried up to 100,000 bales of Indian cotton annually and China exported Nankeen silks, tea and porcelain.

However profitable this trade might seem for the English, there were serious drawbacks. The ships' captains often suffered exasperating delays in port at the hands of the mandarins; the seas were infested with pirates and crews ashore were frequently ambushed or involved in brawls. As a result of Russian influence, American interest in the trade waned and she sent only smaller merchantmen of about 350 tons, fitted-out at Boston, New York and Salem.

Some Spanish ships came from Manila, and very occasionally there were French and Scandinavian ones. One of these was *Le Bordelais*, 200 tons, which in 1816 reached China from France, via Cape Horn, Chile, California and Hawaii. An unpleasant reception awaited her; she found that the customs dues imposed were far higher than for the English merchantmen. Even worse, after a wharf at Whampoo had been placed at *Le Bordelais'* disposal for careening, it was found to be a nest of pirates. The local shipchandler was a rogue, who levied a private fee on all stores sold that was fixed at 500 piastres, whether one bought a sack of rice or an entire cargo.

The three-masted American ship *Bazaar*, 1832, painted by François Roux in profile and three-quarter view. These types of ship heralded the arrival of the clippers. (*Bibl. Hist. de la Marine*)

A ship's cargo up for auction. Popular American engraving, 1840.

THE UPSURGE OF TRADE

On the eleven islands of the Hawaii group lived half a million natives, from which excellent replacements might be found for undermanned ships. Excellent canoeists and born seamen, several of these natives were found aboard the American Pacific traders, but they could not make the passage via the Horn, because in spite of their courage, they would have died from the cold. Sandalwood, cotton and tobacco (rated almost as highly as Virginian leaf) were important articles of trade. Sugar cane also thrived in the islands, but the costs of harvesting and processing were too high in comparison with the imports from China. Throughout the Pacific, English, German and American ships traded successfully in silks, textiles, wines and spirits, copper, rope, clothing of all kinds, footwear and jewellery. The main operational base for these activities was California.

The English and German traders were more successful at selling their countries' manufactures in the Pacific islands than in South America, where the preference was for French de luxe goods. From California the major traffic was in the shipment of furs to China, but here English sea captains engaged in private enterprise came up against the monopoly of the English fur trading companies.

On the northwest Pacific coast of America, the merchant ships did a profitable trade with those articles recommended by Marchand and Mortlock in the past: woollen goods, cloth, linen, lead shot and powder, guns, rice, biscuit and woodworking tools. In return, they took on cargoes of fur: otter, fox and sable. But in the opinion of every captain, the people in those parts were "hard and dangerous".

The small American ships (300 to 400 tons) out of Boston and Providence, which rounded the Horn despite their size, readily traded in silk, cloth and wines with China, in return for furs at a handsome profit.

During the first half of the nineteenth century, California formed part of the Mexican Confederation, dominated first by Jesuits and then by Franciscans. This land of monks and Indian fur trappers boasted the towns and ports of Monterey (seat of government), San Diego, San Francisco and Santa Barbara. All the livestock was in the hands of the missions, the main trade being in cowhides.

In his famous account of the voyage of the *Pilgrim* in *Two Years before the Mast* (1840), Richard Dana has given a vivid picture of seafaring and life along the Californian coast.

Steam assisting sail. A donkey engine driving a pulley-line for unloading bales of wool. Anonymous contemporary drawing, *ca.* 1850.

Peruvian priest at an open-air altar. Anonymous aquatint. *(Bibl. Nat. Estampes)*

The ship lay at anchor in the open roadstead, tied to a buoy and swinging free—a necessary precaution because of the prevalent southeasterlies, upon whose arrival the ship beat up against the wind until calmer weather allowed a return to the anchorage. The captain sent small parties ashore to collect the furs, which were then brought over the sandbars to his ship lying offshore, by dinghies carrying as many as three hundred skins each. The work ashore, and of ferrying the cargo to the ship and packing it in the holds was very laborious, often taking fourteen hours in the day. Dana's account of the disposal of the cargo is picturesque—the little booths on board which transformed the ship for a short time into a bazaar; the arrival of the buyers, great

Tortuga Bay on the Peruvian coast. Unsafe shelter, with its open roadstead and current-swept anchorages. *(Institut de géographie, Paris)*

Street-trader in a Peruvian market. Anonymous aquatint. (*Bibl. Nat. Estampes*)

and small. Sunday was the day of rest. The crew roamed the countryside, astride ancient hired nags; if they were out of pocket, they called upon the generosity of some hospitable missionary. Over them stood the unquestioned authority of the captain.

The Spanish yoke in South America was gradually broken. California in North America won its freedom and then in 1821 Peru joined the ranks of colonies becoming free republics. Callao became the principal meeting-place of the American, Russian and English whalers. Louis Philippe of France recognized the importance of trade relations with the new South American republics in spite of the rise in import dues.

We have seen how Spain could not meet the commercial demands of her colonies, as Gouin de Beauchesne had discovered. From about 1820, a great market began to develop in South America, especially Chile and Peru, for all kinds of French produce: wine, liqueurs, glassware, mirrors, cloth, silk, apparel, hats, footwear, gloves, olive oil, perfumes, butter, salted provisions, dried fruit, books, prints, furniture, clocks, saddlery and weapons. The only obstacle was the high import duty, which even the South Americans themselves were eager to evade. Hear Captain Joubert, in his *Annales Maritimes et Coloniales*, written in 1826:

When a merchant ship arrives in a Chilean port, there is only one customs officer to look after everything; he is usually on friendly terms with the ship's captain. Although his job is to see that nothing leaves the ship without his authority, he cannot be everywhere at once. While he sleeps or lingers over his meals, many opportunities occur for unloading goods illicitly and warehousing them nearby. The customs officer is frequently led astray by the captain's attentions, so that he neglects his duties in day-time as much as at night.

This was how smuggling flourished, and illicit goods quietly slipped in, after which one returned to Le Havre and Bordeaux, perhaps this time to ship over Spanish colonists to harry the rebels.

D'Urville's *L'Astrolabe* painted by François Roux. Illustrated in Admiral Pâris': "Souvenirs de marine conservés". *(Bibl. Hist. de la Marine)*

"STAOUËLI" AND "L'ASTROLABE" AT CAPE HORN (1839–1840)

The liberation of the Spanish South American colonies brought large numbers of European ships to Cape Horn. However, despite progress in the hydrography and cartography of the Pacific little had been done in the field of meteorology, and Maury's wind charts were still in the future. Great problems remained. What was the best time of year to round the Horn? What rules must be followed during the passage? Opinions differed widely as to the solution of these problems.

Several relevant works appeared at this time, including Lieutenant Barral's *Digressions sur la Navigation du Cap Horn*, published in the *Annales Maritimes et Coloniales*, of 1827. Barral concluded his book by quoting Cassini's famous dictum:

It is far better not to know where one is, and realize that one does not know, than to be certain one is in a place where one is not.

Another in the same journal, describes the voyage of the Nantes merchant ship *Staouëli*, under the command of Captain Isnard. Published in 1839, the little ship's adventures in the icy seas south of Cape Horn, are vividly told.

"At 7.30 a.m., being about 56° 41′ S. and 60° W., a sudden fall in the temperature told us of the presence of icebergs." About 2 p.m. they surrounded the ship on every side. There seemed to be a clear channel to the south but it was actually found impassable. As a result, they had to turn north, beating up against the wind under reduced sail. During the night progress was impeded by pack-ice while the wind increased. Captain Isnard decided to play his last card. He gave orders for crowding on sail and the *Staouëli* raced on.

For the first time, both I and the crew began to reflect what would happen if one of these huge masses of ice, between two and twenty feet thick, crashed into the ship's side

L'Astrolabe at Port Carteret, New Ireland. From Dumont D'Urville's atlas, 1837–1840. *(Service hydrographique, Paris)*

Dumont d'Urville's *l'Astrolabe* and *Zelée* held fast in the ice, 16 February 1838. Lithograph by Lebreton. *(Bibl. Nat. Estampes)*

Cape Horn at a distance of nine miles. Drawing by Bayer from D'Urville's atlas. (*Service hydrographique, Paris*)

during the night ... nor could we forget the speed with which storms arose in these latitudes and against which we had struggled so long. Our disquiet was increased by the melancholy calls of the penguins and petrels. At two in the morning, we passed close to a huge iceberg, so large that one of its sides formed a horseshoe-shaped bay, in which small craft might have sheltered from the storm. But other dangers lurked there, for, even as we admired its cold beauty, one of the icy walls of the bay disintegrated with a mighty roar into the sea.

But the little ship ultimately gained the Pacific, her sides scored and dented by the bergs.

Dumont d'Urville made his return voyage via Cape Horn, passing from west to east. In the high latitudes beyond 40° S., they encountered the "Roaring Forties" in their full strength. It became stormy and cold. *L'Astrolabe* reached Cape Pilar, at the western end of the Magellan Strait. The captain went down with scurvy and almost the entire crew became incapacitated. Luckily the following wind required only that the yards be braced; shortening sail or reefing would certainly have been beyond the crew's ability.

As d'Urville told the first mate: "With only ten able-bodied men left, we are lost unless we find Cape Horn to the southeast." Such was the malevolence of Cape Horn, that the winds around her blew west against those attempting to reach the Pacific, and east against those sailing on the opposite course. By good fortune the wind held northwest or southwest, enabling *l'Astrolabe* to round the Horn close-in.

Although Captain Hall has described the cape as: "a high, precipitous rock rising sheer from the nearby land in such a way as to be visible far out at sea as a solitary pinnacle" ..., d'Urville was content to liken it to one of the headlands of the Brittany coast. No one, however, quarreled with his description of the atrocious weather.

A BRETON PAINTER AT CAPE HORN

M. Dauguy, the Breton artist, was a passenger aboard the frigate *La Persévérante* when she weighed from Brest on 28 August 1855, bound for Chile. Here are extracts from his diary:

We left harbor in tow of the steamship *Le Souffleur*, which took us out beyond Ushant. The weather was bad and winds dead against as Brest was lost to view ... my native land seemed infinitely dearer at that moment, but enough said. My cabin measures 2·10 by 2·35 meters. There are two beds including a hammock, a chest which forms a convenient desk, a cupboard and a washbasin. As the cabin is just above the water line, it is lit by a small porthole; what pleases me most is that it is one of the farthest from the galley ... my materials are in order and my oils have not moved out of place ... I have taken with me for the voyage two sets of eating utensils, washing things, a wide-brimmed straw hat, a woollen shirt, cloth and rubber shoes, also candles, sugar, rum, brandy and tea ... I have a cabin boy as servant; the fare on board is excellent, with two meals a day. For lunch: fish, cutlets, eggs, sweet and coffee; for dinner: soup, three entrées, two meat courses, two side dishes, sweet and coffee. At both meals we drink claret or madeira, and at dinner champagne as well!

The frigate is an excellent sailer, but like the proverb: "Good sailer, good roller"; she pitches and rolls so much that one expects her to split at any moment ... The

Three-masted trader of about 1840. 600 tons but able to steer well in bad weather. Painting by François Roux. *(Bibl. Hist. de la Marine)*

captain has kindly put at my disposal two cabins near his, from which I can compose my seascapes after nature ... At Gorée, I saw for the first time negroes in their original habitat. They are almost naked and those in the interior are completely so. They are ruled by a host of petty kings. One of them, the King of Dakar, sent his general of cavalry on board to sell straw for hat making. The general invited us ashore and spoke volubly to me in bad French, intimating that if I were to present him with an old suit of clothes he coveted, I should become his friend for life. As this was the last thing to be wished for, I gave him nothing.

Upon *La Persévérante's* approach to Cape Horn on 21 November 1855, Dauguy's diary goes on:

At five in the morning a violent gale struck us with all sails set; it came so suddenly that there was hardly time to shorten them. The surface of the sea was covered with foam, which seemed to boil at each successive gust of wind; we shipped water as the frigate struggled on at four leagues per hour, under bare poles except for the fore stay-sail. The wind increased in force until six a.m., and for ten minutes blew with such violence that we expected to be dismasted. But then it dropped, as if by command, to

Topmasts tottering or carried away, the frigate rides out the gale. But will her slung-out boat ever be able to rescue the other ship, which is sinking? Lithograph by F. Perrot, 1834. *(Bibl. Nat. Estampes)*

136

Hauling in the mizzen and mainsail aboard a man-of-war. The maneuver was much less coordinated aboard a merchantman, as each sail had to be taken in singly. Note the long studding-sail booms above the yard. Drawing by Morel-Fatio, from *La Marine*, 1844.

a fresh breeze with which we were carried to within a hundred leagues of Cape Horn without further incident.

27 November. We are fifty leagues from the Cape and will reach it tomorrow, just three months since we left Brest. Terrible squalls ever since yesterday evening with huge seas running; the ship has been a-hull to the wind for the last twenty-four hours and rolls horribly. The icy wind and flying spray make the cold weather almost unendurable; we are entering the seas of Cape Horn and they are indeed terrifying.

12 December, Wednesday. At last we are on the other side of Cape Horn, having rounded it yesterday; we are thankful it took us only a fortnight to sail the last terrible 150 leagues. Nonetheless we have been roughly handled. After nearly capsizing last night, the captain caught sight of the shore of Staten Island, once the wind had moderated. But hardly had we passed beyond it than an even more terrible gale struck us; the sea heaved into waves which were literally mountains of water. We sailed under bare poles through this howling, seething chaos, as the gallant *Persévérante* scudded before the tempest. Everything on board was battened down and stowed; but we rolled so heavily, that the ship's boats, thirty feet above the water line, were broached. In the bows, the anchors each weighing about 4,000 kilos, were dislodged from their cables by huge waves which broke over the ship.

In such moments one can neither sleep nor eat much and one tires very easily. The ship creaks and groans until it seems she will break up. But the ship is very seaworthy, in spite of carrying sixty guns and enormous masts; we have suffered only half the damage to be expected in any other ship ... the barometer has behaved abnormally throughout, with the mercury completely out of sight, several degrees below the "storm" mark.

Six days later a fresh gale drove the ship southeast in the direction of Graham Land, and the original course was regained after enduring snow and hailstorms ...

We are now only 140 leagues from Valparaiso, being in the latitude of Valdivia. The entire Magellan Strait was traversed in the teeth of ceaseless gales; these are terrible seas in truth.

A lady of Lima, followed by her valet in livery. Anonymous washdrawing. *(Bibl. Nat. Estampes)*

Dauguy reached Valparaiso on 28 December, where he stayed for a few days in a luxurious but reasonably priced hotel (2 piastres or 10 francs a day):

Society here is rather snobbish, with an English veneer of manners; no one would dream of being seen without a top hat.

Dauguy next crossed the Cordilleras and finally returned to Paris four years later.

Not far from Valparaiso, Pallu de la Barrière came across other visitors from Europe, English ships of 1,500 to 2,000 tons and others from Hamburg, Bordeaux and Marseilles. It was in the open roadstead of the great guano center—the Chincha Islands. Here Chinese volunteers and negro slaves, cuffed by their Peruvian warders, chipped and scraped off the centuries old deposits of yellowish-white bird droppings which covered the ground; they gathered it into sacks under a blazing sun and in clouds of dust which hurt the eyes, throat and lungs. How many millions of gannet, pelicans, sea larks and petrels had since the dawn of time excreted upon the arid soil of these islands and made the fortunes of the Peruvian government and the sea captains? Guano remained the principal fertilizer until the development of the nitrate industry. Ships lay offshore the guano islands in open roadsteads, awaiting the island governor's permission to load.

Right: The guano islands off Peru brought wealth to the sailing ships in the 1840s. The sea birds' e: ment, several meters thick at the nesting grounds, fetched £10 a ton in Ireland as fertilizer. The carg○ no more than the effort of collecting it in sacks and carrying it home. The black masses on the islan not woods, but dense flocks of birds. *(Institut de géographie, Paris)*

The guano islands. The density of the sea bird population is clearly shown. (*Institut de géographie, Paris*)

Four examples of whales' teeth, pricked out with a needle to depict scenes of life aboard. The work of American whaling ship seamen. *(Mariners Museum, Newport News)*

The captain. The eternal question: where is the whale?

The first mate—the second in command —writing up the accounts in his cabin. Note the solid sea chest under the desk.

THE WHALERS AND CAPE HORN

Who did not hunt the whale? Ships, great and small, from Nantes, St. Malo, Le Havre, Bordeaux, Hull, Bremen, Hamburg, Amsterdam, New Bedford, Salem, Boston and Nantucket crossed half the world in pursuit of the whale. In the Middle Ages whale were found in the Bay of Biscay, but with hunting had gradually dispersed to Newfoundland, the Arctic and Greenland. No one knew the ways around the icebergs or the secret channels better than the whaling captains; it was they who in 1903 helped Amundsen find his famous Northwest Passage. Cook saw whales in the Pacific in 1775; three years later, whalers left London to hunt them off Chile, Peru and the Galapagos, and later, California, Japan and Australia.

All rounded the Horn with great skill. On the way many paused in the strait to hunt for walrus, whose fat was prized as much as the whale's for candles. The whaling captains were superb seamen, their ships nearly always at sea. To avoid desertion by the crew, they rarely put into port, anchoring only in some remote bay to wood and water.

An able-seaman sewing a jib on the boom.   The second mate sharpening a bit.

These men gambled with the sea. When it was at its worst, they never lost sight of their objective, and when it was fine they were ready to launch their boats. And what boats! Masters of oar and paddle, they fought the sea to reach their prey. The whalers interested themselves in everything, returning to port with information, logs of their voyages, souvenirs, "curios". If they were not great draughtsmen or surveyors, their memory and experience was precise enough for hydrographers to follow. So the routes of the whalers assumed great geographical importance.

Masters of the harpoon from the North Pole to the South, they searched the bays and creeks of the Seven Seas; nomads of the ocean, their business was weighed in blubber and whale oil. They saw things upon which no other men had ever gazed and brought back strange tales from the deep.

Their ships wallowed in steam and smoke, the sails streaked red by the reflection of the ship's fires at night; on board, the bearded crew, begrimed with soot and grease, worked on oblivious to their appearance and the appalling stench. These iron men, as brave as they were undisciplined, submitted to the lash of the cat-o'-nine-tails long after it had been abolished

Late 18th century marine barometer. How many anxious fingers have tapped its glass, hoping the mercury would rise? Nicknamed by seamen, from early days, as a bringer of bad weather— "the sorcerer". *(Mariners Museum, Saint-Malo)*

elsewhere. Stripped to the waist, their hands lashed to the shrouds, they took their punishment, aware that the next day they would once more hunt the whale, harpoon in hand.

Perhaps the most memorable account is that by Richard Dana of the whaling ship *Wilmington* of New Bedford, which arrived back in California in November 1835, after an eight-months cruise. The picture of decay, disorder and filth aboard the brig, yards askew and paintwork peeling, aroused the unmerited wrath of the whole whaling community.

... Her captain was a Quaker, dressed in a brown suit and wide-brimmed hat; he used to pace the deck with long strides, his head lowered like a ram. His men looked more like fishermen and peasants than sailors, with their thick woollen multi-colored trousers with pockets for thrusting their hands into, and their fancy braces.

But even if Dana believed they did not look very seamanlike, appearances were deceptive. These were the same men who could remain continuously at sea for eight months and whose passage of the Horn at the worst season of the year, earned them the honored title of the "Cape Horners".

THE MISFORTUNES OF "LA CONFIANCE" (1833–1834)

A passage in A. Bouteiller's: *L'Histoire de la ville de Dieppe*, tells the tale:

La Confiance was a three-masted whaler of 539 tons, commanded by Captain T. C. J. Olivier and owned by Messrs. Blondel & Morisse of Dieppe. With a crew of thirty-four she sailed from Dieppe on 15 August 1833; against a head wind, she was towed out by the steam vessel *Mounteneer*. The first part of the voyage went well enough; the Horn was doubled on 18 January 1834 and already two whales had been captured which yielded 140 barrels of oil and 25 crates of whalebone.

Once in the Pacific, course was steered for Mocha Island, in latitude 33° S., and some forty miles off the Chilean coast. Only horses and wild pig lived upon this remote island, where Captain Olivier decided to wood and water. He stayed there only one day, however, as he knew of the area's reputation for storms. On 6 March, high seas were running and the wind reached gale force; *La Confiance* ran before the wind with reefed topsails. About four in the afternoon, they lost sight of land; the captain ordered four boats out to hunt whales, but they later returned empty-handed.

The squalls continued with increasing force, when at 2.30 a.m. the lookout, seaman Leroux, shouted "land ahoy!". The captain came on deck and ordered the anchors to be cleared in case of need. The sky was inky black, out of which fell torrential rain and the wind was so strong that the ship sped along at four leagues per hour. The captain took every necessary step to halt this speed which would obviously have had fatal consequences; sails were hauled in or shortened and the starboard anchor thrown out, but she dragged it. The captain was about to order the port anchor out, when suddenly the ship heeled over and lay to across the wind; huge waves broke over the gunwhales, rails and boats.

In this crisis, the captain ordered the crew to the stern and said to them: "Well, boys, we shall have to fight to save the ship! You, Cotin, who are as strong as four men, cut the main mast down because it's more trouble than it's worth at the moment". His words were addressed to a red-haired giant of about thirty, who replied readily enough: "Whatever you begin, Captain, I'll finish".

It was hardly the time for debate, so the captain seized an axe and began hewing at the mainmast; Cotin grabbed it from him, and set to with tremendous strokes until the mainmast fell with a crash. Soon afterwards the mizzen mast went overboard snapped

by the storm, followed twenty minutes later by the foremast and the bowsprit. The completely dismasted ship rolled drunkenly and about 4 a.m. began to break up; two hours later, when it was clear that nothing more could be done, the crew sought to abandon ship and reach shore which was only two cables away.

The captain allowed four men to jump into the sea, but it was so rough they came back and one disappeared under the waves. The first mate, who was a good swimmer, then tied a rope round his waist and finally swam to the shore. Securing it to a tree-trunk he made a life line by which the crew were saved. Scarcely had they all been brought ashore when natives were seen approaching. *La Confiance* had been wrecked on the Chilean Coast at Imperial Bay, 39°2′ S., 76°15′ W.

The natives proved to be Araucanian Indians, tall of stature and copper-skinned, who seemed friendly. The next morning the weather became calm and everything which could be recovered from the ship was brought ashore, during which time more Araucanians appeared on the scene. The following day their chieftain called upon the survivors to surrender, and they had no choice but to obey. During the next two days they let themselves be driven towards Valdivia, the chief Araucanian town. They were deprived of their weapons and marched in their torn clothes under the surveillance of a mounted guard. They came to a large river which had to be crossed; many of the seamen

Le Havre whaler, *ca.* 1840, painted by François Roux. Following the whales wherever they sounded, these stout ships often circumnavigated the globe before returning home laden with blubber and whalebone. *(Bibl. Hist. de la Marine)*

143

Station Bay, Floriana Island in the Galapagos. Engraving by Berard after the atlas to Dupetit-Thouars' voyage in the *Vénus*, 1836. *(Le Tour du Monde)*

couldn't swim and Captain Olivier asked the guard how it could be done. He smiled and demanded money for his help. At this final insult, the captain called upon the giant Cotin to deal with him which he proceeded to do with vigour and then seized hold of his horse.

The account does not explain how the river was crossed, but captain Olivier and the survivors reached Valdivia on 17 March 1834. After the captain had made a full report to the local magistrate, several of the crew decided to remain there. The rest set out for Valparaiso and reached it on 29 May.

On 2 July, the captain and his cabin boy, named Clement, departed in an English merchant ship, the *African Packet*, which arrived at London on 10 November. From there they went to Dieppe; in time most of the crew got back to France, while the rest remained several years in Chile. One of them, indeed, commanded a small schooner that plied along those far-distant coasts. Some never returned to their native land and their fate remains a mystery.

PART III

The Royal Way of the Pacific Sailing Ships

In 1848 gold was discovered in California; the prospectors took over every ship that could be found and headed for San Francisco. With the enthusiasm of a young nation, the Americans created the clipper and a merchant marine, epitomized in the genius of Donald McKay. Having rounded Cape Horn, the fleets of Europe and New England crowded on sail for the west; it was an era of record voyages and brilliant maritime exploits. After the great ages of discovery, exploration and hydrography, now came that of industrial and commercial exploitation of the Pacific. The ships were accustomed to long overseas voyages; the American, Matthew Fontaine Maury, had unravelled the secrets of the winds.

Gold was also found in Australia, the emigrant ships arriving there via the Cape of Good Hope; with the wind behind them they came back via the Horn. These immense voyages inspired the English shipbuilders to create a special type of vessel, and at this point the naval architect James Baines enters upon the scene. But gold was not inexhaustible and the flow of emigrants slackened; a high percentage of the enormous tonnage that had just been built remained unused, but many shipbuilders were saved from ruin by the guano of the Chincha Islands. Meanwhile, agriculture developed in California and Oregon and timber was felled in the ancient forests of Puget Sound.

In Australia, the pioneers' countless flocks of sheep gave up their wool to the shippers of Sydney harbor; in Chile, a wonderful fertilizer, nitrate, brought wealth to a desert coast. Manpower, tools, machinery, cement, rails, clothing were needed everywhere. Cottons from India, weaves and prints from Manchester, clothed the South Sea islanders. English coal fed the boilers of railway engines in California and desalination plants in Chile. New South Wales developed her own coal mines, and New Zealand the export of frozen meat. Zones of influence, both commercial and political, began to develop in the Pacific.

Wooden ships became obsolescent; from the Clyde in 1880, ships of iron

Contemporary American illustration.

Baltimore in 1840. Drawing by Bartlett; engraved by S. Fisher. (*Bibl. Nat. Estampes*)

Reminiscent of the little Baltimore clippers—the American pilot-cutters with their raked masts; this one being the Norfolk, Va., pilot. (*Mariners Museum, Newport News*)

were built, then of steel. Although sailing ships had suffered successive blows, in the opening of the Suez Canal in 1869 and in the unceasing development of the steamship, whose speed and comfort began to erode her monopoly of passengers and cargoes, they still retained certain advantages—they never needed to put in for coal or water at remote places, and the wind in their sails was free.

Since the general costs of a voyage did not increase in proportion to tonnage, France, Germany and the North European powers built bigger and bigger sailing ships, to carry increasingly heavy cargoes. As the time taken for the voyage remained almost the same, greater profit could only be achieved by carrying more. While American sailing ships entered a bad period, the English merchant marine rose to preeminence. Competition was fierce; crews worked twelve, fourteen, even sixteen hours a day. Only absolute devotion to duty made such endurance possible in conditions of great risk. For the seas off Cape Horn had not moderated since the days of Schouten, nor had the "Roaring Forties" lost their power. And all this for 75 francs a month, biscuit, fat and beans to eat, and a quart of wine to drink, for a voyage which might take over a year to accomplish.

By the beginning of the present century, only France and Germany were still fitting out oceanic sailing ships in competition; it was a strange rivalry, soon to disappear. The opening of the Panama Canal, the outbreak of the First World War, the advent of submarines and commerce raiders all contributed to the decline. Many of the remaining sailing ships survived until about 1920, when it was time to build new merchant fleets to replace those lost during the war. This was the end; one by one the great birds of Cape Horn, at the end of their magnificent careers, suffered the ignominy of being broken up at the breakers' yards.

1 *The Age of the Clippers*

BIRTH OF THE AMERICAN MERCHANT MARINE

Despite England's efforts to keep her American colonies in ignorance of maritime problems, the young nation developed her own shipyards, seamen and ships, from New England to Pennsylvania. After small beginnings, the quality of American frigates and privateers matured during the War of 1812. The American yards were able to build ships without reference to previous English designs and to evolve such famous types as the Baltimore clipper, which in 1812 became the wonder of the world.

In 1783, on the morrow of the War of Independence, merchants of Boston, New York, Salem, and Philadelphia had taken stock of their maritime future. The following years saw their ships reach Europe, the Indian and Pacific Oceans and round Cape Horn, their seamen developed under the schooling of Paul Jones, Murray and Bainbridge. This commercial ardor began to alarm merchants on the other side of the Atlantic, even after the Treaty of Ghent which marked the end of the Anglo-American naval war in 1814. The English merchant navy emerged from the Napoleonic wars in a bad state, with construction straightjacketed by obsolete tonnage restrictions,

The *Great Republic*, an aquatint by François Roux. Never seen like this at sea, this great ship—the largest in the world at the time—was no sooner launched than she caught fire at New York. After two years repair, the *Great Republic* reappeared with three masts instead of four. In 1872, having sprung a leak she was abandoned off Bermuda. (*Bibl. Hist. de la Marine*)

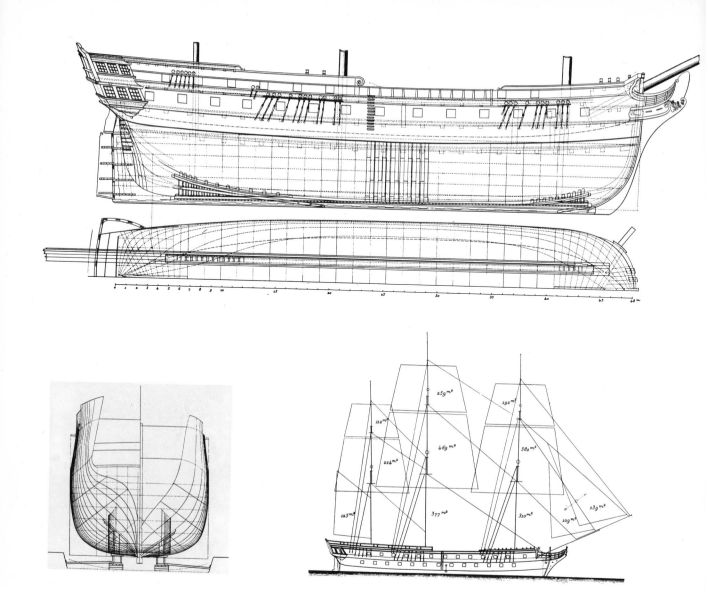

Draught and sail-plan of an East Indiaman, *ca.*
1800–1830. Surprising echo of the Elizabethan
past, compared with the racing clipper form of
the American sailing ships of her day. The East
Indiamen were slow sailers, but sure. The figures
in the illustration represent each sail's area in
square meters. From Admiral Pâris: "Souvenirs
de marine conservés." (*Bibl. Hist. de la Marine*)

and shipowners crippled by taxation. Shortly after the creation of *Lloyd's
Register of Shipping* (1843), a Parliamentary enquiry found that the more
modern and faster American merchant ships were preferred by the shipowners; the gravity of the situation led to the formation of the Marine
Department at the Board of Trade in 1847.

The monopoly wielded by the East India Company, little changed since
Elizabethan times, continued to suffocate private enterprise; the lack of
competition had long given emphasis to heavy cargoes, slow voyages and
the avoidance of all risk. But in 1832, at last, the special privileges of the
Company were abolished.

In 1816, 500-ton American ships of the Black Ball Line, made the crossing
between New York and Liverpool in ten days. Other shipping companies
with ships of 1,000 to 1,500 tons followed in hot pursuit—the Swallow Tail
Line, the Red Star Line, the Dramatic Line. Wagers of 10,000 dollars were

struck on the fastest New York—Liverpool crossing. In 1837, the Black Baller *Columbus*, at a speed of twelve knots, beat the Dramatic Line's *Sheridan* in a sixteen-day crossing. This intense competition marked the opening of a new era for sailing ships, side by side with the trading clippers.

At the time when the Atlantic packets were locked in rivalry to gain passengers, small English schooners had for some years been engaged in the lucrative traffic in opium between India and China, sailing deep into the China Sea to catch the monsoons and outdistance the pirates. Profits exceeding £300,000 attracted shipowners and, by 1846, American and English clippers lay alongside each other in the harbors of Foochow, Amoy and Ningpo.

The trade encouraged the evolution of special ships—the opium clippers—a large number of which were over 600 tons and built in American yards. Their design became characteristic—cutwater stem, concave shape in the bows and contoured stern. Their sailing records were outstanding—New York to Canton via Cape Horn in less than ninety days became commonplace—and certain ships, *Rainbow, Ariel, Sea Witch,* established records. The value of the trade in tea, spices and silk pushed American mercantile tonnage up to 1,241,313 tons by 1847. With this sort of rivalry, it became essential for the antiquated English Navigation laws to be amended—laws rightly condemned by Captain Clark when he said: "It would be difficult to find such crass stupidity expressed within such small compass".

Amendment began in 1849, but too late to prevent a number of English yards from closing down. Nor could the formidable rivalry of the American merchant fleet be eliminated just like that. Consternation in British shipping circles, for instance, greeted the arrival of the American clipper *Oriental*, 1,600 tons, at the West India docks in 1850; her cargo of tea fetched £6 a ton, against £3 obtained by English clippers.

American sailing ships prospered in the boom caused by the North Atlantic passenger demand, and the development of the opium and tea trades; they forged farther ahead as a result of the California gold rush. The fantastic enthusiasm of the American clipper captains was epitomized in men such as the Cape Horner, Captain Waterman of the *Natchez*. He became legendary for the way in which he "nailed" the lines to the topsails and refused to take in sail whatever the weather; his type of determination inspired the young captains and crew of the clippers.

Figurehead of the *George R. Skolfield*, launched at Brunswick, Maine in 1885. Carved by Emery Jones. (*Mariners Museum, Newport News*)

American shipbuilding yard. Contemporary illustration, *ca.* 1850.

THE RISE OF SAN FRANCISCO

On page 1581 of Bouillet's *Dictionnaire de Géographie* (Hachette, 1842), you will find the entry: "San Francisco: fine Californian port, situated at the mouth of the rivers San Sacramento and San Joachin". In fact, Yerba Buena was a Mexican village comprising a few small dwellings, a trapper's store and a chapel. It was the chosen rendezvous of Russian, English, and American whalers and the ideal port for small brigs like Dana's *Pilgrim*, trafficking in furs and tallow.

However, it was not until nearly two centuries after Drake's visit (1576–1577) that the bay was rediscovered by Spanish ships (1769). The Mexican War and the conquest of California brought an American warship—the *Portsmouth*—(1846); but after the American flag had been hoisted and Yerba Buena renamed San Francisco, torpor returned in the heat of the Californian summer. It was not for long. Colonel Sutter's gold nuggets shattered the calm. In 1849 alone, nearly eight hundred ships from every American port brought 100,000 people to San Francisco in search of gold. This was truly an extraordinary transformation as people ran to the placers almost before ships had dropped anchor, in a port, where only a short time before, few ships had ever been.

View of San Francisco on the morrow of the Gold Rush. Anonymous drawing. *(National Cultural Center, Washington, D.C.)*

Mission Street Quay, San Francisco, ca. 1860. Engraving by Moyart. (*Le Tour du Monde*)

Overnight a forest of masts appeared at Yerba Buena; ships of all types and sizes congregated there, beaching hastily in the shallows to discharge their passengers or more often, being totally deserted (as happened to nearly a hundred ships) while the crew led by their captain rushed to the gold fields. The nuggets were far more tempting than their wages; after the rush had started, $150 to $200 monthly was being offered to persuade them to make the return voyage.

Prices rose astronomically. Dockers were engaged at $30 a day; people put up where they could, regardless of price, even squatting on the ground. Abandoned ships were beached and placarded with notices: "Hotel—rooms to let". Freight rates between New York and San Francisco soared from $13 per ton in 1849 to $60 per ton in 1850; one voyage was sufficient to recover a ship's original cost.

Some captains, having managed to enlist crews, returned via China, where they took on cargoes of tea for London; from London they came back to Boston laden with English emigrants—future gold-seekers—thus trebling the profits of their voyage. Fantastic fortunes were made in shipping circles during the gold rush, which lasted until 1860. Strangely enough, however, there was no class of professional seamen in the United States at that time. Captains and mates, even without their "tickets", had the necessary experience, but most of the seamen were volunteers who learnt as they went along. "They would rather navigate between the dance halls of Cherry Street and the pubs of Waterloo Road, than along the routes of the Indies and China, and if they worked like horses they spent their money like asses."

Terms of engagement were fixed before sailing and applied for the duration of the voyage; there was no way of recruitment or discipline, except the rope's end and the bark of command. Crew were furnished by the peddlers

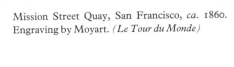

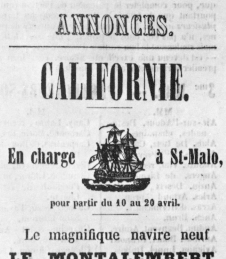

Advertisement in "La Verité" (formerly, "Messager Breton"), 11 July 1850. (*Mariners Museum, Saint-Malo*)

151

Panorama of San Francisco Bay in 1855. Of the 400 ships lying at anchor, more than half had been abandoned by their crews. A gold mine was better than a sailor's wage. *(San Francisco Maritime Museum)*

Broadsheet. "Roll up, gold diggers! New York to San Francisco via Cape Horn in 110 days!" *(Mariners Museum, Newport News)*

Advertisement of a company's claims to a gold strike and 5% annual interest upon the capital. Were social services also included? *(Mariners Museum, Saint-Malo)*

A tempting advertisement! Who could resist dashing off at once to California with the certainty of finding wealth in the gold fields? (*Mariners Museum, Saint-Malo*)

American sailor, *ca.* 1850. Popular engraving.

in human cargo, the shipchandlers and the innkeepers. Drunken brutes were shipped aboard on the strength of three months' pay in advance and their clothing. Undermanned ships often picked up more crew members on the quayside; anchors aweigh, their unfortunate victims awoke to the heave of the windlass.

The captain had officers who knew how to wield the belaying pin, the traditional cudgel aboard ship. Hardly had they got to their feet, before the raw recruits were ordered to the capstan bars or to the ratlines, up which, perhaps for the first time in their lives, they had to climb and unfurl the sails from dizzy heights. And who were these men? Of every race, creed and profession, really: farmers, artists, craftsmen, shopkeepers, policemen, hardened criminals, even clerics—all "shanghaied", under the influence of drugs and fine promises. It was the captain's job to control from the outset this motley collection, defiant and often dangerous though they might be. As soon as the ship had sailed, they were mustered in the waist while the captain delivered some plain speaking from the poop. Thus Captain Halyard, described in Basil Lubbock's *Down Easters*:

"You there! I am Captain Halyard and master of this ship and I wish to make some things clear between us. We have a long voyage ahead and plenty of work. You can see that there must be discipline on board and it is up to you whether we have heaven or hell. All orders will be obeyed, as you have been enlisted and paid to work. If you do so, all will be well; if not, there will be trouble. The first one who wavers, I'll drill holes in him with this (whereupon he brandished a vicious-looking revolver). If anyone tries

154

anything, it will be the worse for them. I have heard some of you have come from the *White Swallow*, on which there was recently a mutiny on board in Chinese waters. This is NOT the *White Swallow* and you've got Jack Halyard in person to deal with. Now you know who I am and what to expect. To your stations!"

But it was not enough to set the pattern of behavior on departure; it had to be maintained. On board the *Challenge*, Captain Waterman once found that fifty-nine of the crew were in league against him soon after sailing, and quite incapable of doing any work. Obviously their only intention had been to board ship in order to reach San Francisco. Waterman, his mate and boatswains were armed and when two men attacked with knives, the captain did not hesitate to fire and both were killed. Five other men died of illnesses en route to San Francisco, and seventeen lay sick in their hammocks.

As soon as the ship had anchored, the crew rushed to engage the services of a "sea-lawyer", the sailor's friend. In this particular case the so-called "Vigilance Committee" of San Francisco threatened to lynch Captain Waterman and his first mate and sink their ship. Had it not been for the firmness of the sheriff, a mob of five hundred, incited by the crew would have put their threats into action.

There are many instances of captains and mates quitting their ships as soon as anchors had been dropped, in order to avoid any revengeful action by their crew. But the latter in general had much less cause for complaint than their predecessors. Accommodation aboard the clippers was infinitely better than the cramped airless conditions of the past. Food was plentiful; if the men were not drinking to excess, they were eating to repletion. Pay was good, the ships were new and on the whole well fitted-out. On the other hand, many ships and their captains were hated from the first, by men who had no pride in their work. Only the captains aboard the clippers seemed to possess a faith and innate realization of their purpose and commercial interest.

American mutineers at New York, *ca.* 1860. *(National Cultural Center, Washington, D.C.)*

The American clipper *Tornado* dismasted at Cape Horn. *(Gleason's Pictorial)*

The *Flying Cloud*, one of the fastest clippers of the 1850s, with a tail wind and studding sails out. Painting by Frank Vining Smith. *(Mariners Museum, Newport News)*

THE ENGLISH AND AMERICAN SHIPBUILDERS

The cargo boom to San Francisco was immediately followed by the construction of numerous clippers. Typical of 1850 were *Surprise* and *Staghound*, displacing 1,500 tons with dimensions 70 × 12 meters and a molded depth of 7 meters. Yards crossed attained a tremendous length of 25 meters. The crew comprised forty seamen, cabin boys and apprentices; two boatswains; one carpenter; one sailmaker; two cooks (usually negroes); one steward; two or three lieutenants; a first mate and the captain. The crew was vitally important when one remembers that in the last days of sail the entire complement might number only 25 to 28 men, including officers.

The launching of those ships was always a great occasion for festivity and rejoicing, and a fine spectacle: the vessels dressed overall, gleaming on the slipways, fully rigged, their masts and yards stepped. Little time was lost in fitting-out, and within a hundred days, they were en route to Cape Horn and San Francisco.

Around 1851, the American yards launched 2,000 ton clippers; everything lacking in California had to be brought by sea—building materials, equipment, machinery, raw materials, victuals, coal, tools. That year 31 clippers were launched, including the famous *Flying Cloud*, 1,783 tons and the *Challenge*, 2,006 tons. The *Golden Gate's* manifest showed a cargo worth $78,000. The freight compelled the crowding on of sail. An 89-day voyage of the *Flying Cloud* from Sandy Hook to San Francisco was undertaken as follows: from Sandy Hook to the equator, 21 days; from the equator to 50° S., 25 days; from 50° S. in the Atlantic to 50° S. in the Pacific, including round the Horn, 7 days only; from 50° S. to the equator, 17 days; from the equator to San Francisco, 19 days. Sometimes results were much less spectacular;

Launch of the *Flying Cloud* at McKay's yard in 1851. This great ship once sailed from New York to San Francisco in 89 days. *(Gleason's Pictorial)*

contrary winds, disablement or an incompetent crew could make the voyage last seven months.

The year 1852 marked the appearance of the famous English ships—the China clippers—which used to sail between Shanghai and London in 87 days. Due to fierce competition from Donald McKay's Boston clippers undercutting freight, it took some time for the English shipowners to draw level. English naval construction began to lean towards iron ships; but many problems still remained, notably in the rolling of sheet metal, in riveting plates and in careening. Regarding the latter, marine vegetation still fouled the hulls even when coated with paint, a problem unknown to the copper-bottomed wooden ships.

The years 1850 to 1857 marked the apogee of the American shipbuilders, Donald McKay and William H. Webb. The former's ships were supreme: the *Sovereign of the Seas* reaching 22 knots, and the *Champion of the Seas*, 20 knots. Exceptional distances—up to 400 miles in one day—were covered by McKay's clippers.

Launched in 1852, the *Sovereign of the Seas* (2,050 tons, 77 meters overall

Frank Vining Smith's painting of the *Sovereign of the Seas*: 1,500 tons; dimensions 60 × 15 meters; built by Donald McKay in 1868. (*Mariners Museum, Newport News*)

The *Great Republic*—McKay's masterpiece. Built at Boston in 1853. Dimensions 98 × 15 × 12 meters; displacement 4,555 tons; sail area 3,770 square meters; diameter of mainmast 1·12 meters; length of mainyard 37 meters. A 15 horsepower steam engine operated the winches. Thirty-six tons of water were stored on board. Material used in construction

68

105

148

210

290

370

109

160

207

81

GREAT REPUBLIC

Donald McKay, the most famous American clipper builder. Popular engraving.

included the following: 3,810 cubic meters of pine; 2,056 tons of white oak; 336 tons of iron; 5·6 tons of copper, for sheathing and bolts. The hull occupied 50,000 working days; 64,648 meters of canvas were used for the sails. In the diagram the number on each sail indicates its surface area. From Admiral Pâris: "Souvenirs de marine conservés". (*Bibl. Hist. de la Marine*)

Unloading from a clipper. Contemporary
American engraving.

length with a crew of 105) had an inauspicious maiden voyage. She was dismasted off the Horn while carrying too much sail, a frequent risk with this type of ship. One by one the masts came down, the mizzen being fouled by the enormous boom. However, the clipper was able to rig a jury mast at sea and proceed to San Francisco. If the seas were hard, the men were harder, and Captain Clark told how the clipper captains used to row across to each other in appalling weather in the Tierra del Fuego channel, to dine and exchange news.

The American clippers could claim in their prime to be the most elegant, best rigged and best kept ships anywhere, despite some shortcomings in

Figurehead of the *Belle of Oregon*, launched at Bath, Maine in 1876. (*Mariners Museum, Newport News*)

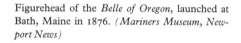

The American clipper *Ocean Herald*, 1855. F. Roux aquatint.

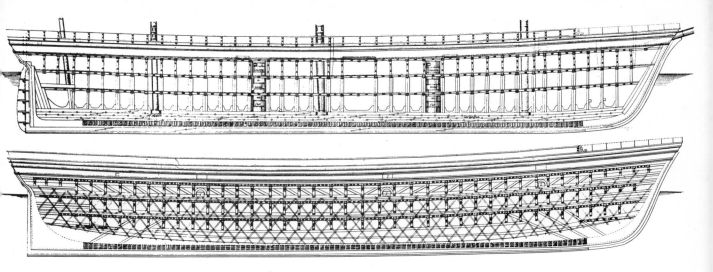

accommodations. Thirteen were launched from American yards in 1850; 31 in 1851; 40 in 1852; 51 in 1853—the record year. Thereafter construction declined—to 20 in 1854; 13 in 1855; 8 in 1856 and 3 in 1857.

On 4 October of that record year, 1853, McKay launched his renowned *Great Republic,* 4,555 tons, 98 meters long and 15 in the beam. This clipper had double topsails and a 15 h.p. steam engine on the deck for hoisting them from the yards; the mainyard measured 37 meters and the truck was 69 meters above the deck! The lower masts were supported by tarred stays of 30 centimeters circumference and the main anchors each weighed four tons.

More than 3,800 square meters of sail, excluding stay- and studding-sails were required to propel this colossus. Sixty thousand people attended the launching, which was the climax of McKay's genius; hundreds of ships' carpenters were involved in her construction. What industry, what labor! Two men manipulated the handsaw, cutting out to shape the sections roughly hewn by adze and hatchet. Each pintle hole had to be pierced in the planking and frame, each timber dovetailed between the stem and the keel, the stern and the buttock-frame. The *Great Republic,* scheduled by McKay for the Australia run, went first to New York but there caught fire in December 1853. After repairs which lasted a year, she took part in the Crimean campaign and subsequently became a troopship in the Civil War.

Cross-section of the *Great Republic*, showing the interlacing beams and struts, which strengthened the internal frame. *(Bibl. Hist. de la Marine)*

MAURY—THE PILOT OF WINDS AND CURRENTS

Everybody knows that for thousands of years, the sea winds which used to be so placid and favourable, have become wild and malignant. All ships rowing against them endured long and painful voyages. One day a ship's captain in too much of a hurry gave his soul to the devil in return for the power to capture the winds, which lived upon an uncharted island at the other end of the world. The ship belonging to this accursed captain—who kept the winds locked up in the hold for his own use—happened to strike a rock near her port of arrival and all on board were drowned. The winds regained their freedom, but they did not remember the way back to their island, and from that day to this they have continued to blow across the seas looking for their home!

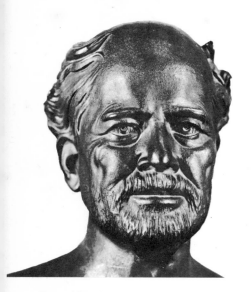

This delightful fable reached the ears of a young officer in the U.S. navy, Lieutenant Matthew Fontaine Maury, but the fatalism of the old mariners did not appeal to his scientific mind. The winds certainly were free, and if one could not put them in a cage, at least their habits and moods could be studied; if they were uncontrollable, something could be done to profit from their great strength. That was what must be done.

Maury worked upon his father's farm before embarking on the frigate *Brandywine* at Washington in 1830. There he found his vocation—a seaman in the widest sense, more concerned with navigation than seamanship or strategy. After a short time at sea, he realized how little was known about winds and currents and what extraordinary errors were made by navigators in this direction. He remained a navigator for nine years but went ashore as the result of an accident. Maury was then appointed director of the newly founded *Bureau of Cartography and Navigational Instruments* at Washington, which became through him a mainspring of contemporary hydrography and meteorology.

Maury decided to regard past records—ships' logs and journals—as the main basis for his *Wind and Current Charts of the North Atlantic*. The idea was sound. Information supplied by a number of ships about seas crossed at the same period of the year, could provide valuable statistics for a study of the

Bust of Matthew Fontaine Maury, whose pilot charts revolutionized sailing ship navigation. *(Hydrographic Office, Washington)*

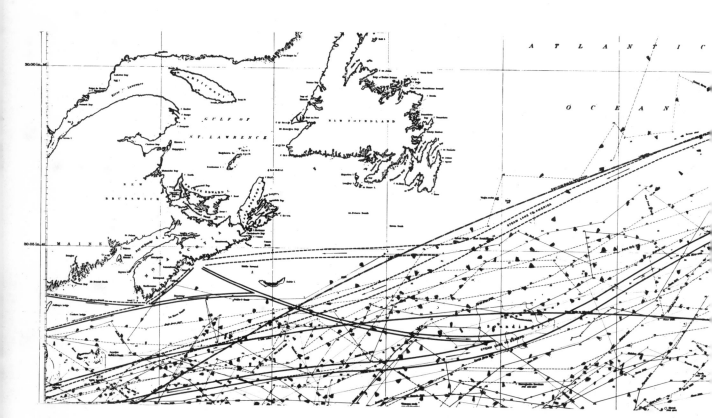

Example of Maury's wind and current chart (Washington, 1853). The tracks shown across the North Atlantic are plotted according to the most favorable winds and currents. The year 1853 marked the end of the pilot's guesswork and mumbo jumbo, and the dawn of scientific navigation. *(Hydrographic Office, Washington)*

direction of oceanic currents and prevailing winds. Maury's first wind chart comprised a series of diagrams, upon which the estimated wind proportion and strength was separately plotted for each month; these were followed by two bulky volumes, entitled *Maury's Sailing Directions*, designed to be used in conjunction with the charts.

From these tabulations, rather than steer a course more or less in a straight line, it was possible to determine the prevailing wind in any given area at all times of the year. This new method had a profound effect upon sailing ships. Distance mattered little in comparison with the weather, and in order to avoid the areas of little wind or doldrums, clearly shown on Maury's charts, the clippers went in search of winds wherever they could be found.

At an international meteorological conference held at Brussels in 1853, Maury proposed and won the adoption of a standard nomenclature. The days when this knowledge had been jealously guarded by pilots and schools of navigation were past. The assembled data enabled a complete chart of winds and currents throughout the world to be put together: equatorial calms, trade winds, "Roaring Forties", monsoons, typhoons. Definite routes were recommended and even whalers found something of advantage, when the Bureau of Ordnance and Hydrography published a whale chart for the Atlantic and Pacific in 1852. Our modern pilot books owe much to the fantastic work undertaken by Maury. A result of major importance was time gained on the voyage to San Francisco via the Horn, saving shipowners millions of dollars. Fifty days were saved on the Liverpool-Melbourne run, so that the 120 days of torment which English emigrants had to suffer between decks were reduced to 70, if not less. Maury's charts were so useful that returning east from Australia via Cape Horn was no longer considered risky. Others as well as Maury made important contributions in this field: the American William Redfield and the Englishman Piddington are examples. The latter's studies of storm behavior and the first attempt to avoid the path of hurricanes were relevant developments.

Detail from a pilot chart of the North Atlantic by Maury (Washington, 1853). Each 5° area of the chart contained a wind diagram, divided into sixteen sectors. In each sector, the position of the figures represented one of the twelve months of the year. The figures themselves gave the number of days throughout the year in which the wind blew in the direction indicated. With this data, the navigator could plot his course to make best use of favorable winds. The pilot charts of today are only a modification of Maury, for instance showing the wind data plotted graphically as a percentage. To complete his colossal task, Maury analyzed many thousand merchant ship and warship logs between 1810 and 1852. *(Hydrographic Office, Washington)*

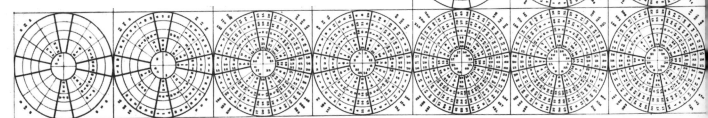

AUSTRALIA

News of the discovery of gold in Australia in 1851, induced 340,000 English emigrants to take ship from Liverpool (notwithstanding what had happened in the Californian gold rush). The oldest ships, manned by highly improbable crews, set sail on the four-months voyage via the Cape of Good Hope. The stop at the Cape allowed many of the wretched emigrants, after being cooped up between decks, to contract infectious diseases and die of them before reaching Port Phillip Bay; it was worse still when the deck was sealed off, as if they were negro slaves.

Just as had happened at San Francisco, a forest of masts sprang up in the harbors and again entire crews deserted, more than 50 ships being abandoned in this way at Hobson Bay. If diseases contracted on the outward voyage reduced hundreds almost to the condition of wild beasts, the return voyage was terrifying for other reasons. As soon as the barrels of gold dust were loaded into the ship's hold, the officers stayed armed to the teeth in the stern while the crew was confined in the bows; with the exception of the helmsman, all the latter were forbidden access to the poop deck.

This period saw the beautiful English clippers *James Baines* (built in Boston by McKay for the British owners of that name) and *Marco Polo* set out from Liverpool for Geelong and Melbourne. Built to last forever, with stout oak and copper sheathing, they showed themselves stronger but heavier than their softwood-hulled American rivals. The vessels of the Black Ball and White Star Lines transported emigrants—not only poor Scots and Irish—across the Atlantic in 75 days.

James Baines, shipowner and shipbuilder of the Black Ball Line, was

Melbourne and Hobson Bay. Engraving by A. Willmore. *(Société de géographie, Paris)*

Geelong seen from the bay. Engraving by J. Tingle from a drawing by S. T. Gill. Extract from: "Victoria Illustrated", Sydney, 1857. (*Société de géographie, Paris*)

England's equivalent to Donald McKay. The exodus to Australia made his fortune and by 1860 he employed 86 ships, 300 officers and 3,000 seamen. But the height of his career lasted only one decade, 1851–1861, the latter year marking the launching of his first steamship. Baines loved sailing ships and steam ruined him.

The struggle for greater speed re-awakened the rivalry between the Black Ball and White Star Lines; both companies agreed to pay the government £100, for each day exceeding the 68 days allocated for the passage. The famous *Marco Polo* under the command of the redoubtable Bully Forbes circumnavigated the globe, via the Horn, in five months and twenty-one days.

Forbes' ideas of captaincy and navigation were very much his own. On one occasion, fearing his crew might desert at Melbourne he had them all locked up in jail under a trumped-up charge of insubordination, and was delighted to have them released in good health just before departure.

Short of tonnage, the Black Ball Line chartered the *Sovereign of the Seas*. At the same time the *Lightning*, the *Champion of the Seas*, the *James Baines* and the *Donald McKay* were commissioned by James Baines, and the White Star Line replied by placing orders for the *Red Jacket* and the *White Star*. Nor must we forget among these famous ships built in England, the *Sobraon* and the *Schomberg*. Whilst the United States was torn with civil war, supremacy in the overseas clipper trade passed to England.

Red Jacket amid ice floes off Cape Horn, August 1854, en route from Australia to Liverpool. Drawing by J. B. Smith, lithograph by C. Parsons.

During this first period of Australian voyages, sail remained supreme but from about 1856, at the close of the Crimean War, the struggle against steam became severe. The iron steamship *Argo*, 1,850 tons, took 69 days to reach Melbourne from London in 1854, and only 63 days for the return voyage. Two years later the development of the Peninsular and Orient Company (P. & O.) began to threaten the position of sailing ship owners on the Australia run. In the latter days of the golden age of the American clippers, although a crisis was clearly at hand, both owners and captains pinned their faith on their beautiful ships, with their black painted sides and the lofty polished masts. They did not for a moment believe that the public would lose confidence in the clippers. The English Government's decision in 1849 to abrogate the "Navigation Act" served to revitalize the country's ship-yards and their ships were better in 1856 than they had been four years earlier. But iron came into their construction: iron frames planked with oak.

The English, a patient race, much preferred a lower but continuous return on outlay, to bursts of frenzied speculation. Experience had taught them the fundamentals of modern maritime trade: rapid turnaround, reliable contracts, economy of expenses, adaptable ships, big and small operators. Although much publicity was given to the famous tea-clipper races in which the first to arrive took the glory and the prize, those which arrived later were still able to dispose of their cargoes at the same price. The great exoduses to Australia, California, and China hardly disturbed the peaceful and profitable trade with Africa and the East and West Indies.

Queens quay, Melbourne. Engraving by J. Tingle after S. T. Gill. Extract from: "Victoria Illustrated"; Sydney, 1857. *(Société de géographie, Paris)*

Sydney and Port Macquarie. Engraving from drawing by Fleury, 1853. *(Société de géographie, Paris)*

Boston, Mass., in 1857. (Mariners Museum, Newport News)

THE "DOWN EASTERS", THE CLIPPERS OF NEW ENGLAND

The gold fever did not only bring prospectors, bandits, saloon keepers and fan-dancers to the Far West; many who came by land and sea realized that wheat growing could also make their fortunes. The Californian plain did not take long to reward their efforts and hopes, showing also that cereals grown on the Pacific coast were better than those in the east. The farmers came to the aid of the sailors; without the "grain rush" of 1855, the ship-owners would have had no alternative but to sell their ships and close down the yards.

Many of the elegant clippers sprang their seams under the continual rough treatment meted out by the storms of the Southern Ocean, so that their repair became uneconomic. Other ships took their place—the grain carriers, less marvelous perhaps, but more suitable for heavy cargoes. These were built in the Eastern United States—the New England coast and especially farther south at Newburyport, Massachusetts, etc.—which was why they were called the "Down Easters".

During the vintage grain harvest of 1862, 145 American ships and 405 English, German, French, Norwegian and Italian craft took on cargoes at

San Francisco and Tacoma, either of bulk wheat or flour in cask. Despite having shorter masts, less complex construction, no studding sails and only half the crew of the clippers, these ships proved to be fine sailers. The crews were invariably tough and could only be controlled by force; in port they drank vast quantities of alcohol, especially the famous "tarantula juice", made up of two quarts of spirit, cooked peaches and tobacco juice diluted with water. Remembering all the supposed injustices they had suffered during the voyage, they became aggressive and planned revenge, especially against those professional seamen, of whom so many 21- and 25-year-olds came from the puritanical stock of New England. In his first class book *The Down Easters*, Basil Lubbock has given an excellent portrait of such men—Bert Williams of the *St. Paul*, Jim Murphy of the *David Brown*, David S. Babcock of the *Young America*, Burgess of the *David Crockett*, Limeburner of the *Great Republic*, and many more. . . .

San Francisco in 1877. After the gold rush, she became a grain and general cargo port. (*Société de géographie, Paris*)

2 Sail against Steam

PROBLEMS OF FITTING OUT THE SAILING SHIPS

From about 1875—when steam had invaded not only coastal but oceanic trade, when the progress of the industrial revolution was accelerating with great rapidity—it is relevant to consider how and why sailing ships could still be built and fitted out; their apparent slowness, irregularity of passage and poor rates of pay for crew were all factors sufficient to discourage shipbuilders and they seemed doomed to become historical relics in museums.

Why, therefore, England and Germany continued to build sailing ships may at first be difficult to understand. Sentiment for their past achievements, felt by owners, builders and crew alike, was partly the reason, but it was not the main consideration for the continued investment of large capital sums in these vessels. Certain sea routes simply could not be used by steamships with profit, for lack of coaling or repair facilities in many parts of the world and by reason of all such overseas costs being payable in the national currency, with the inevitable result of trading at a loss.

On the long-distance voyages, including circumnavigation of the globe, the sailing ship long remained supreme because she could remain entirely self-sufficient throughout. The wind cost nothing; moreover, despite an obsolete outward appearance, the sailing ship could be economically operated by a small number of people. In the works of Louis Lacroix, for example, one reads with what skill the fleet of A. D. Bordes was administered by a staff of five plus two clerks, and it numbered fifty ships!

These sailing men, too, could judge exactly when to make insurance and when not, for either ship or cargo; the shipowners often endeavored to safeguard their ventures by the creation of limited companies with shareholders.

The premium on navigation, which brought a renaissance to French sailing ships between 1893 and 1902, modified the spartan outlook of the family concerns. But until then, in France, England, Germany, the United States and Scandinavia, one invariably found the head of a sailing ship company to be both owner and manager, able administrator and mariner—surrounded by other members of his family and supported by a very small staff and the devotion of his ships' captains. Thus by great individual effort, they could often eclipse the performances of much larger companies, with their complex departmental organization—general secretariat, supplies, legal, technical, development, personnel.

These were the reasons why so many sailing ships still operated on the high seas in 1875, after control of passengers and freight had largely fallen into the hands of steam. The following tables extracted from the *Bureau Veritas* for that year (although it does not list ocean-going ships exclusively), gives an indication of the position by country:

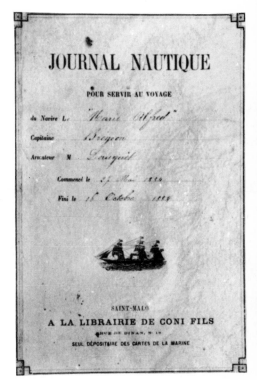

Log of the sailing ship *Marie-Alfred.* (*Mariners Museum, Saint-Malo*)

English model of the *Maud*, made more by a marine enthusiast than a professional sailor. However, despite many inaccuracies in the masts, rigging and sails, the overall result is delightful. (*Mariners Museum, Saint-Malo*)

Flag	Number of Sailing Ships Registered	Total Sailing Ship Tonnage
	Units	*000 tons*
England	19,709	5,543·6
America	7,312	2,387·9
Norway	4,718	1,360·7
Italy	4,469	1,222·8
Germany	3,477	853·3
France	3,877	751·9
Spain	2,888	551·2
Greece	2,092	418·7
Netherlands	1,471	403·8
Sweden	2,018	389·1
Russia	1,759	383·8
Austria	980	330·0
Denmark	1,291	176·9
Portugal	444	107·2

The following table, published as: *Décadence de la Marine Marchande à voile* in *l'Illustration* of 1910, is also significant. If the decline continued until the last years of the 19th century, it was a very slow one:

PERCENTAGE OF SAILING SHIPS IN TOTAL MERCHANT FLEET

Flag	*1888* %	*1908* %
England	41	12·6
Germany	62	19
Norway	91·9	54·6
Japan	35·8	24·7
France	47·9	47·2
Italy	80	47
U.S.A.	80·7	30·9
Sweden	75	34·2
Spain	43·2	6·3
Holland	59·3	11
Austria	59·5	7·5
Belgium	6·4	0·8
Portugal	78·9	48·9

France, it is clear, was one of the last countries to have an important overseas sailing ship fleet, whereas by 1914 things had greatly changed in Germany (2,090 steamships, 298 sailing ships = 5·5 m. tons) and in England (8,587 steamships, 653 sailing ships = 19·25 m. tons).

Just as some sailing ships on certain routes and trades had to give way to steamships, in other cases the latter failed to become an effective alternative. This duality and rivalry of sail against "the stovepipes" was more a question

A Newcastle shipyard in 1850. (*Nat. Maritime Museum, Greenwich*)

The *Macquarie*, a true English three-master. After voyaging to Australia as the *Melbourne*, she became a training ship. (*Nat. Maritime Museum, Greenwich*)

Southwick's Yard, Sunderland in 1860. English shipyards built medium-sized wooden clippers; their age of supremacy came after the use of iron from 1870. (*Nat. Maritime Museum, Greenwich*)

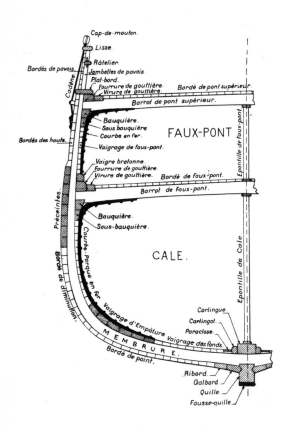

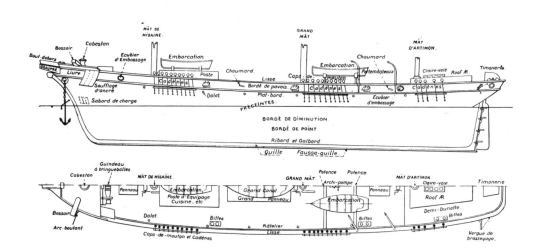

Wooden construction. An extract from Challamel: "Gréement et Manoeuvre".

A. d'Orbigny, Faustin & Cie. — La Rochelle, le 25 Juillet 1905.

LA ROCHELLE

M

M

Nous avons l'honneur de vous confirmer notre lettre du 20 Juillet 1904 et de vous remettre, ci-contre, le Compte d'Inventaire des Quatre Mâts *Asie* et *Europe*, (7ᵐᵉˢ voyages aller et retour) et d'après lequel il y a à répartir, aux co-participants, une somme de ___ F. 60.000 " soit 8% d'intérêt de la valeur agréée au 1ᵉʳ fixée à F. 750.000 " Ces navires sont en outre assurés sur bonne arrivée pour F. 250.000 "

Total ___ F. 1.000.000 "

Il vous revient, pour vos /630ᵉ de la somme ci-dessus de F. 60.000 ___ F.
que nous vous réglons par notre mémorandum ci-joint.

Nous vous donnons aussi, au verso de la présente, le Compte d'Amortissement de ces voiliers, s'élevant à ___ F. 76.144.25

Cette somme est représentée, comme vous le verrez, par des valeurs de 1ᵉʳ Ordre, qui sont déposées à la Banque de France.

Veuillez agréer, M ___ nos salutations respectueuses.

A. d'Orbigny, Faustin & Cie

Doit — Compte d'Amortissement "Europe" et "Asie" — Avoir

Doit			Avoir		
Balance formant l'importance des compte et représentée par les valeurs suivantes :			Importance du Compte remis le 20 Juillet 1905 ___ F.	32.468	05
1° 73 Oblig. Midi 500 fr. 3% anciennes achetées le 20 Juillet 1904 à 445 fr. 37½ soit ___ F. 32.512.37			Encaissement 1° du 7 Janvier 1905 de 73 coupons oblig.ⁿˢ Midi 500 fr. 3% anciennes qui ont produit F. 491.35		
2° 1315 fr. rente 3% achetés le 25 Juillet 1905 à 99.42½ et frais, soit ___ F. 43.630.25			2° du 13 Juillet 1905 de 73 coupons oblig. Midi et intérêt ___ F. 503.25	994	60
3° Somme en caisse F. ___ 1.63	76.144	25	Prélèvement opéré sur les bénéfices à l'inventaire actuel ___ F.	42.681	60
F.	76.144	25		76.144	25

* N. B. — Ces 73 Obligations sont cotées F. 33.507." (Bourse de Paris du 20 Juillet 1905. Nous avons pris le cours d'achat parce qu'il est le plus bas.)

Quatre Mats "Asie" et "Europe"

"Asie" — 7ᵉ voyage aller et retour. = Fin du déchargement à Emden, du précédent voyage le 31 Décembre 1903 = Départ de Emden, avec partie de chargement de rails, le 7 Janvier 1904, pour Angers. = Arrivée à Angers le 12 Janvier 1904 (Complète son chargement de rails). Départ d'Angers, le 29 Janvier 1904 pour Hobart-Town = Arrivée à Hobart le 31 Mai 1904 pour ordres = Départ de Hobart Town le 1ᵉʳ Juin 1904, pour San Pedro (Californie) = Arrivée à San Pedro le 23 Août 1904 (opéré son déchargement de rails) = Départ de San Pedro, sur lest, le 8 Octobre 1904, pour Portland (Orégon) = Arrivée à Portland le 3 Novembre 1904 = Départ de Portland avec un chargement, le 30 Novembre 1904, pour Birkenead (Angleterre) = Arrivée à Birkenead le 25 Avril 1905 = Fin du déchargement le 14 Mai 1905 =

Europe — 7ᵉ voyage aller et retour. = Fin du déchargement à Hambourg, du précédent voyage le 24 Mai 1904 = Départ de Hambourg, sur lest, le 31 Mai 1904, pour Hobart Town (Tasmanie) = Arrivée à Hobart Town, le 16 Août 1904 pour ordres = Départ de Hobart Town le 20 Août 1904, pour Portland (Orégon) Arrivée à Portland le 8 Novembre 1904 = Départ de Portland avec un chargement, le 6 Décembre 1904, pour Ipswich (Angleterre) = Arrivée à Ipswich, le 10 April 1905 = Fin du déchargement, le 18 Mai 1905.

Inventaires arrêtés au 31 Mai 1905

	Asie		Europe				Asie		Europe	
Salaires, conduites et rapatriements des équipages F.	43.800	31	32.025	25	Remises et remboursements divers d'avaries, ristournes, etc F.	3.441	85	5.067	50
Nourriture des équipages F.	17.337	13	14.764	18	Produits des frets, etc F.	182.349	20	89.394	70
Dépenses d'entretien et approvisionnements divers F.	30.631	08	20.763	88	Prime à la navigation aller et retour F.	124.781	48	122.433	70
Lestages, délestages, embarquements, débarquements F.	27.688	55	12.145	05	Vente de lest de vieilles chaînes F.	1.509	70	924	30
Frais de port, remorquages, pilotages, etc F.	51.315	59	32.213	05	Approvisionnements divers restant à bord F.	2.235	"	3.409	50
Frais divers, hospitalisation, petites avaries, etc F.	6.921	90	5.167	41					
Commission d'affrètements aux courtiers, etc F.	12.505	55	9.709	"					
Assurance des navires, des frets, des primes d'Assurances F.	51.865	72	43.877	50					
Balance des Intérêts à 4% sur avances suivant Cte C/C F.	4.498	21	5.236	23					
Bénéfices F.	68.763	60	45.327	"					
F.	314.325	73	221.229	10	F.	314.325	73	221.229	10

Répartition des Bénéfices.

Bénéfices par "Asie" F.	68.763	60		Commission d'Armateur, 10% des bénéfices F.	11.409	"	
Bénéfices par "Europe" F.	45.327	"		Somme portée au Cte d'Amortissement F.	42.681	60	
				Solde des bénéfices à répartir F.	60.000	"	
F.	114.090	60		F.	114.090	60	

For those who like figures; the sailing accounts of two three-masters, published by Compagnie d'Obigny.

London, 1890: south West India Dock. *(Nat. Maritime Museum, Greenwich)*

of flexibility than a conscious realization of the need to adapt both modes of transport to the circumstances.

The European sailing ships, laden usually with English coal or general cargo, monopolized certain routes leaving Europe. From that point the destination was New York or Philadelphia, where cased petrol might be taken on for the Far East. After rounding the Horn, the return voyage was made via Australia, the American Pacific coast or Chile. For Australia (Sydney, Newcastle, Geelong, Port Pirie, Melbourne) and New Zealand, one loaded heavy goods, tiles, machinery, etc., and returned to Europe with cargoes of wool or frozen beef; or, sometimes carried Australian coal to Chile, and from there brought back nitrate to Europe. Freight bound for the American west coast was equally mixed, but often ships left in ballast and came back with grain. Higher up the coast, grain and lumber were loaded at the ports of Portland, Seattle, Tacoma, Port Townsend and Vancouver.

From the English ports—often coal loaded at Newcastle, Cardiff or Barry

—the sailing ships went to the Chilean ports—Talcahuano, Valparaiso, Coquimbo, Mejillones, Antofagasta, Caldera, Taltal, Iquique, Caleta Buena, Pisagua—to bring nitrates back to Europe, and discharge them at Dunkirk, London, Bruges, Antwerp, Rotterdam and Hamburg. From New Caledonia in the Pacific, nickel was loaded at Thio, Canala, Kouaoua and Gomen by sailing ships, which brought the ore back to Glasgow and Le Havre; the outward cargo in ballast was often supplemented by European coal supplied to, and paid by the Nickel Corporation. These Pacific voyages were very typical but, of course, in this case they involved a straightforward two-way passage via Cape Horn.

Very different were the sailing "tramp ships" which crossed most of the world and called at innumerable ports. One of these might, for instance, leave a French port in ballast, take on petrol at Philadelphia destined for Yokohama or Hong Kong, leave Japan in ballast and proceed to Australia, there taking on New South Wales coal for Chile. There saltpeter was loaded for California, discharged and then grain was taken on at Portland, Oregon and carried on the last stage of the voyage to Falmouth in England. But it was unusual to know where all these ships were at one time; while a simple outward/inward voyage to Chile might take six months, these extraordinary long-distance world voyages might last over two years. For forty years, the latter remained almost a monopoly of the European sailing ships. The following typifies the fantastic schedule involved:

Europe to Australia via the Cape of Good Hope:	75–80 days
Australia to Europe via Cape Horn:	120 days
(i.e. Australia to Cape Horn: 50 days;	
Cape Horn to the Channel: 70 days)	
Europe to Chile (10,300 miles)	90 days
Ushant to San Francisco or Puget Sound	120–130 days
Valparaiso to New Caledonia	60 days
New Caledonia to Cape Horn	45 days
Cape Horn to Le Havre	80 days

The speed of the average daily run was sometimes very high (14–15 knots, reaching 17–18 over short periods); but the mean for the entire voyage, including days becalmed and bad weather, was extremely low, $4\frac{1}{2}$ to $6\frac{1}{2}$ knots at best, although the real figure was a little higher due to differences in navigational methods aboard the sailing ships.

Unloading cargo at an English port. Drawing by Mellery. (*Le Tour du Monde*)

Three-masted French barque.

Four-masted French barque. The drawing is taken from Captain Ludwig Albrand's "Westward Ho!" (*Bibl. Hist. de la Marine*)

The *Biessard* in dry dock at Le Havre, *ca. 1900*. (*Augé Collection*)

THE STEEL SAILING SHIPS

Woods selected and treated for the keel, frame, side timbers, and stern timbers; English oak and elm; yellow pine for the decks; Danzig fir, Douglas fir, Danzig oak, African oak, mahogany, American elm, Quebec oak, pitch pine; adzes, augers, caulkers, carpenters—these were evidence of a glorious past which vanished in the smoke of the Clydebank shipyards or under the hammer blows of the riveters of the Gironde, the Loire and Bremerhaven.

The steel sailing ship's relationship with her wooden predecessor is rather like that between the locomotive and the stagecoach; it may seem distant, but the form of the steel sailing ship grew from the curved side timbers of the wooden ship. More bulbous and heavier, it was infinitely stronger at sea—with steel braces and stays, iron masts and yards—than its forebears of wood and hemp.

The steel sailing ship of the period displaced between 2,000 and 3,000 tons and had a length overall of 70 to 80 meters; it was only in the first years of the twentieth century that the huge four- and five-masted barques and four-masted square-riggers made their appearance.

The hull of the steel ships closely resembled their predecessors, along the whole length of the keel from stern to sternpost. Steel sections, flanged at the corners were joined together, held by the Kelson and floor timbers beneath and the beams and stay-plates above, and formed the framework of the ship; holes were pile-driven in the plates, which were then riveted together. Afterwards came the fitting-out of the hull itself: two or four hawse holes straight from the forge; the helm port, where the end of the rudder could pass through and be joined to the base of the poop. The deck of the rudder was itself a fine piece of steel, with a protective layer of sheet iron. All was made with the care needed for a masterpiece of maritime art. From the forge also, came the mooring bitts, the gear knightheads, the cleats,

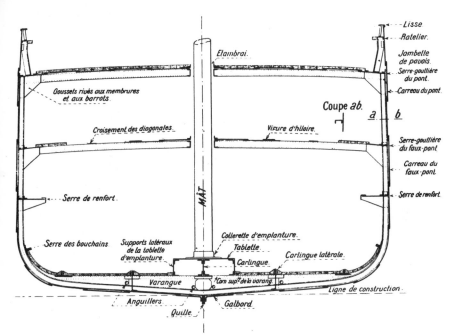

Lisse.
Ratelier.
Jambette de pavois.
Serre-gouttière du pont.
Carreau du pont.

Coupe ab. a b

Serre-gouttière du faux-pont.

Carreau du faux-pont.

Serre de renfort.

Etambrai.

Goussets rivés aux membrures et aux barrots.

Croisement des diagonales.

Virure d'hiloire.

Serre de renfort.

Serre des bouchains.

MÂT

Supports latéraux de la tablette d'emplanture.

Collerette d'emplanture.

Tablette.

Carlingue.

Carlingue latérale.

Varangue.

Corn supⁱˢ de la varang.

Ligne de construction.

Anguillers.

Quille.

Galbord.

Cross-section of a ship's hull, at the mainmast. Extract from Challamel: "Gréement et Man-oeuvre".

France II under construction at the Gironde yards; advanced stage, 23 May 1911. *(Le Tour du Monde)*

The appearance of the hull strakes. *(Lacroix Collection)*

The laid-down keel of the five-masted *France II*, at the Gironde yards, 6 March 1911. (*Le Tour du Monde*)

Josiah Emery's marine chronometer, late 18th century. Precision to the last half-second and fully modern design. There were few improvements made to chronometers in the 19th century. (*Conservatoire des Arts et Métiers*)

the capstanheads, the windlass drums, the cathead sockets, the partners, the housings for the steam-winches and, of course, the anchors and cables.

Except for the iron keel, laid on its line of blocks, everything else was first blueprinted on the design floor and then fitted on piece by piece after forging. The rivet holes were pierced beforehand and the operation was done by two men, standing one on each side of the steel section, hammering in the molten rivets, which were then sealed off in smoke and a shower of sparks. Lowly work, perhaps, but absolutely vital for the ship's safety. How could a billet of wood be pushed into a badly fitted rivet hole, possibly situated in the hold beneath 4,000 tons of cargo, during a voyage? And even so, would it withstand the water pressure at a depth of perhaps six to eight meters?

Next followed the stepping of the masts, the fitting of the hatch coamings, the pump-well, watertight doors and internal bulkheads. With the end of the steelwork, a team of carpenters came aboard to install decks and orlop, poop and forecastle, rigging-racks, gratings, planking for the holds and orlop, hatch covers, wooden superstructure and deckhouse. Then came the machinery: steering mechanism, windlass, capstan, boiler, galley stove, distillation unit, winches, pumps, catheads—fitted, while the seams were filled with oakum and the decks resounded with the blow of the caulker's hammer and burin, and the smell of tar mingled with the paintwork of the hull.

Then the joiners and cabinetmakers, whose interior décor of the officers' quarters achieved wonderful skill in this area. Proof was shown in the polished teak panelling of the cabin walls, ornamentally moulded; doors and decklights; grooved barlings; table, bunks and armchairs; glass-racks and decanter-holders—a style which was both pleasing and functional at sea, based on centuries of experience. Even the smallest bronze lock, door hook, angle-bracket and belaying pin possessed this functional beauty which was

Feminine influence and comfort. The saloon of the *Eva Montgomery*. (*San Francisco Maritime Museum*)

not destroyed by usage. The economy with which the fine materials were used—precious woods and copper—only underlined the good taste which was evident throughout.

The outlay which shipowners were prepared to make towards decoration of the poops in their ships naturally varied, but the English and American ships excelled in this respect. Upon them, there was often astonishing luxury in the shape of Dutch stoves in faience, inlaid revolving chairs, upholstered sofas and fine wood panels, mottled, striped, flecked and inlaid

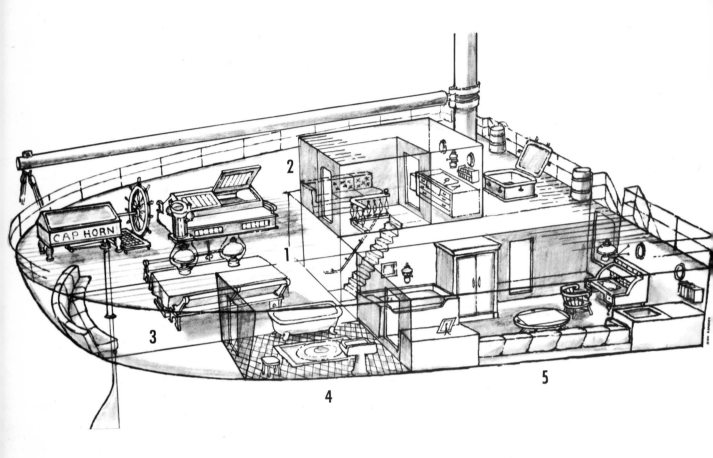

THE POOP *(starboard side) :*

Stern fittings; the arrangement of the poop is simple and characteristic of most sailing ships. There is neither captain's saloon nor officer's mess, both the captain and his officers messing together.

1. The wardroom is lit by Cardan oil lamps and decklight. A large table in the center is flanked by two collapsible sofas. When the table is not in use, it is covered by a baize cloth in functional green or dark red. A semi-circular sofa is at the far end of the room. The walls are elegantly panelled and the whole effect is sober, austere and dignified.

2. The captain reaches the chartroom via a companionway on the starboard side. At the head of the companionway is the signal locker; in front is the chartroom table, containing charts, telescope, sextants, distress signals, log and other navigational instruments. The order book is kept on the table. At the rear of the chartroom is the captain's couch, where he can snatch some sleep in between moments of

crisis when his constant presence on deck is needed. The chartroom is the captain's private sanctuary; except for recording entries in the day order book, no officer may frequent it, their proper place being outside. The entry points to the chartroom have to be firmly closed in bad weather and the use of the companionway from it to the main cabin is restricted to the captain and his cabin boy.

3. Here, accessible only through the captain's cabin, are kept the fine table linen, silverware, ships valuables, and victuals preserved for special occasions.

4. The captain's bathroom is equipped with a tub and a lavatory. The cabin boy runs to the galley to fetch buckets of hot water for the captain's ablutions.

5. The captain's cabin is situated on the starboard side of the stern. The cabin is clean, simply furnished and equipped with a bunk of reasonable size. A hanging cupboard is fitted to

the bulkhead. There are a chest of drawers, a couch and a table in the middle of the room; also a roll-top desk which is securely locked as it contains the ship's safe. Marine chronometers are fitted to the walls. Normally the captain's cabin contains few extra furnishings—perhaps an occasional photograph, picture, or model made by a member of the crew and presented to him at the end of a voyage. Perhaps, also, a gun for shooting sea birds, a few books, and mercury and aneroid barometers mounted on Cardan fittings. Many of the charts and the ship's orders were also kept in the captain's cabin. The duties of the officer of the watch were confined to keeping the ship on course and observing wind and weather. The captain alone made the astronomical calculations and decisions regarding the course.

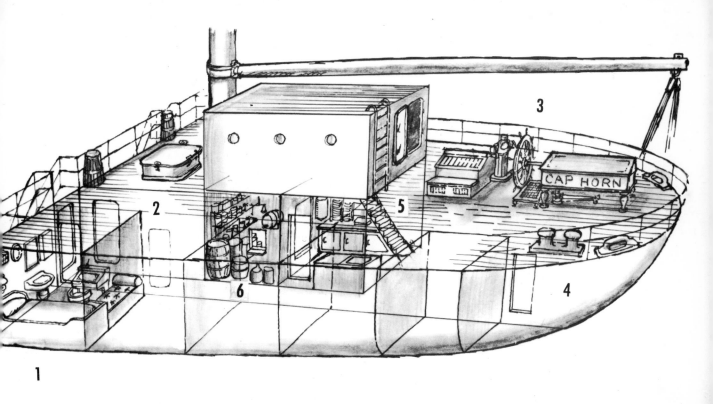

THE POOP *(port side)*:

1. In separate quarters on the port side were the officers' cabins. The first forward belonged to the first mate. There was the usual simple furniture inside: a bunk, with fitted drawers below; a couch; a small desk, on which he wrote his reports and kept his accounts; a lavatory, which drained into a bucket and certainly did not have running water; a few books; one or two portholes. The first and second lieutenants' cabins were even more spartan; right at the back was the cabin boy's cubbyhole, with only a very narrow bunk inside. The pilots slept in the small deckhouse along with the boatswain and carpenter. Sometimes one of the unoccupied cabins would be taken by a supercargo, or used as an isolation room for a seriously ill member of the crew.

2. This was the sail locker, reached by a small hatchway overhead on the poop deck. All types of sails were kept here in reserve, graded according to condition: new sails for bad weather; previously used sails which, for economy, could suffice in fair weather. All were carefully folded and stowed in racks and marked with their names in prominent black letters for ease of recognition. In wet weather, the sailors worked in the sail room and in very heavy weather sheltered there, when it was impossible to regain the main deckhouse.

3. Behind the chartroom—with its two couches where no one ever remembered the captain resting—the door led out on to the poop deck. There were the compass on its polished teak stand and binnacle burnished by the cabin boy; the port and starboard lights; the wheel and helmsman's grating, in front of the "turtle" —that curious sort of wooden coffin which protected the tiller, and upon which the ship's name was usually spelled out prominently in large letters. Some steeringwheels were surrounded by a small wooden shelter to protect the helmsman.

4. In this compartment, directly accessible from the cabin, were kept the ship's stores bonded under custom while in port—tobacco, matches and alcohol.

5. This was called the pantry. Here the cabin boy kept the plates and dishes from the galley before serving the captain at table. Other equipment here comprised a small sink for washing up the dishes; perhaps a tiny cooker or warming-plate, where warm drinks for the crew could be prepared if the galley was flooded.

6. The upper storeroom contained the reserve supply of victuals and also those for immediate consumption: beef, olive oil, lard and biscuit. Through a hatch in the storeroom the officer in charge of rations distributed wine to the men and victuals to the cook. And, it was past this hatch the men filed when they drew their rum ration in bad weather. The upper and lower storerooms were connected by a hatchway. All the main stock of victuals were kept in the lower storeroom, which was situated astern between decks. The lieutenant in charge of stores kept a very strict account of everything in his charge. Even if energetic, however, he was fighting a losing battle against worm, damp and, above all, rats. *(Sketch by the author)*

Oil lantern, used more for illumination than signalling; 19th century. *(Mariners Museum, Saint-Malo)*

by methods known only to the English cabinetmakers. Double spirit lamps richly ornamented hung from the ceiling, swaying ceaselessly to the roll of the ship.

The plan of the poop varied very much according to the type of ship—long, short or even non-existent, if the accommodation was grouped centrally, like in steamships. Certain ships had a captain's cabin, saloon for the officers and additional cabins for passengers; the lighting everywhere was by spirit lamps, mounted on Cardan universal joints. At the end of the period electric light was to be found on some ships, but only as a subsidiary to oil lamps. The poop deck carried the steering mechanism, round which was a grating 20–30 cms. above the deck so that the helmsman did not get wet feet, and nearby lay the charthouse, the captain's second place of refuge.

The helm was, in some ships, shielded by a wooden or metal hood; a device which sheltered the helmsman from following seas, those dreaded "poopers" whose waves could suddenly sweep over a ship from the stern.

At the top of the companionway were installed two water tanks, securely fastened. Among flush-decked sailing ships, those with one continuous deck from stem to stern (that is with neither poop nor forecastle) were uncommon. The platform of the quarterdeck was prominent forward of the poop, and from it two ladders gave off, connected to the deckhouse and forecastle by a companionway; the latter became very important in the dangerous moments when the ship rolled heavily and the well-deck became filled with tons of water. Between the mizzen and the mainmast was sited the small deckhouse —the quarters of the boatswain, carpenter, cook and pilot. Inside was a smaller replica of the officers' quarters, but more soberly furnished—bunks against the bulkheads, sea chests lashed to the deck, tables and chairs, the natural daylight of a portlight and, one spirit lamp for the hours of darkness. On the roof of the deckhouse was found the standard compass, since in this area the ship's magnetism seemed to be most in equilibrium.

Between the mainmast and foremast lay the main deckhouse, which comprised the port and starboard quarters and messes, the galley and boilerhouse. This arrangement was typical only of the later large sailing ships, as we remember that in those of the '60s and '70s the crew lived under the forecastle. Even before they occupied the forecastle, the forepart of the orlop deck had been their home, an area without air or light. The transfer of berths to deck level improved the seamen's health and sleep, which had been so disturbed in the past; there was more light and air from scuttles, ports and decklights. Even so, despite its height above water level, the sea sometimes reached the deckhouse when waves broke over the well-deck, and in bad weather it was very damp. Otherwise, however, it was very habitable.

The cookhouse in the last sailing ships was wedged between the messes and the boiler house, "wedged" being the best word to describe this narrow thoroughfare pierced by doors at either end. It was not unknown for the wind to tear open one of these doors and allow the sea to pour in and engulf some of the cook's most appetizing preparations, even the cook himself.

Nothing was more depressing than to see the galley awash, with margarine tins, saucepans and sacks of flour floating on the surface. In preparing meals for the crew, the cook had at his disposal a galley fire (whose draught varied according to the wind direction and the position of the staysails), an assortment of pots and pans, and a working area of limited size. At the rear of the

The galley of the *Cutty Sark*.

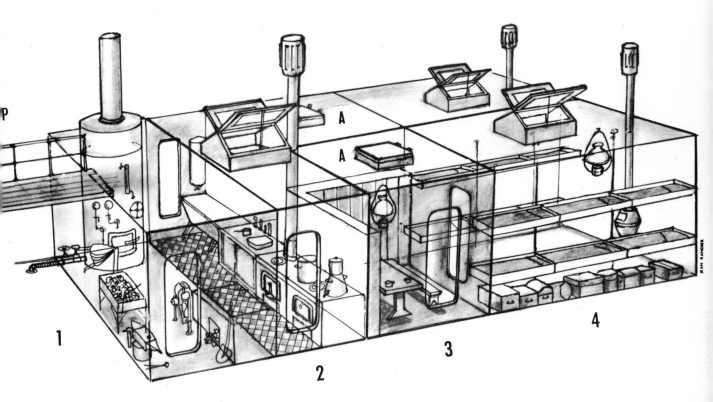

THE MAIN DECKHOUSE:

The weather needed only to be moderately bad for waves to break over the decks, and it was dangerous to open the deckhouse bulkhead doors or decklights for fear of flooding. Another danger came from water penetrating through the hatch covers (marked "A") from which metal ladders led below. The roof of the deckhouse was reached from the poop by a gangway ("P"), which ran across the sea-filled well-deck.

1. The boilerroom was the kingdom of the carpenter and engineer. As well as the boiler, which provided steam for the pump, winches and sometimes the windlass, there were tools, forge and anvil and a small stock of coal. Frequently also a small stove and unit for the distillation of sea water into fresh.

2. The galley, the nerve center of maritime gastronomy, was very practically equipped: a water cask, a kneading trough, a movable butcher's table with its rack of knives, and a cupboard full of utensils and cutlery. The kitchen stove, with its cauldron and coffee pot, was coal-fired.

Ventilation in the galley was obtained through the two side doors and the decklight. Water frequently flooded the galley, the waves slopping from side to side carrying off food, cooking pots and furniture to the scuppers—until one wondered if the cook deserved to receive such want of courtesy from the sea.

3. The starboard mess. Sometimes both watches were joined in one large mess, running right across the width of the deckhouse. Narrow cupboards hung from the walls used by the men to stow their dripping oilskins, sou'westers and seaboots after coming off watch. A table, two benches and an oil lamp completed the décor.

4. The starboard sleeping quarters—those on the port side were identical. A dozen wooden bunks were secured to the deckhouse bulkheads and held in place by stanchions. The bedding comprised a palliasse (provided by the sailor himself) and a thin coverlet, which had to last the whole voyage. Lots were drawn for the bunks—upper or lower, inside or out, near the decklight or stove. The sea chests were stowed underneath, lashed by ring-bolts to the deck. The room was illuminated by decklights and oil lamps, after dark. Heat came from a coal stove, but it was pretty cold while it was being cleaned out or lit. Clotheslines were strung between the bunks, to hang out the washing. In spite of the raised level of the doors and padded lining at their edges, water always got in somehow. It flooded the floor, slopping from side to side to each roll of the ship. In bad weather everything in the deckhouse was damp. (*Sketch by the author*)

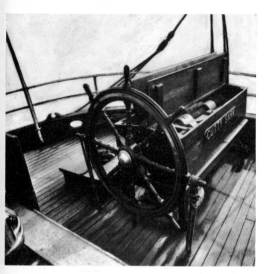

The wheel of the *Cutty Sark*, showing the spindle-threaded right and left screw, controlling the rudder. *(J. Freeman)*

main deckhouse were to be found the boiler, engineer's and carpenter's tools, forge, coal scuttle, and a water-distillation unit, for providing the boiler with fresh water.

The forecastle was decked in wood, as were other appointments in the ship, and was dominated in the center by the capstan, symbolic of the many hours which the chanting crew spent working at its bars. Forward were the anchors, their stocks stowed either above the ship's side or alongside, according to the type of construction; these iron monsters were made fast to immovable ringlets. Small sheers on the forecastle enabled them to be swung out on to the catheads prior to anchoring; the catheads themselves, of wood or iron, jutted out from the stern. At the back of the forecastle were the fire lockers, solid round structures and fire screened, to which the duty seamen went at dusk to put on the navigation lights—red for port, green for starboard—visual testimonies of adherence to the laws of the sea.

Under the forecastle, and on each side of the ship at deck level, were situated a number of ill-lit compartments—stowed with gear, which in some ships had to give place to the jib-boom or underpart of the bowsprit—plugged with tow and smeared with fish oil. One typical compartment contained paint and brushes, lamp materials, petrol, steel wire sockets, pulleys, block and tackle, winding gear, rope, tarpaulins, swabs, buckets, potash, bricks for the deck and coppers, tow bungs, rags and an assortment of oil, greases, tools; not forgetting the well polished harpoons, which would be seized from their racks at the first sight of a whale.

Between the two rows of storerooms stood the massive windlass, hand operated from above by the capstan, or, eventually, by steam from below by a system of rods and pistons. At sea the hawse holes were sealed, the unshackled anchor chains being lowered into the cable wells. Beneath the forecastle the navigation lights were stowed, and here the lamps were lit and extinguished.

The carriage of livestock under the forecastle head must not be forgotten, nor the celebrated function of "lieutenant in charge of caged birds"! An area of the front of the forecastle was set aside for a cow or two, some pigs, even sheep, and either perched in the deckhouse or in boxes in the forecastle were hens, whose clucking disturbed the early hours. This practice was not confined to sailing ships alone; as late as 1948, some steamships, without refrigeration, carried live cattle on long voyages.

On deck were the four ship's boats, covered with tarpaulins and equipped with davits for launching them into the sea. On the starboard side there was a launch on a cradle ready to slip down with the help of the derricks; on the port side was a whaler used as a lifeboat. If catheads were lacking, as was often the case, two girtlines were attached to the lower main and mizzen yards, which enabled the boats to be lowered. On the roof of the main deckhouse were a second whaler and a dinghy, both of which were launched in the way just described.

The hatch covers over the holds were of great importance, not only because they were the cargo's means of entry and exit to the ship, but any defect in their construction would let in the sea with fatal results. They were solidly built in reinforced hardwood, with the upper surface of the covers being surmounted by one or two layers of tarpaulin and held rigid by transverse rods which fastened on steel lugs at the edges. Planks fixed as crossbars on

English four-masted barque *Clan Galbraith* at Tacoma grain wharf. A well appointed and cared for ship. *(San Francisco Maritime Museum)*

Unknown four-masted square-rigger. Model in a bottle and framed. Sailor's work. *(Mariners Museum, Saint-Malo)*

The *Japan*, English sailing ship, *ca.* 1850. Silk embroidery. Sailor's work. *(Mariners Museum, Saint-Malo)*

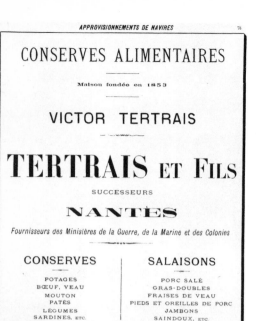

Were the special victuals aboard ocean-going ships better than the ordinary fare? What did the sailors think about it? Advertisements in maritime journals, 1903.

the hatch covers served as breakwaters. Finally, situated forward was a raft made of timbers or bits of a mast or yard; it was a sinister reminder of what might be necessary when the ship was dismasted and the cry went up to abandon ship.

The following list enumerates the stores typical of a sailing ship of the period, which of course varied a great deal, this being the inventory of the Bordes Company's ship *Almendral* for 1907, as described in the Nantes archives. It is interesting to note the farsightedness of those who prepared them; they fully realized that for resources they were entirely dependent upon themselves, the sea, and, in most cases, the nearest port.

ANCHORS AND CHAINS: 3 best bower anchors, one of 1,950 kg., two of 1,400 kgs.; 3 kedge anchors, of 228, 150 and 126 kgs.; 2 cathead chains of 550 and 39 mm.; 2 cathead stoppers; 4 shank painters.

CABLES: 1 3½″ steel towing cable; 1 10″ steel towing spring; 6 steel hawsers of circumference 18 cms. (2), 16 cms., 13 cms., and 12 cms. (2); 1 cat fall; 2 winding tackle falls; 2 boat tackle falls.

SHIP'S BOATS: 1 longboat of 5·70 m., with rudder and helm; 17 oars, 13 of oak and 4 of pine; 14 iron rowlocks; 1 ship's boat of 5 m.. with rudder and helm; 1 boat hook, with handle; 12 cloth fenders; 1 whaleboat of 7 m., with rudder and helm; 1 small ship's boat of 4 m., with rudder and helm, 4 bolster-bitts of cork.

DECKGEAR: 1 iron ship's tiller: 1 rudder, with wheel ropes; 1 copper binnacle; 3 scant lings; 12 float-scantlings; 1 scuttlebutt; 2 hold-pumps, with accessories; 1 stern-pump 2 copper fire-pumps; 1 rubber hose, with couplings; 1 bilge-pump; 10 hawse-plugs, 2 for the chains, 2 for the cable-wells, and 6 for the spring; 2 capstans—one on fore castle, one on poop; 1 windlass, with levers; 4 portable winches; 2 main winches, 1 for the chains; 5 iron davits; 1 accommodation ladder; 1 gangway; 4 poop ladders (2 of pine for the sea); 2 quarterdeck ladders; 2 deck ladders; 2 storeroom ladders; 1 between decks ladder; 1 station ladder; 1 set of gratings; 2 bucket-pens; 1 pig pen; 1 hencoop 17 capstan bars; 2 windlass handles; 1 platform-scales; 6 wooden fenders; 1 washtub 15 deck-awnings; 10 hatch covers; 2 lantern carriers.

BOATSWAIN'S STORES: 1 anchor-hawser; 1 mast cable; 1 winding tackle; 2 deck tackle-blocks; 1 whip tackle-block or burton; 2 cat blocks; 2 top-rope blocks; 4 lower-sail blocks; 4 hoisting pulleys; 4 reverse pulleys; 5 sheaves; 16 ballast shovels (10 pointed, 6 square); 3 large mallets; 3 burtons; 6 chain-hooks; 3 drums of oil; 1 drum of petrol 2 canisters of linseed oil; 1 large tow-hook; 1 tail-hook; 2 chain-clamps; 1 spare windlass drum; 2 barrel-flukes (pair); 2 chain slings; 4 rope slings; 4 boat's gripes, cloth-covered 16 float-lines; 1 scuttle-line; 1 forecastle bell; 4 splices; 2 stowing clamps; 10 deck brushes; 5 mast chairs; 8 pulley-hooks; 20 jib-rings; 15 assorted bull's-eyes; 18 pulleys, 10 double-pulleys; 12 round return sheaves; 20 ordinary return sheaves; 6 swabs; 5 kg. copper piping; 1 iron cramp; 8 wooden thimbles; 15 pipes, various; 1 crew's lamp.

CARPENTER'S STORES: 1 lower fore topmast; 1 fore topmast; 1 foretop yard; 1 mizzen topmast; 1 topmast yard; 2 boat's masts; 1 boat's yard; 4 water casks; 1 wooden funnel; 8 deck buckets; 1 cast-iron mast sheave; 18 various shackles and links, 4 for the anchors; 1 chain drift-bolt; 3 anchor-pins; 6 shackle-pins; 25 iron toggles; 50 wooden toggles; 1 workbench, with vice; 1 clamp; 8 chocks; 5 sledgehammers, 4 round and 1 pointed; 9 hammers, of 3 different kinds; 4 cold chisels, 1 mask chisel; 6 gouges, various; 1 carpenter's mallet; 8 caulking irons; 1 rave-hook; 2 bradawls; 1 wire-cutter; 1 hatchet; 1 small axe; 1 rabbett-plane; 1 trying-plane; 1 jack-plane; 4 ordinary planes; 1 marking-gauge; 1 square; 1 bevel-square; 1 screwdriver; 5 assorted files; 2 three-cornered files;

2 double-handled knives; 1 brace and bit; 5 saws (2 tenon, 1 compass, 1 hack and 1 rat-tail); 1 adze; 1 boxwood rule; 1 pair scissors; 4 mortise chisels; 4 augers; 4 gimlets, assorted; 1 pair pincers; 1 sounding-hook; 1 adjustable plunger; 1 mortar trough; 1 mill-crank; 1 millstone; 2 sounding irons; 6 iron and 4 wooden scrapers; 1 oilcan; 1 derrick (forward in the orlop deck).

SAILMAKER'S STORES: 2 foresails; 2 mainsails; 5 lower topsails; 4 upper topsails; 4 mizzen topsails; 2 gallant sails; 4 main- and fore-topgallants (2 upper, 2 lower); 2 mizzen topgallants; 2 brigantine sails; 3 fore staysails; 2 main staysails; 2 flying jibs; 2 mizzen-jibs; 1 mizzen head; 10 galvanized iron clubs; 1 longboat sail; 1 poop-awning; 1 stern-post awning; 1 cloth windsail; 9 tarpaulin hatch covers, in sets of three; 6 canvas hoods, various; 2 spare tarpaulins; 2 sailmaker's benches; 2 wooden gravers; 30 sailmaker's needles.

STEERAGE STORES: 1 ship's compass; 1 standard compass; 1 azimuthal compass; 1 hanging compass; 1 boat's compass; 1 compass case; 1 speaking-trumpet (or hailer); 2 fog-horns; 1 pair of bellows; 1 aneroid barometer; 1 thermometer; 1 binnacle clock; 1 15-second thermometer bulb; 4 sounding leads; 4 fixed lights; 3 red and 2 white navigation lights; 2 binnacle lamps; 2 compass lamps; 3 ensigns; 1 international code of signals; 1 pilot's timepiece; 4 lead-lines, various; 1 sounding-cleat; 1 patent log; 2 lifebuoys; 1 French navy list; 1 adjustable glass (red); 4 cloth strainers.

SHIP'S FURNITURE: 2 assorted mirrors; 1 mahogany table; 4 curtain rods; 2 upholstered benches; 1 waxed table cover; 5 sofas, various; 1 armchair; 1 folding chair; 2 stoves, with accessories; 1 medicine cabinet; 8 lamps; 2 copper candlesticks; 4 cabin curtains; 2 napkins; 15 serviettes; 1 water filter; 1 cruet; 1 salt-cellar; 2 tea urns, one enamelled; 2 sugar-casters; 1 sugar tongs; 2 carafes; 2 lids; 10 table knives; 25 spoons; 15 forks; 2 soup ladles (one faïence, one metal); 7 large dishes; 46 plates; 16 glasses; 1 bucket; 1 fish-slice; 6 tea-bowls; 10 coffee cups and saucers; 2 salad dishes; 3 egg-cups; 1 butter dish; 1 fruit platter; 1 wash basin; 1 pepper mill; 1 coffee mill; 4 brushes and brooms; 1 shovel; 2 coffee pots; 1 stove for the crew; 1 wooden spittoon.

STOREROOM FURNITURE: 2 biscuit barrels; 16 demijohns; 120 empty bottles; 2 mess-kettles; 1 drum; 2 beam-balances; 1 set of weights and measures; 2 funnels and 1 pump of tinplate; 2 rubber siphons.

GALLEY FURNITURE: 1 cook's bench; 1 coal scuttle; 1 kneading trough and cupboard; 1 cooking oven; 1 coal shovel; 1 poker; 1 bucket; 1 flour sifter; 1 coffee grinder; 1 pudding-mould; 3 copper pots; 3 casserole dishes; 4 lids; 2 kitchen knives; 1 meat chopper; 1 pâté knife; 2 spoons; 2 skimmers; 1 meat hook; 1 spice cabinet; 2 frying pans; 1 American coffee mill; 2 roasting dishes; 1 coffee roaster; 1 mincer; 2 iron platters and 1 metal spoon; 1 meat grill.

STORES: 10 casks of wine; 4 barrels of vinegar; 2 casks of brandy; 4 barrels of salt pork (100 kg.); 4 barrels of white beans; 2 barrels of lentils and peas; 60 kgs. of coffee; 2 kgs. of tea; 1 sack of sugar; 40 kgs. of salt; 16 kgs. of candles; 100 boxes of matches; 18 liters of olive oil; 30 liters of cognac; 1,200 ship's biscuits; 6 sacks of coal; 500 bottle corks; 45 tins of lard; 85 tins of beef; 150 kgs. of jam.

OILS AND PAINTS: 115 liters raw linseed oil; 200 liters distilled linseed oil; 30 large and 10 small brushes; 550 kgs. white paint; 50 kgs. black paint; 20 kgs. green paint; 40 kgs. yellow paint; 125 kgs. white lead; 45 kgs. red lead; 15 kgs. mastic; 20 packets drying compound; 95 liters petrol; distemper, 1st and 2nd quality.

ROPE AND CANVAS: 2 lanyards of $4\frac{3}{4}'$; 2 of $3\frac{1}{4}'$; 3 of $3'$; 2 of $2\frac{3}{4}'$; 2 of $2\frac{1}{4}'$; 1 of $2'$; 1 40' length of rope; 170 m. steel wire bolt-rope; 10 fathoms of lead line; 120 kgs. spun yarn; 2 mooring ropes; 2 fishing lines; 14 pieces of canvas cloth; 1 piece of tarpaulin; 11 gauges and 1 extinguisher for the coal furnace.

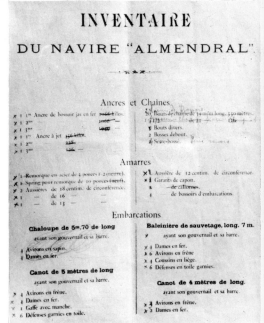

Every ship carried an inventory, which listed everything on board from the windlass to the quartermaster's pen case. (*Mariners Museum, Saint-Malo*)

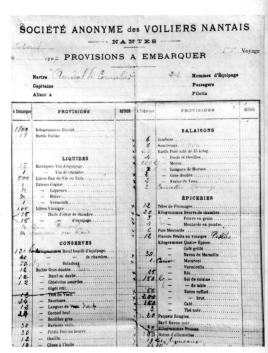

Victuals in the storeroom; showing the basic ration tables. (*Mariners Museum, Saint Malo*)

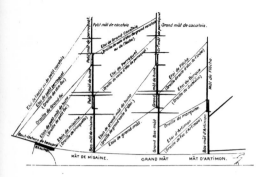

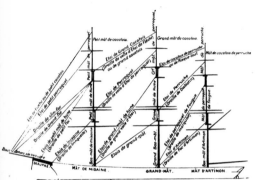

The stays and girtlines of a three-masted barque and three-masted square-rigger. Challamel: "Gréement et Manoeuvre".

Nothing in front of me except the masthead, with its truck, rolling through the frightening expanse of sky. The way to heaven began there, for those who lost their grip fell and broke their necks 60 meters below. (Henri Jacques: *Cap Horn.*)

Sixty meters aloft, with nothing to cling to but the steel rungs set in the masts and yards, buffeted to and fro by the motion. It was like the spider's web with which Vulcan ensnared Aeolus and resisted Neptune's attempts to rescue him. The great scaffolding of masts was an astonishing sight that seemed to defy both the laws of gravity and dynamics and to imperil the counterweight of the hull.

Some of these sailing ships were launched fully rigged, others had their masts stepped afterwards. The shipyard riggers first stepped the lower masts and the jib-boom, held in place by the steel braces; then followed the mast tops and caps, and the small jib-boom, equally secured by the backstays and other shrouds. To crown all, the gallant and topgallant yard masts were added.

The masts were tilted slightly backwards—the rake—and the shrouds, therefore, lay a little back from the masts, to counterbalance the wind's action upon the sails. To hold the whole complex structure together, a centuries-old system had evolved—by which, for example the jib-boom and bowsprit supported the foremast in three places. The bowsprit was held in place at the stern by wires and cables. A similar arrangement was adopted for the stays bracing the main and mizzen masts, depending on the number of masts the ship carried.

Then the yards were erected—fixed yards first, then lower yards, gallant and topgallant yards, swivelling on stirrups fixed to the masts.

The guy and brigantine gaff were next fitted, followed by the lifts and swifters and their supporting spars. Once the standing rigging was in place, attention was given to the running rigging, the downhalls of the staysail yards knitting with the braces of the main yards. After ratlines had been attached to the shrouds, and the standing rigging parcelled and wrapped with yarn, and finally coated with paint against corrosion, it was time for the sails to be hoisted, for the skeleton of masts to be clothed with triangular, square and fore-and-aft sails.

First came the set of jibs and staysails, held by rings to the stays and by girtlines to the bowsprit. The girtlines were used to hoist them, the braces to control them and the edges of the sheet were held on each side by tackle blocks. These blocks were heavy enough to crack the skull of the unwary, if they came down at the swing of the boom. Between the foremast and the mainmast were the main staysail, the fore staysail, and the topgallant staysail; and between the mainmast and the mizzen, the mizzen staysail, the marquee, the mizzen topmast-staysail and the mizzen beam stay, with all their various attachments.

The triangular sail between the mizzen crutch and the beam was known as the "driver" and filled the gap between the other sails in that area. Here, also, the brigantine carried her only fore-and-aft sail astern, which in rough weather was replaced by a very small sail—the trysail. Finally, and towering over all, came the square sails on the foremast: foresail, fore topsail, fore topgallant sail, foreroyal and fore skysail. On the mainmast: mainsail, main

Ready to sail. The *Richelieu* at Port Lincoln.

topsail, main topgallant sail, mainroyal and main skysail. On the mizzenmast: mizzensail, mizzen topsail, mizzen topgallant sail, mizzenroyal and mizzen skysail. These were named, as we can see, after the masts which carried them. Some sails—for instance the fore and mizzen staysails and the topsails—were by tradition hardly ever furled at sea, even in the roughest weather; for this reason, they were made of the strongest canvas, oo gauge.

The square sails were held to their yards by toggles and dead eyes at regular intervals, steel cables lacing trapezium patterns along the sails. Aloft the bolt-ropes held the billowing canvas, as the sails bellied over the yards; at these points the corners of the sheets were restrained by cables which ran back to two pulleys. It was this weight which controlled the sails, as they shivered or ballooned according to the pace of the ship.

The extended sheets of the sails were taken in to the yards in folds and held there by rope bands which stopped them billowing out again in the wind. In order to furl sail, the crew clambered up the mast and with feet anchored on the manrope and stomachs against the yards, they hauled in the sail with both hands. Normally the ship was under-sailed a little to reduce the billowing of the canvas before furling. It was impossible to furl a large

Hauling in the mizzen aboard the *Garthsnaid*. *(Nautical Photo Agency)*

Hauling in the mainsail aboard the *Garthsnaid*. The helmsman has altered course slightly to mask the sail and assist the operation. (*Nautical Photo Agency*)

sail without brails; the latter were ropes which ran up from the deck to reversible pulleys in the yards, By hauling on the brails on the deck, the bolt-ropes could be brought nearer to the yards, the sails slackened, thereby allowing the topmen to get a hold on the canvas.

The sheets and brails were connected with the ratlines running from the foot of the masts, in such a way that every sailor knew where they were, even on the darkest nights. There was no room for mistakes—the slightest error meant disaster—nor could time be spent in groping about, when speed was so essential.

With braces, halyards, downhalls, sheets and brails, a three-masted square-rigger could undertake about three hundred different maneuvers. The astonishment of a cabin boy on first sighting this incredible apparatus can well be imagined, and he was expected to know every detail of it in three months. It was not unusual, on American clippers or, later, on European ships returning from Oregon, to have a scratch crew, of whom only the first mate or the boatswain knew the ropes or how to sail the ship. In such cases the captain had to summon the watch and send the men aloft—without expecting them to know what they were doing, or even teaching them the names of the ropes in English, French, German or Swedish. What was needed above all were arms to haul in the canvas, and a watchful eye upon men, who might be at sea for twenty years before they knew what a brigantine staysail was.

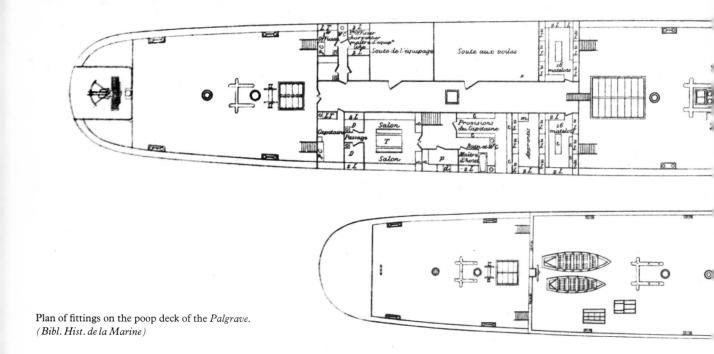

Plan of fittings on the poop deck of the *Palgrave*.
(Bibl. Hist. de la Marine)

Poop, without charthouse or shelter.
The three-masted square-rigger
Ariadne of Hamburg. *(San Francisco Maritime Museum)*

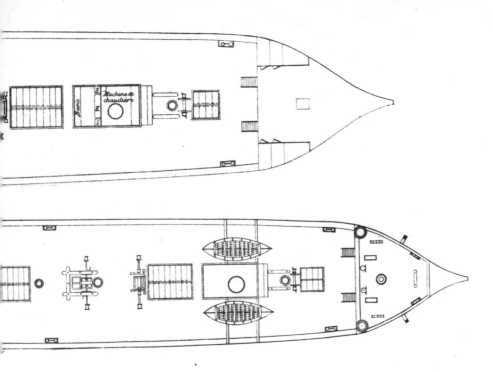

To assist the crew's hauling and furling, ships were usually equipped with capstans, two on the bridge near the mainmast and two on the poop opposite the mizzen. Other men also manned winches at the foot of the masts—useful machines, upon whose conical drums the steel cables of the yard-braces could be wound round. Thus, two men with a couple of turns on its handle could control the braces and affect the ship's entire course—a wonderful saving from the old days, when the whole watch had to struggle with the tackle-blocks and feed the cable onto the capstan. As always, the more picturesque operation had to give way, the songs of the capstan men being gradually relegated to the museum of ocean sailers.

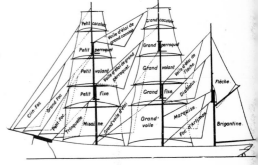

The sails of a three-masted square-rigger and three-masted barque. Challamel: "Gréement et Manœuvre".

FIVE HUGE MASTS ON COLOSSAL HULLS

Of all the square-rigged sailing ships built, the five-masted *France II* was certainly the largest. Launched at Bordeaux in November 1911 by Chantiers de la Gironde for Messrs. Prentout and Leblond, her dimensions were 126 × 16·9 × 10·54 meters, her gross tonnage was 6,255 tons, and she had a dead-weight capacity of 8,000 tons. An interesting innovation was the use of water as ballast in place of the normal ballast, whose capacity (1,1106 m.³) and weight helped keep the ship's equilibrium; in addition, deep fresh-water tanks were fitted (1,126 tons).

The rigging and masts were however the most extraordinary feature, the trucks of the mainmast being 64 meters above the water. Other statistics quoted by Captain Lacroix were: weight of masts—258 tons; weight of rigging—198 tons; surface area of 20 principal sails (excluding the 12 stay-

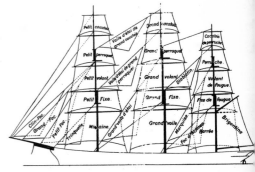

English iron ship *Palgrave*. Dimensions: 94 × 14.94 × 7.8 meters. Sail area; 3,013 square meters. Built at Glasgow in 1888 by William Hamilton. This fine four-master is an excellent example of the bulk English traders of the 19th century. Pâris: "Souvenirs de marine conservés". (*Bibl. Hist. de la Marine*)

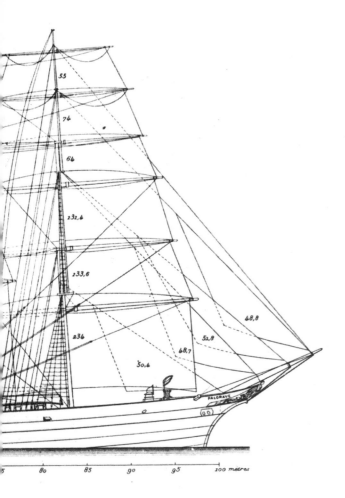

Three-masted American square-rigger.

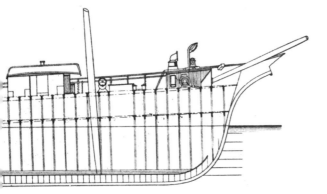

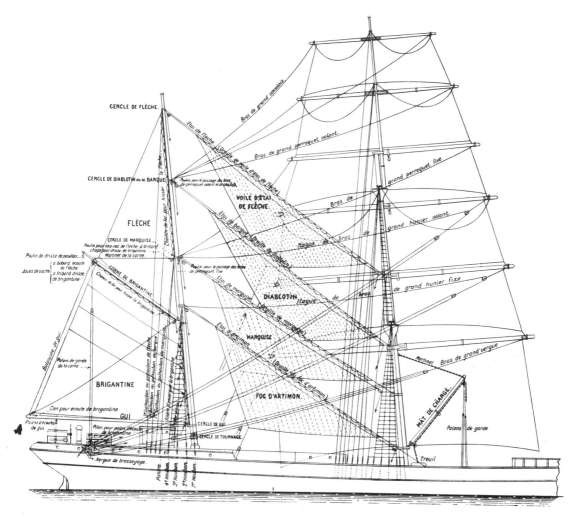

Position and nomenclature of the stern rigging of a three-masted barque. Challamel: "Gréement et Manoeuvre".

sails)—6,350 square meters. The running rigging had a length of 48 kilometers and there were 871 tackle-blocks in use. *France II* also carried two 900 h.p. motors (240 revs per minute capacity), which were finally dismounted in 1919.

For nine years she evaded German submarines and commerce raiders, icebergs, reefs, sandbars and doldrums to carry English coal to New Caledonia, via the Cape, Tristan de Cunha and Tasmania, and return with nickel ore via Cape Horn. Sometimes she carried wool and tallow between Australia and New Zealand. Her best outward passage took 90 days, less than 100 days were required for the return. On 11 July 1922, she was becalmed off Nouméa and then dashed against the shore by a tidal wave. She could have been salvaged, but the post-war slump in nickel depressed the value of the derelict to 300,000 francs. Thus ended the career of the giant Cape Horner.

Her predecessor was the Bordes Co.'s ship *France I*, launched at Glasgow on 2 September 1890, and the first five-masted sailing ship in the world. At the time, English shipbuilders were dubious of the sailing qualities of ships of this size—with masts 51 meters high, dimensions 114 × 14.9 meters, 4,520 square meters of canvas and a crew of 46.

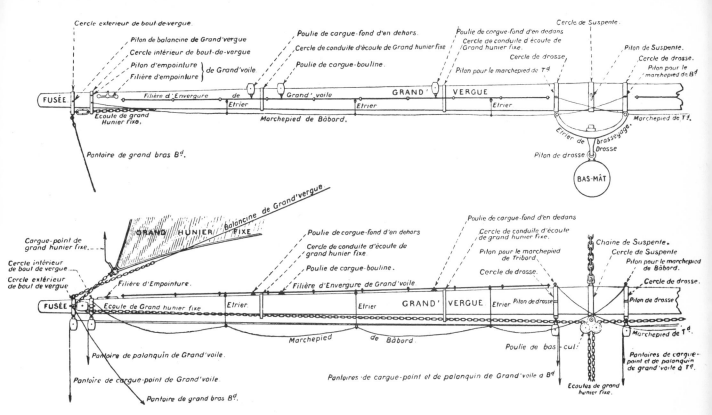

The rigging of the mainyard. Challamel: "Gréement et Manoeuvre".

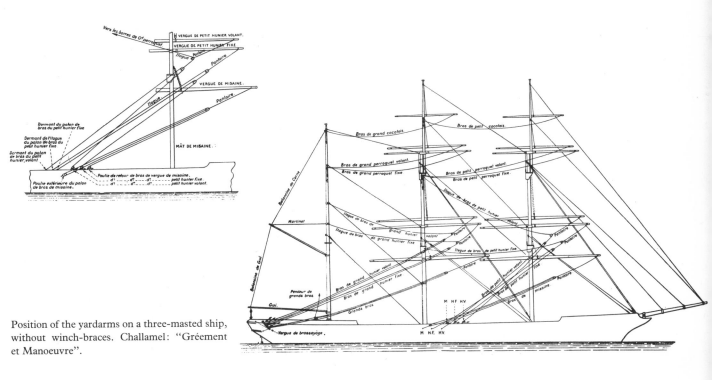

Position of the yardarms on a three-masted ship, without winch-braces. Challamel: "Gréement et Manoeuvre".

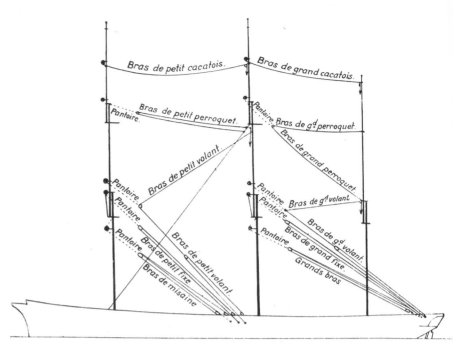

Position of yard-braces on a three-masted barque.
Challamel: "Gréement et Manoeuvre".

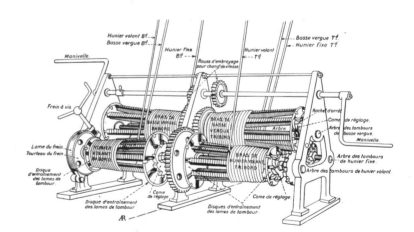

Strong and reliable! The brace-winches, one of
the few machines available to seamen aboard the
later sailing ships to assist them in their arduous
duties. Challamel: "Gréement et Manoeuvre".

Plan of the running rigging of a three-masted barque. No one on board had an excuse not to know
the exact position of every rope, even on the darkest night. The safety of the ship depended on
handling the rigging speedily. For clarity, the location of the braces for the staysail sheets has been
omitted from the diagram. They are situated at the base of the masts. *(Diagram by the author)*

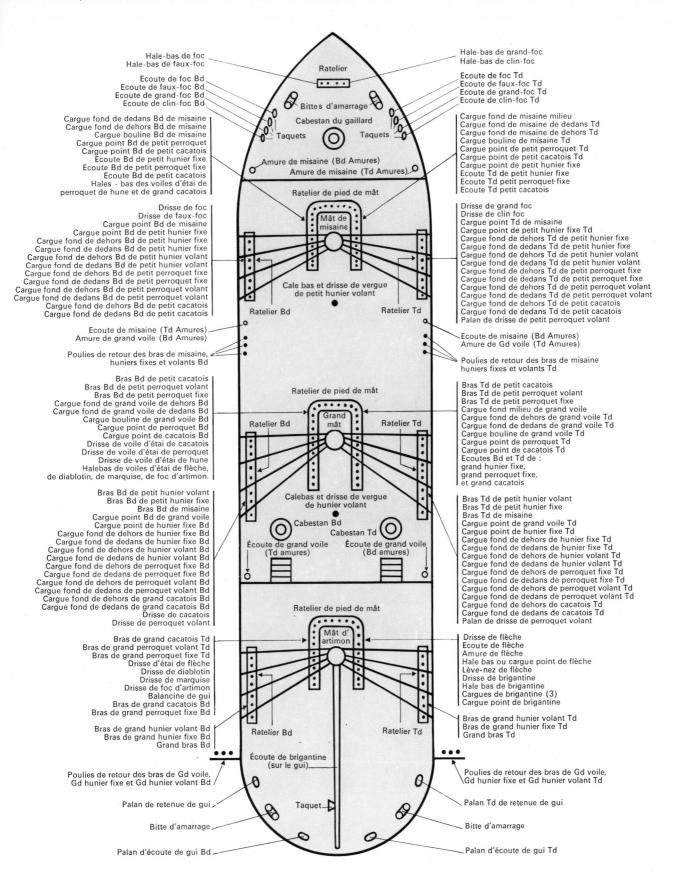

Hale-bas de foc
Hale-bas de faux-foc

Ecoute de foc Bd
Ecoute de faux-foc Bd
Ecoute de grand-foc Bd
Ecoute de clin-foc Bd

Ratelier

Bittes d'amarrage
Cabestan du gaillard
Taquets

Hale-bas de grand-foc
Hale-bas de clin-foc

Ecoute de foc Td
Ecoute de faux-foc Td
Ecoute de grand-foc Td
Ecoute de clin-foc Td

Cargue fond de dedans Bd de misaine
Cargue fond de dehors Bd de misaine
Cargue bouline Bd de misaine
Cargue point Bd de petit perroquet
Cargue point Bd de petit cacatois
Écoute Bd de petit hunier fixe
Ecoute Bd de petit perroquet fixe
Ecoute Bd de petit cacatois
Hales - bas des voiles d'étai de
perroquet de hune et de grand cacatois

Taquets

Amure de misaine (Bd Amures)
Amure de misaine (Td Amures)

Cargue fond de misaine milieu
Cargue fond de misaine de dedans Td
Cargue fond de misaine de dehors Td
Cargue bouline de misaine Td
Cargue point de petit perroquet Td
Cargue point de petit cacatois Td
Cargue point de petit hunier fixe
Ecoute Td de petit hunier fixe
Ecoute Td petit perroquet·fixe
Ecoute Td petit cacatois

Drisse de foc
Drisse de faux-foc
Cargue point Bd de petit hunier fixe
Cargue fond de dehors Bd de petit hunier fixe
Cargue fond de dedans Bd de petit hunier fixe
Cargue fond de dehors Bd de petit hunier volant
Cargue fond de dedans Bd de petit hunier volant
Cargue fond de dehors Bd de petit perroquet fixe
Cargue fond de dedans Bd de petit perroquet fixe
Cargue fond de dehors Bd de petit perroquet volant
Cargue fond de dedans Bd de petit perroquet volant
Cargue fond de dehors Bd de petit cacatois
Cargue fond de dedans Bd de petit cacatois

Ratelier de pied de mât

Mât de
misaine

Cale bas et drisse de vergue
de petit hunier volant

Ratelier Bd

Ratelier Td

Drisse de grand foc
Drisse de clin foc
Cargue point Td de misaine
Cargue point de petit hunier fixe Td
Cargue fond de dehors Td de petit hunier fixe
Cargue fond de dedans Td de petit hunier fixe
Cargue fond de dehors Td de petit hunier volant
Cargue fond de dedans Td de petit hunier volant
Cargue fond de dehors Td de petit perroquet fixe
Cargue fond de dedans Td de petit perroquet fixe
Cargue fond de dehors Td de petit perroquet volant
Cargue fond de dedans Td de petit perroquet volant
Cargue fond de dehors Td de petit cacatois
Cargue fond de dedans Td de petit cacatois
Palan de drisse de petit perroquet volant

Ecoute de misaine (Td Amures)
Amure de grand voile (Bd Amures)

Poulies de retour des bras de misaine,
huniers fixes et volants Bd

Ecoute de misaine (Bd Amures)
Amure de Gd voile (Td Amures)

Poulies de retour des bras de misaine
huniers fixes et volants Td

Bras Bd de petit cacatois
Bras Bd de petit perroquet volant
Bras Bd de petit perroquet fixe
Cargue fond de grand voile de dehors Bd
Cargue fond de grand voile de dedans Bd
Cargue bouline de grand voile Bd
Cargue point de perroquet Bd
Cargue point de cacatois Bd
Drisse de voile d'étai de cacatois
Drisse de voile d'étai de perroquet
Drisse de voile d'étai de hune
Halebas de voiles d'étai de flèche,
de diablotin, de marquise, de foc d'artimon.

Ratelier de pied de mât

Grand
mât

Ratelier Bd

Ratelier Td

Bras Td de petit cacatois
Bras Td de petit perroquet volant
Bras Td de petit perroquet fixe
Cargue fond milieu de grand voile
Cargue fond de dehors de grand voile Td
Cargue fond de dedans de grand voile Td
Cargue bouline de grand voile Td
Cargue point de perroquet Td
Cargue point de cacatois Td
Ecoutes Bd et Td de :
grand hunier fixe,
grand perroquet fixe,
et grand cacatois

Bras Bd de petit hunier volant
Bras Bd de petit hunier fixe
Bras Bd de misaine
Cargue point Bd de grand voile
Cargue point de hunier fixe Bd
Cargue fond de dedans de hunier fixe Bd
Cargue fond de dehors de hunier fixe Bd
Cargue fond de dedans de hunier volant Bd
Cargue fond de dehors de perroquet fixe Bd
Cargue fond de dedans de perroquet fixe Bd
Cargue fond de dehors de perroquet volant Bd
Cargue fond de dedans de perroquet volant Bd
Cargue fond de dehors de grand cacatois Bd
Cargue fond de dedans de grand cacatois Bd
Drisse de cacatois
Drisse de perroquet volant

Calebas et drisse de vergue
de hunier volant

Cabestan Bd
Cabestan Td

Écoute de grand voile
(Td amures)

Écoute de grand voile
(Bd amures)

Bras Td de petit hunier volant
Bras Td de petit hunier fixe
Bras Td de misaine
Cargue point de grand voile Td
Cargue point de hunier fixe Td
Cargue fond de dehors de hunier fixe Td
Cargue fond de dedans de hunier fixe Td
Cargue fond de dehors de hunier volant Td
Cargue fond de dedans de hunier volant Td
Cargue fond de dehors de perroquet fixe Td
Cargue fond de dedans de perroquet fixe Td
Cargue fond de dehors de perroquet volant Td
Cargue fond de dedans de perroquet volant Td
Cargue fond de dehors de cacatois Td
Cargue fond de dedans de cacatois Td
Palan de drisse de perroquet volant

Ratelier de pied de mât

Mât d'
artimon

Bras de grand cacatois Td
Bras de grand perroquet volant Td
Bras de grand perroquet fixe Td
Drisse d'étai de flèche
Drisse de diablotin
Drisse de marquise
Drisse de foc d'artimon
Balancine de gui
Bras de grand cacatois Bd
Bras de grand perroquet fixe Bd

Drisse de flèche
Ecoute de flèche
Amure de flèche
Hale bas ou cargue point de flèche
Lève-nez de flèche
Drisse de brigantine
Hale bas de brigantine
Cargues de brigantine (3)
Cargue point de brigantine

Bras de grand hunier volant Bd
Bras de grand hunier fixe Bd
Grand bras Bd

Ratelier Bd

Ratelier Td

Bras de grand hunier volant Td
Bras de grand hunier fixe Td
Grand bras Td

Écoute de brigantine
(sur le gui)

Poulies de retour des bras de Gd voile,
Gd hunier fixe et Gd hunier volant Bd

Poulies de retour des bras de Gd voile,
Gd hunier fixe et Gd hunier volant Td

Palan de retenue de gui

Taquet

Palan Td de retenue de gui

Bitte d'amarrage

Bitte d'amarrage

Palan d'écoute de gui Bd

Palan d'écoute de gui Td

With winds against her *France* veered completely off course within fifteen minutes. The colossal span of the main canvas made it difficult to correct this tendency and could not be counterbalanced by the influence of the jibs and staysails, which were almost totally ineffective. (Notes by *France I*'s first captain.)

Struck by a violent gust of wind from a "pampero" off Brazil on 10 May 1901, *France I*'s cargo shifted and she developed a 45° list. When the German sailing ship *Hebe* was sighted, Captain Forgeard decided to abandon ship, and he and his crew arrived at Valparaiso on 9 June 1901.

The *R.C.Rickmers* had a 1,000 h.p. engine and was launched at the Rickmers yard, Geestemünde in 1906. She displaced 5,548 gross tons and her dimensions were: 134·5 × 16·6 × 9·2 meters. Until the outbreak of war she operated in the Far East for the company, but was interned in an English

View from the deck of the five-masted *France II*, an imposing array of yards, masts, running and standing rigging. Altogether 45 men had to cope with 6,350 square meters of canvas.

The five-masted barque *France II* in a river estuary. Although painted with "batteries" on her topsides in early days, she stood out among the Bordes fleet by the absence of a large black rubbing-strake below the deadlights. During the war she was painted a uniform gray. *(The Yacht)*

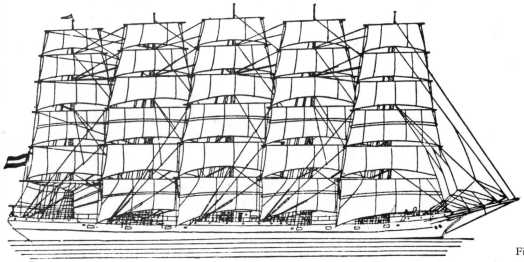

Five-masted German square-rigger.

port in 1914. Renamed, and under a British flag, she was torpedoed and sunk off Ireland in 1917 by U.66. The *Thomas W. Lawson* was a seven-masted American fore-and-aft schooner launched at Quincy, Mass., in 1902. She displaced 7,500 tons and her dimensions were: 132 × 16·6 × 8·1 meters. She first carried petrol from Texas to the eastern United States but later voyaged to Europe. In 1907 she was wrecked off the Scillys, only two of the crew being saved.

The *Preussen* (second of the name) was commissioned in 1902 for the celebrated ship owner Laiesz. Her displacement was 5,081 tons gross, 7,850 tons deadweight and her dimensions were 122 × 16·4 × 10·3 × 8·2 meters. The *Preussen* was the masterpiece of the sailing shipmaster Robert Hilgendorf, and in 1903 reached Iquique from the Lizard in 58 days, as a nitrate clipper. On 6 November 1910 she was in a collision with the British steamer *Brighton* in the Channel; towed into Dover, she was grounded and became a total loss.

Built in 1895, the *Potosi* was the first German five-master, and at that time the largest in the world, displacing 4,026 tons and with dimensions: 111 × 15·6 × 9·5 meters. Her captain, Hilgendorf, formerly of the *Preussen*, once sailed her from Europe to the west coast of South America in 97 days, but he never repeated the successes he had achieved with the *Preussen*. The *Potosi's* greatest exploit was to reach a speed of 11·2 knots over a period of eleven days in December 1908. During the war she was interned in Chile but was returned to France at the armistice and later sold to the Chileans who renamed her *Flora*. On 19 October 1925, en route to Valparaiso with a cargo of coal, she caught fire in the Atlantic and was abandoned.

The *Copenhagen*, a five-master with an auxiliary engine, was launched in England in 1921 and became a training ship. She had an overall length of 122 meters; in 1928 she was lost in the southern ocean with all hands.

Coming out of the shipbuilder's yard. The five-masted *Preussen*, pride of the Laeisz fleet. Built at Geestemünde in 1902; overall length 144 meters; sail area 5,562 square meters. One of the finest Cape Horners ever built. (*Society of Cape Horners, Germany*)

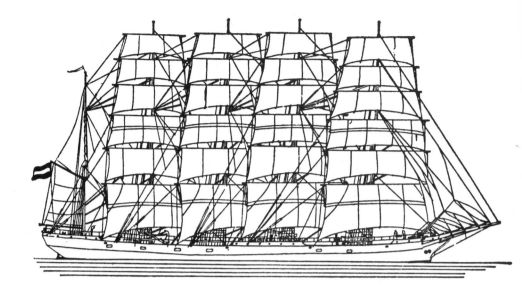

Five-masted German barque.

SHIP HANDLING AND THE VIRTUOSOS OF CAPE HORN

To sail from one place to another, a ship must have wind in her sails, beat against it and follow the course that gives the maximum speed. There are six main ways of sailing, dictated by the wind's direction in relation to the axis of the ship: on a wind; close to; wind on the beam; running free; off the wind; and, dead before the wind. On a wind and close-hauled, the ship sails best at a 45° angle of the eye of the wind, although she may heel. There may be no alternative, however, if the ship must round a hazard. The yards are braced to receive little wind and the foresail is brought round on the tack. Unfortunately, in heavy weather the ship may easily become strained on this course, and in the hands of an inexpert helmsman suffer badly from the seas; there is always the risk of the deck being awash with a large wave running from the stern and sweeping the men overboard. In such a situation, the need is to tack and keep tacking in order to hold the course.

With the wind on the beam, the course is most favorable and in fine weather the entire canvas is working with the yards braced, bisecting the angle between the wind's direction and the ship's axis. All the staysails are out, with the topmast sails being furled only in blustery weather.

To maintain a running free course, off the wind, there is little deviation as the sea is running on the ship's quarter and the sails may be fully hoisted without risk. For this reason it is an excellent course that a good helmsman can keep for long periods without effort.

The wind dead before is very different in its effect, however. The staysails and the jib must be brought in, since their utility is completely blotted out by the square sails. The rolling is severe due to the sails' inability to provide stability. The force of the seas at the stern and under the counter has the unpleasant effect of pushing the ship across the waves and can even force the rudder out of the water, in the troughs between the wave crests.

In this sort of maneuver an experienced and daring man at the wheel is required. By holding the course for long periods—twelve or twenty-four

Bowling along in a fine breeze. Note the confused sea at the stern. *(Lacroix Collection)*

Hauling in the spanker. *(Lacroix Collection)*

hours, sometimes less—the ship is well founded and, with a full canvas, gains in stability and speed. Thereby the danger of waves from a following sea breaking over the poop is minimized. The watch officer's business above all is to judge the various strains being placed upon his ship and to know, for instance, how much canvas can be crowded on without undue risk. This ability is particularly necessary in squally weather and in areas

The five-masted barque *Copenhagen*, fitted with an auxiliary engine. At one time a Danish training ship, she was lost with all hands in the South Seas in 1929.

Each rope has its appointed place. On board the *Richelieu*, sailing from Port Lincoln, Australia.

where the wind is very changeable; those in charge must always be ready to order the bracing of the yards, hauling in or letting out sail, in order to take the utmost advantage of every opportunity offered. The art of the pilot lies in this ability to work right to the limits of the narrow dividing line between the possible and the impossible.

This game played against wind and sea has its own rules. For example, when a three-master meets thickening weather close to the wind with all her sails set, the officer of the watch will give the following orders in succession to reduce canvas:

Haul in the main skysail, the mizzen topgallant staysail, and main royal staysail—bring down the fore royal—bring down the main royal—lower the flying jib and the main topgallant staysail—haul in the upper mizzen topsails—bring down the mizzen topmast staysail—take in the brigantine sail—rove in the mizzen heads—reef in the upper main topsail—furl the lower mizzen topsail—reef the upper fore topsail, and lower the main staysail—reef the foresail—reef the upper main topsail—lower the mainsail and haul down the main staysail—lower the upper fore topsail—bring in the outer jib and lower the upper main topsail. With this done, the ship is running under minimum canvas—with reefed foresail, inner jib, mizzen staysail and jib. (Sailing instructions quoted in Massenet, Vallerey and Letalle: *Gréement et Manoeuvre*.)

This sequence of taking in sail applies equally to a three-masted square-rigger sailing off wind. Of course, the sequence of hoisting sail is exactly the reverse of the foregoing. To take up a new tack, the ship either turns to cross over the path of the wind or wears to luff, the wind astern. In the first case, being on a wind, the vessel's speed increases in trying to keep with the wind; the brigantine boom is swung over and as soon as the lower sails begin to shiver, the order: "ease off the jibs" is given. Then when the ship swings dead into the wind, the mizzen yards are braced on the opposite tack upon the command: "Haul about". Only the mizzen sails continue to give the ship some forward impetus and the influence of the rudder brings her

Bending the main topsail aboard the *Suzanne*. *(Mariners Museum, Saint-Malo)*

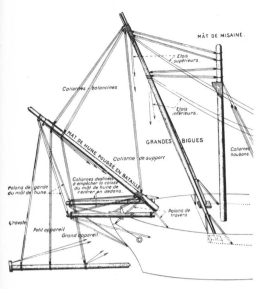

The art of the rigger: how to step a bowsprit. Extract from Challamel: "Gréement et Manoeuvre".

round to the desired course. The moment the wind is felt in the new quarter, the jibs, foresail and brigantine are hauled taut, and the ship proceeds on her new course.

Sometimes the ship, in spite of a skilful crew, fails to turn enough, or too lightly, to execute the maneuver. The fault may be incorrect trim aboard. Or, in heavy seas, the ship's headway is checked before the maneuver can be got under way and her speed is then drastically reduced by the onrush of successive waves at right angles.

In such a situation the ship must come round dead before the wind or by wearing on the luff. To begin this maneuver the brigantine and mainsail are hauled up and while the foremast yards alone continue to pivot, the crew "shut" the mainmast and mizzen yards at the command "Brace and secure". At this critical moment the sails are almost shivered, but as soon as the ship has come round dead before the wind, the jib and brigantine fill again and the foresail can be braced square. Under the influence of the cross wind the brigantine is hauled close and then the entire canvas fills and the ship takes up her new course.

This maneuver "dead before" is always successful, but not without the crew viewing with apprehension the fact that the ship has twice to lie hove-to at right angles to the waves, with the sea breaking over the poop and well-deck. With the violent rolling of the ship which frequently accompanies these alterations of course, it is difficult to keep the sails shivered, at the risk of spoiling the maneuver. The ship's sudden waywardness may in an instant

If the winches for bracing the yards gave all round control, operated by only two men, at least they should not work with their feet in the water. On board the *Richelieu*.

A wrong maneuver by the *Ditton* in the harbor of Newcastle, N.S.W. in 1902, led to her becoming entangled in the rigging and bowsprits of two other sailing ships, *Port Crawford* and *Peeblesshire*. A lengthy repair job for the riggers.

lose all the precious gains made previously, but often there is no possible alternative.

The countless ways of handling a ship as practiced by these great sailers would make a fascinating subject for research. It is only necessary to glance at the seamanship manuals used by these captains to realize their skill. They knew their ships' capabilities like the best yachtsmen. Even if one maneuver miscarried, they were able at once to fall back on another and as if by magic could conjure up some fresh ruse.

In very high seas, when the strain placed upon the ship became too great, it was necessary to run before the wind. In this situation, with all sails in except for the foresail braced square and the inner jib, the ship scudded on at more than eight knots, under almost bare poles and with the waves creaming at her taffrail. The rolling was very severe, with the ever present risk of her lying-to across the waves and the poop being submerged with water. At all costs the ship's axis must be kept perpendicular to the waves' crests, and to this end, dragging an anchor or a length of cable from the stern could give the added stability necessary.

In sailing ship days, it was frequently said that many ships were lost with all hands in a squall, having held their course running before the wind too long. This is readily understandable when it is realized that at the moment when she swings round to take her head, the roll is very pronounced—carrying with it the risk of dismasting and the displacement of cargo and ballast. At the same time the amount of water shipped in the well threatens to break open the hatch covers. Thus it rests upon the captain's skill to judge the right moment to haul round.

Lying-to is when the ship has the wind on her beam and only her inner jib, reefed foresail and lower fore, lower main and lower mizzen topsails out. In this position the ship drifts, lying between the breaking waves and

The *Junon*, her rudder broken, rigging up a jury. Drawing by Jules Noel. (*Le Tour du Monde*)

Three-masted Nantes ship *Duchesse Anne*, dismasted off Bermuda on 8 February, 1894, running before the wind under jury-sails. Painting by M. Mohrmann. (*Lacroix Collection*)

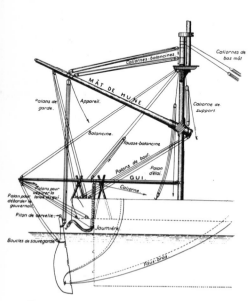

Fitting and removal of a rudder at sea; a difficult operation, undertaken only in fine weather. Challamel: "Gréement et Manoeuvre".

their troughs of forty meters or so, before the next crest. The skill here is to prevent the ship making too much way forward or astern—in either case she is liable to come out of the protection of the troughs. If the ship is sailed too slackly, there is too much headway in the bows and only the stern will be sheltered by the backwash of the waves. The safety of the ship depends on a strict control of the sails. At one time good results were achieved in keeping the ship's balance when hove-to by pouring oil on the surface of the sea.

This drifting hove-to could only be done before the sea. Drifting about three knots on a 65° bearing, the ship may have to sail for days in this dangerous state. Then comes the moment when the captain must boldly alter course in a moment of calm weather, at the risk of losing his ship in the maneuver. Sometimes, also, a sailing ship must heave-to (for a ship hove-to does not come to a standstill)—when arriving off a port at dusk. Waiting until daylight, she will signal for a pilot. Heaving-to sailwise entails the lowering of all the main canvas, the ship maintaining her course and balance by means of jibs, staysails and brigantine alone.

As well as these maneuvers at sea, the sailors had also to be able to navigate rivers under sail, enter and leave ports and roads without tugs, find their anchorage, get under way in difficult bays, negotiate twisting channels, and struggle with the vagaries of wind, tide and, sometimes, their own craft.

Moreover the seamen of this golden age, as well as being skilful topmen and steersmen in all kinds of weather, knew the art of repairing the common misfortunes that could strike their ships such as damage to the masts, the sails, the rudder; leaks, which could ruin the cargo; running aground; collision, and fire. Their skill in devising jury-rigs was supreme. The numerous running repairs aloft could only be done on the spot—along the yards, and in the topmasts. Pulley-blocks, purchases and sheers were used with genius in this work, so much so, that tons of metal were moved about in the air with the ease of an electric crane.

When it was a question of the running rigging, one bit of rope was as good as another. But acrobatics aloft in bad weather were altogether different, especially when broken spars swung crazily in space, letting off showers of sparks. For the rest, the boatswain managed to do something, whether it was broken yards, a shattered bowsprit, cracking masts, or even partial or total dismasting. The treatises on rigging describe the methods and apparatus for making repairs, but only the courage of the crew, working in bad weather, enabled such problems to be solved in cold blood.

In each case, several means of repair were put forward; for instance, there were many ideas as to the best way to rig a jury-mast or rudder. Captains Pakenham, Bassière, Lucas, Cabaret, Marco Stareich, Fabvre, Prat, Quoiam, Roberts and Duris all had ingenious solutions. But it was for the crew (who were being tested, not by examining captains but well and truly by the sea) to transfer these ideas into practice under the worst conditions. But this they did with a consummate skill that has always evoked universal admiration. Indeed, this ability to triumph over adversity has always been a hallmark of the mariner.

In 1900, the *Jacques* went up the Tancarville canal on her way to Rouen. Insufficiently ballasted, she capsized at the quayside after being struck by a sudden gust of wind. Her masts had to be cut down before she could be righted.

3 Mates and Crews

Coming out of the shipbuilders' yards, almost every sailing ship had the same hull and rigging. But gradually they drew apart, taking an individuality which was formed by their careers. Some made wretched voyages at the hands of melancholy captains and bad crews; others, driven to the limits of achievement in expert hands, earned the homage of the maritime world. Yet others began brilliantly only to succumb to some disaster, whereby their career was suddenly cut short by shipwreck. The old saying is true: "All ships are good; it is the men that sail them who decide their fate."

As the crew liked to see themselves—serious, but at ease, grouped round their captain in bowler hat, and officers with cravats. Best recollection of all was their mascot, the ship's dog, to whom they raised their glasses. Photograph taken on board the *Marguerite Dollfus*, Captain Bidon. (*Mariners Museum, Saint-Malo*)

The harmony of fine rigging. The masts of the *Richelieu*.

SOCIÉTÉ ANONYME DES VOILIERS NANTAIS
2, Rue Cambronne - NANTES

CONDITIONS DE COMMANDEMENT
du Capitaine *A. Bidon*
à bord du trois-mâts *Amiral de Cornulier.*

Conditions it were best to adhere to, if one wanted to remain in the shipowners' esteem. *(Mariners Museum, Saint-Malo)*

THE CAPTAINS, THE 24-YEAR OLD VETERANS

Maritime law, commercial treaties, legal decisions hardly affect shipping companies—their directors, shareholders or their vessels. They really have only one lawmaker—the captain.

Until the last days of the sailing ship and even in our age of steam—although gradually navigation shed its aura of far-off expeditions of discovery and trade—the captain remained king of his little domain. He represented the commercial interests of the shipowner and took administrative charge of the voyage. With almost unlimited disciplinary powers over those aboard, he was criminal judge against the wrongdoer and civil lawgiver regarding births, deaths, and wills. He was doctor and surgeon when the need arose. Above all, he was looked upon as "le vieux", the old man—who had risen successively in the regard of his shipowners, through the ranks of seaman or pilot, lieutenant and first mate, to captain. Some had reached this position at the age of twenty-four, and were in command of a four-master ship worth a million francs.

In the Master Mariners' Museum at St. Malo there is an intimidating document of three pages entitled: *The Conditions of Command*. This document, once sent by the Sailing Ship Society of Nantes to Captain A. Bidon, in command of the three-masted barque *Amiral de Cornulier*, defined the terms of agreement between the two parties. Its equivalent may be found in every merchant fleet throughout the world during the period:

1. The pay is fixed at 259 francs per month.
2. The allotted commission is 1% of the overall freight and net premium of the voyage.
   In ballast the commission is 2% of net premium.
   A commission of 10% is allotted on the fees paid by the pilots carried by the captain.

Lieutenant in 1899; captain in 1904. The rapid promotion of an excellent officer, shown by the entry in the muster roll. *(Augé Collection)*

The Taylor Navigation School, San Francisco, *ca.* 1900. All these candidates for a captain's ticket had had plenty of experience in practical navigation. *(San Francisco Maritime Museum)*

3. The captain is responsible for the goods carried by him and loaded with his knowledge. He must supervize its storage and ensure that the ship is in good trim. If the cargo is in bags, he must see that they are not opened and keep a tally of the number, since any missing will always be claimed as full by the recipient. (A ship has recently at Dieppe been forced to pay 15,000 francs damages for a less than 2% discrepancy in the itemized cargo, although its full weight corresponded with the manifest.)

4. The captain will under no circumstances hire out the ship without authorization by telegram or written permission from the owners.

5. No victuals or preserves, salt provisions, livestock, wine, brandy, biscuits, meal, etc. (except chickens at the port of departure) will be taken on board, unless to supplement the ship's stores. The ship will be fully provided with gear, sailcloth, rope, etc., beforehand, and no purchase of these materials should be made unless in emergency and with the shipowners' authority.

6. It is agreed that vegetables, fruit and fish may be purchased in each port on the scale of 4 francs a day; the daily meat ration is extra.

7. No private packets or parcels may be carried by the captain without the shipowners' permission for each voyage.

8. After fitting-out, the captain will maintain a record, listing all the stores taken on board at the outset of the voyage. The record of consumption will be kept daily and be based according to the ration scales. An exact copy of this record must be sent to the owners on arrival at each port, and a full return supplied upon return to Europe at the end of the voyage. The record must include the "per caput" consumption and the stores remaining. The stores consumed should correspond with those originally taken on, less 2% for ordinary victuals, 7% for wine and 10% for brandy.

9. On arrival at every port, the captain must regularly supply the owners with the shipment certificate, and take care to include the name of the port, date and seal,

A warrant of authority issued by Bordes Co., to their captains. (*Mariners Museum, Saint-Malo*)

countersigned by the consul, with it. It is important that the name of the ship-owners is correctly spelled on the certificates.

When the ship reaches a foreign port and the captain is compelled to replace sick or deserters, only French seamen may be signed on. If there are no Frenchmen available and the crew must be made up with foreign sailors, the captain must send a certificate to the French consul of the port concerned, stating that no other means of obtaining men had been found.

10. Loading and unloading should always be done by the ship's crew; the captain may, if necessary, use local stevedores as well, except in those ports where it is forbidden. Should he negotiate with a docking contractor, the captain must take out an accident policy as safeguard.

11. The captain must render an account of his expenses, with receipts, at each port visited. This must be recorded on the forms supplied: in column 1 the amount, in foreign currency, should be filled in by the captain; in column 2, its conversion into francs at the current rate of exchange. Any monies advanced to the crew during the voyage and in port, which are in excess of the amount allocated, will be placed to the captain's account. Record of these transactions must be signed by the parties concerned, countersigned by the consul and a copy sent to the owners.

12. Upon arrival in port, the captain must *himself* telegraph the owners, using the house code. During his stay, he must report his progress by each courier, taking care to include details of loading and discharging cargo and any other important information, particularly instances of delay. Upon departure he must notify the volume of cargo loaded and, in his final letter, the ship's draught AV and AR.

13. The ship's log must be kept by the captain *himself*, in which all the incidents of the voyage are recorded. A copy must be forwarded to the owners on arrival at each port.

14. In the event of damage, whether in harbor or as a result of storms, the captain must immediately telegraph the occurrence to the owners and subsequently furnish a full report by letter. If the damge is considerable, he must obtain the services of the French consul and report developments to the owners. If there is

The captain in the comfort of his cabin. (*Augé Collection*)

Not a total of a hundred years amongst the four of them: the captain of the *Anne of Bretagne* is 24, the first mate 23, the lieutenant 21 and the boatswain 25. (*Augé Collection*)

Captain Angus MacKinnon of the three-masted *Kinrosshire*, accompanied on the voyage by his wife and small son. *(San Francisco Maritime Museum)*

an insurance agent in the vicinity, the captain must seek his support, but remember that in the long run, it is himself who is solely responsible. In any event, the captain must not undertake any repairs or replacements, without first acquainting the owners of the approximate cost and obtaining their authorization.

But what was the point of this legal contract and detailed instructions, if the captain's abilities could not be given free rein in the enterprise? From the purely nautical point of view, his duty might be summarized thus:

To take his ship and her cargo to the destination by the best route, in the shortest time and with the least expense.

There remains the commercial angle. Very often, for want of an agent or broker, the responsibility for the freight, according to the charter-agreement, and the safeguarding of the shipowners' interests, rested with the captain alone. The heated discussions and arguments over the terms of the contract (which was frequently signed, on departure, by a shipper unknown to the consignee) began as soon as the ship arrived in port. What sailor cannot remember the profound feeling of disenchantment which this petty haggling over trifles caused at the end of a long difficult voyage? The captain had had time during the voyage to know every detail of the charter-agreement, but he had to fight hard to make any profit out of it.

Personal expenses had to be recorded down to the last halfpenny. Here is an example, from the page of a diary kept by a Captain Augé, describing an excursion he made to Hamburg in 1904:

Ticket—Paris to Hamburg	76 frs. 10 cent	
Luggage	75 ,, 10 ,,	
Tips and Transport	8 ,,	
Tax on the German border	4 Marks	
Two Lunches	9	,, 50 Pfennig
Note: Meyer's Hotel	13	,, 85 ,,
Dinghy for baggage	6 ,,	
Transport	7 ,,	
Tramway, 20–27 March	7 ,,	
Interest on 3 months loan	0	,, 40 ,,
Lunch, 25 March	2	,, 10 ,,
Cab, 25 March	2	,, 50 ,,
Tramway, 27 March	0	,, 6 ,,
Telegram	1	,, 95 ,,
M. Reusser's charges	146 francs 10 cents	

The purchase of food and equipment was always done through invoices. Only in the case of shipchandlers' stores did the captains enjoy any freedom, a tradition which was accepted by the shipowners. On the other hand, the disposal of old rope, canvas and other worn-out equipment was always debited to the ship's account.

Damage sustained during a voyage usually required immediate decisions to be made, leaving no time to obtain instructions from France. By maritime law the ship was held in custody under insurance cover, and any additional expenses were only deemed valid after a full assessment had been made. The captain was always alone in defending himself in such cases. Although often well-pleased, the shipowners were chary of congratulation and the captain consoled himself with the thought: "If they don't say anything, all is well".

So sparing were owners in their appreciation, that in one case—the captain of the *Maria Rickmers*—it had fatal results. That fine five-master was launched in 1890, and her owners expected wonderful things of her. With a cargo of coal from Barry docks, the ship reached Singapore after a lengthy passage of 82 days. The owners expressed their disappointment in a cable which reached the captain upon his arrival. Having put everything into the voyage, and feeling exhausted and ill, he was unable to withstand the shock of the telegram and fell down dead on his quarterdeck.

The captain of the English windjammer *Dimsdale*, with his daughter who appears to have found her sea legs. (*San Francisco Maritime Museum*)

SEAMEN'S PORTRAITS

An astonishing variety of people comprised the sailing ship captains—a race now almost extinct. The list included men of the coast or inland, former cabin boys who had climbed the ladder of success, banished sons of wealthy families. They might be huge, cantankerous, evil-tempered giants or seedy little men, dry and hardened old sinners. (For example, there is the case of Captain Peattie of the *Leicester Castle*, who received four bullets in his body after being shot at by a seaman, taken on at San Francisco. No operation could be performed and after a day in bed, he got up and took his ship to Queenstown, Australia, where the mutineers were tried and the bullets extracted.) Other captains were constantly ill, but remained indomitable although prostrate with seasickness every time they went to sea.

There were drunkards and melancholics, busybodies and men consumed with suspicion, bitterness and fear. There were daredevils and family men who doted upon their crews; young, cultured men of science; soapbox orators and merchants. There were sportsmen and puritanical preachers. Almost all had nicknames, such as: "Port-tack"; "Every-ready"; "Sweet Tornado"; "Old Junk"; "Headman Jake"; "Straight-on-Course"; "Peg-leg".

Here is a description of the captain of the Cape Horner *Stella*, upon which Léopold Pallu de la Barrière sailed as a lieutenant in 1875:

I then met Captain Wilhem Olfus, whom I had heard beforehand was an old whaling man and an Alsatian by birth. He was of small build and wore a rough woollen shirt, stained with whale oil. His crooked nose, flaming beard, strange dress and curious gestures gave him an astonishing appearance, which was softened by the kindness in his blue eyes. He spoke a few words of welcome and apologized for not being notified of my arrival.

... Although M. Marcel, the first mate, had taken some nautical observations which were nullified by the overcast weather, the captain showed his disbelief in these scientific methods: "We can steer without them." And, indeed, he proved that he could.

The *Stella* reached Callao from San Francisco in this way, and I heard later that Captain Olfus became so tired after ten days, that gross navigational errors were apparent in his calculations every day; in fact, on one occasion there was a dispute whether the ship's position was among the peaks of the Andes or in the valleys of lower Peru! This excellent man had not been able to count since the age of five, and in pretending to make logarithmic calculations he could not conceal his ignorance, in thinking that "2+2 = 5". Despite all his intelligence, this ability had deserted him from the age of eight; he therefore shut the table of logarithms and delegated all the

The chief of staff of the *Pilier* of Nantes: the captain, first mate and lieutenant. (*Mariners Museum, Saint-Malo*)

The three-masted Nantes barque *Jean* running before the wind off Cape Horn, 1908. Painting by M. Mohrmann *(Lacroix Collection)*

English wool clipper *Eliza Houghton*. Painting by R. Hard, 1881. *(Mariners Museum, Saint-Malo)*

The *Anne of Bretagne* in the trade winds. (*Augé Collection*)

calculations to the first mate. It was remarkable that they reached the 50° latitude and then anchorage, forty-five days out of San Francisco, without mishap. The sea is big and the rocks and reefs are small by comparison. It would be hard otherwise to explain this type of navigation which was a throwback to the crossbow, the *Sea Torch* and the first nautical almanacs.

Nevertheless Captain Olfus of the *Stella* was a first-class mariner, fully capable of overcoming all the dangers to be met with at sea.

Commandant Augé paints the portrait of another captain, (who shall be nameless), with whom he shipped as lieutenant aboard a 2,800 tonner, a new vessel built in Rouen in 1900.

Augé was twenty; the first mate, an experienced officer, was forty. But the captain himself was only thirty-two, a master mariner whose experience of sailing ships was limited to two voyages to the Caribbean as a cabin boy.

We were roughly handled coming out of the Channel. The rigging became entangled 45 meters up the steel masts, and there was a serious risk of the halyards and shrouds being severed against the handrails. The first mate took in hand the tautening of the steel wires, but the captain insisted that the rigging would work loose of its own accord. The struggle between them was clear to all—the mate full of commonsense, the captain jealous and ill-tempered, sowing discord among the crew. Thereafter the captain took every opportunity to impose his will.

The poop was bridged over with wood, and lined with tow and pitch to keep it water-tight. But after a fortnight, if a bucket of water was thrown over the poop, water was found to be seeping into the cabins. The captain got the crew to caulk the poop, except over the first mate's cabin, and mine which was adjoining ... meanness in distributing the rations harmed the crew's morale ... We arrived at Melbourne after an 102-day passage. The crew's caulking work had kept the poop dry, except over the first mate's

Sometimes a tough crew got out of hand and had to be disciplined. The punishment book recording the offence and the sentence of punishment. Captain Lacroix' notebook. *(Nantes Archives)*

cabin and my own. I had to rig a piece of sailcloth over my bunk to catch the water drops, but this did not solve the problem of excessive humidity, which gave me terrible rheumatism.

In the Antarctic the captain abolished the afternoon rest, and in these terrible seas, the result was 16 hours on duty and 8 hours off.

We reached Dunkirk after 95 days at sea and everyone left the ship without any regret. I visited the shipowners at Rouen and they introduced me to a fine seaman and a gentleman, Captain Ladonne. I sailed $3\frac{1}{2}$ years under him on the *Biessard*, days of happiness which made me forget those 241 days of misery beforehand. Both were my apprenticeship to taking up command of the *Anne de Bretagne* at the age of $24\frac{1}{2}$.

On occasions, an unexpected development would shatter the growing harmony aboard. An example is quoted by C. Walter in *Der Albatros*.

In January 1904, the four-masted barque *Mneme* of Hamburg fitted-out for Peru. She was a fine modern vessel with a young energetic crew and harsh efficient officers—characteristic features of German and Scandinavian ships of this period.

After rounding Cape Finisterre, a drama unfolded one morning. Captain Hansen demanded that the stealer of sausages from the pantry be found; but although the crew were interrogated, no one confessed. Punishment was severe—rations of 250 grammes potatoes and 250 grammes molasses only per man daily henceforth. After two weeks fasting, during which everyone came under suspicion, the cabin boy said the culprit was the old ship's dog. A kentledge was then tied round the poor creature's neck and it was thrown into the sea.

But the captain insisted that the rationing continue and the crew arrived at Callao weak and undernourished. After three weeks spent in unloading, the men were allowed on shore but were refused loans by the captain. But this did not dampen their spirits; one inspired sailor thought of taking their musical instruments with them, and having passed through an acquiescent Peruvian Customs, they were literally able to sing and play for their suppers. In a perfectly orderly manner, the crew returned to the ship at the appointed time, much to the surprise of the officer of the watch. At nightfall they put away their fiddles, but the following day the performance was repeated exactly as before. Hansen was beside himself with rage.

The rationing of food was even more severe on the return voyage and it was a starving crew which brought the *Mneme* into Rotterdam. Little suspecting what had happened, Malitzki, the director of the shipowning company, made an inspection of the ship, including the storeroom. He was astonished to find the latter crammed with provisions of every description. Hansen was congratulating himself on his good management but the owner gave him no time to enjoy it: "I gave you stores for your crew, the best to be found throughout the whole German merchant marine, and you bring back a collection of skeletons. I have taken a lot of trouble to improve the company's reputation and enlist good men. Now, thanks to you, I am entirely unable to find another crew. Pack your bags, Hansen; you're fired!"

The narrator made the point that not one member of the crew ever thought of, or dared to consider, complaining to the German consul at Callao. German crews of those days were accustomed to being harshly treated.

Upon all the sailing ships, irrespective of nationality, the work was hard, the weather was hard, the crew and officers were hard. They had to be, to

The violent rolling of the ship threatens to smash the chronometers along with everything else in the cabin. The captain protects his precious instruments as best he can until the ship rights herself. (*The Graphic*)

survive. At the risk of incurring comparisons with negro slavery, a twelve-hour day seemed normal aboard ship. The social behavior and conditions of today ought not to affect our understanding of the position then. Not so long ago a capable sea captain could say: "In 1907 I arrived in the Pacific, to learn that a number of ships' crews were in mutiny. This news appeared quite unbelievable to us and we were certain that our profession was about to disappear".

The penal and disciplinary code in use in the merchant navy appears harsh, even today, but it has to be remembered that the maintenance of law on land and at sea are very different matters, and special jurisdiction is required for the latter. The law distinguishes minor offenses, major offenses, misdemeanors, and crime on the high seas, the latter not necessarily implying only murder.

Wilfully losing one's ship, for instance, constitutes a maritime crime. There is, besides, a code of written laws applicable on board ship, which the captain, by virtue of his role as supreme legal authority, interprets. Beyond the fact that he cannot throw the whole crew in chains or put them under arrest—thereby endangering the safety of his ship—his word is law. On the other hand, his powers must be used with discretion, and he cannot punish before a full examination of the case has been made.

THE CAPTAIN AND LIFE ON BOARD

Turning over the pages of *L'Amicale internationale des Capitaines au long-cours cap-horniers* at St. Malo, one reads the captains' terse accounts of their life at sea, written in their own hands. Here are recorded a wealth of personal details: sailing dates, shipping lines and names of individual ships, ranks obtained, date of masters' certificates, first command, particular incidents during voyages, groundings, shipwrecks and notable storms. The struggles to round Cape Horn, the endless hours on watch, the agonizing decisions to be taken, the reliance upon the captain's skill and courage, the heavy weight of his responsibilites—all come to life in the old pages.

In moments of peril, petty quarrels were put aside and no one disputed the captain's supreme authority and wisdom. At such times, even crews nursing a grievance subordinated their claims and rights. The captain's rare compliment: "It is good" was sufficient for them. Perfect accord between the captain and his crew was thus the uppermost sentiment, and the old complaints were buried in times of crisis. Even if the officers fed on chicken and the men on lard, when the storm came they were all equal. The old man, in oilskins and seaboots, remained on the poop for 48 hours, swept with spray and numbed with cold—just as his crew did. Their gratitude came at the end of the voyage; when they were paid off they would often bring small gifts to their captain—a model, a ship in a bottle, a walking stick, made from a shark's vertebrae and the beak of an albatross for the handle—which they had made themselves during their rare moments of leisure.

In retirement the men always began their reminiscences: "I was sailor aboard the *Président Félix Faure*, Captain Stéphan", or: "I was mate of the *Antonin* under Captain Lecoq", thus closely associating the ship with a particular captain, and unconsciously emphasizing that they would not have been so lucky if it had been otherwise.

A shark's vertebrae threaded to a metal rod, a ferrule of carved wood; and the beak of an albatross made a very elegant cane. Often given by the crew to their captain at the end of a good voyage. *(Lacroix Collection)*

Straw-hatted on the poop, the captain traces out the lines of a new sail, delicate work. The sailors seated at the right, stitch with needle and palm. How many thousands of stitches to a 25-meter sail, how many hours of patient toil? *(Lacroix Collection)*

On board *L'Union*; a lesson on the anatomy of shark—the fins will be used for a soup. On the left of the photograph is Captain Le Mentec, in straw hat and slippers. *(Mariners Museum, Saint-Malo)*

On board *Le Cassard*. On the poop, beside the water butt, its copper hoops gleaming after being polished by the ship's boy. The time for photography; it was with such large cameras, as the Kodak held by the first mate, that pictures were then taken, even up the rigging in bad weather. *(Mariners Museum, Saint-Malo)*

Apart from preparing the journal, doing his accounts and reports, the captain invariably had his own hobby.

Keeping the ship in good order was a favorite subject of discussion between the captain and his officers; they spoke of the rusting of the ship's plates, the paintwork, the state of the gear and rigging, and plans to put this or that program into operation. Often the captain supervised the making of sails himself and the ship's sailing qualities expressed his own character. Some were over cautious, and ordered all sail to be hauled in at the first sign of bad weather for fear of damage; others boldly carried full canvas right to the last possible moment, and did not hesitate to take full advantage of the first puff of wind.

Yet others were interested in science, or meteorology, or medicine, and were able to perform miracles out of the pitiful stock of remedies in the cabinet. To pass the time, the captains did odd jobs, read or wrote letters; a number of them played a musical instrument—the piano, the flute, the violin, or even the horn. Others sketched, painted or coached their crews in cricket, boxing or rowing in preparation for matches when they returned to port. Other hobbies on board were fishing, catching sea birds, or, if the conditions were suitable, photography. For the latter they risked clambering up the masts or along the boom in order to take snaps with their primitive box cameras. The prints, poorly made, have come down to us yellow and faded; but, at least, something can be seen, and they possess great historical interest today.

These professional recluses used to pass many days, even weeks, without speaking more than half a dozen words to each other during the day. They would hurry through their meals in the saloon, the only sound being the clatter of cutlery. And then, one day, they might feel loquacious and demand an audience; thereupon they could be seen striding the quarterdeck, flanked by the first mate and lieutenant, both badly in need of sleep. Their conversation might cease almost as soon as it had begun, and their subordinates

A group of albatrosses taken on board the *Richelieu*.

Bowling along in fine weather with full canvas; the captain is content. On board the four-masted *Nord*, one of the finest vessels in the Bordes fleet, 99 meters long and 5,150 tons gross tonnage. (*Lacroix Collection*)

wondered: "What sort of mood will the old man be in tomorrow?" Their humors were as changeable as a barometer; good in stormy weather, bad in calm, excited the day before reaching port, melancholy in fog, impatient in port.

Some were colorful personalities, including the captain who played the hunting horn, as described in Commander Hayett's charming: *Us et Coutumes*. And who can ever forget the delightful story told by R. Rauh in *Der Albatros*?

In the year 1905, Captain Jochensen of the four-masted barque *Pindos* of Hamburg rounded Cape Horn with a cargo of cement for San Pedro, California. After having passed through the southeast trades, the ship entered the doldrums. Not a breath of wind for several days. Jochensen became as furious as a caged lion and tacked his ship endlessly to port and starboard in an effort to find a breeze; but the sea remained like a millpond.

The God of Winds remained deaf to his pleas and the ship lay in a dead calm, which threatened to jeopardize a voyage which up to then had been very speedy. Then Jochensen decided to stake his all; he found an old pair of carpet slippers, twirled them round his head so that the Gods could see, and then pitched them into the sea. But the Gods remained unmoved; undeterred, Jochensen reappeared on deck brandishing a bottle of brandy. Removing the cork, he took a swig and then with a theatrical gesture threw it overboard, crying: "Your good health!"

This second sacrifice appeared to move the God of the winds, because scarcely was the ceremony over before small wavelets began to ruffle the ocean's surface. As one man, the captain and the officer on watch shouted: "Man the braces!" The sails began to fill and, little by little, the *Pindos* glided forward. Apparently, in the heat of the moment,

The sails are the ship's motor; they must receive the greatest care and attention. On board the *Port Jackson*. *(National Maritime Museum, Greenwich)*

Jochensen had thrown the label and the method of manufacture along with the bottle of brandy, because the spirit was so much to the wind god's taste that a violent south-easterly storm soon made up the four days which the *Pindos* had lost in the doldrums.

So many men, so many characters, so many fates: and when the old "shellbacks"—as the English captains were called—looked back upon their memories of the past, it warmed the cockles of their hearts. Fate had added miles to their log lines . . .

"MISTER MATE"

The law, the shipowner and the broker recognized the captain. But who recognized his mate? He was called "Mr. Mate" by his captain, "Mr." by the crew and persons ashore. His cabin was tiny and undistinguished; in any case, he was hardly ever there—being the first to rise, the last to retire, and always at everyone's beck and call. This was why the mate was affectionately known as the ship's dog, faithfully serving the ship and his master.

Sometimes he was a middle-aged man who had never been in command. Why? Usually there was a background of a break in service or insufficient qualifications shown in the company's books. More often he was a young man gaining experience for his sixty months' navigation qualification, which was required before he gained his master's ticket. He soon found that he had bargained for too much rather than too little, as he bent to his work under a hail of reproaches from the captain.

The mate was in charge of the crew on board ship, which explains why American and German captains preferred husky types so that the men were kept in order. He was responsible for discipline and, if he did not give out punishments himself, he referred them to the captain, a thankless task. In order to save money, most of the crew were paid off as soon as the ship reached a European port, and the captain himself quitted the ship, leaving the mate to take charge of cleaning up.

In his *Mirror of the Sea*, Joseph Conrad described how he became mate for the first time in his life, and spent several weeks of the winter of 1881–1882 in Amsterdam, alone aboard a sailing ship except for a Dutch watchman, and waiting for a cargo which the barges could not bring because the canals were frozen over. When it came at last, he had to keep a watchful eye on the stevedores and the stowage of the cargo, because on his ability depended the prospects of future promotion.

In harbor, the mate rigged up the derricks and the winches and organized the crew into its various duties. He had a special responsibility during unloading to ensure that the weight in the holds remained centrally balanced for safety reasons, ensuring that the ballast did not shift forward or aft to affect the ship's trim. At the end of a hard day, the captain coming back from ashore in the whaler, might greet him with: "And how many tons today?" When the long-suffering mate had given the answer, he might receive the dry rejoinder: "Ah! Well, Mister Mate, the German behind has managed to take on two hundred more".

At sea, the mate organized the port watch, on twelve-hour duty, which did not prevent him looking after his men as well. In several ships, he was a familiar figure in blue denims and clogs, squinting through the sextant to take the meridian. So much of the upkeep of the ship depended on him: combatting rust, looking after the paintwork, periodical checks on the rigging, masts, anchors and chains; examining the cargo in port and at sea; maintaining the sheers, winches, capstans, boiler, windlass and steam pipes; replacing worn-out ropes and blocks; organizing makeshift repairs and jury-rigs; supervising re-rigging and re-masting, or alterations to the sails, as circumstances demanded in certain ports, or in order to pass under certain bridges. It was up to him to train an efficient boatswain and crew, in whom he had absolute confidence. Otherwise it was a continuous struggle, with poor results; and at the end of the voyage, there would be a bad report to the shipowners that put an end to his hopes of a future command.

Aboard ship, the mate's orders were not always well received by the old boatswains and veteran seamen, who never failed to grumble. Great subtlety and understanding had to be shown by the mate as he walked the tightrope between the captain and the lower deck hands. His best friends on board were usually the pilot or the lieutenant.

Mealtimes were often an ordeal; hurriedly taken in silence with tension in the air. Many captains took a delight—and who can blame this human weakness?—in making their mates start the conversation. If all was well, the captain would be full of praise or agreement; if not, reproaches soon fell upon the unfortunate mate's head. This pantomime was normal aboard ocean-going ships, but not universal; in some, great friendships were formed between captains and their officers.

Between supervising the painting and inspecting the rigging, the officer on watch must not omit to take a sight. On board *Le Cassard*. (*Mariners Museum, Saint-Malo*)

LIEUTENANTS AND PILOTS

If the position of a young first mate was difficult, what about the lieutenant, with or without his "ticket"? Much depended on his ability to mix socially and fit in between the ship's commander and the older members of the crew.

The first lieutenant sometimes had his certificate and was waiting his time to succeed as mate. His main duty was looking after the sails, and the men of the starboard watch under his direct control comprised the best sailmakers in the crew. With them, he supervised the preparation of new sails and kept a record of their dimensions and condition.

The first lieutenant's watch, like that of the mate, was frequently spent in busying himself with a pot of paint or a marlinespike. Like the rest of the crew he was often dressed in blue overalls; he lived in a tiny cabin on the starboard side and like the mate was entirely subservient to the captain's bidding. On the smaller ships, the boatswain often acted as lieutenant. Usually an older man who spoke little, he exerted authority by reason of his long experience at sea.

The second lieutenant was always a young man, often in his 'teens; formerly the pilot, he shared the watch with the mate and frequently sported a small moustache as evidence of his maturity. His province was the ship's books and charts, and everything connected with navigation. In addition, he was the captain's secretary and kept his papers in order. He also wound up the ship's clocks every day, and, if there was no third lieutenant aboard, took over the thankless task of the storeroom. When the rations were issued he weighed the portions of food and measures of wine. It was a thankless occupation because no one was ever satisfied: the captain, anxious over the dwindling supplies; the crew, certain they were not getting their right share; the cook, always labelled the "arch-robber" of the ration stores. It required plenty of spirit to function under these conditions.

The second lieutenant was also the ship's rat-catcher, and the hunter of all the other nameless creatures, which he pursued with hurricane lamp in the dark recesses of the storeroom. Quite a disenchantment for a lad of twenty who had run away from the village store and gone to sea on a Cape Horner dreaming of adventures and white sails crowding! The livestock in the bows were also in his charge and he fed the pigs, the cows and the hens. After all this, he was glad to stand watch on the poop, beneath the slap of the sails along the yards.

In the English and German merchant navies, the young officers gradually acquired their certificates of competence, depending on their experience of navigation and the number of voyages made. This was particularly the case of English apprentices, who had to have the sea in their blood to endure four, five or six years service doing everyone's bidding.

In France, a youth who was beyond the age of cabin boy or apprentice could only sign on as pilot, and not as an extra seaman or officer. The seventeen-year old lad was taken on—provided he paid for his keep—after a recommendation from a relative or friend, which was sent to the shipowners. The apprentice pilot, unpaid, shared the deckhouse with his superiors. At once he became the friend or foe of the crew, boatswain or petty officers. "I came aboard the French three-masted barque *Versailles* on Tuesday 25 November 1902", one reads in the young pilot Ravasse's autobiography:

Apprentices of the *Port Jackson* fishing for dorado and bonito from the bobstay of the bowsprit. (*National Maritime Museum, Greenwich*)

Love of the sea, and the lure of the unknown as personified by the great sailing ships, sometimes encouraged adventurous young lads to become stowaways. Hunger would drive them from their hiding place. The captain makes a show of anger but the courage of the little chap is after his own heart. The youngster is instantly made cabin boy, his zeal heightened by the attentions of the mate's boot. (*After a painting by Anton Otto Fischer*)

Impressions durant mon premier voyage. "I was introduced to the captain who seemed very charming, if a little brusque. I did not meet the first mate, but had ample opportunity to get to know the lieutenants. They were all very friendly and helpful, showing me that evening where to make my purchases. These were very numerous, as one could not set out on such a long voyage without preparing for every contingency. The next morning the captain took me to the harbor office at Dunkirk, where I was signed on as a member of the crew. On leaving the captain said something, which put me on my mettle. These were his words: 'Now you see, my lad, that in future if you get into the slightest trouble you will come up before judges in uniform and not judges in court.' Then he turned me over to the mate".

So you can picture our little pilot boy busily shining the copper on the poop, the drinking tank, the wheel, the clock, the compass-binnacle and holystoning the handrails and the deck. This was performed under the watchful eye of the mate, who was inwardly amused by the fact that he had done just the same only a few years before: down on all fours, with bucket and scrubbing brush, with one's heart in one's mouth and ready to weep.

Many of these youngsters made voyages, which they recalled for the rest of their lives, like service in the army. Some, only a few years later, rose to take command of the great Cape Horn sailing ships, of which they had dreamed in their youth.

THE MEN OF THE DECKHOUSE

The boatswain—the master, after the captain, after God—ruled over the crew in his infinite wisdom. Former cabin boy, former apprentice, former seaman, topman and quartermaster, he knew so much about the sea and how to wield a marlinespike that any complaints were quickly silenced. Big of hands and heart, he was the toughest among a crew of tough men, and all of them gave way before him.

Thus Conrad said of him:

Of all the creatures which lived upon land or sea, only the sailors did not allow themselves to be deceived of the truth; only they cared for the bo'suns as much as the captain, because they knew that the bo'sun, as they themselves, was the body and soul of the ship.

The first fresh meat since setting sail. It was not enough to be butcher; one had to be cook as well. (*Mariners Museum, Saint-Malo*)

No part of the ship escaped the boatswain's attention, not a rivet, cable, pulley, rope, plank nor awning. Years after he had left the ship, he could recite with his eyes closed details of dimensions, weight and area, with incredible accuracy. A man of great skill and ingenuity, he was the only one aboard to whom the captain, figuratively speaking, doffed his cap. As well as his knowledge, he possessed a wonderful ability to size up a man at once and to find the right words when needed. In the worst moments of a voyage he stood firm.

How could the captain or mate have carried on without the boatswain, whose shrill whistle summoned the weary men from their slumbers below, like the trumpets of the last day of Judgment? If there was already a first lieutenant on board, the boatswain did not maintain a watch, but in bad weather, whatever the time of day or night, he came into his own.

Another inmate of the deckhouse was the cook. No watch for him, no hauling in the sails with pandemonium aloft; undisturbed nights, perhaps, but he—the "doctor" as he was frequently called—paid dearly for this privilege.

The crew never spared him their sarcasm: "Shammer, spouter, poisoner, ration-stealer ... " The poor man might have been a chef at the Savoy or a village baker, who wanted to go to sea. His job in the galley was to try to compose a culinary symphony, with only two or three notes at his command. He made coffee in the morning, the mid-day meal and supper; as we often read in novels, he was also ready to serve something hot during the ship's moments of crisis.

The cook ate by himself in the kitchen; on many of the English and French ships he was a negro. The much maligned cook often got his own back in the evening, when the cabin boy waiting at table brought back the news and remarks made by the officers as they ate. He thus became, in his retired position in the galley, aware of many things and a holder of secrets.

On the Bordes Company's sailing ships, the normal menu for the crew was lard, potatoes, bully beef (often referred to as "monkey"), beans, salted cod, soup, biscuits and coffee. Possible extras were a jar of pickles, fried potatoes and a chicken, on Thursdays and Sundays. But the cook's reputation stood or fell by his twice-weekly baking, according to whether his loaves of bread were crisp, light and crusty or indigestible and as heavy as the "sounding lead".

Between them, the cook and the second lieutenant slaughtered the pigs, the first one usually on leaving the Bay of Biscay, the second on approaching Cape Horn. When that happened the crew temporarily enjoyed double rations. After slaughtering, the cook took the carcass down to the salting-tub after which it was cut in pieces, and black puddings, sausages and pâtés were prepared, just as in a butcher's shop.

In fine weather, the catering was not too difficult; but around Cape Horn the cook would find himself rolling about in seaboots in his narrow galley, choked by the fumes and constantly banging his head against the pots and pans. If the soup was not ready at mealtimes, he was roundly cursed; even more so when the chickens were tough eating, although he could hardly be blamed for their muscles having become so hard due to the ship's perpetual rolling.

In some ports the cook had to provide thirty or forty extra meals for stevedores during unloading, in addition to the crew's dinners. And for all this work, forty hours a week for an eight weeks voyage, he was only paid 110 francs a month.

The carpenter also lived in the deckhouse. A former ordinary hand, he qualified as leading seaman because of his wood- and iron-working skill. If the sailors were handy with the marlinespike, and the sailmaker's palm and needle, the carpenter was more concerned with the actual parts of the ship. Pumps, ship's boats, spars, tackle blocks, capstans and everything made of wood and iron were his province. After storm damage they could be repaired by him to look as new. A movable workbench, a personal set of tools and a portable forge comprised the equipment of this invaluable member of the ship's company. Although not officially on call during the night watches, the carpenter was not averse on occasion to revive old memories and stand-to on deck, as good as the next man.

The latter-day sailing ships, with drastically reduced crews, were formidable things to manage. It must be remembered that the accepted ratio of 150

Despite the bad weather (note the seaboots), and a hand injured in some accident, there is always the pleasure of modelling ships in bottles. (*A. Hayet Collection*)

The carpenter of the *Port Jackson* at work on the deck.

An improvement upon the daily menu on board the *Tijuca*; a large dorado being cut up.

square meters of canvas per man had gradually fallen to only 40 by the turn of the century. To compensate for this loss of manpower, boilers, steam engines, winches and windlasses were installed. At this juncture the engineer appeared on board the sailing ship.

In France, the engineers usually came from Le Havre, St. Nazaire or Paris. They were looked upon as strange creatures by the crew, robots whose speech and behavior fell quite outside normal life on board. These curious misfits—often however wide awake in other directions—were in the early days an object of amusement, due mainly to their ignorance of purely maritime matters. Their kingdom comprised the steam-boilers, engines, winches, and pipelines. They often helped the carpenters in repair work because their mechanical training had taught them how to forge, tap, thread and fit together all the ironwork aboard. Unfortunately the tools available did not match their ability; usually only hammers, anvils and monkey wrenches were to hand. The engineer dossed down with the carpenter in the deckhouse and shared his meals with him. He worked ten to twelve hours a day, stood no night watches and remained blissfully ignorant of the ship's maneuvers and course.

Hauling in the square canvas aboard the *Dieppedale*. (The smudges on the sails are due to the poor quality of the early photograph.) *(Augé Collection)*

236

What were the owners thinking about when they ordered the crews to put on these "Potemkin" caps? Although they had only to be worn on special occasions or for photographs, they were not very popular, judging by the expressions on the faces of the crew. The crew of the *Léon Blum*. (*A. Hayet Collection*)

JACK TAR, Prince of Storm-clouds, Duke of Marlinespike, Marquess of Palm and Cable-wire

"What made you become a sailor?" He started, regarded us vacantly, and then replied, as if to himself, "One foggy evening I seemed to find the way . . . I knew this was the way I wanted to go" (Bernard Frank: *The Yard*). . . . .

What other choice was there, as the eldest of ten or twelve children of a Breton or Welsh fisherman's family? What else, when he had been on his father's boat between the ages of eight and twelve, when his father, grandfather and great-grandfather had done the same thing and his schoolmates were already at sea? He had to follow suit.

Strapping lads of twelve or thirteen began as cabin boys aboard the ocean-going ships. Certainly it was not the worst way to start. The voyages might be long, but there were compensations being cabin boy to the officers and servant in the deckhouse. It was infinitely better than being a slave aboard a coaster or Newfoundland banker, beaten and terrorized by a brutal master. If the cabin boy did not earn very much, at least he learnt his job and cost his family nothing. He lived in the small deckhouse with his superiors or in the cabin and did not stand night watches. If there were two, one looked after the stern quarters, the other the bow, and both served the officers at table, ran errands, and did the other minor duties on board. When the boatswain rolled his eyes and grabbed them by the ears, trouble was in store.

The boys learnt the ropes little by little and there were plenty of ways of teaching them. Holding a capstan at arm's length for an hour; numerous

A model of a five-masted German barque in a bottle. Sailor's work. (*Mariners Museum, Saint-Malo*)

English rolling pins. Given by sailors to their wives or sweethearts, these pastry rolling pins of opaline, decorated with ships or romantic verse, were plights of troth. Normally purely decorative, holes were sometimes pierced at the ends and they were used as salt-cellars. Contrary to popular belief, their fragility did not allow their being thrown into the sea to carry messages to the crew's loved ones. (*Mariners Museum, Saint-Malo*)

circuits of the deck under a deluge of buckets of water; astride the bowsprit in bad weather or in cold; a spell in the crow's-nest—were all lessons in this hard school.

By their second voyage, the cabin boys had risen to become apprentices and were a little better paid; thereafter they became, in time, able seamen and ultimately first class seamen. There was a break at the age of twenty for French boys for military service, which might detain them four years before they re-engaged. Some took the easy way out and left the sailing ships for steam. But the real seamen returned to their first love—the sailing ships, despite the poverty it brought. Seventy-five francs a month was their reward for turning their backs on progress and a comfortable life ashore. They returned because only at sea could they find the comradeship they sought.

So here is our lad, older now, coming aboard again. On what basis will he be signed on? He must conform both to the mercantile code and the company's regulations:

Article 1—At sea, and while the ship is in harbor, every enrolled man is instructed to perform his duties in all weathers, particularly those relating to getting under way, anchoring, working the ship, and in person to being properly turned out, and at all times when the safety of the ship or its cargo are in jeopardy.

Article 2—Excluding the above conditions, the enrolled man is not liable for further duty outside his turn at watch, but he cannot refuse to obey orders given to him.

Article 3—Any work undertaken outside the circumstances specified in Article 1, or off the ship, or relating to the handling of coal or other cargo, is classified as supplementary, in extra time.

Article 4—The hours of duty are regulated according to conditions at sea: four-hour watches alternating with four-hour periods off duty.

One reads in the contract used by the Company of Nantes Sailing Ship-owners, the following passage:

The crew undertake to carry out all loading and unloading of cargo, the maintenance of the ship and all work connected with towing and with manning launches and ship's boats, as is necessary in regard to the ship.

The captain is also empowered to order the crew on deck in the afternoons when he judges it necessary, in order that the upkeep of the ship and her boats should be maintained, between latitudes 30° N. and 30° S.

The duty was regulated on board according to a time-table, which varied little in every merchant navy. The crew were divided into two watches:

A pretty example of patient craftsmanship: the crucifixion in a bottle. (*Mariners Museum, Saint-Malo*)

First Watch		*Second Watch*	
0000–0400	on duty	0000–0400	rest
0400–0730	rest	0400–0800	on duty
0730–0800	breakfast	0800–0830	breakfast
0800–1200	on duty	0830–1130	rest
1200–1230	dinner	1130–1200	dinner
1230–1600	rest	1200–1600	on duty
1600–1800	on duty	1600–1730	rest
1800–1830	supper	1730–1800	supper
1830–2000	rest	1800–2000	on duty
2000–2400	on duty	2000–2400	rest

MARINE ET COLONIES.

RÔLE POUR LE LONG COURS, LE CABOTAGE, LE BORNAGE ET LA GRANDE PÊCHE.

ARMEMENT(1) *en long cours*
ANNÉE 1873.

L'Amiral Jurien de la Gravière 3 mâts

allant a(2) *Long cours*

RÔLE D'ÉQUIPAGE *de dix-train mats* , construit en l'an 1865 *à St Malo* , du port de *441.13* tonneaux, muni d'une machine de   chevaux, tirant d'eau, chargé,   mètres   centimètres, et non chargé,   mètres   centimètres, et non chargé,   pont, gaillard, appartenant à Mᵐᵉ *Secour Parterle & Cⁱᵉ* armé a *Nantes* par   , sous le commandement du sⁱ *Baudouin*

QUARTIER
d' *Nantes*

PORT
Nantes

PIÈCES DONT EST MUNI LE CAPITAINE

Un certificat du directeur de la poste aux lettres.
(Dépêche du 16 août 1816.)

ARTILLERIE
ARMES ET MUNITIONS.
(Ordonnance du 12 juillet 1847.)

ESPÈCE.	VALEUR.

ARMÉ SOUS LE Nº *261*

IMMATRICULÉ AU QUARTIER
Nantes
f° 510 nº 1529

(1) Mettre ici l'une de ces trois indications :
AU LONG COURS.
AU CABOTAGE OU AU BORNAGE.
À LA PÊCHE { de la baleine.
{ de la morue.

(2) Indiquer ici la destination pour les navires armés au long cours.

Les salaires de l'équipage courent du *19 Mars* 1873, et ont cessé le   187   inclusivem.ᵗ

DÉSARMÉ AU PORT
187   nº

CONDITIONS GÉNÉRALES DE L'ENGAGEMENT.

L'équipage s'engage à suivre le navire dans toutes ses opérations commerciales et renonce à la faculté exceptée en cas de naufrage, de maladie ou de revente du navire à l'étranger. Au bout d'un an le capitaine aura la faculté de remplacer le vin par la boisson du pays.

APOSTILLES ET MOUVEMENTS CONSTATÉS PAR : 1° Les administrateurs de la marine ; 2° Les consuls ; 3° Procès-verbaux en forme.	NOMS, PRÉNOMS, ÉPOQUE ET LIEU DE NAISSANCE, FILIATION, DOMICILE, TAILLE ET SIGNES PARTICULIERS, quartiers, grade au service, spécialité professionnelle.	A : Fonctions à bord. B : Gages ou parts. C : Taxe par unité. D : Décompte des services à bord.	AVANCES au départ.	DÉCOMPTE AU DÉSARMEMENT. Montant des salaires (gages ou parts)	Frais de Justice (D.P. ou autres)
Nº 1	*Baudouin, Jean Marie* né le 17 8bre 1831 à *Cancale Ille et Vilaine* fils de *Jean Marie* et de *Modeste* , domicilié à taille : un mèt. signes partic. : Inscrit à *Cancale* f° X nº *14* comme *Cap.ⁿᵉ au Long cours* spécialité : Incorporé à dater du 18	*Capitaine* 250	750		
Nº 2	*Besnard, Julien Marie* né le 12 juin 1850 à *St Briac Ille et Vilaine* fils de *Julien Marie* et de *Agathe Godet* , domicilié à taille : un mèt. signes partic. : Inscrit à *St Malo* f° X nº comme *Cap.ⁿᵉ au L. C.* spécialité : Incorporé à dater du 18	*Second* 150	450		
Nº 3 *L'ligue à sa femme Anne Bihan demeurant à la Bernerie un mois sur trois mois soit trésorerie agréée par le Commissaire de l'Inscription maritime.*	*Chesneau, Jean Louis* né le 27 Xbre 1825 aux *Moutiers Loire Infᵉ* fils de *Jean Louis* et de *Marguerite Caillaud* , domicilié à taille : un mèt. signes partic. : Inscrit à *Bernerie* f° X nº *16* comme *Maître au Long cours* spécialité : Incorporé à dater du 18	*Mᵉ d'Équipage* 85	255		
Nº 4 *L'ligue à sa femme Anne Hélène Vaillant demeurant à Montoir un mois sur trois mois soit trésorerie agréée par le Commissaire de l'Inscription maritime.*	*Morand, Jean Baptiste* né le 28 9bre 1844 à *Montoir Loire Infᵉ* fils de *Jean Marie* et de *Perrine Poitrin* , domicilié à taille : un mèt. signes partic. : Inscrit à *St Nazaire* f° 3333 nº *136* comme *Matelot* spécialité : Incorporé à dater du 18	*Maître Charpentier* 75	225		

Muster roll of the three-masted *Amiral Julien de la Gravière*, commissioned at Nantes. All ships carried such a list, being an official statement of their complement. If a seamen was registered on the muster roll, he was bound by all the provisions of maritime law. *(Nantes archives)*

Danish sea chest, *ca.* 1870, to hold the sailor's few precious possessions. (*Danish Maritime Museum, Elsinore*)

Smoking tobacco, chewing tobacco and soap: the only articles for sale on board. (*Nantes archives*)

The second watch was invariably summoned on deck during the afternoon, to undertake general maintenance between 1 and 5 p.m. Thanks to this ingenious schedule, and the mounting of short afternoon watches—4 to 6, and 6 to 8—both watches were fully interchangeable, so that neither had to undertake the same two hours running. The mealtimes also suited the cook: breakfast 0730–0830; dinner 1130–1230; and supper 1730–1830.

The crew therefore worked fourteen, sometimes sixteen, hours a day. In English and German ships, Sunday was respected to the extent that, outside the watches, the crew were not on deck duty during the afternoon. By French law, the granting of this weekly period of rest was left to the individual shipowners to decide. Until 1907—an important year for maritime legislation—and even afterwards, a seaman was not in a position to claim pay for more than the hours he had actually worked. Commenting on seamen's conditions aboard sailing ships about 1900, André Moufflet wrote:

> The sailor who broke his contract was branded as a deserter, and the entire legal apparatus was directed in favor of the shipowner compelling him to undertake the service he had signed on for.

How could the sailor sign on if he knew neither the captain nor the ship-owner? He went to the "crimp", who dealt in the hiring and engagement of crew. The "crimp" received from the shipowner a sum of money, half of which was paid in order to engage men, and the balance as soon as they were brought on board.

A cabin boy was paid three francs, a seaman five and a boatswain ten. But these fixed rates were often exceeded in practice; as much as 50 francs or even $\frac{2}{3}$ of the total sum being given on occasions. A law promulgated in 1904 put a stop to these abuses. Henceforth the "crimp" had no hold upon the seaman, and his only function was to act on behalf of captains and shipowners looking for crew; as such, he was the shipowners' representative at the moment of signing-on and responsible for the sailor being given three months' pay in advance. Unfortunately for the recruit, the "crimp" also sold clothes and equipment for the voyage—at a price—so that the former had little of his advanced money left by the time he had stumbled out of the shop.

Further improvements in the recruiting system took place about 1900, when seamen were entitled by the Marine Office to carry an "embarkation license", verifying their identity and terms of service. But here again the nefarious "crimps" took care to obtain these permits from the young recruits—perhaps in pawn for purchases—and thus had them in their power. It was tragic to see how these simple, brave fellows became enmeshed in the schemes of unscrupulous shipchandlers and other rogues. Often it was better to serve under a brutal captain than fall into the clutches of these oily and obsequious gentlemen, against whom they were powerless. When the young sailor was in harbor, waiting to sail, his only concern was the "crimp". But when he returned at the end of a voyage, he might see the quay thronged with strangers, eager to help him spend his money. Offers to stay at lodgings kept by a friend or a charming hostess came thick and fast.

The cost of lodgings might be very modest—4 or 5 francs a day—but our naive sailor wanted to "paint the town red". He drank, gave parties for friends he hardly knew, and in a few days his hard-earned 600 or 800 francs had gone up in smoke. If he spent more, it was only by signing away future wages in a loan, which was repayable at 50 francs per month as a seaman, 75 francs as a leading seaman and 90–115 francs as a boatswain.

The combined efforts of the "crimp" and the hostess were therefore well able to force Jack Tar back to sea soon enough. But what about the seamen's hostels, one might ask, where daily board was only 2 francs? The answer comes from a member of the naval recruiting board, who wrote in 1898: "These establishments are contrary to our interests. Seamen are quartered there under police surveillance, compelled to keep fixed hours, and submit to the moral guidance of almoner and matron." The men just back from the Horn obviously had better ideas of how to spend their shore leave.

It is not necessary to generalize; without the "crimps" and hostesses, the men would have got back to their ships very ill-satisfied, deprived of vivid memories of carousing and girls. As for personal gear, they normally took with them seaboots, sailcloth trousers and shirt, sou'wester, oilskins, one or two overalls, underwear, slippers and socks. The rest they often made at sea—cloth cap and rope-soled sandals. One other item they also brought for their bunks—a miserable straw palliasse costing about three francs, known aboard English ships as the "donkey's breakfast". The poor seaman, thrown from side to side by the ship's rolling, his clothes often soaked through or damp, had to lie prostrate on this crude bed, or sway in a hammock. Sometimes it was possible to improve matters by padding the mattress with seaweed, covering it with wool or cotton and adding a pillow of old sailcloth, stuffed with wood shavings from the carpenter's shop.

Once the men were aboard with their kitbags and chests, they were immediately divided into the two watches. The mate and the lieutenant or boatswain took a roll-call and then selected their men, one by one. When this was done, the men were immediately set to work. From that moment, their

Thirty to forty men in the crew, and only a small medicine chest with a few flasks of remedies. *(Mariners Museum, Saint-Malo)*

Since the age of Colbert, a law of the sea—three months' pay in advance of departure. *(Mariners Museum, Saint-Malo)*

243

Keeping fit; a boxing match on the poop of the *Versailles*. *(Mariners Museum, Saint-Malo)*

professional and social life began. The sturdier ones soon made their mark, while the weaker members fitted in as best they could.

Gradually the rough edges were knocked off and a real crew began to emerge. The men became aware of the characteristics of the ship, their officers and companions. As chaos could not be accepted on board, it depended upon cooperation between the officers and the older and more experienced sailors to achieve harmony. In this respect, it became tacitly understood that certain functions were reserved for the best seamen—such as easing off the sheets. In such cases there was no question of the inexperienced members of the crew being jealous; they admired those who could do it.

The different atmosphere aboard British, Scandinavian and American ships always surprised French crews, which by law were composed only of people of their own country. The officers of the former had to be extremely capable in order to control these Towers of Babel. Some French captains faced the same problem when they had no alternative but to "shanghai" in American ports, in order to man their ships.

I had to ship [wrote Captain Griénais] some extraordinary characters, when it became necessary to replace some of my men who had fallen sick. For the voyage back to France from Chile, I had an Australian jockey and a Canadian painter, and it was a mystery how these two poor devils had got stranded on such an inhospitable place as the Tarapaca coast in the first place. They had to be fully togged up with clothes, since all their money had been taken by a "crimp". But we managed to give them sailcloth trousers, seaboots and wooden clogs, made by the carpenter. They had a pretty rough time, because we had to take them on at a much higher rate of pay than our own men (225 francs against

A melancholy register—the sick list. Fractures, cuts, boils, sunburn, blows, dysentery. Only a few very serious cases obtained exemption from all duties. *(Nantes Archives)*

90), so there was bad feeling all round. On another voyage, I remember, a husky young Scandinavian sailor tried to take the law into his own hands but a few turns round the foremast soon cooled him down until we reached port.

Another instance of the difficulty of sailing with mixed crews may be found in R. Rauh's account in *Der Albatros* of the voyage of the four-masted barque *Pindos* of Hamburg. The *Pindos*, under her notorious Captain Jochensen, swept magnificently one day into the harbor of San Pedro, California, and dropped anchor with great precision. But it was learned that the crew had been fed very badly on board the German ship, so the American vessels in the port invited them to share their victuals. A local journalist made the most of the situation: "Famine aboard the *Pindos*, while her captain relaxes at a spa ... American sailors come to the rescue of the crew of the *Pindos* ...".

When Jochensen, "the devil of Hamburg"*, returned on board, he was bellowing with rage and threatened to take it out of the men during the voyage home. But the next morning, four of the crew had left the port in an American schooner and during the days that followed, many others deserted, until only two officers and four seamen remained willing to sail back to Hamburg with the captain. So Jochensen had to find another crew. The first attempt produced a horrible crowd of lascars who stayed on the ship only long enough to throw a tureen of soup at the captain's feet. The next comprised the human dregs of the local prison at Sing-Sing; this rabble came on board, ate a meal, spat on the deck, refused to work, demanded to be paid and then left the ship.

Twice outwitted, Jochensen determined to succeed the third time. He returned to the town, leaving his two officers and four men with instructions to cast off the moorings, ready for the ship to be towed out of San Pedro harbor. Soon a tug appeared, with Jochensen aboard surrounded by a group of strangers.

One by one they were hoisted aboard the deck of the *Pindos*, while Jochensen shut himself up in his cabin with the "crimp" to get down to some hard bargaining. The crew later surrounded the new arrivals while they were still asleep and relieved them of their pistols, hatchets, bludgeons and American knuckledusters. The sails were set, the weather was fine and, for the moment, Jochensen could retire untroubled to his cabin, while the *Pindos* set course for Taltal, Chile.

The next morning, the loyal members of the crew, with revolvers concealed in their jackets, awakened the new intake who staggered from the hold. Jochensen, his humor restored, addressed them from the poop: "You have not come to us from the 'crimps'. If you mutiny you will be thrown into prison. That is the law in Germany, and you are on board a German ship. At this moment the *Pindos* is 100 miles from land, and only real sailors can operate a ship like her. In three or four weeks' time we shall have arrived in our home port and then you may air your grievances; but, until then don't cause trouble and let's get on with the work".

The new intake were a motley crew: two seamen and two stokers off a steamship; farm laborers, drovers and a parish beadle. Only four were capable

Sunday morning. Freshly washed and shaved, hanging the washing out on the poop of the *Richelieu*. (It looks like the captain's laundry drying on the line.)

---

*Other "devils of Hamburg" were so named for their unpleasant dispositions, tendencies towards parsimony, or uncanny skills. The most famous was Hilgendorf of *Potosi*, known as the "Devil of Hamburg" for his skill in making the most of the weather for a fast voyage.

Bare-headed, the crew listen to the captain reading the burial service. Soon, the body of their comrade, sewn up in sailcloth, will be consigned to the deep.

of scaling the masts and reaching the main yard; the rest, afraid of heights and the ship's rolling, refused to leave the deck.

On the way to Chile, the *Pindos* met very bad weather, which shifted her ballast. Having jibbed at going aloft, the new men worked below, restoring the stone ballast to its original position. As soon as Taltal was reached, they got off the ship with all speed, their sole intention being to get back to San Francisco and square accounts with the "crimp" there. Once more, Captain Jochensen faced the same problem in Chile as he had in California. But, luckily, this time some professional seamen were bailed out of the local jail, and the homeward voyage via Cape Horn passed without further incident.

What a medley of different temperaments and strange characters were revealed in men suddenly thrown together by force of circumstance. Uncommunicative they were, perhaps, in the long hours of lookout watch and working on deck and with the sails, but certainly not insensitive. Despite often humble origins, the crew managed to remain cheerful and calm, even in the worst moments.

In their life on board, many seamen regaled their audience with wonderful stories, in the forecastle or at the capstan in fine weather during the evening watch. Others revealed a capacity for infinite patience. Some were avid readers or kept private journals of the daily incidents. Occasionally one was revealed as an outstanding personality, of whom the others whispered among themselves that he must be a captain who had lost his rank. But generally the men looked after their own affairs; they might talk a lot about the ships or the captains under whom they had served, but rarely of personal matters, and it was better so.

Sometimes personal animosity got the upper hand, and an individual officer or man might be ignored by the rest. But the nature and arduousness of the work on board soon tended to bury these differences.

The finest traditions aboard the sailing ships were usually found among crews entirely composed of men from one country. Clearly there were customs and traditions peculiar to one country or another which found common expression in this way. Thus those preserved aboard French ships have been immortalized in the works of Captain Armand Hayet. How was this possible aboard American ships or even some European vessels, where the crews were mixed and frequently only passengers for a single voyage? There was a world of difference between these tyros, these awkward and clumsy louts and the dedicated, professional seamen, who were the hallmark of the noble spirit of the ocean-going sailing ships.

SAILORS' WIVES—BLACK-VEILED WOMEN OF HOPE AND DESPAIR

It was not a life which the seaman willingly chose, nor indeed any woman who had married one; but they had to accept and adapt themselves to its hardness. Women there certainly were of all kinds—married, single and those of easy virtue—for the sailors, because they were prepared to take the situation as it stood.

Maritime literature abounds with tales of captains' wives who sailed with them; who helped them at critical moments and even, if their husbands died, took over the ship and brought her back to port at the head of a mutinous crew. Others showed bravery in a shipwreck or during the perilous return in the lifeboat. Yet others were remarkable for understanding their place in the marital relationship.

One remembers Conrad's charming description of the wife of his first captain, in his book *Youth*. These women had to show a delicacy and gentleness to counterbalance authority and prestige, which was vested in their husbands as captains. Upon this point, the sailors' opinions varied. If the "lady" was genteel, it was not always very agreeable to have to watch one's language, avoid unseemly jokes, refrain from appearing naked on deck, hide one's often erotic tattoo marks and stop spitting out untimely jets of tobacco juice! However, the men were never lacking in respect. On the other hand, some sensitive captains were so jealous, that their wives' daily promenade was restricted to a small area of the poop, or even to the cabin itself. More frequent were the nautical viragos—shrews, who might or might not be tamed by the life at sea—who, as soon as they had set foot on the gangplank, turned the ship into a veritable hell.

Matrimonial discord could spread rapidly beyond the cabin and saloon, quickly reaching the ears of the men in the deckhouse, hiding like naughty schoolboys from the teacher. The unfortunate cabin boy was uplifted into the realms of qualifying as the ideal domestic. The influx of a feminine régime brought disturbing consequences: Madame's sofa, the sun-awning on deck, small helpings at table, no noise here, no singing there; a lack of

In such moments, one is master of one's ship and one's family. (*Jean Rio Collection*)

conversation, more formality in dress, no music; even morning and evening prayers, Sunday school, hymnsinging, lessons in writing and reading. Where would it all end? Mercifully, such instances were uncommon and the shipowners felt that the morality of their crews was sufficiently cared for already.

The *Thomas Stephens*, a fine wool clipper, lost her reputation as a fast sailer the day after the captain brought his wife on board. She disliked the discomfort of the ship sailing under full canvas, so it was reduced. Another example comes from Basil Lubbock's story of the American clipper *William H. Connor*. In the face of heavy weather her captain, John G. Pendleton, managed to maintain full canvas, while the unsecured articles in the cabins were thrown hither and thither. In spite of the fury of the gale and the soaking of her light clothes, Mrs. Pendleton appeared on deck and approached her husband, standing like a rock on the poop.

"Everything is flying all over the place in the cabin, my dear," she said, "don't you think some of the sails should be taken down?"

The astonishment on the good man's face on hearing this extraordinary suggestion can well be imagined—one which none of his senior officers had ever put to him throughout his whole career. He was struggling to hide his emotions when, at that moment, the main topsail came down with a crash and was carried off by the wind.

A man of intuition, the captain at once replied to his wife: "Well, there you are, my dear; there's one big sail down for you." She, a little reassured and no doubt pleased with her demonstration of nautical knowledge, then retraced her steps to the cabin. But the best part of this little story is that she had hardly got there before a new topsail had been hoisted and put in place!

Those wives, who remained on shore and only followed their husbands' interminable voyages in their imagination, deserved the greatest credit.

They stayed at home, alone, always dreading the arrival of a telegram with

Fine weather with a slight breeze. A lady and her cat enjoying the voyage aboard the *Dieppedale*, 1907. (*Photo Augé*)

Is this a suite at the Carlton Hotel? Only the decklight and the anti-rolling lamp betray the fact that one is in the saloon of a sailing ship. Captain Fraser of the four-masted barque *Lynton* enjoys family life. (*San Francisco Maritime Museum*)

the shipowners' condolences. They brought up the children, kept house and put on a brave face to the outside world. Few captains' wives met their husbands at their home ports at the conclusion of a voyage; they waited until they came home. As for the boatswains' and seamen's women—very few of whom were in fact married—the cost of going to the port put such a journey out of the question. They had to wait patiently for the arrival home of their men. Men who, moreover, were as little accustomed to being shut within four walls, as an albatross pinioned to the ship's deck. All these circumstances were difficult to endure. The children hardly knew a father who returned at such long intervals, and the mothers were in constant dread of the moment of parting once more. Often, only a worn-out ruined man remained as a companion for their old age.

When the leave was over, a further separation, sometimes for two years, ensued. They parted with mixed feelings; sad that a few weeks was insufficient time to get to know how to live together. Many men were a little bitter, but also, curiously, a little relieved to get away again. The wife took up the rhythm of her life once more, punctuated by letters received from all parts of the world; the husband returned to the reality of life on board, the only place where he felt utterly at ease.

Lastly, girl friends and prostitutes played an important part in the sailors' emotional life. The brief encounter or whirlwind romance softened the hearts of men inured to the hardships of a voyage. In addition, there were the matrons of lodging-houses and hostesses, whose motherliness and hospitality gave many sailors a welcome that could not otherwise be found, outside their own families.

Souvenirs; photographs—faded, scratched, crumpled, and damp; the snapshot of a girl with a new hair-do, popped into a letter to Yokohama; memories and images, distorted by time and distance: who can tell enough about women's influence upon the lives of the men of the sea?

A young wife happy to accompany her husband, captain of the *Dieppedale*, on the long voyage to New Caledonia, 1907. (*Augé Collection*)

Between ships one stayed 'en pension' or in hostels, and forgot for a time the monotony of the ships life and food. (*Lacroix Collection*)

4 *The Cape Horners of the West and the Pacific Trade*

THE GREAT PORTS OF THE EUROPEAN SAILING SHIPS

At the very end of the nineteenth century, there was not a port in Europe that did not boast, alongside the steamships, its quota of ocean-going sailing ships. Their crowded masts climbed higher than the bell-towers and cathedral spires.

They were to be found everywhere—in floating docks; in twos and threes, with their yards braced, lying alongside the quays; in river estuaries, anchored against the current; sometimes, moored to posts, known as "Dukes of Alba", in the roadstead, if there was no proper anchorage, in which case the cargo was discharged into lighters. Frequently the ships were berthed close to, with their bows right against the quayside and their sterns moored to a dolphin. In this position, the wonderful sweep of their stem overhung the quay, and the figurehead and boom seemed about to break into the houses alongside.

No Sunday promenaders who came to gaze upon them, thought them out of place because they knew that they were just as much a part of the contemporary scene as the steamships. Many different people saw the activity and were eager to come aboard: river pilots and harbormasters; moorers, inshore pilots, sailmakers, riggers, careeners, wharf-keepers, shipchandlers, compass-keepers, navigational instrument makers, chart sellers, dockers and stevedores. These were the professionally interested, but others were hardly less so: brokers, clerks, commercial travellers, shopkeepers, café and boarding

The entrance to the port of Le Havre at high water; one tug to two sailing ships.

house proprietors, hostesses; outfitters, craftsmen, tattooers, painters, photographers, souvenir sellers and pawnbrokers. Finally came the accordion players on the quayside, and the coachmen whose circuit of the docks was much appreciated by their fares. This whole colorful world of the sailing ships, their cargoes and their crews, has completely vanished today, never to return.

Every port has its own particular flavor and atmosphere. Bordeaux with its Quai des Chartrons, fine shipowners' residences, little cafés and gay life, was Cockayne land for the ocean sailor. Le Havre and its St. François district, full of sailors' haunts, bearing fantastic names: *The Pressure-Gauge, The Sextant, North Star*, to which the officers also resorted, in disguise. In these places, it was one man's job to hide the accordion or pianola, if the constable arrived after closing time. At Antwerp, prostitutes were to be found at Place Falcon and in the Rue Shipper. In the city's big department stores pretty shop girls sold bars of soap and writing paper to the sailors.

London had its dockland. During opening hours, vast quantities of beer were consumed in the innumerable "pubs", to wash down the fish and chips. The English coal ports were very sinister; while the stevedores propped themselves up in the bars, drinking stouts in quick succession, the pallid women roamed the mean streets of the slums, trying to profit from what remained of their charms. In Nantes, it was the Quai de la Fosse that attracted the sailors, and in Hamburg an entire district, with its shop-fronted streets became their haunt. In the noisy saloons of Sanct Pauli, thousands of seamen consumed vast quantities of pork and beer, and afterwards burst out onto the pavements to vent their quarrels.

Perhaps the most surprising feature of this period—the end of the nineteenth century—was the gross discrepancy in cargo-handling capability at the various havens. In the coal ports, loading and unloading was quickly and

An exceptional moment of friendliness between three deep-sea sailors and two policemen. The latter, called "square heads" after their headgear, entertained very different feelings towards seamen at the time the ships sailed. (*Lacroix Collection*)

View of the port of Hamburg, Sanct Pauli district in 1890. (*Société de géographie*)

mechanically performed; also, elevators were in use for the handling of grain. On the other hand, some mixed cargoes and timber could only be unloaded very laboriously by manpower or some crude machines. Horses could sometimes be used on the quayside, but all the shifting of the cargo on board and the manipulation of the capstan could only be done by men. The whole business was carried out in the bustling noise of steam-winches intermingled with the hooting of the tugs' whistles and the churning of the water, as they nudged the ships into position.

The Straits of Gibraltar witnessed the passage of sailing ships returning from the Pacific, homeward bound for Marseilles and Genoa—Frenchmen, Italians and later Americans, laden with Oregon wheat or guano. Gibraltar was a picturesque rendezvous, under the Mediterranean sun, of both the modern overseas trade and the local traffic, which had changed little since the days of Rome. Moored alongside the square-rigged three-masters, were the polacres, brigs, and schooners, manned by Mediterranean crews in motley clothes.

The larger ships from the Pacific, carried on northwards. Some entered the Gironde estuary, en route for Bordeaux; at its mouth they were normally met by a pilot cutter off Verdon—since the passage was dangerous, owing to the westerly wind, the strength of the ebb tide and the number of treacherous shoals. Occasionally, it was possible to waft in with the tide, anchors at the ready, as far up as Bacalan.

Bordeaux was traditionally the port for the West Indies, Africa and India trades—coffee, cotton, sugar, wine, etc., and also the terminus of the earliest line of sailing packets to the Pacific. Their ships were the "Peruvians", the clippers which brought the mail to and from Lima and Colon. In company with the ocean-going ships at Bordeaux, were the Newfoundland tankers and a whole fleet of smaller square-riggers. From 1847, Le Quellec and Bordes' vessels set sail from Bordeaux for Chile, carrying valuable cargoes

Discharging grain at Marseilles in 1870. The ships' bows are right against the quayside, the bowsprits are retracted and the sacks are unloaded one by one down the gangplank. Painting by A. Moutte.

Nantes; the Quai de la Fosse in 1900.

of French manufactures; and to Bordeaux they returned, with guano, nitrate, rawhides, copper, silver and island copra. Twenty years later these Cape Horners that plied so regularly between France and South America, flew the famous house-flag of A. D. Bordes.

Nantes lies fifty-five kilometers from the sea. However, the tide and following winds are strong enough to carry ships up, without their being towed. Passing famous shipbuilders' yards on the way—Dubigeon, Chantiers Nantais, Chantiers de la Loire—they all reached Nantes in this way: the big ocean-goers, the little three-masters, the West Indian brigs carrying sugar, rum and cocoa, and finally the notorious slavers. Although from about 1890, Nantes built a number of sail trampers, which carried coal from England, the port in general had little trade with the Pacific.

The ports of Cork and Queenstown in Ireland received a number of ships, with grain from California and Oregon, guano from Peru and nitrate from Chile. But most of the oceanic trade across the Irish Sea and St. George's Channel was bringing Australian wool and Indian cotton to the huge docks

Alongside the coal-hopper. The French four-master *l'Union* loading at Port Talbot in 1906. (*Bohé Collection*)

in Liverpool and Manchester, entrepôts for the textile regions they served. The ships' return cargoes—unless they were in ballast—often comprised heavy goods and machinery from the steel foundries and mills of Birmingham, Bristol and Glasgow. Most important of all was the activity of the Clyde, whose shipyards built steel vessels of the highest quality for Britain and abroad.

For generations, the South Wales ports had been indelibly associated with coal; they were the main area where sailing ships loaded with it before crossing the Atlantic to Chile. In South Wales, as on the northeast coast of England at Newcastle, coal reigned supreme.

Sailing ships, from as far away as Hamburg or even the Baltic, came to South Wales. According to the time of year, they were ballasted with 700 or 900 tons of sand. No time was lost as soon as the ships came alongside the quays. Discharge spouts were maneuvered over the hatches, forward and aft; a hydraulic elevator lifted the 10-ton coal waggons and then tipped them up. With a thunderous roar the coal poured into the inky black holds. After perhaps a thousand tons had been loaded in this way, the ship hauled off to her mooring in the roadstead and the crew then unloaded the sand ballast into hoppers.

Since several thousand tons of coal had to be taken on and the ship's rolling threatened dangerously to shift the whole mass, the crew took great care beforehand to construct a long partition-wall around the hold, to prevent any displacement; between it and the stanchions on the quay, large planks were fixed in position side by side. Later on, four steel tubes, 8 meters long and 6 centimeters in diameter, and pierced with holes at regular intervals, were set in position—two in the holds and one on each side of the ship. These were used to measure the temperature of the cargo at different levels, by

Discharging coal. A sort of ladder is lashed to the mast, upon which the combined weight of four of the crew going up and down it, operates the coal-tip. Labour was cheap in England in the 1860s. (*The Graphic*)

means of a thermometer that could reach the bottom of the tube, whatever the depth of hold. Once the ship had reached the correct laden capacity, the moorings were cast off and tugs pushed her out into the estuary. Under the eyes of the boatswain, the steam pumps disgorged a torrent of water and the decks were scrubbed until a black river of coal ran through the scuppers to the sea. The ship could not sail before she was clean.

Taking on coal could be hazardous, and at one time or another vessels had unnerving experiences. The constant friction of the coal lumps could raise the temperature enough to produce combustion. If a fire broke out, one way of trying to extinguish it was to seal off the hatches, coal chutes and other ventilators, so that air could not reach them; or, alternatively, pump water or steam down the temperature-tubes. If these methods failed, it was necessary to shovel away the coal to reach the center of the fire, unless a fire-damp explosion had already blown off the hatch covers. Each type of coal carried its own special risks; that from Cardiff was not handled in the same way, for instance, as Newcastle or Australian coal.

Fire at sea was the greatest danger of all on a voyage. If steel ships might seem less likely to go down as a result of fire than their wooden predecessors, they had none the less to be abandoned just as quickly. The vessel soon became quite uninhabitable, through heat, poisonous fumes, white hot steel plates, the subsidence of the mast steps and the ever present danger of explosion.

Here, for example, is an account of a fire aboard the *Cedarbank*, as told by Basil Lubbock. In June 1893, the English sailing ship *Cedarbank* set course for San Francisco with a cargo of coal from Newcastle, Australia. Thin smoke was seen coming from the middle hatch cover and the thermometer reading confirmed that the cargo was on fire. The smoking hatch cover was opened and attempts were made to shovel away coal to reach the seat of the fire; but the heat inside the hold was unbearable, men passed out in the fumes and even soaking the coal for days on end failed to extinguish it.

The heat continued to rise, until after three days, the hatches were blown off and great flames began to lick up the masts. In this extremity, the openings had to be sealed off at all costs, even though everything was burning to the touch. The crew worked with the fever of despair, expecting the masts at any moment to crash down upon them. Fortunately a fair wind drove the *Cedarbank* towards San Francisco; the day before her expected arrival there, further explosions blew the hatch covers off again.

They were replaced and time was even found to paint over the hull's smoke-blackened plates. The paint job was so well done that the master of the tug who came alongside noticed nothing amiss. He was, therefore, quite astonished to take in the ship's signal: "Run me ashore, I am on fire". Thus, thirty-six hours after the beginning of the disaster, the ship was grounded on the mudbanks outside San Francisco, where the fire on board was at last successfully put out.

Nitrate clippers from Chile, grain clippers from Australia, timber carriers from Oregon, made their first landfall at the Scillies. Having passed the Lizard they received their orders by semaphore at Falmouth, concerning the last stage of their voyage to Dunkirk, Le Havre, London, Antwerp, Hamburg, Ghent, Bruges or Zeebrugge.

It was not enough, however, to have sighted land successfully after weeks of "blind" reckoning and bad weather; the Channel and the shoals off the Pas de Calais had still to be negotiated, a prospect which the ships' captains never relished, especially when the wind was freshening from the east. Sometimes it was necessary to tack forty times between the entrance to the Channel and the Isle of Wight, keeping anxious watch for steamers and sailing ships that might cross one's path. An account of shipwrecks and collisions in the Channel and Irish Sea would by itself fill a large book. The number of fine sailing ships returning from Cape Horn, which foul winds and fog have destroyed at the Scillies, the Lizard and the approaches to Falmouth, is beyond counting.

Normally a pilot was taken on from a cutter cruising at the entrance to the Channel; at night he was signalled in by a blue rocket. Only when the ship got into difficulties were calls sent out for English or Dutch tugs, with whom the shipowners had made contracts. "Before starting negotiations, the tugmaster made a close inspection of the ship, paying particular attention to the double-hull, rigging, helm, ship's boats and anchors." This was very important because their conditions and workability determined whether the tug was towing a ship or a wreck. Agreement was usually made verbally and at once by loud-hailer, under conditions which did not favor protracted dispute or haggling.

The captain might be surprised that a less powerful tug had been sent out than he thought necessary; or, the tugmaster might find at daybreak that he had only charged the standard rate to tow a vessel that was clearly a wreck. Thereafter, whatever the weather, the sailing ship was entirely in the hands of the tug and her towing cable, drawn along at four knots—through

In dry dock at Falmouth. Ships often signalled messages by semaphore from Falmouth before reaching their home ports in Europe. The presence of this signalling station saved many ships, coming in from the Atlantic to their first landfall, in fog or bad weather and uncertain of their true position. (*Lacroix Collection*)

the channels and banks of the Pas de Calais and North Sea, at the approaches to the Thames and Dunkirk or the Frisian Islands. Sea fog and ocean current tested the tugmaster's abilities to the utmost. A broken tow, mechanical breakdown or a navigational error invariably led to the shipwreck of her charge.

In April 1913, the *Parnassos* of Hamburg, a steel full-rigged ship, homeward bound with 3,000 tons of Chilean saltpeter was taken in tow in the North Sea by the English tug *T.O.Joliffe*. The weather worsened and soon after sighting the lightship *Elbe I*, *Parnassos* was suddenly struck a shuddering blow beneath the water line. In the dark icy night she had grounded on the Terschelling Bank, and was pounded by the heavy seas.

Every effort was made by the tug to pull her clear, but it was too late; she was water-logged, with the water rising in her hold. The tug steamed away to seek help, while the ship tried to keep afloat until daybreak. As soon as the Terschelling lifeboat had taken off the last man, Captain Karl Jung, the *Parnassos* capsized and disappeared.

Richard Peter, in an article in *Der Albatros*, tells another story of a shipwreck. The three-masted *Marie Hackfeld* set sail from Hamburg under tow of the *Vulcan* in November 1909, bound for Honolulu. The weather was extremely bad at the mouth of the Elbe, but got worse in the open sea, fifteen miles west of Heligoland. The tug was peremptorily ordered back and had to leave the sailing ship to fend for herself.

Taking advantage of a shift of wind, the captain hoisted a rag canvas and headed for the Elbe estuary. Unluckily he came in too far north of the *Elbe I* lightship, and saw ahead, too late, the breaking surf on the Holstein shore. Although she was carrying very little canvas, her forward impetus was still too great. Both bower anchors were thrown out but their chains broke off. It was a frightful place to be stranded, exposed to a fierce cross wind, with waves breaking over the ship and the hull being pounded against the bank. The only thing left to do was to fire distress rockets and endeavor to survive the night. At dawn six tugs were standing by, but they were unable to get near the wreck due to lack of water around her. Two lifeboats managed to rescue some of the crew—nineteen in the first boat and five in the second, including the captain, who was wounded and unconscious. The ship became a total loss for her owners, J.C.Pflüger, and much of her cargo, intended for Hawaiian islanders, found its way into the less scrupulous hands of those who lived on that North Sea coast and were specialists in the taking of booty.

The approaches to many of the North Sea ports—Dunkirk, Bremen, Hamburg, London, Newcastle—were tricky at all times, in spite of lightships and buoys marking the channels. The sandbanks shifted their positions too often and the currents were very treacherous.

The huge, muddy estuary of the Thames was the gateway to the port of London, where a mighty concourse of great ocean sailing ships, steamers, and small craft jostled. Here, amongst many other things, came cargoes of wool, cotton and fertilizers, while London exported her famous mixed cargoes, manufactures and other finished goods. Sailing ships found in the city the shelter of wet-docks, situated below London Bridge. The entrance to these docks was as hidden as that of a rabbit's burrow; only the huge forest of masts betrayed their position. Joseph Conrad has given a disturbing picture of them:

A sloping runway for the unloading of coal, Newcastle-on-Tyne, 1910. *(Le Tour du Monde)*

It was painful to see these magnificent vessels as it were tied and hemmed into each quayside; clustered together in square patches of black and oily water, poor reward for a voyage well performed . . . I have seen ships emerging from some of the docks like half-dead prisoners from a dungeon; worn and crushed by the filth, the whites of their crews' eyes standing out from the dirtiness of the rest of their faces. Even the smoky, grimy atmosphere seemed to partake of the sordid appearance of the whole scene.

Coming up the Thames from the sea, past Gravesend, the great docks came into view in succession: the Tilbury, Royal Victoria and Albert, King George V, East India, West India, Millwall, Surrey Commercial, St. Katherine's and finally London Pool, near London Bridge.

Newcastle-upon-Tyne, North and South Shields wore the same grimy, unhappy face as Cardiff, often the last view of Europe which many sailors took away with them to the Pacific. Like Cardiff, too, there was much activity in the shipbuilders' yards.

Dunkirk and Calais traded in nitrate and timber, the former being the

The *Belen* of Nantes (later the *Jeanne d'Arc* of the Bordes' fleet), aground outside Dunkirk having missed the channel, 12 December 1904. With the aid of harnessed horses, the crew take off part of the rigging to lighten the ship. Ten days later, the *Belen* was refloated at high water and towed to drydock for repairs. Note the amount of weed and other marine vegetation on the hull. *(Lacroix Collection)*

259

London docks, north quay in 1900. (*Port of London Authority*)

headquarters of the Bordes Company fleet. There were local shipyards, but the drawback in Dunkirk at least was the port's possessing only one lock gate, the Trystram lock. On the banks of the Elbe and Weser, the German shipyards were flourishing. With respect to sailing ships, both Bremen and Hamburg sought to be hailed as the last strongholds of these craft, in competition with Antwerp and Mariehamn. Bremen and Hamburg imported fertilizers, cotton and wool, and exported mixed cargoes—including heavy machinery and equipment to the Pacific and Far East. Old photographs of Hamburg and Rotterdam, taken at the turn of the century, show the anchorages crowded with sailing ships and prove the strength of the German merchant navy in this period.

All of the users of these ports, of course, knew the route to and from Cape Horn well. Before the great steel ships followed it, we know how many little merchant ships bound for the Pacific, how many whalers seeking their prey in the southern seas—Scandinavians and Englishmen, Frenchmen from Bayonne, Bordeaux and Le Havre—had gone that way.

Unloading a ship at Calais, *ca.* 1900. Only one small hand-machine to handle 2,000 tons of cargo.

Last in this survey of important ports comes Le Havre. Le Havre—where so many whaling ships had been fitted out since the Napoleonic Empire; where great prosperity had followed the opening of the sailing packet service to North America; where superb clippers—the "Rio Swallows" and "Cape Pigeons"—set out to conquer the world. Moreover, at the turn of the century Le Havre saw her sailing ships prosper in another direction—the growing trade in nickel from New Caledonia. The shipowners of Le Havre and Rouen enjoyed a complete monopoly on this traffic.

FROM THE CHANNEL TO CAPE HORN

Maison Bordes' instructions to their captains

In general, neither our ships nor their cargoes are insured; the captain must, therefore, be very careful to avoid damage. If it happens to him, he must effect repairs out of the resources available on board; if this is not possible, he must do so at the nearest port, making use of companies known to us, or, if all else fails, obtain consular intervention.

The captain must furnish the consul with a full report of the circumstances of the accident and details of the damage, a copy of which must be forwarded to us. Great care must be taken to avoid collision at sea. Upon this subject we refer you to: *Regulations on the use of Flares, Signals and Maneuvers to avoid collision*. We direct that a lookout be at the crow's-nest at all times, and that there should be two there in foggy weather. We are sure you are aware that most of the ships lost with all hands at sea are caused by collision following faulty lookouts.

Great vigilance must be exercised around Cape Horn and the Falkland Islands, due to the prevalence of icebergs. When rounding the Horn, experience has shown that it is best to hug the land up to the cape and then keep well off the western side of Patagonia. Every opportunity should be taken in these areas to make the most of the changeable winds. Jettisoning cargo or equipment at sea is forbidden unless a critical situation demands it.

All unnecessary putting into ports is to be avoided at all costs; in difficult circumstances the captain should rather be able to rally his crew and continue on to the fixed destination. Only in very bad weather, or when the ship is likely to sink or has suffered serious damage, should course be set for the nearest port. In South American waters, if

Hauling in the towline hand over hand. On board the *Richelieu*.

you have to put into port, Valparaiso is much to be preferred to Callao; in fact, Valparaiso is the best port of any on the American Pacific coast for this purpose.

If calling at a port cannot possibly be avoided, and the charter party is willing, the captain must put his ships in the hands of our local agents :-

         Messrs. G. Wilms at Valparaiso
              „   H. Christophersen at Montevideo and Rio de Janeiro
              „   Rimbaud & Co. at Fort de France (Martinique)
              „   A. & C. Gunet at Lisbon.

On instructions from the charter party, the cargo should be handed over to the consignees' agents, but the captain must not hesitate to discuss the costs fully with the parties concerned and do everything to see that they are as low as possible. If the cargo is our own, the captain must ensure on arrival at a port that he keeps the ship under canvas and stands to, awaiting instructions. Thereby the harbor dues, anchorage, towing and other charges—which are pure loss if he is bound elsewhere—will be avoided. Ships bound for Valparaiso should in difficulties proceed to Curaumilla and signal that they await further instructions. Normally captains returning to Europe will receive our final destination instructions via the pilots taken on. In any event, every captain is advised to make for Falmouth, and to transmit their intended messages at the Scillies and the Lizard. Every captain entering or leaving a British or North Seas port must use a pilot, at a fee previously arranged.

The captain must furnish a full report of the incidents of the voyage, but only in the event of actual danger to the ship is it necessary to go into details regarding bad weather. In this connection, it is worth remembering that any exaggeration of bad weather and danger at sea will be reported in the press and can only harm the company's reputation. Your report must only be sent through our agents or other competent authorities.

THE VOYAGE

Passing St. Catherines, Isle of Wight, coming from the Tyne; through the St. George's or Bristol Channels—the tug lines were cast off, and the pilots came down the sides, bringing the last letters for the shore. The sails were hoisted, the tug blew three farewell blasts on her whistle and turned back for the shore. The great voyage had begun.

The wind whistled in the rigging, the great masts began to creak and bend;

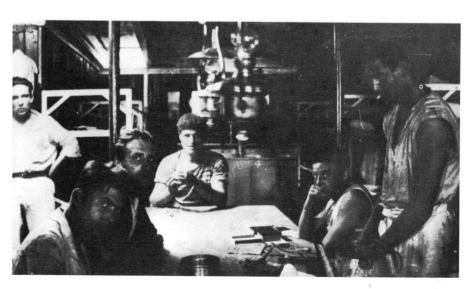

Last maintainers of a great tradition; young seamen of the *Richelieu*.

262

Overleaf : Dunkirk. While a Bordes four-master berths and the crowd of relatives and friends throng the quayside, an English sailing ship negotiates the dock entrance, nudged by two paddlewheel tugs. A magnificent scene, hardly noticed by the plaice-fishers in the foreground of the photograph. *(Vaugham Collection)*

On tow in the Channel. On board the English windjammer *Glenalvon*. *(Vaugham Collection)*

the stem ploughed a furrow in the sea. The waves parted before it, throwing up white crests that ran along the length of the hull and then disappeared in the foam made by the rudder at the stern. Life on board began all over again, with the unbroken rhythm of day and night watches, recorded by the sound of the ship's bell. The ship belonged to no one then but her crew.

The mate's first care was for the anchors—unshackling the chains, lowering them into the wells, sealing off the hawse holes and securing the two bower anchors to the cathead. Everything was then made shipshape—running rigging, boats, equipment—ready for inspection. If the frequent Channel and Biscay squalls removed the coal dust from the masts, they could not clean the deckhouses, poop or forecastle. That was when the potash, the swabs, the deck brushes and holystones came into play ; later came the attack on rust and poor paintwork.

The crew was divided into the two watches, and then subdivided into three categories according to their function aloft : first, the sail men—the old sailors, experts in handling the canvas. Then the topmen, one for each mast, whose job was to maintain the masts, the standing and running rigging. Finally, the apprentice seamen and novices who worked the lower sails, and did the general duties like cleaning, de-rusting, painting and occasionally took a turn at the wheel in fine weather.

Whatever the weather, the morning watch swabbed down the decks at dawn, then made any necessary adjustments to the rigging and brought coal and fresh water to the galley. The part of the crew who stood watch after breakfast, then worked for eight hours under the orders of the mate. The whole daily routine was based on the written instructions in the captain's orders.

The sailors used to bring their benches up on deck in fine weather, to do

The tug hoots farewell, the ensign flutters at the mizzen peak, the sails fill, the course is passed to the helmsman. The long voyage of the *Maréchal de Castries* has begun. *(Bohé Collection)*

The day's work began with scrubbing the decks. From forecastle to poop, each plank was holy-stoned. (*Vaugham Collection*)

The Walker patent log; an English instrument, with built-in dial. Only the back revolved in the water. It was taken back on board at the end of each watch, and the number of miles shown on the dial recorded. (*Photo J. Randier*)

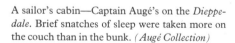

A sailor's cabin—Captain Augé's on the *Dieppedale*. Brief snatches of sleep were taken more on the couch than in the bunk. (*Augé Collection*)

their sail-mending and -making. In bad weather this work which required so much patience and skill was carried on below in the sail room. At 9 o'clock the daily rations were issued to the member of each watch who was on mess duty that week. In addition, the lieutenant in charge of stores gave out every Monday, certain weekly provisions: coffee, sugar, oil, vinegar, salt, pepper, mustard. At the same time the cook received his weekly rations of flour, salt and lard. At 11.30 a.m. the first watch went to dinner, and at noon relieved

Anchors lashed to the deck, weighing a ton apiece. On board *La Françoise d' Amboise.* (*Augé Collection*)

their comrades on the 8–12 watch, who in turn took their meal. "Going to dinner" aboard an ocean-going sailing ship at the turn of the century, was certainly an exaggerated way to describe the scene as the men sat eating on their sea chests, or with their legs dangling from their hammocks.

As soon as the bell was rung, the men formed up below in watches, with their plates, mugs and spoons and then took their places at table. The junior seaman served the food, being also responsible for washing the dishes and sweeping up afterwards. The issue of wine and rum was also undertaken by the seaman on mess duty that week, who incidentally had first call on any surplus.

The men ate slowly and in silence, almost reflectively, as they did most other things. They used to cut off long slices of bacon or cod and spread them on bread or biscuits, from which they had carefully knocked out the worm and weevils beforehand. They then swallowed their plateful of cooked food washed down with a draught of wine. Afterwards, having wiped their moustaches and noisily smacked their lips, they retired to their hammocks for a rest.

In the afternoon, all hands worked on deck, except in extremely bad weather, when they were permitted to rest below. During the daytime it was not necessary to post men in the bows, the topmen aloft being sufficient look-out in clear weather.

Once out of the Channel, the sailing ships strove to find the most westerly course before giving Cap Finisterre a wide berth. " . . . one could never find too much westerly . . . with the barometer high and steady, the wind blowing hard from the north or northwest, one would bowl along splendidly in the northeast trades. But if the wind slackened and veered easterly and the barometer fell, then one must be ready for the sou'westerlies".

Such were the guide-lines of an age that had no broadcast weather bulletins upon which to rely. Their courses were shaped initially by the orders given by the shipowners, Messrs. Bordes & Company.

As soon as Finisterre had been rounded, the next step was to steer a course one hundred miles west of Madeira, giving the Canaries a wide berth

The patriarch of maritime gastronomy—the ship's biscuit. Teeth made little impression upon its surface, and it often had to be broken by a hammer wrapped in cloth and left to the soup to dissolve it. (*A. Hayet Collection*)

Ebony English sextant, with ivory movement, *ca. 1860. Obsolete, but efficient. (Mariners Museum, Saint-Malo)*

and then pass within fifty miles of San Antonio, Cape Verde Islands, in order to avoid the Doldrums. "Having passed the Cape Verdes, the problem was not, as one might imagine, to decide where to cross the equator, but rather how to pass from the northeast to the southeast trades with the minimum of delay".

In the fine weather within the trades, the ship required little maneuvering. The crew worked on deck during the day, and could sleep on deck during the night—all that is except for the helmsman, the deck watch, and the duty officer on the poop. As long as fine nights with a constant breeze and calm sea lasted, the ship carried the fullest possible canvas, the fine weather sails replacing those set when she sailed from Europe. Changing the sails was a considerable undertaking. It involved the hoisting of new canvas, properly dried, patched and folded, and was made more difficult by the fact that some of the sails weighed nearly a ton. During this time all the topmen, sailors and novices worked together aloft and in the rigging, adjusting the pulley-blocks and clewing the sails, if necessary.

As his ship forges ahead, the captain is content at last, his taciturnity of the previous week being succeeded by an unusual volubility. He offers his men coffee, liqueurs, even a cigar after their Sunday lunch. Sundays are invested with a special dignity. The boatswain mans the pumps, as each man files past with his bucket and draws the weekly allowance of six liters of fresh water.

The men only washed once a week, with a ceremony which became almost ritual; they made little piles of their dirty clothes, with the dirtiest on top. Having carefully scrubbed and washed themselves, they saved the rest of the fresh water to rinse out their clothes. Shaved and clean, they put on jersey,

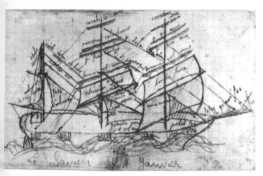

In order to remember the sails and spars, the young pilot Ravasse drew this sketch in his diary. *(Mariners Museum, Saint-Malo)*

One by one, with the help of brails, the sails are hoisted up the mast to the yards. On board the *Suzanne.*

The meridian. Three observers are better than one; the captain's calculations setting the pace for the rest! Aboard the *La Rochefoucauld*.

Looking down the mainyard, the impressive wake of the *Richelieu*.

trousers and rope-sandals and finally a wide-brimmed straw hat. Meanwhile, their washing, hung out on the gantlines, dried quickly. Some old sailors who had hoarded their whole week's ration of rum (28 centiliters), now indulged themselves to the full. This was the day for reflection and mending one's clothes; sometimes the men sang and danced to the accordion.

On board the wool clipper *Macquarie*. Fine weather: having a haircut in the open air and the running rigging laid out to dry on the deck. (*Nat. Maritime Museum, Greenwich*)

Exceptional Sunday relaxation. Dancing on board the *Françoise d'Amboise* to the sound of the accordion and the beat of the deck mop. (*Hayet Collection*)

Sunday aboard *l'Union*. Cabin boys playing a favorite game, "bones". (*Mariners Museum, Saint-Malo*)

But these happy times were followed by many depressing hours, like those described by the pilot Henri Jacques in his book, *Cap Horn*:

We are in the doldrums and for six days the ship has rolled horribly in the swell, with no wind in her sails. The royals and topsails flap drily against the yards; the ship sways clumsily from side to side against a background of melancholy noises: straining ropes, grinding braces, screaming pulley-blocks and distended backstays. The sounds make us nervous, and each movement of the three masts seems to indicate imminent collapse; but no, the sickening rolling continues unabated. For six days, too, it has rained continuously—a slow, steady, enervating downpour. Having been forced to handle the wet ropes unceasingly, the crew's hands have become soft and split open, the rope strands making them bleed.

These are the regions of little wind and overpowering calms, dreaded by sailing ships and crews alike. No clear skies or visible horizon, but an embracing, suffocating haze, from which drops of tepid water are squeezed out. Sometimes a watery sun appears struggling against the immense lines of sullen clouds lying parallel with the pale waters, between which the ship appears to hang suspended. The whole atmosphere evokes unreality and menace; the incessant groans of the stricken masts is matched by the shock of seeing other ships nearby, trapped in the same mists and grossly distorted by the curious reflective effects. Farther off, a three-masted ship glitters with a deathly whiteness amidst the somber patches of fog. In this restless, unhealthy region she appears a ghost ship abandoned there by the devil.

After the calms of the Doldrums, there came torrential rain, which blocked the scuppers and turned the well-deck into a swimming pool. Fifteen centimeters of water in less than an hour were a godsend—washing the decks and replenishing the water casks. The men soon became worn out in this Turkish bath heat, amidst which, dressed in oilskins and seaboots they had continually to brace the yards, searching for a wind. The captain fretted his heart out, but at last a puff of wind came and the ship crossed the Equator.

What followed is well described by the young pilot, Léon Ravasse:

Great preparations on board for the baptism; at 2 o'clock everyone is in costume and there are seven of us to be initiated. We are daubed with paint and wear only a pair of trousers. Father Neptune sends his lieutenant aboard to take command of the ship, while the captain sends us seven to different parts of the ship. Our little group looks very funny (as shown in my sketch): two lieutenants, two cabin boys, an ordinary seaman, an engineer, and myself.

Father Neptune comes on board, reads a proclamation to the captain, and then his minions come to look for us. I was the second to be caught; after being soaped all over, I was suspended over a water cask and then ducked in it seven or eight times. Then I was led to the end of the poop and had to read out some doggerel; afterwards I had to swallow some sea water through some oilskin trousers. So the baptismal ceremony was over and

The Doldrums. Not a puff of wind but an appalling swell which threatens to roll everything overboard. On board the *Richelieu*.

Entry showing night orders; signed by the captain and counter-signed by his officers.

271

The *Glenalvon*, 1903. Making every effort to use her sails, but there is not a puff of wind. The helmsman stands disconsolately by the wheel. (*Vaugham Collection*)

we all threw water over each other. Then the captain ordered a good meal to be prepared: chicken with rice, vegetables, coffee, rum, wine, cigars; and we all drank champagne with him.

Fishing lines were always put out, lashed since the start of the voyage to stanchions in the stern. From them were caught tunny, dorado, and bonito. Porpoises were attacked by harpoons in pursuit of which the first mate used to clamber down to the bobstay of the bowsprit. The dolphin's tail hanging from the end of the boom was thought to bring good luck. Sharks, whose presence was betrayed by the wake of their fins, were caught by massive baited hooks, attached by swivelchains to the lines. They were very dangerous, and had to be landed with great care, being still able to inflict terrible bites from their seven rows of sharp pointed teeth. Flying fish came on board by themselves, landing on deck during the night, from which they could be collected at daybreak, before the ship's cat had made her tour of the deck. The flying fish brought a welcome change to the usual menu and it was customary for the captain to issue a quart of wine for each one caught.

Then came the southeast Trades. It was important to steer southwards as far as possible, to round Cap San Roque, avoid entering Bahia Bay, and then

Crossing the line on board the transport *Loire* in 1870. Drawings by J. Mauger: "the baptismal font"; the police; the barber; Neptune and his pilot. *(Mariners Museum, Saint-Malo)*

Modern version of crossing the line. Pilot disguised as Neptune's aide; on board the *Tijuca*, 1900.

cross the Tropic of Capricorn about 120 miles off Cape Frio. It was here that ships bound for the Indian Ocean and Australia parted company, leaving their companions making for Cape Horn, to continue southwards. The southeast Trades are stronger than their northeast counterparts, and off Brazil and the estuary of the Plate sudden and violent gales frequently occur. Thanks to the steam-winches the fine weather sails are, in three or four days, replaced by the storm canvas, for Cape Horn ahead. Now storms are more usual; flashes of light appear at the yards and run down the masts and braces. These are the St. Elmo's fires, a bad omen for the sailors.

The ship holds her course under lowering clouds, running over seas growing colder, darker and more tempestuous. One hundred miles from La Plata, the sea water is colored by the discharge of surplus coal overboard; the trim of the cargo is checked and tarpaulins tied over the hatch covers. At the same time the captain orders a massive breakwater—made of large cross-pieces of timber, bolted down and held in place by cables—to be built over the hatches. Its purpose is to protect the hold from waves coming in over the side. Also in this region, the pig is slaughtered on board, an event celebrated by a double issue of wine to the crew.

273

A stiff breeze and salt spray. On board the sailing ship *Garthsnaid*.

Suddenly the barometer plummets down; a large copper-colored cloud appears from the west, often with a bank of black clouds in its wake. This is certainly a "pampero". At the first signs of it, all the canvas must be brought in, except for the topsails. The arrival of the great black cloud, heralded by distant thunder, is awaited with ominous silence on board. Then it strikes with tremendous force against the ship, heeling her over, as the seas grow ever larger in the minutes which follow. For several hours, all hell is let loose and woe betide any ship that carries too much canvas, as it would be stripped by the first big gust. Shipwreck would immediately follow a shifting of the cargo and rupture of the hull—as was the fate of the sailing ship *France I* and many other Cape Horners.

The cold weather returns. The crew, in seaboots and oilskins on the spray-swept deck, stand by, ready to alter the rigging and sails. Already the weather has chapped their hands, and their necks and wrists are gashed by rubbing against their oilskins. Schools of cachalot and whale can be seen in the raging seas, but not the sun. The impossibility of making an observation from the sun, prevents any determination of the ship's position. Rope hand-rails have been fixed along the companionways and around the compass binnacle; on the poop, a canvas structure has been rigged up to shelter the man at the wheel. Forward, in the mizzen shrouds, a large square of sail protects the officer of the watch.

The lookout remains on the forecastle, retreating to the main deckhouse only in very heavy weather. His job is to report the sighting of lights, breakers or land ahead, by a pre-arranged ringing of a hand bell, indicating the direction. At the end of his watch, he returns to the poop, reporting to the officer on watch with the familiar words: "Nothing to report on lookout, the lights are clear".

The senseless change of watches continues: first lieutenant replacing first mate, and vice versa; the change of helmsman is carried on in the same fashion. The seabooted officer on watch paces the poop deck for four hours, continually asking himself whether there is too much or too little sail being carried.

Page from a meteorological journal, personally kept by a keen young captain. (*Augé Collection*)

Rolling in heavy seas aboard the *Françoise d'Amboise*, 1908. (*Augé Collection*)

Near the Argentine coast, the fair weather canvas of the tropics is taken down and the "oo" gauge sails are hoisted in readiness for Cape Horn. *(Lacroix Collection)*

The helmsman arriving on duty is told by his colleague already at the wheel: "The course is sou'sou'west, no change".

The lieutenant comes up on deck, shouting "Who is not here on this watch?"

The men coming off watch, entangled by their heavy sea clothes, stagger below, to snatch four hours rest, while the ship drives along through the dark seas, crested with foam.

CAPE HORN, DAYS OF MISERY

Gulls, terns, mews, and petrels rest on the water, far astern in the ship's wake; cape pigeons, brown and gray mollymauks, black cormorants with yellow beaks, albatrosses and frigate birds wheel and bank round the ship—heralds of bad weather and the days of torment that lie ahead. The course hugs the coastline as far as Port Desire and the Bay of Patagonia, and here the seas are not as terrible as in the more open waters.

The object is to pass within sixty miles of the Cape of the Virgins and find both the right latitude and longitude to reach the Le Maire channel. Eventually, in lowering visibility and under leaden skies, the broken cliffs of Staten Island appear on the port bow and the three unmistakable hillocks known as the Three Brothers show on the starboard bow. At this point, two choices lie open to the captain. If the weather is settled and the wind constant from the north, it is best to proceed immediately into the Le Maire channel; if not, it is advisable to round Staten Island and obtain sea room, to forestall the effects of a sudden southwesterly gale.

Staten Island, her white and blue cliffs smothered in surf, is rounded under an inky sky, and then the full force of the Cape Horn seas strike the ship, wave upon wave. She is tossed up and then races down into the abyss, the troughs separating the mountainous waves, twenty meters high. The wall of water that bursts against the bows is carried by the force of the wind along the decks in a stinging spray, which lashes against the bulkheads of the deckhouse and the men's oilskins.

We were all clad in heavy oilskins, and seaboots, scarcely visible in the gloom shed by the dark clouds above us [writes the Cape Horner Henri Jacques]. The men clambered awkwardly along the deck, in their sou'westers and shining oilskins, their seaboots reaching up to their thighs. All looked grave and tense, constantly gazing at the sky and the rigging.

The distance between New Year lighthouse (on Cape St. John, the most easterly point of Staten Island) and Diego Ramirez Island was about 220 miles, or approximately one day's sailing for a ship with a good following wind. From Staten Island to the meridian of longitude 85° W., which must be

The sea pours into the well of the *Garthsnaid*. Note the lifelines for the men to grab in case of need.

Hoisting in the upper main topsail. Despite the help of brails, the men cannot hoist in the last bit of sail and the topman at the peak is shouting to the helmsman to luff the ship so that the wind can be reduced. Gouache by Oswald Pennington. *(Hon. Company of Master Mariners Collection)*

reached before one could steer north, the distance was 600 miles. But in this area, such estimations were practically valueless. The wind blew a gale from the west throughout most of the year; the waves were colossal and if there was a lull in the weather, the current carried the ship back fifteen to twenty miles in one day. So, in this contest between wind and sea, one was likely to lose in one unfortunate moment all the progress made in a hundred laborious maneuvers.

In tacking [wrote one of the Bordes Company's captains] it was essential not to prolong starboard too far south, but rather return northwards within a reasonable distance of the shore. The seas are less mountainous there and, once past the longitude of Cape Horn itself, it is possible to make use of the changeability of winds in order to reach the line Diego Ramirez—Cap Pilar to the west. One holds to the course 75° W.—

even 85° W., if one is proceeding to Valparaiso—as a port tack with the wind in the west will take one there directly. In summer, the Cape Horn gales are less continuous, but frequent and severe and the days are longer. In winter there are occasional winds blowing from the east, and therefore helpful; on the other hand, the days are very short and the combination of thick haze, snow and intense cold are serious complications. Contrary to general belief, the barometer, upon which the old navigators relied so much, is a very reliable indicator. Readings could sometimes fall below 720 millimeters in these regions and it was essential to take note of all the barometer's variations.

Another serious danger was caused by the sudden shifts and changes of wind, which could easily take the ship right aback and dismast her.

Fishing for albatross aboard the transport *Loire*. Drawing by J. Mauguer. *(Mariners Museum, Saint-Malo)*

Great attention had to be paid both to the sails and rigging, to guard against the notorious stripping of canvas, which might happen quite unexpectedly; to this end it was necessary to make the most of a lull in the weather. The welfare of the men, also, required the greatest attention in these latitudes—an increase in rations, a pot of tea during the night, care in ensuring that their sodden clothes were properly dried, were all ways of doing this.

Above all, it was essential that the vessel's position should neither be too far south when the wind blew from the north or northwest, not too near the coast when it blew from the south or southwest. The wind force was usually much greater during the day than at night, owing to the pronounced northerly declination of the moon in its new and full phases.

It is June 1905. The three-masted barque *Susanna* of Hamburg, with 25 men on board, arrives off the Horn. A northwesterly gale drives her from latitude 60° S. to the exit of the Magellan Strait. Then the wind shifts southwest before returning to west. The ship is weighed down with ice and snow, and the crew try to chip it off the rigging and melt it off the yards with hot water. The mate is knocked down by a pulley-block and breaks his nose on a spar; the cabin boy fractures a leg and the cook, chased out of the galley by a wave, cracks two ribs against a bulkhead. The men's fingers are frozen and there are still six weeks to go before they reach Cape Horn.

Day and night they toil at the pumps in water up to their chests. Tacking to the north keeps the ship in sight of land; tacking to the south brings them to 60° and 62° S., but no further, without the help of a following wind. Seven men are confined to their bunks, with broken or frostbitten legs and arms; soon to be joined by others, stricken with scurvy. Two cases of typhus occur on board. Only cold food can be served, as the galley has long ago been flooded out. The saloon skylight has been carried away by a giant wave, which smashed two whaleboats and the poop deck companionway. There is a shortage of water and when the *Susanna* at last reaches 79° W., there are so few fit men aboard, that the yards have to be braced at the capstan. (From an account by Chr. Jensen in the journal *Der Albatros*).

Around Cape Horn, a ship's well-deck was always filled with salt water, which dashed against the bulkheads, drowned the winches and capstans, penetrated the deckhouses and seeped in everywhere—into the crew's boots and oilskins, irritating the skin of their hands and faces. The men, haggard with fatigue and numbed with misery, were only able to carry on through the ingrained disciplines, order and routine on board. These were the defenses against the uncertainty and chaos, and once they were broken down, all was lost.

Cork float and triangle, baited with closely packed lard. The albatross' beak got hooked in the triangle and it could not get free. It was then only necessary to haul the bird in. *(Mariners Museum, Saint-Malo)*

JANVIER 1887.

HEURE MOYENNE.	DISTANCE.	LOG. 3ʰ différence	ARG. Δ.	HEURE MOYENNE.	DISTANCE.	LOG. 3ʰ différence	ARG. Δ.	HEURE MOYENNE.	DISTANCE.	LOG. 3ʰ différence	ARG. Δ.
Soleil O.		Samedi 1.		Aldébaran E.		Samedi 1.		α Pégase O.		Dimanche 2.	
0	78.55.51	0,3769	0	0	68.20.22	0,3068	0	0	29.59.36	0,4668	0
3	80.16.51	0,3766	0	3	66.51.32	0,3065	0	3	31. 2. 2	0,4519	1
6	81.37.55	0,3462	0	6	65.22.37	0,3061	0	6	32. 6.38	0,4387	1
9	82.59. 4	0,3457	0	9	63.53.38	0,3057	0	9	33.13. 6	0,4269	2
12	84.20.19	0,3452	0	12	62.24.33	0,3053	0	12	34.21.17	0,4164	2
15	85.41.40	0,3446	0	15	60.55.22	0,3047	0	15	35.31. 3	0,4069	3
18	87. 3. 8	0,3440	0	18	59.26. 5	0,3042	0	18	36.42.16	0,3985	3
21	88.24.43	0,3433	0	21	57.56.40	0,3036	0	21	37.54.50	0,3907	4
24	89.46.26	0,3426	0	24	56.27. 8	0,3029		24	39. 8.40	0,3836	
Mars O.		Samedi 1.		Soleil O.		Dimanche 2.		α Bélier E.		Dimanche 2.	
0	53.19.41	0,3377	0	0	89.46.26	0,3426	0	0	27.50.51	0,3789	0
3	54.42.25	0,3373	0	3	91. 8.17	0,3418	0	3	26.36.15	0,3863	1
6	56. 5.15	0,3369	0	6	92.30.18	0,3410	0	6	25.23. 2	0,3952	2
9	57.28. 9	0,3364	0	9	93.52.28	0,3401	0	9	24.11.26	0,4058	2
12	58.51. 9	0,3359	0	12	95.14.48	0,3392	0	12	23. 1.43	0,4185	3
15	60.14.16	0,3353	0	15	96.37.20	0,3382	0	15	21.54.13	0,4340	3
18	61.37.29	0,3347	0	18	98. 0. 3	0,3371	0	18	20.49.19	0,4529	4
21	63. 0.50	0,3340	0	21	99.22.58	0,3360	0	21	19.47.30	0,4763	4
24	64.24.20	0,3333		24	100.46. 6	0,3349		24	18.49.18	0,5056	5

A page from a nautical almanac of 1885. Fingers which gripped the rough ropes had also to run down the columns of small figures in these tables to make the necessary nautical calculations. (*Service hydrographique, Paris*)

The bottle which contained this message was found in Lampaul Bay at Ouessant, four months and fourteen days after being thrown overboard, having covered a distance of 660 miles. (*Mariners Museum, Saint-Malo*)

L'Union, the Bordes' fleet first straight four-master. In 1914, she was sunk after being captured by the German raider *Kronprinz Wilhelm*. Launched on the Clyde in 1882, *L'Union* crossed the Pacific 36 times during her career. Her dimensions were: 87 × 13 meters and she could carry 3,360 tons of cargo.

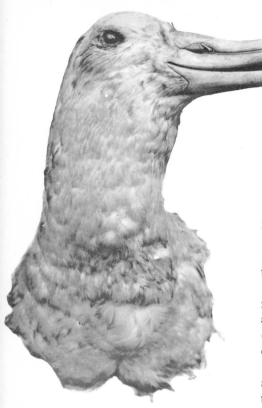

A hooked beak 20 cms. long, able to crack the skull of a man as easily as a pickaxe. The wings of the albatross spanned three meters. *(A. Hayet Collection)*

Body, mind and spirit flinch under the fury of the storm; the men are tired and beaten, but still remain alert. There are lulls between the long days of misery, when the weather is calmer.

Crouching aloft on the yards, the topman sees all. While the ship buckets, rolls, heaves and shudders, he stands fast, his yellow tobacco stained teeth shining from a beard turned white by the salt spray. His torn nails spill blood upon the frozen sails, and his hands are smeared with vaseline in an attempt to reduce the sensation of appalling cold. The sheet cables strike against the yards in a shower of sparks. The men begin to wonder if it is worth going on; if they fell from aloft onto the deck or into the sea, the end would be sudden and complete. But they conquer their exhaustion and fear, and will only come down when all the work on the sails has been completed, in spite of the difficulties of working under such appalling conditions.

And now there is the task of bringing in the sail, as it thrashes in the wind—awkward and uncooperative. It has frozen as hard as iron; one crouches below, thumping, pushing and grabbing it by the throat—once, twice, ten times, almost falling over in the process—until at last it is brought into the yard, folded and lashed by the ropes. Time passes quickly; soon one is back at the topmast and returning down the companion-ladder and ratlines, against which one is flattened by the force of the wind. The deck is reached at length and one stumbles across it to the stern, awaiting the next order of maneuver. Then the next watch comes up from below, numbed, sleepy shivering as the gusts strike them. The mate shouts above the storm: "All not on watch, below; all not on watch, below".

Eight bells ring, and the new helmsman takes over the wheel. The old watch return to their quarters, dodging the waves that are breaking over the well on the way there. The last to arrive slams the steel door shut. Inside, amid the clamor of the rolling ship and the water on the floor slapping from bulkhead to bulkhead, the crew, wet and dazed, try to rest. The oil lamp smokes, the dirty stove belches steam as the prostrate men, still in oilskins and seaboots, snatch some sleep before they are roused by the boatswain's cry: "Watch on deck; watch on deck; to the yards and mainsail!"

Before the boatswain has finished, they are on their feet. And if it is the main topsail to be reefed it won't be easy, needing perhaps both watches working together. The work will only cease with the command: "Reef the mizzen home!" These are magic words to their ears for it means they can stumble below, and file past the storeroom hatch with mugs in their hands to draw the rum ration or take a swig from the bottle, as the storeroom lieutenant marks off the amount with his thumb. For a brief moment their spirits revive with the grog.

Outside on the poop deck, it is inky black. The officer of the watch sees the boiling seas at the wake and glances at the helmsman standing like a rock at the wheel, his eyes smarting against the spray. In the cabin, a sudden roll of

Right : In the westerlies, on board the *Richelieu.* *(Degard)*

A "mollymauk", smallest of the albatrosses. They were captured in stormy latitudes. On board *l'Union*, 1907. (*Mariners Museum, Saint-Malo*)

The steeringwheel of the wool clipper *Northern Monarch*, after being smashed by the huge wave of a "pooper".

Opposite: Track charts round Cape Horn used by Captain Lecocq of the Bordes Co. The tracks of the four vessels—*l'A.D.Bordes, Le Chili, Le Gers* and *l'Antonin*—enabled him to profit by their experiences. The east-west route re-entered the Gulf of Patagonia and then stood well off the Chilean coast to the Pacific. The west-east route hugged the coastline and then converged east of the Falkland Islands. (*Mariners Museum, Saint-Malo*)

the ship throws the men over, one on top of each other; shaken and cursing, they get to their feet again. Trying to make themselves comfortable, they settle down once more and attempt to sleep, if need be standing up, shaken from side to side and soaked to the skin.

The masts and spars stand out black and ghostly against the overcast sky; the moon appears fitfully, zig-zagging its pale light through the swaying rigging. The masts and yards swing in crazy curves like diabolical metronomes. At this crisis, the sails can only be worked from below, by men standing at the foot of the masts, or in the well-deck, avoiding the waves that break over the side. "Watch out! Watch out! Man the braces!" Then they grope forward in the darkness amidst the tangled rigging.

Everyone is suffering and groaning. Will the ship survive the onslaught? What more can be done—reduce sail, run before the wind, spur the crew to more efforts or get out the boats? In his mind the captain seesaws between taking too many risks or being over cautious. He listens for any unusual sound the ship might make, as a portent of danger. She is battling well against the waves, if a little heavily; but is there too much water in the bilges, indicating that she has sprung a leak? Should he order the carpenter to investigate, or put his men to man the pumps? The deck is awash with the sea pouring over the sides, but nothing can be done until the wind moderates and the waves are calmer.

Keeping a cool head is his most important need, trying to give the crew confidence while carrying on as if nothing was amiss. Above all he must wait and see; the ship will survive if the crew keep her under control, even if they have to submit to many days of assault, waiting for the weather to relent. For the captain, it is neither the moment to dream nor to seethe with impatience.

The worst moment comes when the whole vessel shudders, as if in despair, and seems about to go down. Her whole forecastle is under water and she appears overwhelmed. "Come up, old ship, come up"! Little by little, the bow emerges from the waves, and a green sea breaks like a battering-ram against the front of the poop, its spray reaching right up to the mizzen peak before falling back again. The scuppers pour forth torrents of water and the enormous wave having swept under the ship's keel, reappears on the other side, the thousand white horses of its ruffled crest seeming to bid farewell.

284

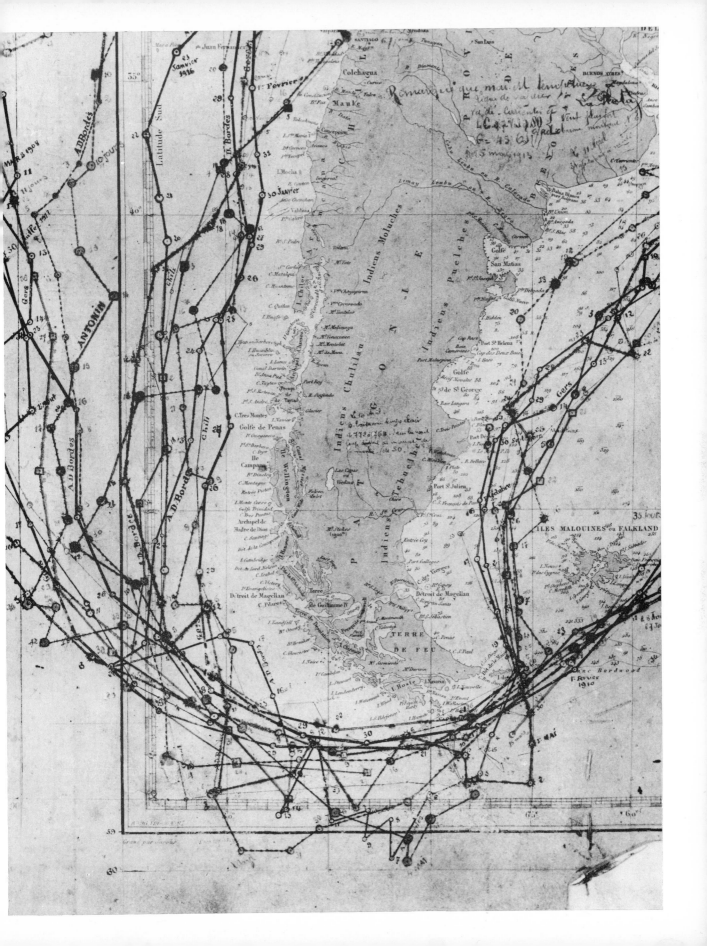

Heavy weather on board the *Richelieu*.

The hull has dropped into the abyss of the wave trough and the ship lies helpless across the rollers, tossed to and fro, awaiting the *coup de grâce*. A second huge wave breaks over the ship, cascading against the bulkheads, smothering and heavy over her, it does not retreat. The crew hold their breaths, and the seconds seem like hours. This looks like the end; the list becomes so pronounced that the extremities of the mainyards are lying in the water and the barnacles and seaweed on the lower parts of the ship's side are clearly visible.

The crew seem resigned to their fate as the ship is about to capsize. There are heavy rumblings below deck as if the cargo has shifted. But at the last possible moment, a miracle occurs. With agonizing slowness, the masts begin to rise again and the ship rights herself. Not a word is spoken aboard at this supreme moment of crisis; the degree of danger is reflected in the faces of the men, who seem to have aged several years in the process.

The ship gets back on course with companionways smashed, an injured crew, two boats washed away and the hencoops lying in the scuppers. At last the officer can come off watch and go below to the cabin. There, overwhelmed with fatigue, he sits at the green baize table writing up the entry in the log, while the sea water rolls off his oilskins and spurts out of the top of his seaboots on to the floor. Overhead, the oil lamp sways and the huge waves crash over the roof with the noise of an express train crossing an iron bridge.

Here are extracts from the log of the *Hélène*, which rounded Cape Horn, October–November 1910:

17 October, 1910: In sight of Staten Island; strong sou'westerly wind. Lower sails and gallants furled. Barometer: 747; thermometer +5; noon position 54°59′ S., 65°15′ W. Ship sailed 12 miles and made three changes of course. Chronometer checked off Staten Island.

18–19 October: Strong breeze from the northwest, freshening. Gallants, flying jib and brigantine sail taken in. Noon position 56°18′ S., 66°25′ W.

20 October: Westerly gale. Heavy rain and gusty squalls, high seas. Lower sails reefed and gallants furled. Sailed 48 miles on southwesterly course. Barometer: 760; thermometer +4; noon position 56°41′ S., 67°22′ W.

21 October: Bad weather continues with enormous seas; the deck is breached by every wave. A packet ship seen on ENE course. Three changes of course during the day, running under topsails and reefed mizzens. Covered 70 miles on course 40° W. Noon position 55°57′ S., 68°43′ W.

22 October: Storm from the west. During the night the spar of the topsail yard broke under the strain of the braces, and was followed by the snapping of the main topsail yard in a gust of wind. Colossal seas made the ship roll 27°. At dawn both watches on deck repairing the damage. Barometer rose slowly to 758; thermometer +6. Noon position 56°54′ S., 68°55′ W.

23 October: In sight of the Cape Horn islands—Deceit & Barneveldt. Position taken by bearings 55°54′ S., 69°02′ W. Wind got up from the northwest, rapidly reaching gale force. Lower sails reefed; proceeded 31 miles on course 42° south by west. Barometer: 758; thermometer +6. At 1510 hours we were 30 miles off Cape Horn.

24 October: WNW. gales veering SW., with violent gusts. Colossal seas. Under bare poles except for flying jib and reefed mizzen. Covered 59 miles on course 5° south by east.

25 October: Bad weather continues. Wind changes constantly SW., NW. & NNW. with raging seas. Changed course at 0800 hours using both watches; same sails as before. Barometer: 756; thermometer +6. Covered 22 miles on course 39° south by west. Noon postion: 57°09′ S., 69°18′ W.

26 October: Winds moderate and blow NNW. Sighted southern point of Diego Ramirez Island, bearing 47° south by west. Hoisted full sail at noon. Covered 64 miles on course 45° north by west. Noon position: 56°22′ S., 70°34′ W.

27 October: Reasonable weather with stiff northerly breeze; St. Ildefonso Islands and the west coast of Tierra del Fuego in sight. Barometer: 753; thermometer +6. Covered 68 miles on course 80° north by west. Noon position: 55°59′ S., 75°17′ W.

28 October: NNW. gale. Gusts of rain and snow throughout the night. At daybreak hoisted the gallant royals and main staysails, with lower sails reefed. Barometer: 748; thermometer +6. Noon position: 55°13′ S., 81°36′ W.

29 October: Bad weather, sea very rough: gallants and lower sails reefed. Covered 99 miles on course 84° north by west. Noon position 55°06′ S., 86°49′ W.

30 October: Changeable weather, with winds veering and threat of storms; barometer falling rapidly. Covered 81 miles on course 78° south by west. Noon position: 56°23′ S., 86°11′ W.

31 October: Gale force winds from W. and WNW. A ship believed to be German sighted to the south. Barometer: 748; thermometer +5. Covered 200 miles on course 24° north by east. Noon position: 53°21′ S., 83°52′ W.

1 November: Northwesterly gale. Very bad visibility in driving rain; heavy seas. Lower sails and gallants furled, mizzen reefed. At 0800 hours changed course and ran to the south. Barometer: 751; thermometer +7. Covered 95 miles on course 24° north by east. Noon position: 55°55′ S., 82°59′ W.

2 November: NW. and WNW. gale. Very high seas with rain and hail; barometer swinging between 755 and 760. Mainsails reefed and topgallant royals furled. Covered 90 miles on course 3° north by east. Noon position: 50°25′ S., 82°38′ W.

3 November: Severe storm from NNW. and WNW. Lower sails and gallants furled, mizzen reefed. Ship rolling badly. Barometer: 750; thermometer +6. Covered 21 miles on course 19° north by west. Noon position: 50°05′ S., 82°49′ W.

At this point the passage of Cape Horn could be considered over. Thus, from 17 October to 3 November 1910, the *Hélène* had struggled through seventeen days of appalling weather and raging seas, in a temperature which averaged 5° C. That was what rounding the Horn meant. In this case it was

CONNAISSANCE

DES TEMPS

ou

DES MOUVEMENTS CÉLESTES,

A L'USAGE

DES ASTRONOMES ET DES NAVIGATEURS,

POUR L'AN 1887,

PUBLIÉE

PAR LE BUREAU DES LONGITUDES.

PARIS,

GAUTHIER-VILLARS, IMPRIMEUR-LIBRAIRE

DU BUREAU DES LONGITUDES, DE L'ÉCOLE POLYTECHNIQUE,

SUCCESSEUR DE MALLET-BACHELIER,

Quai des Augustins, 55.

Septembre 1885.

Without this handbook, no longitude! (*Service hydrographique, Paris*)

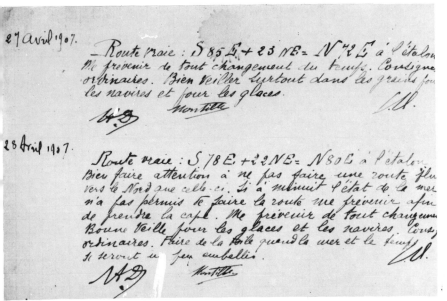

Daily orders: "Make sail!" (*Augé Collection*)

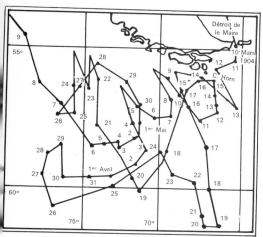

The ordeal of the four-masted American barque *Edward Sewell*, March–April–May 1914. The diagram needs no further comment.

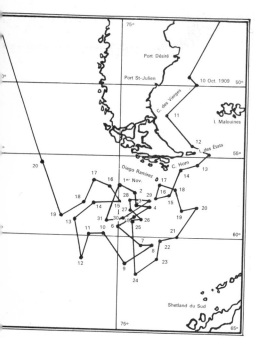

Track of the three-masted Nantes barque *La Rochejaquelein* around Cape Horn, October 1909. (Based on the notes of Commander Bourgues and his second in command.)

only a hard passage with no serious damage; others were not so lucky. Thus the story of the *Thekla's* experiences in 1911, adapted from the account of W. Nommensen puplished by the *Führerzeitung* in 1936:

On 6 July 1911, the four-masted barque *Thekla* of Hamburg was rounding Cape St. John, Staten Island. Having tacked to the south, she turned north again under fixed topsails. At 7 o'clock on the evening of 9 July, the second lieutenant, who was aloft on the mainsail yard checking the reefings, suddenly noticed in the fading light the flash of breakers dead ahead. Despite the high winds in the rigging, he reached the deck with all possible speed and told the captain, who shouted to the helmsman: "Port the tiller, port the tiller".

But it was too late; the impetus of the ship carried her forward to destruction. Waves engulfed the bulwarks and tore away the four lifeboats. The masts stayed upright and the crew tied themselves to the ratlines of the shrouds. An appalling night followed, with the men being swept by wind and sea in sub-zero temperatures. Dawn revealed the wreck lying on her side, against which huge waves broke and then thundered upon the rocks three hundred yards beyond. The surviving crew tried to rig up some rafts and save some provisions, in order to reach the shore. In a slight lull in the storm, they set off but six were drowned in the attempt. The 24 freezing survivors took refuge in a small shelter, lit a fire and killed a seal. Nearby they discovered the wreck of an English four-masted ship which had been plundered.

A fortnight passed and then on July 24 a ship hove in sight; sighting the survivors' signals, she launched a boat despite the bad weather. Nine sick men were rescued, including the second lieutenant, and taken aboard. Three more days passed in worsening weather, before the ship—which was the *Isebek* of Hamburg—reappeared. She was sighted by the men on shore and then was lost to view; the fifteen survivors began to lose hope, and night and day they squatted round the fire and kept lookout.

The *Isebek* had not abandoned them, but failing to meet any steamer, had been unable to give the alarm until she reached Antofagasta. The shipwrecked men, nearly dead from hunger, repaired a canoe wrecked on the shore; three of them embarked in her but were never seen again. At length on 6 September, a party of Argentinian gold diggers reached them, having set out on mules from a village seven days' march away. At the same time an Argentinian steamer from Punta Arenas came to the rescue. The survivors were saved and taken back to Punta Arenas, where they were reunited with their nine companions who had been picked up by the *Isebek*. Eventually all the survivors reached Germany.

Another disaster of the same period—this time on a homeward voyage, rounding Cape Horn west to east—is recounted in the annals of the German Cape Horners.

The three-masted English sailing ship *Criccieth Castle* had left Ballestos, Peru bound for Queenstown, Ireland, with a cargo of guano. She sailed down the South American coast without incident and rounded the Horn on 13 July 1912, scudding under reduced canvas before a severe westerly gale. The wind increased in force until the danger of running before the wind too long decided the captain to beat up against it and alter course.

Unfortunately at 2 a.m. on 15 July, the ship pitched so violently that the cheek of the rudder broke, tearing a hole in the helm–port. The leak in the stern brought a rush of water into the hold, and—another disaster—the

The three-masted Nantes barque *Babin Chevaye* amongst the icebergs of the southern seas, 1907.
Painting by M. Mohrmann. *(Lacroix Collection)*

The Nantes straight three-master *Amiral Cecile*; long poop and close-hauled. *(Mariners Museum, Saint-Malo)*

Lying-to, under rag-canvas, amid the fury of the Cape Horn seas. *(Lacroix Collection)*

shafts of the pumps became jammed by the cargo of guano, which became viscous after contact with the sea water. It was necessary to abandon the ship, which had on board twenty-two souls, including the captain's wife and son.

The ship possessed three boats, including a 26-foot lifeboat built to hold 34 people. In appalling weather, the latter and one of the smaller ones were got ready; about two o'clock they were lowered into the sea. The captain, his wife, their four-year old son and twelve of the crew were in the lifeboat, with the small boat, carrying the mate and six men, in tow. Course was set to the north in the direction of the Falkland Islands. Night fell and the weather worsened; it was necessary to alter course. By daybreak the small boat had parted company; it was never seen again.

On 16 July, about 11 o'clock, a large gray four-masted barque was sighted on the horizon; they signalled desperately but a snowstorm dashed their hopes. At seven o'clock in the evening a Finnish seaman died of exposure, followed soon afterwards by the cook and cabin boy.

The second night passed at sea. The men were frozen and soaked to the skin, the rum ration having little beneficial effect. On 17 July two more

sailors died; they were put overboard and their oilskins transferred to the survivors. The captain's wife Mrs. Thomas, lay in the thwarts trying to revive her little son. Her desperate efforts gave the men the will to survive. On 18 July, the weather moderated and the small sail was hoisted; the icy south wind pushed them steadily northwards.

"The Roaring Forties": heavy sea, grey skies, cold, miserable weather. On board the *Richelieu*.

Madness began to appear on board; the sailing master imagined he was still on the *Criccieth Castle* and the captain, exhausted by his many hours at the helm, thought he saw a ship. On 19 July, land was sighted. It was not a dream, but the island of Beauchesne. Having struggled ashore, the men lit a fire, warmed themselves before it and then fell into a deep sleep.

At dawn Captain Thomas aroused the men and persuaded them to set off again in the boat. Ultimately they sighted the east coast of the Falklands, but the wind set in strongly from the west and they had to alter course. On the 21st, another sailor died of exhaustion; on the 22nd, the wind came round again to the south and pushed the boat into Port Stanley harbor where all the survivors, including the captain, his wife and child, were taken to hospital. The second lieutenant and a seaman died the next day; because of gangrene,

Close-hauled in a strong gale. The watch are using their weight to keep the mizzen sail to the wind. Gouache by Oswald Pennington. *(Hon. Company of Master Mariners Collection)*

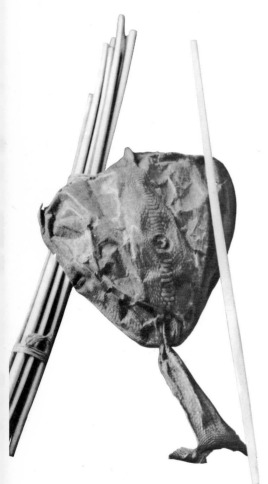

Two or three ounces of fat could be stored in a dried albatross' foot. Its wing bones could be used either as pipe filters or miniature masts and yards for model ships. *(Mariners Museum, Saint-Malo)*

one of the survivors had a foot amputated and others lost some toes. In all, fifteen had died and the rest had only their extraordinary courage and powers of endurance to thank for their survival.

This was the price exacted by Cape Horn—terrible storms, untold suffering to the men, and a fearful ordeal for their ships. The headland, never seen even by mariners who had rounded it many times, far to the south or in a snowstorm, commanded fear and respect. To the seamen it was an implacable foe against whom one fought with might and main. The whole desolate region was a graveyard for ships and their men. In 1883 the steam frigate *La Romanche,* under the command of Lieutenant F. Martial, carried out a meteorological survey of the area. The official account comprises four thick volumes, in which the following passage occurs:

On the small isthmus dividing Port Cook and Port Vancouver, we found traces of men who had been shipwrecked there, including some remnants of sails which had been used as tents, a scorched hearth and abandoned cooking utensils. Nearby, on Saddle Island, was the wreckage of the hull, masts and boats once part of a large English or American sailing ship; but we found no traces of any survivors.

Bougainville's founding of a French colony in the Falkland Islands in 1764, served, among other advantages, to provide a valuable refuge for vessels en route from Chile, who got into difficulties at Cape Horn. Port Stanley, the main port of the islands which became a British colony, was frequented after 1900 by damaged ships and shipwrecked survivors. The cost of repairs there was very high and Montevideo or a Brazilian port were better in this respect. Other possibilities were Ushaia or Punta Arenas, on the

Patagonian mainland, but the difficulty was to reach them, across an uninhabited waste intersected by innumerable channels.

In the 1904 edition of the French Hydrographic Survey's manual on *Nautical Instructions*, the following paragraphs refer to shipwrecks:

Every settlement and mission in these regions will give refuge and aid to shipwrecked mariners. Thanks to the good work of the missionaries the attitude of the local inhabitants has greatly changed. For instance, the Yaghan tribe may be trusted; a number of them speak English and they are on friendly terms with the missionaries. Contrary to what one might expect, the savages living on the banks of Nassau Bay and the Beagle Channel will guide shipwrecked sailors to the nearest settlement.

Therefore if a ship has to be abandoned in the seas to the west of Cape Horn, the boats should make for the Douglas River. If the wind carries them so that they cannot pass between the Hermit Islands and the Hardy Peninsula, the best recourse is to make for Grévy Island, and there attract the attention of the inhabitants of the islands to the north by lighting a fire.

Approximately every four weeks a steamship from Punta Arenas passes Grévy Island. Alternatively the ship's boats should try to reach the head of the La Romanche channel, disembark and cross the mountains to Tekenika.

A later passage in the Instructions offers advice to victims of scurvy:

Hermit Island: at the head of St. Martin Bay itself, and at many other places in the area, large quantities of celery may be found on the shore a short distance above the high water mark. This vegetable is best consumed during December, but will also be found available during the autumn months.

While this sea garden grew on the shores of Hermit Island, Captain Bourgain on the four-masted *Antonin*, homeward bound from Chile, is encountering icebergs in the South Atlantic beyond the Falkland Islands:

On 12 April 1909, our position was 51°20′ S., 48°35′ W., and we were proceeding on a course 40° north by east at ten knots, the weather fine with a fresh SSW. breeze. At 8 a.m., two ice floes were sighted, one twenty miles to the northeast, the other far to the north and only visible from the upper rigging.

Another iceberg was seen twenty miles farther on and the *Antonin* turned northeast to avoid it. At 1 p.m. two more were evaded, and at 2.30 p.m. the

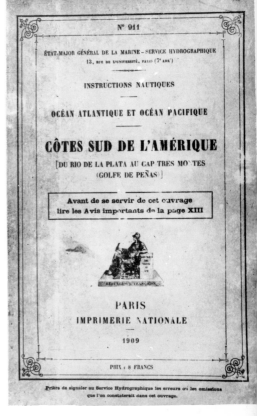

In pink, blue or yellow covers, the seaman's instructions were indispensable. Almost everything he needed was there—weather, ocean, coasts. *(Service hydrographique, Paris)*

Iceberg, 60 meters high and 300 meters long, encountered on 6 May 1905, 900 miles west of Cape Horn. In position 53°23′ S., 88°50′ W., it lay across the route of the New Caledonia sailing ships returning to Europe. *(Augé Collection)*

lookout signalled an enormous floe dead ahead. At 4 p.m. three smaller icebergs broke away from the first, which appeared to be over 125 meters high. In the evening more icebergs were seen to the east and remained visible by the light of the moon, until black clouds obscured its face. Bourgain changed course, doubled his lookouts and sought sea room. "Unfortunately, the icebergs are as treacherous at night as they are fascinating to look at during the day".

About 1 a.m. on 13 April, a whole range of icebergs stretching for seventeen miles was circumvented; at 6 the next morning there was another alarm when a berg 20 meters high was seen in the half-light of dawn. "By 8 o'clock we were surrounded by them within a six mile radius, counting three of 125 meters and fifteen others from ten to twenty meters high".

By 5 o'clock that afternoon the *Antonin* had passed the last of the 42 icebergs and escaped from the dangerous area after thirty-two hours at an average speed of ten knots.

Captain Bourgain had been both skilful and lucky. During some winters the icebergs came right up to the approaches of the Horn, leaving only a narrow channel free. When this happened in July 1906, and the ice reached latitude 44° S., the *Hautot* was caught by them. In 1904, the *Emilie Galine* en route for Portland, Oregon, caught sight of a three-masted ship fast on an iceberg, her masts gone; through the telescope it was seen that nobody remained on board. Other ships were seriously damaged by icebergs—hulls pierced, bowsprits shattered, dismasted. The famous wool clipper, *Torrens*, suffered in this fashion.

If such encounters were to be feared, so, too, were the dangers of collision with other sailing ships proceeding in the opposite direction, at night, perhaps without lights, in the narrow and frequented passage between Diego Ramirez and latitude 60° S.

Calmer weather succeeded the escape from the icebergs. Even so, sudden storms and heavy seas were a constant threat, quite capable of breaking the masts, shifting the cargo or capsizing the ship. Such were the fates of the *Ellenbrook*, capsized in 1895; the *Dreadnought* (in the Le Maire Strait); and the *Deccan* in 1908 (off Cape Tate).

The following extract is from the log of the three-masted barque *Garthsnaid*:

Friday 7th January 1920; estimated position: 58°25′ S., 71°09′ W. Westerly gale with terrible gusts. A huge wave broke over the ship at 3 a.m., carrying away one of the boats and damaging two others. Standard compass torn down; binnacle damaged and compass card put out of action. Central deckhouse breached and port bulwarks pounded up to ten meters high. At 6 o'clock we were struck by a terrific squall which forced us to reduce canvas. Much of the cargo shifted. At 9.30 we altered course to port and in calmer weather hoisted topsails and at noon resumed our original course. But we were later struck by enormous seas which buried the deck, and the ship rolled violently. At 6 o'clock we altered course to starboard and increased sail in improving weather. But at midnight encountered high seas once more.

Despite her buffeting the *Garthsnaid* managed to round the Cape and reach Callao without further delay. But how many other sailing ships coming from the east, had tried to round Cape Horn, been driven back and compelled to go the other way via the Cape of Good Hope, taking nearly 250 days to reach their destination?

Collision with an iceberg could have more serious consequences than breaking a bowsprit. The masts and hull are not damaged, so this ship was lucky. *(Lacroix Collection)*

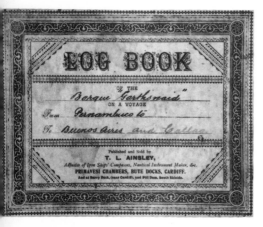

Cover of the log of the *Garthsnaid*. *(E. G. Byrne Collection)*

LOG of the Barque Garthsnaid
From Buenos Aires Towards Callao PATT. No. 5
CHIEF OFFICER'S LOG.
REMARKS, &c. Wednesday Jan 4th 1919
Hard gale with terrific squalls. At 3 am shipped a very heavy sea, shifted life boats, washed Standard Compass away, breaking glass on bowl, Compass Card destroyed and Stand badly damaged. Deck damage. Port midship wash port on bulwarks washed away. Forward wash port on port bulwarks damaged. One bulwark stanchion cracked & several bent and strained. At 6 am Bar. 28.20. Struck by a terrific squall, to save ship from going on her beam ends, let fly M. up. topsail halyards and L. lower topsail sheets, losing lower topsail and all gear attached, also shifted some of the cargo. 9.30 Wore ship (P tack). Gale moderating, bent lower topsail & set it. Noon weather moderating very high sea, decks awash fore and aft. 2.00 P.M. Hoisted M. up topsail. Ship rolling & straining heavily & shipping heavy seas. 6.00 P.M. Wore ship (Stb. tack.) weather moderating, setting sail accordingly. Mid. Light breeze heavy swell & clear.
BEARING AND DISTANCE AT NOON 2068 miles
ON THE LOOK OUT. NAME. LANTERNS HUNG OUT.
Mid – 2 am, 10 P.M. – 12 P.M. Tsunyoshi, Nurse. Sunset – Sunrise
Master. Mate

LOG of the Barque Garthsnaid
From Buenos Aires Towards Callao PATT. No. 5
CHIEF OFFICER'S LOG.
REMARKS, &c. Thursday Jan 8th 1919
Light breeze clear and fine with moderate swell
4.00 am Similar weather
6.30 am Heavy rain squall.
8.00 am Moderate breeze clear and cloudy.
Hands employed getting up coal for galley and variously
Noon Light breeze and cloudy
1.00 P.M. Set in T. gall. sails
Hands employed variously
4.00 P.M. Light airs clear & fine.
8.00 P.M. Similar weather
Mid. Light airs and fine.
BEARING AND DISTANCE AT NOON 2098 miles
ON THE LOOK OUT. NAME. LANTERNS HUNG OUT.
Mid – 2 am, 10 P.M. – mid. Jepson, Brown. Sunset – Sunrise
Master. Mate

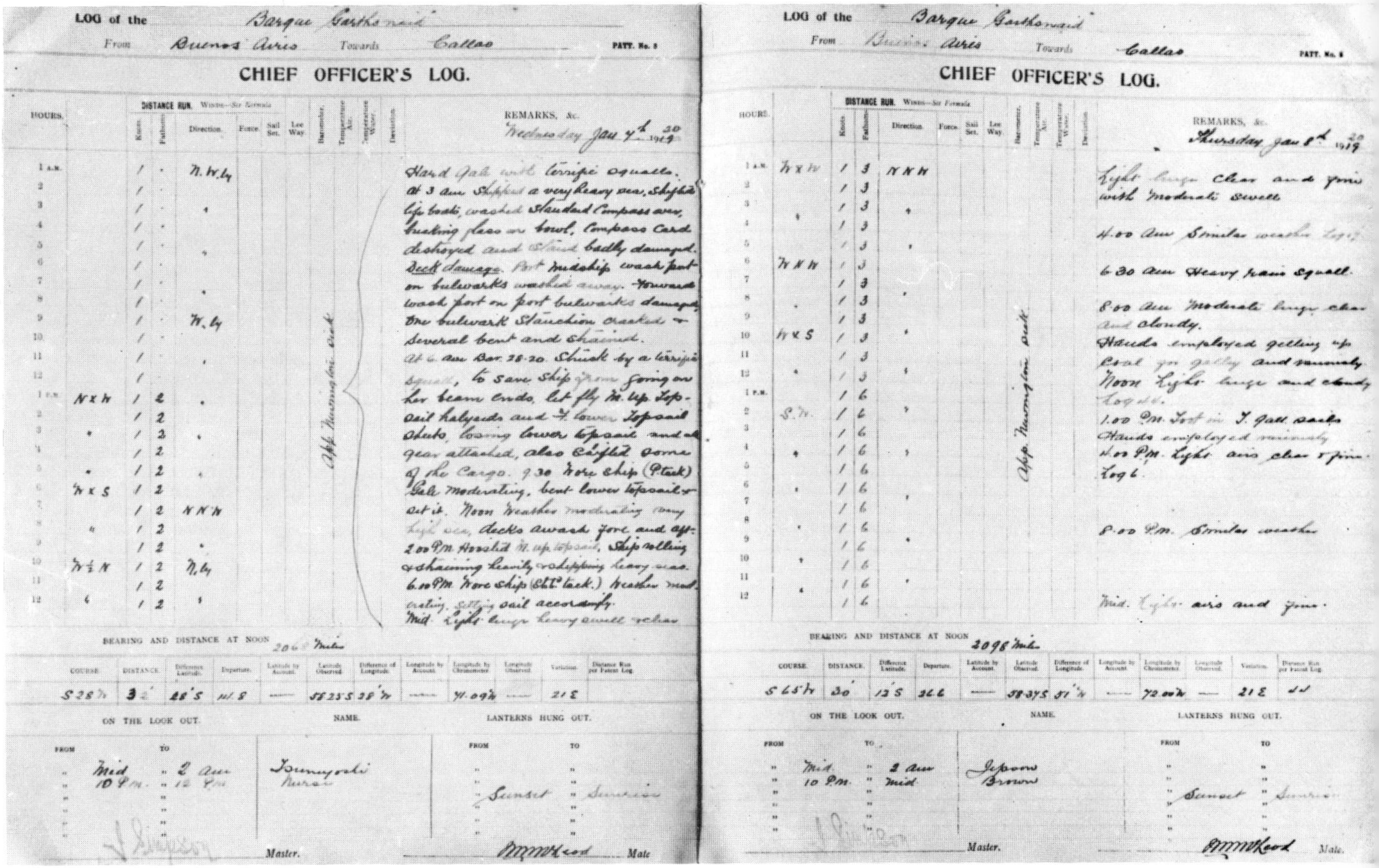

The record seems to belong to the three-masted *Garthwray*, for a voyage she made in 1922. Partially dismasted off Cape Horn, she sought refuge in Montevideo. After repairs there, she proceeded but had to put in at Cape Town for an urgent careening. She then sailed across the Indian Ocean to Hobart, Tasmania. And the time taken by the *Garthwray*, since sailing from England until she dropped anchor at Iquique was 559 days!

The return voyage, from west to east, driven by the colossal ocean swell, was often equally risky; the ships sped on the backs of the waves, pursued by their enormous crests. Frequently the following seas engulfed the poop, smashed the helm and saloon-port, tore away the compass, and often swept the entire watch—helmsman, officers and crew—off their feet, many of whom were injured, being thrown against the rigging by the force of the waves. As always, the sailors met a redoubtable foe in rounding Cape Horn.

Regarding Cape Horn itself, the *Nautical Instructions* give a very prosaic description of its character:

> The celebrated Cape Horn has no particularly remarkable feature; it falls away in black, broken cliffs. To the west it displays a precipitous wall which plunges straight into the sea. The height at the summit is 424 meters.

Insignificant it might appear, but one had to get round it!

Log of the English sailing ship *Garthsnaid*, bound from Buenos Aires to Callao. The drama of rounding Cape Horn.

Lashing up the mizzen sail aboard the four-masted English barque *Garthsnaid*.

A captain's notebook. In the right-hand corner a sketch of Cape Horn. (*Augé Collection*)

TWO WRECKS

When, with infinite patience and great courage, the ship had reached the Pacific and a position 50° S., 85° W., rounded Diego Ramirez, and set a direct NNW. course for Valparaiso, you would have thought the ordeals of Cape Horn were over and this was the entry into calmer seas. But not at all. The great swell of the "Roaring Forties", the north winds in the winter and the fog, did not allow a moment's relaxation. The Chilean coast itself was safe enough, with good anchorages and the height of the mountains gave ample warning of the approach to land. In spite of these favorable features, the stormy weather at sea off this coast was notorious.

The French three-master *Bretagne*, 1,567 tons, owned by M. Raoul Guillon & Co., of Nantes, and with a crew of 23, sailed from Antwerp on 5 April, 1900, bound for San Francisco carrying cement and a mixed cargo. On 20 June, she sighted Cape Horn but could not double it, and therefore changed course to the south. There the trouble started—gales, snow, hail and icebergs. On 29 June, at 57°30′ S., 64°00′ W., the *Bretagne* passed through a series of ice floes, three to eight hundred meters wide and of immeasurable length; on 7 July, at 56°4′ S., 69°01′ W., there was a terrible hurricane.

Cape Horn.

The Laeisz ship *Pinnas*, dismasted off Cape Horn and abandoned by her crew. *(Society of Cape Horners, Germany)*

By 10 o'clock [wrote the captain] I had lost mizzen, topsails, staysail and flying jib, so that the ship was under bare poles ... it didn't stop snowing the whole morning and it was impossible to see the bows from the stern. The snow froze upon the ship very quickly, the temperature in the charthouse falling to −10° C. There was no question of being able to repair the damage to the sails as no man could reach the topsail yard. During the frightful hurricane, and the day after, eleven of the crew suffered frostbite.

By 9 July, with the weather continuing bad and the crew in wretched state, the captain decided, after mutual consultation with his officers, it was impossible to round Cape Horn and the best thing to do was to steer north for Montevideo. But by 13 July the weather had improved and with the wind in the right direction, the captain once more turned about and headed for Cape Horn.

The next day the *Bretagne* found herself in the middle of another enormous ice floe. On 18 July, a squall carried away the main topsail; for several days afterwards it became almost impossible to steer, and it was only by means of boiling water that the pulley-blocks were kept functioning. On 12 August the upper main topsail was carried away and, worst of all, the rudder shattered the next day. Impossible to rig a jury-rudder in the raging seas, the ship drifted on:

Unable to use the sails or yard properly, I had to let the ship drift south, and then east ... the rigging swung crazily, one of the poop companionways was smashed, the cover of the port navigation light was broken ... the cargo in the orlop shifted a lot ... impossible either to open the hatches or work in the hold.

On 18 August, the *Bretagne* found herself in 56°32′ S., 80°07′ W., without rudder or major sail and 2,000 miles from Valparaiso or Montevideo, the only two ports where her damage could be repaired. In the days that followed five ships passed within sight of her—some too far away, the others not responding to her distress signals.

At last about 8 a.m. on 26 August, our approximate position being 57°15′ S., 76° 48′ W., we sighted a ship running to the east. I spoke to her at noon and she proved to be the English three-masted square-rigger *Maxwell* of Liverpool. She signalled she was short of provisions; I replied that we had some, and was it possible for them to take us on board. The lifeboats were got out and while the most incapacitated of the crew (the cook, carpenter and engineer) were lowered into her, the rest of the men brought up the victuals from the storeroom—barrels of lard, beans, flour, fat, biscuits, tinned beef and other tinned goods, coffee and sugar.

After the first boat was got away, we abandoned ship and I was the last to leave in the second, having made sure that no one remained on board. The ship's papers were taken with us, the deck hatches opened, a hole about one meter square was stove in the poop

deck, and, finally, a flag was hoisted at the mizzen, indicating that the ship was no longer under control. By 6 p.m., 26 August, my whole crew were on board the English vessel *Maxwell*, which, I learned, was en route from Iquique to Shields with a cargo of saltpeter.

The deck of the *Pinnas,* a shambles of twisted masts and rigging. Miraculously, the lifeboats remained intact. *(Society of Cape Horners, Germany)*

In 1913, the French sailing-ship *Loire* effected a dramatic rescue of the crew of the English ship *Dalgonar*. The latter, a three-masted square-rigger registered at Liverpool, had weighed from Callao on 23 September 1913 en route for Taltal. On 9 October, in position 31°24' S., 86°25' W., she was struck by a severe gale; an enormous wave came over the starboard side of the ship and she heeled right over on her beam ends; the ballast of shingle rolled right over to port and after a short time, the ends of the lower yards were in the water.

Captain Isbester ordered the rigging to be cut away and the port side whaleboat to be launched, but it was smashed to pieces. The starboard whaleboat was lowered but reduced to matchwood by the waves, and one man was killed. The captain fractured his skull against the sternpost while the first mate, W. A. H. Mull, tried cutting down the rigging. The sea engulfed half the deck and by 8 p.m. the survivors were huddled together on the poop, wet through and shivering with cold.

By midnight the storm had not abated, and every minute they expected the ship to capsize. At 4 a.m. on 10 October, a green light was sighted on the port bow; their signals were answered by a blue light.

The light came from the four-masted French ship *Loire* of Dunkirk, Captain Michel Jaffré in command, which had set sail from Iquique on 1 October 1913 with a cargo of nitrate for Dover. Seeing the wreck of the *Dalgonar*, the *Loire* altered course and hove-to until daylight. In the words of the first mate: " . . . we were sure that the *Loire* would do everything possible to save us". In the middle of the night, the *Loire's* lights disappeared, but by 10 a.m. the next morning, 11 October, she was sighted on the starboard bow. " . . . but her presence could only give us moral support; the storm raged as furiously as ever, and any attempt at rescue was out of the question".

The weather remained atrocious for two more nights and then on the morning of 13 October, the *Loire* hove-to near the *Dalgonar* and lowered the whaleboat, with seven men, including M. Cadic the first mate, aboard. The rescuers managed to throw a lifeline to the whaleboat by which thirteen of the weakest members of the crew of the *Dalgonar* were rescued.

The *Quevilly* sailing under bare poles, all her canvas having been stripped from the yards. The men wait for a lull in the storm to rehoist the topsails. *(Hayet Collection)*

The whaleboat returned to the ship, where we were all gathered on the poop, thanking God and the captain and crew of the *Loire* for having saved our lives at the risk of their own ... when the first boatload of men, of which I was one, were safely on board, I saw that the French captain had tears in his eyes. I ran to thank him and he replied that he would never have abandoned us. By noon of that day, 13 October, and in position 28°58′ S., 89°24′ W., we had all been saved ... with the 26 rescued added to the crew of 33 of the *Loire*, rations were issued to all of us ...

On 10 December 1913, the drifting wreck of *Dalgonar* was sighted by a three-masted French ship; weeks later she was still afloat, being seen on 14 February 1914 by a boat from the schooner *Inca*. Continuing to drift aimlessly westwards, the wreck finally broke up on a coral reef, thousands of miles from where she had first been abandoned.

When the mast is down, the wheel broken, the boats smashed and the ship awash to the hatch covers, what is there left but to pray? *(The Graphic)*

TO VALPARAISO, WITH COAL AND SALTPETER

For those ships that had reached the tropical latitude of the Pacific, the fine weather returned, with sunshine and a following wind. The white sails billowed and the men walked the deck with bare feet. Straw hats were dug out of their sea chests and the fishing lines snaked away from the stern. The nights were calm and still, the stars glittering in a cloudless sky. The course had to be carefully calculated to avoid being driven north of Valparaiso by the force of the Humboldt current. At dawn, a hundred miles off shore, the Cordilleras were visible, dominated by the 7,000-meter peak of Aconcagua. Reaching Curaumilla Point, the ship hove-to flying her flags at the peak and signalling her pennant number. Back came the reply by semaphore: "Set your course for Iquique".

Once Juan Fernandez had been passed, the ship sailed on to the harbor at Iquique, which was recognizable from afar by the countless masts of sailing ships, anchored in serried ranks in the roads. A tug carried the great ship in, where in the silence of the bay—hardly disturbed by the sound of the winches from the ships loading and unloading alongside—she dropped anchor, ninety days out from the Channel.

Soon afterwards, the whaleboat manned by four men, cast off for the landing stage, carrying the captain ashore to meet the company's agent. Dozens of sailing ships—British, German, French, Italian, Scandinavian—lie at anchor in the roads. In the evening, when the captain is back on board, the boat's crew row hard to reach the shore before the other boats. But the crew never saw more of the country than the landing stage, and in Chilean ports they hardly ever got ashore, or at least went inland. Their sole contact with the local inhabitants was with the stevedores from whom they obtained a few bottles of a fiery spirit known as "pisco", in exchange for their old clothes. At nightfall the anchor lights shone from the halyards.

The next day, the beat to quarters was at 6 a.m., and work began at 7 a.m. Launches came alongside, the boiler was lit on board, the steam-winches were started up and the davits were rigged at the ends of the yards. For the next fortnight the crew were transformed into coalmen. Both watches, with the exception of the winch operators, shovelled the coal into sacks, which were sewn by small Chilean men nicknamed "muchachos". The coal was then slung, ten sacks at a time, into a cradle, winched on deck, weighed by the lieutenant and then lowered into the lighters.

Disputes over the cargo often arose on shore, especially when a number of sacks were dumped in the water at the quayside, the "lancheros" hoping that they would be forgotten, so that they could recover them later and make a profitable sale ashore. Discharging coal by hand—eleven hours a day in great heat and dust, with reddened eyes, scorching hands, dry throats and blackened clothes—was a terrible job, but one which was included in the sailors' conditions of employment.

Ships often anchored several miles from the shore. The whaleboat rowed the captain ashore in the morning and back to the ship in the evening. A merry boat's crew. *(Lacroix Collection)*

Open-cast saltpeter mining in the Chilean "pampas". *(Le Tour du Monde)*

An immense concourse of ships, rank upon rank, in Tocopilla roads, taking on saltpeter. *(Mariners Museum, Saint-Malo)*

In sight of the semaphore station at Curaumilla Point, off Valparaiso. The pennant number is signalled before receiving instructions on board the *Cassard*. *(Mariners Museum, Saint-Malo)*

The sloping plateau at Junin and lighters off-shore. A melancholy scene which crews had to contemplate for months on end as they worked at the quays. *(Le Tour du Monde)*

Cable-railway wagons transporting sacks of soda-nitrate down the steep slopes of the Chilean coast to the loading quays. (*Le Tour du Monde*)

Enough ballast had always to be stowed in the bilges, against the effect of sudden cross winds or loss of stability. Several ships capsized in this way, with no hope of being righted. (*Lacroix Collection*)

Throughout this operation, the ship's ballast had to be safeguarded. The fore and aft holds, and the orlop—as soon as they were emptied of coal, and cleaned—were filled with a thousand tons of saltpeter in sacks, before the unloading of the middle hold had been completed. The final load of coal, with the cabin boy sitting astride it, was always saluted with three cheers.

After the hold had been sluiced down, a complex structure of interlocking

Samples of multicolored saltpeter artistically arranged in souvenir bottles. The Chilean "saliteros" sold them to the sailors, or sometimes they were made up on board. (*Private Collection*)

Bazaar at Guayaquil in 1883. Engraving from a photograph. (*Le Tour du Monde*)

With not enough barges available at Pisagua in 1889, the sacks of saltpeter had to be carried to the ships on balsa rafts. The delay and labor of thus transporting ten to twelve sacks at a time, can well be imagined. Extract from W. H. Russell 1890. (*Mariners Museum, Saint-Malo*)

The hurricane of 2 June 1903 at Valparaiso. Having broken her anchor-chains, the *Foyledale* heeled right over and became a total loss. Anonymous postcard.

timbers was fitted on the floor of the hold, to allow air to circulate through the apertures and around the cargo of saltpeter. From this point, the "capataz" and his team of Chilean stevedores undertook the loading of the cargo. In each hold a pyramid of sacks, each weighing about 75 kgs., was formed as the stevedores accurately threw them from their shoulders. About two-thirds of the total cargo was put into the hold, and the rest into the orlop.

Every morning the launches came alongside with the stevedores, only the winch party from the crew taking part in the loading, the rest busying themselves about the ship. There was a break at mid-day. Meanwhile the captain was ashore, supervising the purchase of supplies. This was often a tricky business; the stocks of saltpeter in the warehouses, the number of launches and stevedores were frequently limited and a crew of maybe sixty had to be provided for at the same time.

A month passed in this way; every day ships entered or left the harbor to the cheers of the crews. The day before departure the captain signed the bill of lading and took on food and water. He checked that nothing had been forgotten: his report to the consul ashore; the stevedores, pilot and tugmaster paid; the port dues settled and farewells to friends and professional colleagues made. The hatches were sealed on board and all was ready for the start of the homeward voyage. The sails were prepared and the evening before setting sail, a large wooden cross, to which oil lamps were fastened, was rigged up by the carpenter, and solemnly hauled up the masthead. This "Southern Cross" was saluted by the crews of all the other ships in harbor, and their wishes for a good voyage echoed across the bay. After the cross had been ceremoniously lowered, the captain ordered an issue of brandy and grog.

At first light, the clanking of the capstan in the forecastle was heard, pulling up the two anchor-chains, link by link. The tug came alongside to take up the tow, and, as soon as the mate hailed the captain on the poop: "Anchors aweigh!", indicating that the second anchor was up, the great ship got under way, her sails filling, making for the open sea, Cape Horn and home.

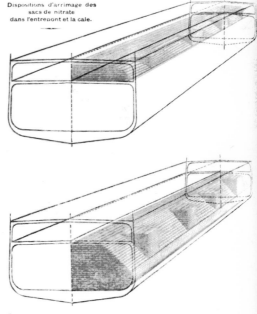

Dispositions d'arrimage des sacs de nitrate dans l'entrepont et la cale.

Stowage plans for saltpeter in the holds and orlop, as laid down in Bordes Co.'s excellent handbook: "Instructions to Captains". (*Mariners Museum, Saint-Malo*)

307

THE NORTHWEST AMERICAN COAST: THE TIMBER AND GRAIN SHIPS

The sailing ships from Europe did not often call at Callao (Peru) or Santa Rosalia and Acapulco (Mexico); it was at San Francisco and Puget Sound that they took on grain. These vessels normally followed the route of those bound for Chile only as far as latitude 40° S. They then stood to the west to pass Easter Island at about four hundred miles, and in the approximate position 20° N., 140° W., steered directly northeast to their destination. Off the Golden Gate they picked up a pilot and then entered the immense bay of San Francisco.

Ahead lay Alcatraz Island with its convict settlement, Yerba Buena on the starboard bow and in the background amid the warm haze, the shipyards of Oakland could be dimly seen. The bay teemed with ferry boats, tugs, sailing ships and all kinds of craft. Suddenly to starboard appeared the immense mass of the city of San Francisco—thousands of white houses where none had stood in 1850. Then the anchorage appeared, crowded with shipping. At the pilot's whistle, the tug heaves-to and takes in the tow.

The American *Lucile* being careened at San Francisco, *ca.* 1890. (*San Francisco Maritime Museum*)

Left: The four-masted German barque *Passat*, with nearly all sails set in a fine breeze.

COAL.
SWANSEA.

HEATLEY & Co.,
LONDON.

TELEGRAPHIC ADDRESS
"OXYLUS LONDON."

London, 26th May 1905

This Charter-Party, this day made and concluded BETWEEN *Messrs. Bureau pères & Baillergeau, Nantes* Owners of the good Ship or Vessel called the *"Babin Chevaye"* measuring 1732 tons register or thereabouts now *on passage San Francisco to Queenstown sailed 20th January as p list.*

And Messrs. HEATLEY & CO., as Agents for Messrs. J. J. MOORE & CO., of San Francisco, Merchants and Charterers. That the said Ship being tight, staunch and strong, and every way fitted for the voyage shall with all possible dispatch

proceed to PRINCE OF WALES DOCK, SWANSEA, and there load in the usual and customary manner in 12 Colliery working days, as per Colliery guarantee attached, a full and complete cargo of ANTHRACITE COAL from the   Colliery, which the said Merchants bind themselves to ship, to be brought to and taken from alongside at the Merchants' risk and expense, not exceeding what she can reasonably stow and carry over and above her Tackle, Apparel, Provisions and Furniture. Colliery terms as to loading, berthing and all other conditions to be accepted by vessel.

The Captain to take a sufficient quantity of Coals on board at Port of Loading for Ship's use for the Voyage, say not less than fifteen tons, such quantity to be endorsed on the Bills of Lading, and being so loaded shall therewith proceed to ~~one or two following ports at Charterers option at time of Loading~~, and deliver the said full and complete cargo in the usual and customary manner, at any safe Wharf or Place, or into Craft alongside, as directed by Consignees, viz. :—

Freight for the said Cargo to be paid on final discharge at the rate of

12/- ~~if ordered~~ to SAN FRANCISCO to discharge at any safe Wharf or Dock within the Golden Gate

~~if ordered to discharge at SAN DIEGO Harbour~~

~~if ordered to discharge at PORT LOS ANGELES~~

~~if ordered to discharge at SITKA, ALASKA~~

~~if ordered to discharge at HONOLULU~~

~~if ordered to~~

per ton of 2,240 lbs., on the quantity delivered, or upon the quantity as per Bill of Lading, and Pit Certificate, at Consignees' option *to be declared before breaking bulk* *ship not to be responsit for natural wastage not on board the delivered except ship's more coal.*

(The Act of God, the King's Enemies, Perils of the Sea, Fire, Barratry of the Master and Crew, Enemies, Pirates, Thieves, Arrest and Restraint of Princes, Rulers and People; Loss or Damage from Fire on Board, in Hulk, on Craft, or on Shore; Collisions, Stranding and other accidents of navigation excepted, even when occasioned by the negligence, default, or error in judgment of the Pilot, Master, Mariners or other Servants of the Ship-owners. Frost or Floods, Fire, Strikes, Lockouts, or Accidents at the Colliery directed, or on Railways, or any other hindrances of what nature soever beyond the Charterers' or their Agents' control, throughout this Charter, always excepted).

All Port Charges, Pilotages, Wharfage Dues, and Charges, on Ship, at ports of loading and discharge, and half cost of weighing at Port of Discharge if freight is paid on weight delivered to be paid by the Ship as customary. Should vessel be free from wharfage during Discharge, the above freight to be reduced by 4½d. per ton.

Payment of Freight to be made as follows: on right and true delivery of Cargo in Gold Coin at the Exchange of $4.80 to the £ sterling

The Captain to sign Bills of Lading without prejudice to this Charter-Party, but at no less than Chartered rates

Charterers' responsibility to cease on cargo being loaded. Owners to have lien on cargo for freight, dead freight and demurrage.

General Average, if any, as per York Antwerp Rules, 1890.

To be discharged as customary, in such customary berth or place as consignees shall direct, ship being always afloat, at average rate of not less than 100 tons per weather working day (Sundays and holidays excepted), to commence ~~two days after arrival~~ and notice thereof has been given by the Captain in writing; if detained over and above the said laying days, demurrage to be at 3d. per register ton per day at San Francisco and as per Colliery Guarantee at Swansea.

Charterers to have the option of discharging at an average rate of 150 tons per day, as above, in which case the rate of freight to be 3d. per ton less, or at an average rate of 200 tons per day, as above, in which case the rate of freight to be 6d. per ton less.

Should Vessel be required to move more than once during discharge, Charterers to pay cost of towage.

The Vessel to be consigned, inwards ~~and outwards~~, to Charterers, or their Agents, at Port of Discharge, paying the usual commissions and Port Agency as follows, say $100 Port Agency, 2½ per cent. Commission on the Total Inward Freight, ~~and usual Commission Outwards, say 3d. per ton penalty in lieu of outward consignment~~

Should the Vessel not arrive at SWANSEA on or before sundown on the 15th August Charterers to have the option of cancelling this Charter Party.

Ship to employ Charterers' Stevedore to take in, trim, and discharge coals, paying current rate for same.

Captain will receive loading instructions from Charterers' Agents at Swansea, whom the Owners hereby accept as Agents for the ship, paying the usual fee.

Lay days not to commence before 15th June unless as Charterers option. ship has liberty to call at a French Atlantic port for bounty purposes. Vessel has also liberty to dry dock.

Penalty for non-performance of this agreement, estimated amount of freight.

Witness to H.C.C.
for J.S. Thomson

For & by authority
Messrs. Bureau pères & Baillergeau
for H. Clarkson & Co
as agents

For & by authority
J. J. Moore & Co Snark
for Heatley & Co
26/5/1905 as agents

this is an usual charter not one of men date from could he which being one he taken to keep vessel.

Charter-agreement or freight contract of the sailing ship *Babin Chevaye* for a voyage to San Francisco. *(Nantes Archives)*

The American wooden three-master *William H. Macy* (2,000 tons, built in 1883), at the quayside, San Francisco. (*San Francisco Maritime Museum*)

"Let go the cable," shouts the mate, followed by the order from the stern: "Drop the starboard anchor-chains away".

The ship drops astern as the anchors make fast and the consignee ascends the companionway. The harbormaster's instructions are awaited, before disembarkation can take place.

San Francisco was the sailors' heaven on earth, with its prospect of crayfish suppers, wonderful wine and, also, the pretty girls of Kearney Street. These were transient pleasures only for the poor sailor because the cost was high. The 1906 earthquake (500 million dollars' damage), was not the cause, but the widespread shortage of so many things there: coal, coke, cement, scrap iron, lime, sheet and bar iron, nitrate, fertilizers, sulphur, glass, bricks, marble, machinery, sugar and salt. The sailing ships made huge freight profits in 1907 but, they had to pay exorbitantly for stevedores (grouped in powerful syndicates) and in port and wharfage dues.

Chinese bankers at San Francisco, *ca.* 1890. (*Le Tour du Monde*)

As for the crews, Master Sullivan of San Francisco was just as concerned with them as his predecessors, the "crimps", had been in the good old days of the clipper ships. Two well known French ships' captains, Rio and Muller, had to turn detectives to retrieve their pilot—on the platform of a low dive downtown, an accordion round his neck and surrounded by dancers with their feather boas and red satin dresses. "What are you doing here?" growled the terrible Captain Rio. "But, Captain, I am only earning my living!" came the reply.

Two hours later, the accordionist was unceremoniously kicked up the gangway and shut in the deckhouse until the ship sailed.

After the cargo had been carefully discharged to maintain the ship's ballast, the loading of grain began. As soon as the hold had been cleaned out, a special timber framework was built and fitted on to the floor, as had been done on the coal ships A jute covering was nailed over the top of the framework to prevent the grain from reaching the pumps. A slipway or slide brought the sacks to the bottom of the hold, where they were stacked by the stevedores in neat rows, close together. As before, two-thirds of the total volume of cargo went into the hold, one-third into the orlop; the sacks were

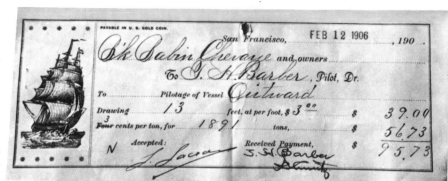

The attractive "pilotage ticket", supplied by the San Francisco harbor authorities to ships' captains for their records. (*Nantes Archives*)

In tow of *Standard No. 1*, coming out of San Francisco Bay. (*San Francisco Maritime Museum*)

always stowed very tightly, to avoid their being displaced when the ship rolled.

In good harvest years, the European ships that took on grain at San Francisco seemed countless. The monthly call took on a routine character: the captains exchanging news and expounding theories at the harbor office and with the agents; the dance halls, the low dives and brothels offering the sailors a world of pleasure beyond that which could be found elsewhere. Some of the brothels were, according to notes made by a captain of the Bordes Co., run on Japanese lines—a kind of "Yoshiwara"—in which the inmates, numbering 200, were graded into distinct categories.

Farther north, the large states of Oregon and Washington carried their grain to Portland on the Columbia river, a hundred miles from the sea. The harbor-bar there was dangerous. Once clear of this hazard and past the lightship, the ships proceeded up river under tow, between banks lined with pine trees. From time to time wooden landing stages and salmon traps were seen, with their waterwheels. Cargoes were unloaded at Portland without the risk of capsizing, since massive timber booms were attached to each side of the ship's hull at the water line to provide stability. After the usual rigging of the timber platform on the floor of the hold, the loading of wheat or barley began.

At Portland possibly even more than San Francisco, the practice of "shanghaiing" crews was prevalent. Following a strong protest by five European shipping groups, the Oregon authorities passed a law in February 1903, that sought to put an end to the nefarious dealings of the "crimps". The law included the following measures:

No seamen's hostel will be established without a license (cost $250). The numbered sign must be displayed outside the house.

A fine of from $400, and imprisonment of from three months to two years, will be imposed on anyone making a seaman desert or corrupting or cheating him.

A *maximum* fee of $30 may be paid by the ship's captain for each seaman engaged. The penalty for payment of excess fees is from $500 to $1,000. The seaman himself pays nothing.

No seaman or officer can be prosecuted for his debts.

However admirable in theory, this law could not prevent widespread boycotting of ships that refused to pay the prices demanded. Basil Lubbock's story of the English sailing ship *Cedarbank* illustrates perfectly the activities of the "crimps" on the west coast:

Nine men had deserted the ship at Hong Kong; Captain Batchelor, nonetheless, proceeded to Portland with a crew of nine seamen and eight apprentices. Hardly had he entered the river, before a boat came alongside with a "crimp" on board.

"The prices have gone up, Cap'n," he shouted, "the blood money is now sixty dollars a man".

The captain's only reply was to have the ship's anvil thrown overboard into the boat: it immediately sank her, and the occupants had to swim for the shore. As soon as the *Cedarbank's* crew stepped on to the quay, two of them were seized and two others assaulted and wounded. The captain rushed down the gangplank and tried to throttle one of the "crimps". As a result, he was jailed for a month, probably because the sheriff was the "crimp's" brother. Very fortunately, Captain Batchelor had a good first mate, and the loading of the cargo continued without interruption.

When the captain came out of prison and regained his ship, he decided not

Ten French ships loaded grain and timber at Portland, Oregon in 1900. Captain Fiaciera of the four-masted *Europe* has invited to his table the other captains—young men entrusted by the owners with responsibility over ships worth more than a million francs each in 1900. In the photograph can be recognised, amongst others, Captains Delignac of *Geneviève Molinos*; Le Dru of *Buffon*; Le Trocque of *Bougainville*; Bonny of *Ville de Mulhouse*; Le Braz of *La Tour d'Auvergne*; Rio of *Sully*; and Corvé of *La Pérouse*. (*J. Rio Collection*)

Lumber chutes running from the poop to the main hatchway. Unidentified English sailing ship.

A telegram in code, sent to the captain by the shipowners. Sometimes the schedule of cargo handling depended on these well-kept secret messages. *(Nantes Archives)*

Opposite: A team of carpenters have soon rigged up a pair of slipways for loading Oregon pine at Tacoma. The picture is of the three-masted barque *Marie* of Nantes, Captain Durieux. *(Mariners Museum, Saint-Malo)*

to replace the deserters. So it was that the *Cedarbank* reached Ireland, manned by five sailors and eight apprentices, after a 97-day voyage via Cape Horn.

Some years before, a notorious "crimp" known as "Shanghai Brown" had on one occasion just obtained his "blood money". Thereupon he was kidnapped by the crew of the *Springburn* and forced to share the perils of rounding Cape Horn in the depths of winter (1889); a fit reward for one who had done the same to so many seamen in the past.

The narrow Juan de Fuca Channel, between Vancouver Island and the American mainland, marked the entrance to Puget Sound, within which were situated the ports of Seattle, Tacoma, Esquimalt, Port Townsend and Port Blakely—names which bulked large in the ships' charters at the turn of the century.

It was a cold region—of snow, humidity, fog and a landscape of pine forests, dominated by the majestic 4,000-meter peak of Mount Rainier. Here it was that the obscure, talented marine photographer, Wilhelm Hester, captured for posterity the great Cape Horners as they rode at anchor. Fortunately, San Francisco Museum had the initiative to purchase his collection of negatives, discovered in the attic of his house after his death.

Bulk grain—wheat, barley, oats—was loaded at the Puget Sound ports by elevator in the usual manner, with timber booms alongside the hull and a platform erected in the hold. What was original here was the method of loading timber, masts and spars (of Oregon pine) which was done by slipways rigged up in the bows or at the stern. Here, too, "crimps" were all too evident and the pilotage and port dues were exorbitant. Even worse were the tug charges. In August 1908, a tugmaster demanded $850 from Captain Walter to tow his ship, the German barque *Herzogin Cicilie*, over the Columbia River sandbar and less than ten miles up river. Walter refused and he hove to off the lightship for a week, unable to proceed because of head winds. But no tug appeared; the local firms combined to defeat him, and the ship retired and set course for Australia.

This sort of behavior was always irritating, but it rarely affected the crews. As Lubbock has described, once the day's work was done they enjoyed the relaxation and companionship, singing songs round the campfire and making the most of their stay in the harbors of Puget Sound.

Port de France, New Caledonia, in 1861.
Engraving by Bérard. *(Le Tour du Monde)*

A Kanaka couple, New Caledonia, 1883. *(Société de Géographie)*

NEW CALEDONIA AND THE NICKEL SHIPS

In the latitude of Bahia, the ships bound for the Indian Ocean parted from their Cape Horn colleagues, and, taking advantage of the westerlies, followed the Great Circle route to the south of Tasmania. Following the 40° parallel of latitude they entered the Indian Ocean, passing to the north of the Amsterdam and St. Paul Islands and to the south of Kerguelen. With the help of the "Roaring Forties", with their following seas and sudden violent storms, they reached Tasmania and rounded Cape Pilar.

Using the southeast trades, they passed between Australia and New Zealand and then altered course to reach Norfolk Island. The Gold Mountain appeared in the distance and soon they were in sight of the pilot station on Amédée Islet, having completed a voyage of 14,000 miles in 90 days, if not less (88 days by Captain Stephan with the *Félix Faure* in 1905).

New Caledonia was bounded by a coral reef, one kilometer wide and over 300 meters deep at the steep outer edge. This was the "Great Barrier Reef" against which the sea pounded furiously. Several natural gaps in the reef—irregularly placed and dangerous to use—made it possible to enter the inland waters, or lagoon, between the island and the reef. Many experienced French captains made it a point of honor to take their vessels through the reef without a pilot, and with all sails set—the boiling surf and breaking waves of the reef just being avoided.

Discovered by Captain Cook in 1774, New Caledonia was named after the Scottish Highlands. Thirty years elapsed between the visit of La Pérouse and d'Entrecasteaux (1794) and Dumont d'Urville's discovery of the Loyalty Islands. Only whalers and sandalwood traders called at New Caledonia, until 1843 when a missionary settlement was established. The native population then comprised 30,000 Kanakas.

France narrowly defeated Britain for possession of the island in 1853, and from 1864 onwards dispatched convicts there, until their number had risen by 1890 to 11,000, including those released. They were taken in

316

specially commissioned vessels, including the celebrated Government transports, *Navarin, Loire* and *Calédonien.* The government, military garrison and colonists numbered 4,000 persons.

Charles Godey's little book: *Tablettes d'un ancien Fonctionnaire de la Nouvelle Calédonie,* published in 1886, paints a lively and cynical picture of this island community:

> The power of money was predominant; on the island, the leading colonist was an Englishman, Mr. Higginson. Do you need a cigar, ten Kanakas, a hundred cattle, a thousand tons of mineral, or a brig? Go and ask Mr. Higginson. Do you want to buy an island there? Once again, go and ask Mr. Higginson.

And, vis-à-vis the colonists:

> To integrate these hardened criminals into accepted society was a concept too Christian, too humanitarian, too philanthropic for the 19th century legislator to consider. The possession of land and a wife were recognized as man's supreme reward by the state. Indeed, the convict was allowed to marry and establish a family; and he enjoyed a limited degree of freedom which was envied by more honest men. Under these cloudless skies, their forced labor was controlled according to their capabilities.
>
> As a result, these scoundrels were everywhere to be seen in the colony, with well-shaven cheerful faces, pouting lips and impudent eyes. One cooked for you and tasted the food beforehand; another looked after your clothes and dressed you. Yet others groomed the horses, waited at table, washed the dishes, tuned the piano, etc. It was a wonder that the mistresses of the houses had anything to do! I have discovered the monstrous fact that over fifty of these villains were employed as house-boys and slept under the same roof as their employer. Should the convict-prison have thus been deserted? It would have been a terrible shame for the colonials if they had not had their servants!

The visiting sailors, with their meager rations and pay, did not share the colonists' attitude towards the convicts.

Except for occasional cargoes of coal, the sailing ships arrived at New Caledonia in ballast. At anchor they discharged part of the ballast, loaded up with a little mineral and then emptied the rest of the ballast before taking on the bulk nickel ore. All the work was done directly alongside, except for the

Searching convicts at the prison in 1909. Their lives often compared favorably with those of sailors. (*Le Tour du Monde*)

317

At Thio, a mechanical tip-transporter able to fill a ship with nickel ore in two to three days. The *Dieppedale* at Thio in 1907. (*Augé Collection*)

Kanaka women posing in front of a photograph of Nouméa, 1885. (*Société de géographie*)

lighters, which were often operated by the crew themselves. Loading might often take as long as a month, except at Thio where a mechanical transporter could load 3,000–4,000 tons of nickel ore in forty-eight hours.

Captain and crew enjoyed the island and the visit. In the evenings the Kanakas danced the pilou-pilou; abundant fish, game, and vegetation and a marvelous climate added to New Caledonia's attraction. Hurricanes were rare and local squabbles did not affect the sailors. Nor were they concerned with the fact that 3,000 convicts had in ten years been unable to cultivate more than 50 out of the 110,000 hectares of land which formed the colony. The colonists, customs officials and police were friendly; tours on horseback —the only means of transport—were a delight.

The ports where the nickel ore was loaded were: Thio, Canala, Kouaoua, Gomen and Pombout.

The homeward voyage to Le Havre, Glasgow or the Belgian ports (where the ore was refined), followed a course north of New Zealand and then the Great Circle route across the Pacific to Cape Horn. Thence the South American coast was followed up to the equator, and course was shaped for Bermuda and the final sweep across the Atlantic to the Channel. In effect, the nickel ships—which in France returned home to Le Havre or Rouen— had circumnavigated the globe.

THE PACIFIC ISLANDS AND THE FAR EAST: SPECIAL CARGOES

The sailing ship *Hautot* took on a mixed cargo at Le Havre for Haiphong. Having unloaded it there, the next consignment included 200 Annamite prisoners, who were to be drafted to New Caledonia to work on building a railway line. Much to the delight of the crew, a number of women of easy virtue were included in the party.

Ships reaching Japan and the Dutch East Indies brought petroleum from Pennsylvania, taken on at New York. The petrol was usually carried in 5-gallon cans, cased in pairs. These voyages enabled ship's captains to demonstrate their prowess in steering and navigation; witness an account written by 25-year-old Commander Augé in 1903:

After a very difficult voyage from New York in December 1903, we found ourselves one morning at 4 a.m. in the Sunda Straits, in company with three English sailing ships and a Dutchman. Together, we set course for Batavia. The easterly winds being changeable, our rivals decided to skirt round the "Thousand Isles". If we had followed suit, we would soon have been left far behind, with our heavy cargo of 3,500 tons of cased petrol against their light cargoes and half empty holds.

We had good charts and were confident of the crew and ourselves; so we took an immediate decision, to sail right through the archipelago. To help the crew, the boiler was lit and navigation of the channels began with everybody on deck. We altered course almost every half-hour, ready to throw out the anchors at a moment's notice; sometimes, we were so close inshore that we nearly fouled the Malays' bamboo fish-traps, much to their alarm. At one place we touched sandy bottom but without mishap, and eventually at 8 p.m. were able to anchor, in fine weather amidst the palm trees, with all sails set. The tropical night passed swiftly, with two men posted on lookout.

At midnight I awoke with a start; squalls, thunder and lightning and shouts on deck overhead. I dashed on deck in my shirtsleeves and helped to raise the second anchor, as everyone scurried to and fro. Under torrential rain, the gallants and topsails were lowered and other sails made fast in case of disaster. We were all drenched; nevertheless the lightning flashes and gusts of wind in the channel made a picturesque scene. Storms were unusual in these parts and it abated before we had completed our maneuvers. A ration of rum was issued to all on board to keep out the cold and we all returned below.

At daybreak we started off again, using every puff of wind in the little channels to our advantage. A large Dutch signal station, surprised to see us venturing in such unfrequented channels, semaphored its congratulations. The Malays cursed as we passed by, not realizing that we were engaged in a race and meant no harm to their fishing nets. At last, the channel widened and that evening we dropped anchor in Batavia roads.

Two days later, the first of our rivals—the three-masted *Hugo Mollenaer*—anchored beside us at Tankjonk Priok. Her captain congratulated us on our ability to handle our 100 meter-long ship like a yacht. One of the English ships did not arrive until a week later; we were delighted to have defended our colors so well.

Cargoes of petrol were regularly shipped to Shanghai, Hong Kong, Tsingtau, Yokohama, Hakodate and Nagasaki.

Tahiti in 1900 had changed little since the time of Captain Cook. The wonderful life it was possible to lead there brought a strong temptation to desert amongst visiting crews. In the island the ships loaded mostly copra and shellfish, the latter being used for mother-of-pearl. Despite the archipelago's appearance of paradise, it was a dangerous area for hurricanes, two thousand people being killed in one in 1905.

Fiji produced cotton; the Gilbert, Marshall and Caroline Islands were noted for sandalwood, palm oil and guano. These were normally taken to the larger ports by local traders; the ocean-going sailing ships rarely visited these islands unless by special charter agreements arranged beforehand in China or America. A few European sailing ships came to Honolulu to ship the island's chief crop, raw sugar, but the bulk of this trade was handled by American sailing ships based on San Francisco. In fact, this traffic was maintained until the last days of sail.

Besides the English, who had trade routes throughout the Pacific, the Germans had won an important stake in the region during the period. By 1885, they had colonies in New Guinea, the Solomon, Caroline and Marshall Islands as well as the Marianas and part of Samoa. This colonial expansion

Chinese boatman, 1886. (*Société de Géographie*)

Honolulu, Hawaii in 1855; the rendezvous of all the Pacific whaling ships. Engraving by Hildebrand from a photograph by J. Howland. (*Le Tour du Monde*)

The roadstead at Hong Kong in 1904. *(Le Tour du Monde)*

Hong Kong, 1886. A captain on his way to see the shipbroker. *(Societé de Géographie)*

ran directly contrary to the policy of Bismarck, wittily expressed by him, some years before: "Colonies for us will be exactly as sable-skin coats to the Polish nobility, who have not even got shirts on their backs".

In order that these island industries could flourish, a more sinister traffic existed in the Pacific. Until the beginning of the present century, the notorious "blackbirders" were rife; these were ships which came to the Solomons, New Hebrides and New Guinea and, willy nilly, shipped off hundreds of natives to work in the cotton or coconut plantations.

Foochow roadstead after the typhoon of 11 September 1893. (*Société de Géographie*)

AUSTRALIA: WHEAT, COAL AND WOOL;
NEW ZEALAND: WOOL AND FROZEN MEAT

The bulk of the European traffic was concentrated upon Australia and New Zealand. Following the meridian 500 miles south of the Cape of Good Hope, the European sailing ship route passed not far from Tristan da Cunha, Prince Edward and Kerguelen Islands. With strong tail winds, the ships followed the prevailing westerlies, with only the great sea birds, whales and icebergs for company.

A little less than three months after leaving the Channel, they reached Kangaroo Island near Cape Borda, an anchorage which had, at all costs, not to be missed, since the winds were always westerly there and the current ran to the east. If they were bound for the Spencer Gulf ports, the ships loaded wheat at Port Pirie, Walaroo and Port Germain. Even as late as 1920, the primitive aspect of these ports, with their wharves of wooden piles and single-track railways, caused surprise, as for instance to C. Lebret, the mate of the *Saint Louis* of Nantes:

> Port Germain is a small village of houses with red-tiled roofs. There are two streets, two shops, a church, and two banks—quite enough for a small community. No Australian keeps his money at home; the farms are very isolated and there are too many robbers about. The bank opens its safe to supply cash on request each time a visit is made to town.

After the ships had been rid of vermin, the loading began; it might take a month to complete, 30–35,000 sacks of grain being brought to the quayside along a small railway line. The visit was often agreeable, the local ranchers being friendly and hospitable. There was an abundance of food—saddles of mutton, rabbits (as distasteful to Australians as frogs to Englishmen) and game. But above all it was the wool trade which, after the transport of emigrants, made the fortunes of the Liverpool shipowners.

Much had changed in Australia since 20 April 1770, when Zachary Hicks, lieutenant on watch aboard the *Endeavour*, told Captain Cook that land had been sighted. The discovery ship had anchored in Botany Bay and taken possession in the name of King George III. Six years later the American War of Independence had broken out, and English interest had turned towards this large southern continent.

Captain Philip's fleet sailed from England, comprising six major warships, two frigates and three storeships, carrying 717 convicts—men and women— and 290 warders. The fleet's arrival at Botany Bay on 16 January, 1780, marked the beginning of the colonization of Australia. That part of New Holland where he disembarked was henceforth called New South Wales. The early days greatly discouraged the pioneers, and their efforts would have

Hong Kong prostitute, 1886. (*Société de Géographie*)

Several of the ocean-going sailing ships used to sign on New Hebrides natives, who proved excellent topmen. Note the lucky charm suspended from the neck. (Société de Géographie)

The stowage of the wool bales in the hold, with the help of jacks, levers and docker's hooks. (Bibl. des Arts décoratifs, Paris)

ended in failure but for the energy of Governor Philip. He watched Captain Baudin's hydrographic surveys along that coastline with disfavor, made at the same time as those of Flinders. Other energetic men succeeded Philip as Governor of New South Wales, including Captain Bligh of the *Bounty*.

By 1821, the colony numbered 30,000, all the land on the coastal side of the Blue Mountains being occupied and settled. Thereafter, Sydney, Port Jackson, Port Macquarie, Port Philip, Hobart (Tasmania), Brisbane, Adelaide, Perth and Bathurst were founded. Deportation of convicts ceased in 1850, and the Scotsman, John MacArthur, pioneered Australian sheep-farming.

By 1860, a decade after Edward Hargraves had struck gold on Summer Hill, the colony's population reached one million. As had happened in California, the gold rush did not last long. Soon the Australian plains were covered with immense fields of wheat and the pasturage supported huge flocks of sheep. The land of convicts, kangaroos, gold and rabbits became a rich market for the wool and grain clippers. The ships having rounded Cape Horn joined up with the European and American vessels, laden with grain and timber from the west coast, on the long homeward passage across the Atlantic.

Mountains of wool in bales stood on Sydney's "Round Quay", awaiting shipment—a scene vividly portrayed by Conrad in his *Mirror of the Sea*. The London wool sales took place in January, February and March. They were stopped as soon as the required tonnage had been reached; thus wool clipper captains en route hastened to declare their imminent arrival by getting off a signal at Falmouth. It was the opposite system to that which had been used by the tea clippers from Foochow, in the sense that in Australia the fastest ships were loaded last.

The on-loading of wool demanded the utmost skill by the stevedores. The ship's trim had to be kept to six inches at the stern, however tightly packed the cargo in the hold and orlop. The bales of wool had to be wedged together with the aid of lifting-jacks, purchases and hydraulic levers. The stench, dust and heat in the holds was overpowering, and in the bilges the ballast had to be coated with copper. The wool could catch fire spontaneously, and one remembers the fire aboard *L'Orient* in 1861, which was only brought under control through the coolness of the passengers and crew.

Many small clippers—of from 700 to 1,000 tons—were engaged in the wool trade; vessels of the "White Star Line"; of Duthie, Devitt & Moore; of the "Orient Line"; of Elder. They normally went out via Cape of Good Hope and returned via Cape Horn, except when they carried passengers, in which case they called at St. Helena on the return voyage.

On the outward voyage, once having passed Cape of Good Hope far to the south, the ships made full use of the prevaling westerlies, the "Roaring Forties", right up to their landfall at Cape Borda. During the passage, the crews hardly knew what it was to have a dry shirt on their backs.

As soon as port was reached in Australia, everyone left the ship, and, as crew for the return voyage, the captain had to rely on whatever was available—farmhands, jailbirds, office clerks working their passage home. Famous among the wool clippers were *Torrens, Sobraon, Berean, Harriet MacGregor, Heather Bell*—all classed A 1, the top category registered by Lloyd's, after fifteen years. Wonderful sailers, they could reach Cape Horn from

Australia in 26 days, and the Lizard from Cape Horn in 67.

In this period of the wool trade, the clippers were entirely wood built; it was followed by the age of steel clippers. Their dimensions rose in proportion, until the *Mermerus* was able to bring back to England a cargo of 10,000 bales of wool, equivalent to the fleeces of a million sheep.

The advent of the steamship and the opening of the Suez Canal marked the end of the Australian wool trade for the sailing ships. Until the First World War they were relegated to the transport of grain, loaded at Spencer Gulf, and to coal, loaded at Newcastle, N.S.W., and destined for the west coast of America.

Side by side with the English sailing ships, the German, French and Scandinavian participated in the Australia trade. The return voyage to Europe followed a course which passed Auckland Island and South Island,

Cutty Sark, with boom retracted, loading wool at Sydney's "Round Quay". (*Nat. Maritime Museum, Greenwich*)

New Zealand. Many of the reefs in these regions were not surveyed or buoyed and caused a number of dramatic shipwrecks.

On the night of 6 March 1907, the lookout aboard the English sailing ship *Dundonald*, as she came out of Sydney, suddenly cried: "Breakers, dead ahead! Breakers, dead ahead!" Nothing could be done in time to save her; the hull scraped on the pebbly beach, the shaken masts fell and the stern swinging round, stuck fast in a fissure in the sixty-meter cliffs. As the sea pounded with fury against the wreck, a lifeline linked it with the shore, but only sixteen of the crew of twenty-eight were able to reach safety.

At dawn, the survivors found they were on Disappointment Island, six miles from Auckland Island. The account does not relate how they were able to survive with so little food. On 31 July, 1907, some of them embarked on a small boat which they had fitted with a sail. After two failures, they brought back some provisions found on Auckland Island. At last, on 16 October, they were rescued by the steamship *Hinémoa*.

The cache of provisions had been established there after the loss of ten wool clippers amongst the islands. The worst was the shipwreck of the *General Grant*, lost in 1866, with 45 passengers and £10,000,000 worth of gold nuggets aboard. Only ten survivors struggled ashore and they had to endure eighteen months privation before they were rescued.

On 15 May, 1905, the French three-master *Anjou* (owned by Guillon of Nantes and commanded by Captain le Tallec) was wrecked on the shore of Auckland Island, with a cargo of wool. No one perished at the time of the shipwreck, but it was a miracle that the three ship's boats managed to cross the raging seas to the shore. "Our fate might almost have been supportable", wrote Captain le Tallec, "if the gales and storms, sometimes raging for three whole days, had not tormented us".

Three months after the wreck, the steamship *Hinémoa*, on her way to re-stock the depôt with provisions, found and rescued them.

In New Zealand, visited predominantly by English sailing ships, frozen meat, tallow, rawhide and wool were loaded at the ports of Wellington and Lyttleton.

THE RENAISSANCE OF THE FRENCH SAILING SHIPS

While England, preaching free trade, had revoked her Navigation Laws and put her merchant marine on its mettle, France re-imposed in 1840 a "flag tax", first promulgated in 1793. This measure remained in force until 1866 and protectionism gained the upper hand. The question to be answered, however, was how far had the French shipbuilders and owners been affected.

In 1881, Dupuy de Lome, far from seeking to prohibit free trade, proposed the enactment of a revolutionary new measure. The decree offered bounties and subsidies to sailing ships built in France, based on tonnage and length of voyage and in inverse proportion to the age of the ship. A second liberal measure gave foreign built ships the right to half premiums on navigation. As a result of these developments, the number of French shipbuilders and shipowners increased and prospered: *Chantiers de la Loire*; *Dubigeon of Nantes*; *Chantiers de Normandie* of Grand Quevilly; *Chantiers du Sud-Ouest* of Bordeaux; *Chantiers de la Mediterranée* of La Seyne and Le Havre; and finally, *Chantiers de France* of Dunkirk.

The four-masted *Nord* of the Bordes' fleet leaving Dunkirk. (*Bohé Collection*)

The *Richelieu* in a stiff breeze.

La Rochefoucauld getting under way.

Close-hauled on board the 4-masted German ship *Passat*.

In the trade winds on board the *Passat*.

Bordes Co.'s vessel *Jeanne d'Arc*, formerly the *Belen* of Nantes. Launched at Nantes in 1910; cargo capacity 3,100 tons; specialized in trade with Oregon ports. *(Bohé Collection)*

The sailing ships could not compete with steamships over the same distances, so they limited themselves henceforth to certain cargoes. Thus emerged distinct types of sailing ships, few being constructed outside their class: vessels displacing 3–4,000 tons, built to carry balanced cargoes.

The law of 1895 gave subsidies for ship construction, on the scale of 65 francs per gross ton for steel ships, 40 francs for wooden ships and 150 francs for machinery. The subsidy for navigation was given on the basis of 1 fr. 70 cent. per gross ton and for every thousand miles sailed by a new ship. The scale decreased according to age. The law of 1902 withdrew the subsidy, substituting a "shipowners' compensation", applicable both to French and foreign construction, on the scale: 5 centimes/day during construction of a ship up to 2,000 tons; 4 centimes to 3,000 tons; 2 centimes between 4,000 and 7,000 tons. The law of 1906 increased the rates again.

Thus, from 1893 to 1906, the French merchant marine experienced unparalleled prosperity. About 1895—at a time when steam was threatening the very life of the sailing ship—the directors of A. D. Bordes of Dunkirk bought several fine sailing ships from English owners at a very low price. By 1900, France possessed 1,235 sailing ships (105 "on premium") ranging from one to ten years old, which amounted to a total displacement of 195,716 tons. At the same time her steamship fleet of the same age, numbered only 431 vessels, with a total displacement of 141,464 tons. Moreover, the pace of steamship construction in France was going down at a time when it was increasing 50%, even 100%, elsewhere. Did not the sailing ships steer themselves; even without freight could they not cover their subsidies?

Several protests were heard, one deputy of the National Assembly remarking: "The winds go free; there is no necessity for us to spend 8 million francs a year on sailing ships". In his: *Le Problème de la Marine Marchande*, published in 1901, Maurice Sarraut has shown that several French sailing ships were making profits between 19% to 33% annually. Far from denying these figures, their owners confirmed them, as an encouragement to their shareholders. At the same time a number of English companies registered in France, behaved disreputably by taking advantage of their position to domicile their ships, and make full use of the French navigation subsidies by only trading between foreign ports and only with foreign goods.

Before arrival. Putting the anchors in the port-wells aboard the *Richelieu*. *(Maritime Museum, Saint Malo)*

The longer the voyage, the greater the profit. As well as petroleum taken on at New York for Tasmania, there were a few cases of mixed cargo, and diversions to be made to Japanese and Dutch East Indian ports before reaching the final destination. In 1908, twenty-seven French sailing ships called at Hobart, Tasmania. It was not the overall increase in the seamen's wages of 65 francs a month which accounted for the ships' rising costs:

Accounts of the *Reine Blanche*, 1,945 tons, during a voyage made in 1897–1898 in 6 months and 5 days from Newcastle-upon-Tyne—Swansea—San Francisco—Cape of Good Hope—New Caledonia—and return to Le Havre.

The four-masted barque *Jacqueline* of the Bordes' fleet. Launched at La Seyne in 1897 and sunk in 1917.

Share Capital: 220,000 frs. Loan Capital: 220,000 frs.

		in francs
RECEIPTS:	Navigation Subsidy	133,481
	Freight	237,642
	a. *Total Receipts*	371,123
EXPENSES:	Swansea & Newcastle	27,812
	San Francisco	31,385
	Cape of Good Hope	13,822
	New Caledonia	10,000
	Le Havre	8,000
	Crew's Wages	25,500
	Commission and Agent Expenses	8,000
	Insurances	34,391
		158,910
	Repairs	9,133
	General Expenses	3,000
	Speed Bonus to the Captain	3,000
	3% of Profits to the Captain	5,910
	Voyage Expenses	16,407·33
	Company Expenses	3,437·50
	Interest & Depreciation on Loan Capital $5\frac{1}{2}\%$	40,132·07
	b. *Total Expenses*	239,929·90
NET PROFIT		131,193·10
	Reserves 5%	
	5% Pay-back on Capital over $16\frac{1}{2}$ months	6,559·65
	3% Pay-back on Reserves over $16\frac{1}{2}$ months	15,125
		24,200
		45,884·65
Leaving for dividend distribution		85,308·45

or, on a capital of 220,000 frs. over 1 year an interest rate of 33·19%

The *Reine Blanche* was not the only sailing ship to show a profit. The *Charles Gounod* gave 25·6% interest; the *Général de Charette*, 25·9%; the *Général Neumayer*, 21·5%; and the *Général de Boisdeffre*, 19·25%.

The French training ship *Richelieu* (ex German *Pola*), in tow. *(Photo Cooper)*

Thus also the accounts of the Nantes Co.'s ship *Cassard*, on a voyage Nantes—Swansea—San Francisco—Antwerp, made in one year and ten days, July 1899 to July 1900 :-

		in francs
RECEIPTS :	Navigation Subsidy for the whole voyage	103,113·27
	Freight	174,527·09
	Various	149
	Total Receipts	277,789·36
EXPENSES :	Crew (Wages, Victuals, Medical)	34,508·08
	Ship's Maintenance	18,207·58
	Expenses of the Voyage, Port Dues, Towing Charges, Commissions, Insurance	102,264·57
	Total Expenses	154,980·23
Gross Profit		122,809·13
Less : Depreciation 6%, interest, general expenses		54,561·15
Net Profit		68,247·98
Share Capital		325,000
∴ Interest for the Year		= 20·95%

The superb three-masted barque *Croisset* of the Prentout fleet. Launched at Grand-Quevilly in 1899, she had a characteristically long poop deck, carried forward beyond the mainmast. Sail area over 3,000 square meters and traded predominately in nickel ore. Sunk in the Irish Sea in 1908. (*Augé Collection*)

Seas breaking over the *Richelieu*.

In spite of corrupt practices in some quarters, there were encouraging compensations: the development of French trade overseas, the increased employment given to French shipyards, from Toulon to Dunkirk. By 1914, the Bordes Company with their 44 ships, possessed the most important sailing ship fleet under one house-flag. Their vessels could transport up to 150,000 tons of freight; 60 captains, 170 officers and 1,400 seamen were in their employ. Their principal trade lay in the carriage of soda-nitrate from Chile to Europe via Cape Horn. Nor were they alone in this trade; other Cape Horners operated from Dunkirk, Nantes, Bordeaux and Marseilles.

At Nantes the shipowners Bureau & Son, Bureau & Baillergeau, the Society of Nantes sailing ship owners, the Société Génerale d'Armement, Guillon, the Nantes Shipowners, Société Bretonne de Navigation, etc.—all sent their vessels to Chile, California and Puget Sound. Fine ships there were in these fleets: *Duchesse Anne*; *Général de Sonis*; *Babin Chevaye*; *Versailles*; *Jean*; *Françoise d'Amboise*; *Maréchal de Gontaut*, and many others.

The Ehrenberg Company and the Society of French Sailing Ships, with offices in Paris, had great success with their *Geneviève* and *Marguerite Molinos*. The d'Orbigny Company at la Rochelle had *L'Asie* and *L'Europe*. The sail tanker *Quevilly* and the giant *France II* flew the flag of Compagnie Prentout of Rouen. Brown & Corblet boasted the celebrated *Président Félix Faure,* and les Voiliers Dunkerquois, the *Brizeux, l'Hermite* and *Bérengère*. ... The rest of the fleets operating from Nantes, Bordeaux and Marseilles voyaged to Africa, the Caribbean and the East Indies.

Captain Lacroix's well-known works admirably describe the history of these firms. His books are essential for an understanding of the last days of the French merchant sailing fleet.

"RULE BRITANNIA": THE POWERFUL ENGLISH SAILING SHIP FLEET

The 1870's—when the first iron ships were built in the Clyde, Mersey, Tyne and Aberdeen shipyards—mark the beginning of the real prosperity of the English sailing ship fleets, a supremacy which remained unchallenged for thirty years. Free trade shaped an economic outlook which demanded modern transport. Iron and steel working, in both of which the British were past masters, provided the means to give Britain a twenty-year lead over the rest of Europe.

The era of the Blackwall frigates and the first wool clippers to Australia was over. Spectacular voyages, such as Captain Forbes' with the *Marco Polo* (Liverpool—Sydney—Liverpool in 5 months, 21 days) were no longer the shipowners' main objective. With the opening of the Suez Canal in 1896, it was not long before steamships began to monopolize the routes to Australia and the Orient. Against the passage times achieved by the steamships, the sailing ships could not compete. There remained the matter of freight; steam went quickly but was expensive. Tea, passengers, mixed cargoes and finally wool were sufficiently profitable to absorb the higher freight rates; coal, timber, grain, rice, mineral ores and nitrates, on the other hand, were not. The sailing ships took what was left to them, specializing in the latter— the bulky, heavy, dirty cargoes. They became bigger and heavier.

Iron construction brought a number of advantages: reduction of internal fittings, which gave greater cargo space; greater strength and durability (the iron built *Antiope* lasted 54 years). The masts climbed higher and higher

The magnificent wool clipper *Torrens*, launched at Sunderland in 1875. A fully-rigged composite ship (iron frame, teak planked), she established a record passage of 65 days between Plymouth and Adelaide in 1881. *(Nat. Maritime Museum, Greenwich)*

The crew of the three-masted English steel barque *Invermark* at Tacoma. *(San Francisco Maritime Museum)*

into the sky—so much so, in fact, that there were a number of dramatic dismastings in the '80s. Those were years of experiment and innovation. English shipyards built for the whole world. Their costs were incredibly low and delays in delivery were much shorter than anywhere else.

The first iron ships ran on the Australia—New Zealand service, then to India and the Orient. This was the golden age of the "Loch Line" of Glasgow (Aitken & Lilburn); "Aberdeen White Star Line" (Thomas & Co.); A.J. Carmichael; the "Orient Line"; Devitt & Moore; Duthie, etc. Even the names of some of their ships reflected the commercial triumph of the companies.

About 1882, advances in the processing of steel permitted its incorporation in marine construction. The gain in weight and strength stimulated the naval architects to further daring. Cargo capacity doubled, gross tonnage reaching 3,000 tons and more. In order to steer these enormous masses, the great four-masted ships with their fantastic rigging appeared—as maneuverable as their three-masted predecessors. An important function of these huge ships was their use as storeships. Some of them were "jumboised", that is, the hull was cut in the middle and a new center section, perhaps 10 or 15 meters long, was added, increasing displacement by 200 to 300 tons.

The year 1888 was a prosperous one for the sailing ships and the *Clan*, *City*, *Castle*, *Fall*, *County* and *Garth* classes of vessel. Although steamships had seized the Australia/New Zealand wool trade, the English sailing ships— like the German, French and Scandinavian—kept hold of the timber, grain and nitrate trade with the Pacific and South America, and the rice and jute trade with the East Indies. There were some colossal ships at this time, for example the *Liverpool*, 110 meters long and 6,000 tons gross tonnage.

From their early days, the English steel ships were known, delightfully,

332

The celebrated English wool clipper *Torrens* becalmed. The captain's state of mind may be imagined! *(Nat. Maritime Museum, Greenwich)*

as "Lime Juicers". As a precaution against scurvy, their crews were given 15 centiliters of lime juice daily per man. Unfortunately it was not realized until later that limes did not possess the same anti-scorbutic properties as lemons. The English seamen drank neither beer nor alcohol on board, still less wine. Tea and coffee in Victorian England had displaced the daily beer ration and the rum first issued as grog by Admiral Vernon. Food on board the "Lime Juicers" was a little more varied than on French ships, but less plentiful. The work on board was very similar, with Sundays respected as rest days.

It has been said that the English ships were handled with care and skill; their captains' preference being to take in sail in the worst weather and await an improvement, thus losing days which might be won by a bolder course. But this prudence was perhaps the privilege of the greatest sailing fleet afloat. All in all, too, the English captains were older than the French.

By English law, the ships were under no obligation to sail with only English crews; most of the shipowners would, in fact, not have allowed it. The sailors on board the "Lime Juicers" were better paid than their French opposite numbers, but they enjoyed far less of the social services (insurance, sickness, management), for which the French shipowners were liable.

La Duchesse Anne of Nantes, sailing up the coast of Chile. *(Lacroix Collection)*

Taking an azimuth on board *Port Jackson*. *(Nat. Maritime Museum, Greenwich)*

With typical realism, the English made full use of their internal resources of coal and steel. Their sailing ships had no building subsidies from the government, as in France. Nevertheless, Britain's fleet of steamships forged ahead. outstripping other European countries. The last sailing ships, built for English companies, were launched in 1895; in the next five years, almost all were disposed of to foreign buyers at very low prices. Shipowners in France, Germany, Italy, Sweden, Norway and the United States acquired them, while the majority of the English sailing ship companies disappeared forever.

The marvellous books by Basil Lubbock tell the whole story of the English sailing ship companies. They are recommended to readers, as much as those of Captain Lacroix in his field.

THE YOUNG GERMAN FLEET

Ever since the days of the Hanseatic league, the North German coastal towns had shown great interest in maritime affairs. The break-up, however, of what ought to have become the North German Confederation prevented united effort. It was left to family businesses, similar to those existing in the United States about 1850, to promote the German merchant marine. Frequently, the captains were themselves the owners, even the builders, of the ships. However, these pioneers possessed little capital and had only themselves to rely on.

Since 1815, ships from Bremen, Hamburg and Lübeck had been seen off the coasts of Africa, the West Indies, South America and even China. German whaling ships frequented the Pacific in the years 1815 to 1840. The "Zollverein" or Customs Union of 1833 was the first attempt made in Germany to define a trade policy that would encourage the shipowners. In the 1840s, the peak decade of emigration to the United States, the ships of the German free ports thrived. By 1848, over 6,000 sailing vessels of all kinds, manned by 45,000 seamen, were operating from Germany's Baltic and North Sea ports.

Maritime organization, however, remained backward. During the Schleswig-Holstein dispute (1860–1863), a few minor Danish warships blockaded the North German ports with impunity, there being no German navy available to oppose them. But the desire to create such a navy at first foundered on economic reality; the shipbuilders depended on England for iron and steel; credit banks did not exist and the customs tariff wall opposed large scale imports. But the proclamation of the North German Confederation in 1870 awoke a national patriotism, which crystalized twenty years later in the German Navy League and the Pan-Germanic movement.

In the words of Doctor Hugerberg at Frankfurt: "The eyes of German citizens must henceforth be fixed upon the high seas, as were those of our ancestors of the Hansa". Emperor Wilhelm II followed the same line of reasoning when he declared at Stettin that the nation's future lay in sea-power. Between 1870 and 1890, the number of German steamships leapt from 147 to 815 and their overall tonnage from 81,994 to 617,911 tons. By 1905, the figures were 1,657 ships and 1,774,072 tons respectively. As for sailing ships, while their numbers had decreased (1890: 2,700 of 688,414 tons—1905:

The *Lisbeth*, four-masted German barque owned by Schmidt of Hamburg; carried nitrate and Oregon timber. Launched in England in 1891 as the *Pendragon Castle*; then voyaged to Calcutta. *(San Francisco Maritime Museum)*

The young crew of the full-rigged three-master *Olinda* of Hamburg, at Santa Rosalia in 1905. They are clearly much more at ease in their shirt-sleeves, than were the crew of the *Léon Blum* [q.v. page 235]. (*Steinmayer Collection*)

2,294 of 493,644 tons), the main loss had been in coastal craft going over to steam; many of the big ocean-going sailing ships continued to operate.

The fleet laws of 1898–1900 and Tirpitz's efforts to build a big German navy required a constant flow of trained personnel and crews. These could only be found in the merchant marine, which had 60,000 registered seamen in 1905. Moreover, Germany had to develop her own shipyards.

As in the case of Britain and France, the German sailing ships concentrated upon the carriage of heavy freight in bulk, a traffic which had been relegated to them by the development of the steamship. Moreover, by requiring seamen to serve several years at sea aboard sailing ships to qualify for officers' licences, the merchant marine contributed to the survival of the sailing fleet.

The leading German sailing shipowners in 1911 were, at Hamburg: F. Laiesz; B. Wencke, Knöhr & Burchard; Alster G.m.b.H.; G. J. H. Siemens; H. H. Schmidt; Aug. Bolten (who became W. Müllers); and Wachsmuth & Krogmann. At Bremen: Rickmers G.m.b.h.; D. H. Watjen; Visurgis G.m.b.H.; and E. C. Schramm (Vinnen). For the most part these companies were equally concerned with steamships.

F. Laiesz was the German equivalent of France's A. D. Bordes, a fine example of a sailing ship company running its affairs despite the encroachment of a machine age. Ferdinand Laiesz's career was a curious one. Starting work as an apprentice in a silk hat factory, then setting up his own business in Hamburg, the young man then chartered a small ship to Rio, with a full cargo of hats. The sail of his silk hats in South America (especially the more colorful ones) was so successful that they could not be crammed into the hold tight enough. Soon he was exporting the raw materials: silk, cardboard, straw and leather, and a chain of Laiesz shops and factories sprang up in

L'Arraccan, ex *S.F.Muntz*. Three-masted composite German ship of the 1870's. *(Mariners Museum, Saint-Malo)*

The three-masted German barque *Winterhude*; owned by Schluter & Maack of Hamburg and launched at Geestemünde in 1898.

South America. In 1842, Laiesz decided to build his own ship for the trade, the *Carl*. Thus began his extraordinary career as a shipbuilder: an amazing transformation from hatter to shipping magnate.

His celebrated fleet—the name of each ship beginning with the letter "P" —did not become the leading one in Germany until around 1877. With the assistance of genial Captain Hilgendorf, Laiesz commissioned two remarkable vessels—the celebrated five-masted square-rigger *Potosi* in 1895, and the

The 3-masted composite German barque *Rialto,* owned by Paulsen Elsferth Company. *(Steinmayer Collection)*

The four-masted German barque *Paul Rickmers.* *(Society of Cape Horners, Germany)*

The three-masted German vessel *Katharina*, Captain Spiller. Painting by H. Petersen, 1892.

equally famous five-masted *Preussen*. The latter's mainmast was 68 meters tall and she carried 5,500 square meters of canvas. Like Bordes, Laiesz's ships did a lot of trade in Chilean nitrate. Side by side with this great company, the shipowners Wencke and Rickmers upheld the German sailing ships' tradition on the routes to the Pacific and the Far East.

With France, Germany was the only country that still continued to fit out sailing ships at the opening of the present century, and to maintain highly trained crews. These men, almost exclusively Germans and subject to a rigid discipline, were invariably very young. They normally served a period at sea before taking their certificates. The German captains kept their ships in good condition and had a reputation as fine steersmen and bold sailors. Although she had entered the race late, the German sailing fleet had, by dint of great efforts, largely caught up with its rivals. Valuable accounts of its history are preserved both in the works of Basil Lubbock and in the issues of the journal *Der Albatros* (the bulletin of the Society of German Cape Horner captains).

MORE THAN A DOZEN FLAGS IN THE SEAS OF CAPE HORN

England disposed of her "Lime Juicers"; those not bought by France and Germany, operated under the flags of Russia, Norway, Sweden, Italy, Greece and the United States. For centuries Scandinavian ships had been seen in every port of Europe, from the Baltic to the Black Sea; after the American gold rush they appeared in the Pacific. With native built ships, first of wood and later of steel, the Swedes and Norwegians carried the bulk cargoes to the Pacific via the Horn, as did the other countries, and foregathered at San Francisco, when the grain harvest in California was a particularly good one.

Even by 1900, the American sailing fleet remained very active, and, strangely enough, most of them were entirely wood built. The wood used was always fir or pine, alone available to the American yards. The first

The Danish Cape Horner *Bertha* of Esbjerg. Formerly the English owned *Silvercraig*, she was lost off the Falkland Islands in 1892. (*Maritime Museum, Elsinore*)

The *Balclutha*—still afloat today—was launched on the Clyde in 1886. She voyaged round Cape Horn until 1899. Renamed *Star of Alaska*, she traded between San Francisco and the north, as part of the Alaska Packers Fleet, 1902–1930. Then followed twenty miserable years touring the west coast of the United States as a "showboat", after which she became a derelict on the San Francisco mudbanks, 1952. She was rescued by the San Francisco Maritime Museum and restored to her pristine glory, at a cost of 13,000 man-hours and 100,000 dollars. A universal object of admiration today. (*San Francisco Maritime Museum*. Photo taken at San Francisco in 1899.)

American steel sailing ship—the *Dirigo*—was not, in fact, launched until 1894. At that, she had only been assembled in the U.S.A., her steel plates and ribs coming from Glasgow. While awaiting the American shipyards completion of steel ships, the owners bought English vessels or placed orders for construction on the Clyde.

The shortage of well-trained crews in the United States at this period was one reason why many ships were built schooner-rigged over there. The Maine shipyards built nearly 400 of these vessels, with four, five, six, and even seven masts. Voyaging from coast to coast via Cape Horn—with cargoes of "mixed", timber, coal, petroleum, cereals, flour or Hawaiian sugar cane—the best of these ships were able to reach Honolulu from New York in 115 days, sometimes less, and Honolulu from San Francisco in 8 to 12 days. One of these "Down Easters" was the *Northern Light*, once commanded by Captain Joshua Slocum, whose name is immortalized in his single-handed voyage round the world in the *Spray*.

Other American sailing ships ended their days in the Alaskan fishing fleets, with a combine known as the "Alaska Packers Association". The fleets wintered at Oakland; at the beginning of spring each ship, with a crew of about thirty, they set off north, fully equipped with everything to net and crate the salmon. With the crews, sailed 150 to 200 Chinese or Mexican fishermen to work the lines. It was normally a four to six weeks' voyage from Oakland to Bristol Bay, Alaska—the fishing and packing center. The voyage along the American coast was not without its dangers due to gales.

A veteran ship in this service was the *Balclutha*, ex *Star of Alaska*; built at Glasgow in 1886, she once made a remarkable passage between San Francisco and Bristol Bay in two weeks (1926). Restored, re-rigged and drydocked by a society of amateur ship lovers in San Francisco, she is afloat today.

Sublime perfection of naval architecture: the bows of the *Passat*.

THE SAILING SHIPS IN THE 1914–1918 WAR

On 27 March 1917, en route from Antofagasta to Europe, the Bordes Company ship *Cambronne* was far out in the Atlantic, in the approximate position 20°00′ S., 28°05′ W. Then she sighted a sailing ship which altered course toward her and closed at considerable speed in spite of the light winds. Two miles off, the strange vessel hoveto, took in her sails and then ran up German colors. Then came the signal: "Abandon ship, or I open fire!", followed by a warning shot across the *Cambronne's* bows.

It was 8 a.m.; the mystery ship with the Norwegian flag painted across her hull, was in fact the German raider *See Adler*. She had 233 prisoners on board, and her commander, Count von Lückner, ordered their transfer to the *Cambronne*.

Once this had been done, she was commanded to proceed to the nearest port, which she did, reaching Rio four days later. Everyone was disembarked, and the *Cambronne* set sail for Nantes. However, on the 8th of July, two days from home, she was torpedoed and sunk off Sein Island by a German submarine.

The *See Adler* which wreaked such havoc among the nitrate clippers was formerly the English windjammer *Pass of Balmaha*. Captured by the Germans in the North Sea at the start of the war she had been converted into a raider, to operate in waters beyond the range of their submarines. Re-named *Irma* and with a crew of 64, she carried Norwegian papers

Bayonne, straight three-master owned by Prentout. Torpedoed and sunk by U-84 in the First World War. *(Bohé Collection)*

Norway being then neutral). Her Atlantic cruise resulted in the sinking of five French sailing ships, three British, one Italian and three British steamships. After a difficult passage around Cape Horn, the *See Adler* entered the Pacific, sank three American ships, but was wrecked on a coral reef in Tahiti. Von Lückner was taken prisoner and sent to New Zealand, but succeeded in escaping. Ultimately he was recaptured and sent home in a steamer in 1919.

The English Channel, infested by auxiliary cruisers and German submarines, became a dangerous area. In one week in 1916 twenty-two ships were sunk there. Sailing ships continued to carry coal from the Bristol Channel ports in order to supply the needs of the warship squadrons. But they rarely ventured to Dunkirk, Le Havre or the English east coast. After being immobilized for more than a year in French and Chilean ports, the bulk of the French sailing ship fleet was chartered by the Government. Chilean nitrate had to be brought to Nantes, Bordeaux, Rochefort and La Pallice for use in the manufacture of explosives. Although the Battle of the Falkland Islands action had made the Cape Horn route less dangerous, the sailing ships—mostly unarmed and very vulnerable when becalmed—crossed the Atlantic at great risk. No praise is too great for the heroism and self-sacrifice of their crews.

Out of the 136 seaworthy German sailing ships in 1914, 60 were interned in Chile and Peru until the end of the war. Of the rest, only 11 managed to get back to Germany. Twenty-four were captured or interned by Britain, three by France.

In 1882, the *Port Jackson* made the passage between the Channel and Sydney in 77 days. A typical training-ship for apprentices making a long voyage. The *Port Jackson* was sunk in the Channel in 1917. Here she is seen in her rôle as training-ship. (*Nat. Maritime Museum, Greenwich*)

The Dale Line's *Torrisdale*, wool clipper to Australia. Run-down but not sunk; fortunately the point of impact occurred well forward at the peak. *(Nat. Maritime Museum, Greenwich)*

At the armistice, a full account could be made. Both England and France had suffered severely; the Nantes fleet alone had lost 36 sailing ships, and the Bordes Company 18. By the peace treaty, Germany was permitted to retain her steamships and sailing ships of less than 1,600 tons. As reparations, she handed over 19 of her sailing ships to Britain, 20 to Italy and 34 to France (including the *Passat* and *Potosi*).

These compensations could not eradicate the loss of hundreds of officers and mariners, who went down with their ships or died in the ranks of the marine corps. Many shipping companies were destroyed by the war. The Panama Canal had been open since 1914, and everything combined to render the continued existence of the sailing ships impossible. It was only the gross shortage of mercantile tonnage after the war that permitted the survival, for a few more years, of the great "birds of the Cape".

346

PART IV

The Seamen of Another Age

The First World War was just over. A large part of the sailing ship fleet had been sent to the bottom of the sea by the submarines and surface raiders such as the *See Adler*. The stay of execution upon the remainder was only because of the general shortage of ships throughout the world. One needed to be a romantic enthusiast in order to equip a sailing ship in those days. Those who did it were opponents to the steamships, to the coal burning vessels whose high chimneys belched forth a plume of black smoke. Right up to the last years before the beginning of the Second World War, these shipbuilders of former days could still find young and enthusiastic seamen and old experienced captains who were willing to sail round the world in these old ships. These men were indeed the last of the Cape Horners.

At Nantes, at Dunkirk, at Le Havre and at Marseilles the great ships, stripped of the last vestiges of their sails and rigging, awaited the arrival of the tugs which would take them to the breaker's yards. Nevertheless, after the demobilization of the "useless State fleet" of 1920, some French sailing ships took on a new lease of life.

The *Ville de Mulhouse,* the *Maréchal de Turenne,* the *Duguay-Trouin,* the *Général de Sonis,* the *Bayard,* the *Général Faidherbe* took on grain at San Francisco for Queenstown Island or for Falmouth. These were slow laborious voyages both ways; in some cases 186 days elapsing between San Francisco and the entry to the Channel, usually via Cape Horn. At least until 1926 some French ships still appeared in Australian ports; for example the Bordes' Company ship *l'Atlantique* operated there for one single voyage. Other vessels occasionally went to the Carribbean. In one case, after lengthy negotiations the *Richelieu,* the ex-German sailing ship *Pola,* was taken over by a nautical training school; after taking grain to Adelaide with a crew of 30 and 18 cadets, the training ship blew up and was lost at Baltimore in 1926.

Almost the only countries that continued to make use of ocean-going sailing ships during this period were Germany, Sweden, Finland and

Buried in the sand, a mast and a yardarm— melancholy symbols, framing the wreck of a Cape Horner in Nouméa Bay.

Denmark, while at the same time English and Italian sailing ships practically disappeared.

At the confluence of the Gulfs of Finland and Bothnia and the Islands of Aland, in the middle of dark pine woods and picturesque fishermen's cottages lies the Port of Mariehamn. In turn Swedish, in turn Finnish and practically independent since 1920, Mariehamn was to become the last refuge of the great sailing ships. The place was a great meeting place for seamen and the total population in 1963 amounted to approximately 30,000 of whom 198 were actual Cape Horners.

One of the very last important owners of sailing ships was Captain Gustav Erikson of Mariehamn. In 1918, at the age of 45 and a wealthy man, he already owned a considerable fleet of sailing ships. At the same time he began to add to them by purchasing other ships at a cost only slightly higher than the scrapping rate. Between 1932 and 1938, Erikson built up a considerable fleet in this way. His ships, bound for Australia in order to bring back grain, normally left Europe in ballast (more occasionally with coal for the remoter corners of South Africa, or with timber for Melbourne), rounded Cape Horn and arrived in Australia in January. The return voyage was made via Cape Horn and usually started in May or the early part of July. However this type of trade was not very profitable to the owners; for example, in 1935, carrying a ton of grain from Australia to Europe—halfway round the world—actually cost less than the carriage of 100 kilos of grain between Paris and Toulon. These were the sort of economies the sailing ships were now faced with. They sailed with old sails and rigging and neither the cargo nor the hull of the ship was properly insured. The crew might consist of only 20 men, plus cadets who were obliged to pay for their passage and a number of amateur sailing men who went on the voyage and who had to contribute 4,000 francs for the voyage to Australia and back. The captain himself might

Mariehamn, last refuge of the Australian grain ships. At anchorage before the next season; in the foreground, the *Archibald Russell*. (*L'Illustration*)

The Martinière Canal in 1921. A long line of sailing ships in perfect condition with no one prepared to commission them. The majority left this graveyard only to go to the breakers' yards. *(Lacroix Collection)*

How better to symbolize Mariehamn than by a fine four-master? *(Postage stamp, 1964)*

349

One of the last two of Laiesz' great fleet of sailing ships, the *Padua*—leaving Taltal with a cargo of saltpeter, *ca.* 1935. (*S. Reyes Collection*)

only receive about 2,000 francs. As a shipowner, then, Gustav Erikson only did it because of his love of the sailing ships.

TABLE OF VOYAGE DURATIONS FOR SAILING SHIPS
BETWEEN AUSTRALIA AND FALMOUTH IN THE YEAR 1934

1. *Swedish sailing ships*
    The four-masted barque *Abraham Rydberg* .... 107 days
    The four-masted barque *C. B. Pedersen* .... 127 days

2. *German sailing ships*
    The four-masted barque *Padua* .... 108 days
    The four-masted barque *Pamir* (sold to Erikson in 1908) .... 119 days
    The *Priwall* .... 108 days

3. *Erikson's sailing ships*
    The three-masted barque *Penang* .... 116 days
    The three-masted barque *Killoran* .... 125 days
    The three-masted square-rigger *Grace Harwar* .... 127 days
    The three-masted barque *Winterhude* .... 126 days
    The four-masted barque *Archibald Russell* .... 130 days
    The four-masted barque *L'Avenir* .... 137 days
    The *Lawhill* .... 121 days
    The *Olivebank* .... 115 days
    The *Passat* .... 106 days
    The *Pommern* .... 110 days
    (In 1936 she made a run from Port Lincoln to Falmouth in 94 days)
    The *Ponape* .... 130 days
    The *Viking* .... 137 days

NOTES:
One might mention in this context that the *Lightning* in ballast took 64 days in 1854 to make the passage between Australia and Falmouth; and the Nova-Scotian schooner *Wanhilda*, with a cargo of grain, took 66 days for the same passage in 1890. In 1938 Erikson's fleet was augmented by the addition of the *Moshulu, Abraham Rydberg* and the *Hougomont*. After 1945 only 6 ships remained in his fleet; these were the *Pamir*, the *Passat*, the *Viking*, the *Pommern*, the *Moshulu* and the *Archibald Russell*, *the second*.

These grain voyages were the last to be made and after the second world war, 1939–1945, the sailing ships did not do more than make occasional voyages between Argentina and London carrying grain. As shown above, Erikson's fleet had by this time dwindled to six sailing ships. In 1950 the *Passat* and the *Pamir* were dismantled at a quayside in Antwerp; a scrap merchant bought them and there seemed no way of preventing their being broken up; however the German government stepped in, took them over and converted them into training ships.

Padua leaving Taltal. *(S. Reyes Collection)*

Although the *Pamir* no longer rounded Cape Horn after 1945, she still carried grain from Argentina to London under the Finnish flag in 1950. The last Cape Horner to make a trading voyage, she was the sister ship of the *Passat*. On 24 September 1957 in mid-Atlantic, the sea settled accounts with the *Pamir*, when a severe gale overwhelmed her in tragic circumstances with the loss of eighty lives.

The log-reel paying out the line over the stern. When the log-glass had emptied its sand every thirty seconds, the knots on the line were counted. *(Nat. Maritime Museum, Greenwich)*

The dramatic end of the *Pamir* is well known. At the beginning of September 1957, she sailed from La Plata bound for London with a bulk cargo of grain. Around 4 o'clock in the afternoon of the 24th, with all her sails set, she was struck without warning by Hurricane Carrie in position 35°57′ N. and 40°20′ W. A very strong gust of wind turned her on her side and the cargo shifted to such an extent that she soon had a pronounced list. Only 6 of her crew, which comprised 86 men of whom many were young cadets, were rescued by ships that came to her assistance.

This beautiful four-masted vessel was, in fact, the last Cape Horner to undertake a commercial voyage. Her sister ship, the *Passat*, belongs to the German Sailing Ship Society.

How many of these great veterans still survive today? The *Cutty Sark* is at London, the *Pommern* at Mariehamn, the *Balclutha* at San Francisco, the *Passat* at Lübeck, the *Viking* at Gothenburg—last survivors of a great age of Cape Horners which had lasted for more than three centuries.

As for the men who sailed them, what has happened to them? In June 1936 thirty veteran sea captains gave a lunch at St. Malo in honor of their former Professor of Hydrography, who was then 76 years old. Commander Briand totalled up the years of service undertaken by all his former pupils there; the result was 900 years in all and included 250 passages of Cape Horn. How many more would there have been if one included all the other survivors from France, England, Germany and elsewhere? Was not this the time to record all these wonderful achievements through the years before they were forgotten?

Thus it was that the Society of Cape Horners was founded. After the war the members of the society held annual conferences, which have taken place in such places as Nantes, Paris, St. Malo, Bordeux, Marseilles, Antwerp, Bremen, Hamburg, Dunkirk, Hoorn in Holland (in 1963) and elsewhere.

The magnificent wake of the *Passat*, four-masted barque of the Laeisz fleet.

Domestic jobs undertaken by young enthusiasts.
Sailmakers on board the Erikson fleet's *Passat*.

Look-out man aboard the *Passat*.

Every ship had to be properly cared for. After the rust had been scaled off, the paintwork
was renewed—so that all the masts were well preserved. On board the *Passat*.

Six husky young men are not too many to wind the anchor-cable round the capstan, bringing the clew of the wind-filled sail home to the forecastle. Aboard the *Passat*.

How many of these fine men still remain today? How many of the "Albatrosses", as the captains of the ships which sailed round the Horn were known? How many of the "Mollymauks", as the mates or lieutenants of these vessels were known? Each year there are fewer and fewer.

They still return to the society's annual meetings if they can possibly do so, despite illness or the great distances they have to travel. Germans, Englishmen, Belgians, Frenchmen, Finns, Dutchmen, Italians, Norwegians, Swedes, and many many others. Now the men, who stand erect despite their age, wearing their blue caps with the badge of the great Cape Horners—a picture of the albatross with his hooked beak gnawing at the fishing net sewn on them—in token of their past service.

When the time for singing old sea songs at the society's meeting comes along, all the old enthusiasm and courage of their former years is revived. In full voice they sing together *We went to Valparaiso*—that song which they used to chant to give courage to their men in times of trial, when the waves were sweeping over the ships and the wind was whistling through the rigging.

If all else was changed, neither the wind nor the sea have softened the aspect of Cape Horn itself. Every day of the year the great west winds blow continuously with savage violence across those seas, veering capriciously from northwest to southwest. The gray clouds scud across the horizon laden with freezing rain and flurries of snow. The heavy swell rolls in foaming crests and the surf explodes against the granite shore of Diego Ramirez and then dashes against the rocks of Horn Island. In the immense waste there is not a ship to be seen and the sea is empty.

On 31st October 1962, however, the Lighthouses and Beacons Department

of the Chilean Government erected on Cape Horn a small wooden structure 4 meters high. This was the "Cabo de Hornos" light tower, 40 meters above sea level. A white light shone from it every ten seconds, with a range of eleven miles and a traverse between eighty and two hundred and forty-nine degrees. Why was it erected, and for whom? For the two lonely Trinity House boats which pass there annually, for the few cargo ships which round Cape Horn on their way to South Africa?

In their noiseless flight, the great albatrosses pass across the revolving beam of the lighthouse. For a moment it catches these great birds of the Southern Ocean in its light; surprised by this last relic of human vanity in that remote area, they blink their eyes.

On tow in the Elbe, leaving Hamburg—last minute checks before the open sea. Extract from Captain Ludwig Albrand's: *Westward ho!* (*Service Hist. de la Marine*)

SELECT BIBLIOGRAPHY

PART I
DE BRY, Theodor: *Grands Voyages.*
HARRIS (J.): *Voyages.*
VIGNAUD (H.): *La Lettre et la Carte de Toscanelli.*
HOWE (S.): *Great Navigators in search of Spices.*
GRAVIÈRE (J. de la): *Les Marins du XVe et du XVIe siècle ; Les Gueux de la Mer.*
ZWEIG (S.): *Magellan.* Cassell 1938

PART II
BROSSES (Ch. de): *Histoire des Navigations aux Terres australes.* F. Cass 1967.
DALRYMPLE (A.): *An Historical Collection of the several Voyages and Discoveries in the*
    South Pacific Ocean. Nourse, Payne & Elmsley 1770.
FROGER (F.): *Relation du Voyage de M. de Gennes.*
DUPLESSIS: *Relation du Voyage de Gouin de Beauchesne.*
DAHLGREN (E. W.): *Voyages français à la Mer du Sud.*
CLARET-FLEURIEU: *Voyage autour du Monde du Capitaine Marchand.*
MAME: *Voyages autour du Monde.*
MADROLLE: *Premiers voyages français à la Chine.*
ANSON (G.): *Voyage round the World.* Dent 1748
FOURNIER (P.): *Hydrographie.*
DANA (R.): *Two Years before the Mast.*
BÉRIOT (A.): *Grands Voiliers autour du Monde.*
DUHAMEL DU MONCEAU: *Traité de la Construction des Vaisseaux.*
DIDEROT-D'ALEMBERT: *La Grande Encyclopédie.*
RAINAUD (A.): *Le Continent austral, hypothèses et découvertes.*

PART III
MARTIAL (F.): *Mission to Cape Horn.*
CLARK (A. J.): *The Clipper Ship Era.*
LUBBOCK (B.): *The Down Easters ; The Colonial Clippers ; The Last of the Windjammers*
    Brown, Son & Ferguson.
LACROIX (L.): *Les Derniers grands voiliers ; Les Derniers Cap-Horniers.*
DUSSOL (A.): *Les Grands Compagnies de Navigation en Allemagne.*
MOUFFLET (A.): *Les Conditions du Travail dans la Marine marchande.*
KEMBLE (J. H.): *San Francisco Bay.*
LAING (A.): *American Sail.* Foulsham 1962
CONRAD (J.): *The Mirror of the Sea.* Dent 1949
HAYET (A.): *Us et Coutumes à Bord des Long-Courriers ; Dictons et Tirades des Anciens de*
    la Voile.
MASSENET, VALLEREY, LETALLE: *Gréement, Manœuvre et Conduite du Navire.*
PALLU DE LA BARRIÈRE: *Gens de Mer.*
JACQUES (H.): *Cap Horn.*
FRANK (B.): *The Barque Magellan : a story of the French deep-sea sailors.* Jarrolds 1938
BEAUJEU (A.): *Dans les Tempêtes du Cap Horn.*
AUBIN (B.): *L'Empreinte de la Voile.*

PART IV
VILLIERS (A.): *Voyage of the Parma.* Bles 1933
            Falmouth for orders. Bles 1929
            By Way of Cape Horn. Hodder & Stoughton 1930

Figurehead of the three-masted *Loch Linnhe.*
(Mariehamn Museum)

GENERAL BIBLIOGRAPHY

Histoire de la Marine ; L'Illustration.

LLOYD (C.): *Ships and Seamen.* Weidenfeld & Nicolson 1961

TRAMOND (J.): *Histoire maritime de la France.*

LOTHURE (R. de): *La Navigation à travers les Ages.*

VAN LOON (H. W.): *Ships and how they sailed the Seven Seas.* Harrap 1935

BAKER (J.): *A History of Geographical Discovery & Exploration.* Harrap 1931

MARGUET (F.): *Histoire générale de la Navigation du XVe au XXe Siècle.*

PARDESSUS (J.-M.): *Collection des Lois maritimes.*

SARRAUT (M.): *Le Problème de la Marine marchande.*

TOUSSAINT (V.): *Code manuel des Armateurs et des Capitaines.*

LA ROERIE: *Navires et Marins de la Rame à l'Hélice.*

BOUILLET (N.): *Dictionnaire d'Histoire et de Géographie.*

BONNEFOUX et PARIS: *Dictionnaire de Marine.*

JAL (A.): *Glossaire nautique.*

CHARLIAT (P.): *Trois Siècles d'Economie maritime française.*

PARIS (Amiral): *Souvenirs de Marine conservés.*

BRUNSCHWIG (H.): *L'Expansion allemande outre-mer.*

Lloyd's lists.

Annuaire du Bureau Veritas.

Bulletins de l'Académie de Marine, Paris.

La Revue maritime.

Revue maritime et coloniale.

Le Tour du Monde.

L'Illustration.

The Graphic.

Der Albatros.

Gleason's Pictorial.

Cartes du Service hydrographique, Paris:

Océan Pacifique (n° 5438)—*Mers de Cap Horn* (n° 5504)—*Archipel du Cap Horn et Canal du Beagle* (n° 4115).

Instructions nautiques n° 911 du Service hydrographique français (Côtes sud de l'Amérique). 1903

ACKNOWLEDGEMENTS

This book has only been possible thanks to the cooperation of all those who have sent documents, memoirs and other material, as well as many others who have given their advice. To all these people I am extremely grateful:

Audouy (G.), Augé (L.), Ameil (G.), Benoit (M.), Berthelot (M.), Bidon (M.), Blandin (E.), Mme. Bohé, Boman (G), Briand (A.), Brisart (R.), Busson (J.-P.), Byrne (E. G.), Cailliatte (F.), Chevallier (M.), Collin-Olivier (M.), Danguy (M.), Demarbois (M.), Disney (H.), Durieux (M), Evenou (F.), Fiault (M.), Mme. Galanis, Glück (M.), Godeau (M.), Gourio (L.), Gruénais (P.), Mme. Gruss, Hayet (A.), Henningsen (H.), Jeannot (M.), Jebens (H.), Kortum (K.), Mme. Lacroix, Lailler (D.), Mlle. de la Roncière, Le Bret (C.), Lecoq (F.), Legros (M.), Le Garrec (P.), Le Goff (F.), Lelièvre (M.), Le Maître (O.), Lidou (J.), Lochhead (J. L.), Louvet (L.), Mareschal (Y.), Marinet (M.), Mme. de Masson d'Autume (B.), Mellert (F.), Menguy (Y.), Motto (U.), Niblock (R. W.), Osbon (G. A.), Person (H.), Phibbs (H.), Pognon (M.), Putois (M.), Rauh (R.), Ravasse (L.), Reyes (S.), Reynaud (F.), Rio (J.), Roquet (M.), Rying (B.), Sauce (M.), Schoof (R.), Steinmeyer (E.), Stéphan (R.), Taillemitte (M.), Mme. Thalman, Mme. Tiercelin (M.), Mrs. Tucker (E.), Vaugham (A. B.), Verhé (C.), von Zatorski (W.).

Libraries, Museums and other collections, for the use of whose material I am extremely grateful in the preparation of this book:

Amicale internationale des Capitaines au long cours cap-horniers, Saint-Malo.
Bibliothèque Nationale de Paris, départements des imprimés, des cartes et plans et des manuscrits.
Service Hydrographique de la Marine, Paris.
Bibliothèque Historique de la Marine, Paris.
Archives Nationales, Paris.
Musée du Long Cours, Saint-Malo.
Société de Géographie, Paris.
Institut de Géographie, Paris.
Musée et bibliothèque des Arts décoratifs, Paris.
Archives de la Librairie Hachette, Paris.
Comité central des Armateurs de France.
Musée des Arts et Traditions populaires, Paris.
Académie de Marine, Paris.
Archives départementales de Nantes.
Bibliothèque de Marseille.
Compagnie de Navigation d'Orbigny.
Chantiers Dubigeon.
National Maritime Museum, Greenwich.
The Honourable Company of Master Mariners, London.
Port of London Authority.
San Francisco Maritime Museum.
The Mariners Museum, Newport News.
U.S. Naval Oceanographic Office, Washington.
Danish Maritime Museum, Elsinor.
Musée d'Aland, Mariehamn.

Figurehead of the four-masted *Hougomont*. (*Mariehamn Museum*)

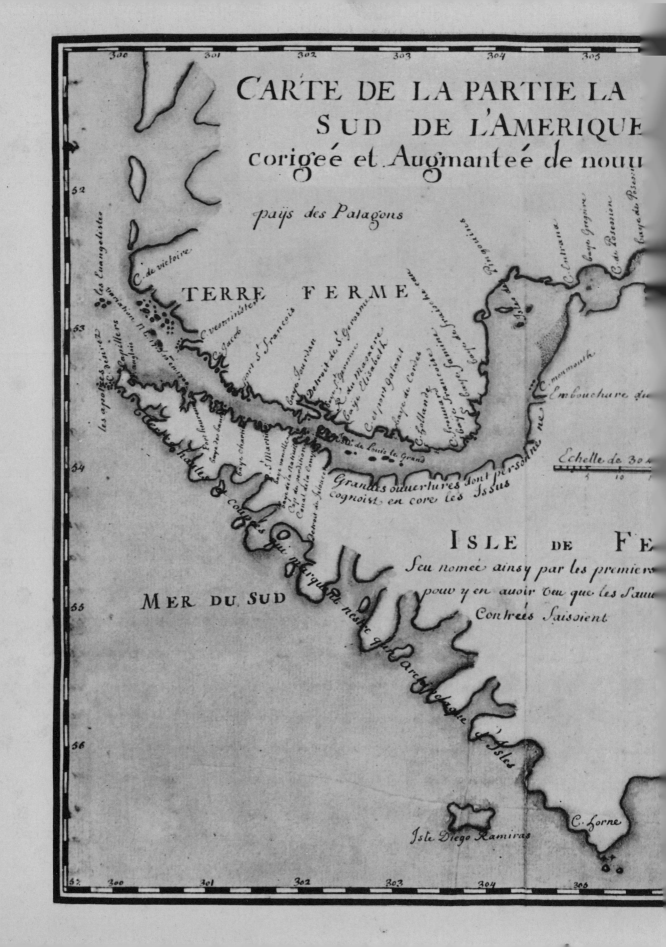

CARTE DE LA PARTIE LA
SUD DE L'AMERIQUE
corigeé et Augmanteé de nouu

paijs des Patagons

TERRE FERME

MER DU SUD

ISLE DE FE
Seu nomeé ainsy par les premiers
pour y en auoir veu que les Sauu
Contrees Saissient

Grandes ouuertures dont personne ne
cognoist, en core les Issus

Echelle de 30

Isle Diego Ramiras

C. Horne